THE PSYCHOLOGY OF GREEN ORGANIZATIONS

THE PSYCHOLOGY OF GREEN ORGANIZATIONS

Edited by

Jennifer L. Robertson

Julian Barling

OXFORD
UNIVERSITY PRESS

OXFORD
UNIVERSITY PRESS

Oxford University Press is a department of the University of
Oxford. It furthers the University's objective of excellence in research,
scholarship, and education by publishing worldwide.

Oxford   New York
Auckland   Cape Town   Dar es Salaam   Hong Kong   Karachi
Kuala Lumpur   Madrid   Melbourne   Mexico City   Nairobi
New Delhi   Shanghai   Taipei   Toronto

With offices in
Argentina   Austria   Brazil   Chile   Czech Republic   France   Greece
Guatemala   Hungary   Italy   Japan   Poland   Portugal   Singapore
South Korea   Switzerland   Thailand   Turkey   Ukraine   Vietnam

Oxford is a registered trademark of Oxford University Press
in the UK and certain other countries.

Published in the United States of America by
Oxford University Press
198 Madison Avenue, New York, NY 10016

© Oxford University Press 2015

All rights reserved. No part of this publication may be reproduced, stored in
a retrieval system, or transmitted, in any form or by any means, without the prior
permission in writing of Oxford University Press, or as expressly permitted by law,
by license, or under terms agreed with the appropriate reproduction rights organization.
Inquiries concerning reproduction outside the scope of the above should be sent to the
Rights Department, Oxford University Press, at the address above.

You must not circulate this work in any other form
and you must impose this same condition on any acquirer.

Library of Congress Cataloging-in-Publication Data
The psychology of green organizations / edited by Jennifer L. Robertson, Julian Barling.
    pages cm
Includes bibliographical references and index.
ISBN 978–0–19–999748–0
1. Management—Environmental aspects.   2. Organizational behavior—Environmental
aspects.   3. Corporate culture—Environmental aspects.   4. Employees—
Psychology.   I. Robertson, Jennifer Lynn.   II. Barling, Julian.
HD30.255.P79 2015
658.4′083—dc23
2014025875

9 8 7 6 5 4 3 2 1
Printed in the United States of America
on acid-free paper

To my parents, Linda and Brian, and my loving husband, Sean

                                                              Jennifer Robertson

To my wife, Janice

                Julian Barling

CONTENTS

List of Contributors ix

PART I: *Setting the Stage*

1. Introduction 3
   JENNIFER L. ROBERTSON AND JULIAN BARLING

2. The Nature of Employees' Pro-Environmental Behaviors 12
   OLIVIER BOIRAL, PASCAL PAILLÉ, AND NICOLAS RAINERI

3. Theoretical Basis for Organizational Pro-Environmental Research 33
   ANGELA M. RUEPERT, LINDA STEG, AND KEES KEIZER

4. Research Methods in Pro-Environmental Research 58
   TIMUR OZBILIR AND E. KEVIN KELLOWAY

5. Diary Methods and Workplace Pro-Environmental Behaviors 95
   MEGAN J. BISSING-OLSON, KELLY S. FIELDING, AND AARTI IYER

PART II: *The Role of Individuals in Promoting Workplace Pro-Environmental Behaviors*

6. Individual Determinants of Workplace Pro-Environmental Behaviors 119
   SIU HING LO

7. The Relationship between Emotions and Workplace Pro-Environmental Behaviors 141
   SALLY RUSSELL AND ELMAR FRIEDRICH

8. The Role of Leadership in Promoting Workplace Pro-Environmental Behaviors 164
   JENNIFER L. ROBERTSON AND JULIAN BARLING

9. Environmental Locus of Control　　187
MARK CLEVELAND AND MARIA KALAMAS

PART III: *The Role of Organizations in Promoting Workplace Pro-Environmental Behaviors*

10. "Green Me Up, Scotty": Psychological Influence Techniques for Increasing Pro-Environmental Employee Behavior　　215
KERRIE L. UNSWORTH

11. Organizational Change　　244
MATTHEW DAVIS AND PHILLIPA COAN

12. Human Resource Management Approaches　　275
ANDREW BRATTON AND JOHN BRATTON

13. Ergonomic Initiatives　　296
ANDREW THATCHER

14. Pro-Environmental Organizational Culture and Climate　　322
THOMAS A. NORTON, HANNES ZACHER, AND NEAL M. ASHKANASY

PART IV: *Tying It All Together*

15. Sustainable Innovation at Interface: Workplace Pro-Environmental Behavior as a Collective Driver for Continuous Improvement　　351
STEVE KENNEDY, GAIL WHITEMAN, AND AMANDA WILLIAMS

Index　　379

LIST OF CONTRIBUTORS

Neal M. Ashkanasy
UQ Business School
The University of Queensland
Brisbane, Queensland, Australia

Julian Barling
Borden Chair of Leadership
Queen's School of Business
Kingston, Ontario, Canada

Megan J. Bissing-Olson
School of Psychology
The University of Queensland
Brisbane, Queensland, Australia

Olivier Boiral
Department of Management
Université Laval
Laval, Quebec, Canada

Andrew Bratton
Strathclyde Business School
University of Strathclyde
Glasgow, Scotland, United Kingdom

John Bratton
Faculty of Humanities & Social Sciences
Athabasca University
Alberta, Canada

Mark Cleveland
Department of Management and Organizational Studies
Western University
London, Ontario, Canada

Phillipa Coan
Leeds University Business School
University of Leeds
Leeds, United Kingdom

Matthew Davis
Leeds University Business School
University of Leeds
Leeds, United Kingdom

Kelly S. Fielding
Institute for Social Science Research
The University of Queensland
Brisbane, Queensland, Australia

Elmar Friedrich
Institute for Economy and
    the Environment
University of St. Gallen
St. Gallen, Switzerland

Aarti Iyer
School of Psychology
The University of Queensland
Brisbane, Queensland, Australia

Maria Kalamas
Department of Marketing and Professional Sales
Michael J. Coles College of Business
Kennesaw State University
Kennesaw, Georgia, USA

Kees Keizer
Faculty of Behavioural and Social Sciences
University of Groningen
Groningen, The Netherlands

E. Kevin Kelloway
Department of Psychology
Saint Mary's University
Halifax, Nova Scotia, Canada

Steve Kennedy
Rotterdam School of Management
Erasmus University
Rotterdam, The Netherlands

Siu Hing Lo
Health Behaviour Research Centre
University College London
London, United Kingdom

Thomas A. Norton
School of Psychology
The University of Queensland
Brisbane, Queensland, Australia

Timur Ozbilir
Department of Psychology
Saint Mary's University
Halifax, Nova Scotia, Canada

Pascal Paillé
Department of Management
Université Laval
Laval, Quebec, Canada

Nicolas Raineri
Department of Management
Université Laval
Laval, Quebec, Canada

Jennifer L. Robertson
Department of Management and Organizational Studies
Western University
London, Ontario, Canada

Angela M. Ruepert
Faculty of Behavioural and Social Sciences
University of Groningen
Groningen, The Netherlands

Sally Russell
Sustainability Research Institute
University of Leeds
Leeds, United Kingdom

Linda Steg
Faculty of Behavioural and Social Sciences
University of Groningen
Groningen, The Netherlands

Andrew Thatcher
Department of Psychology
University of the Witwatersrand
Johannesburg, South Africa

Kerrie L. Unsworth
University of Western Australia
Business School
University of Western Australia
Crawley, Australia

Gail Whiteman
Rotterdam School of Management
Erasmus University
Rotterdam, The Netherlands

Amanda Williams
Rotterdam School of Management
Erasmus University
Rotterdam, The Netherlands

Hannes Zacher
Department of Psychology
University of Groningen
Groningen, The Netherlands

SETTING THE STAGE

1 INTRODUCTION

Jennifer L. Robertson and Julian Barling

Over the course of human history, we have been witness to the outbreak of devastating infectious diseases. From tuberculosis to smallpox, cholera, various plagues, and more recently, HIV/AIDS, humans have been infected by, suffered from, and developed treatments for numerous illnesses. As we move further into the twenty-first century, we are confronted with a new disease that affects a large patient. This disease is climate change, the patient is planet Earth, and the infectious agent is humankind.

Climate Change

The Intergovernmental Panel on Climate Change (IPCC, 2007a) defines climate change as "any change in climate over time due to natural variability or human actions." (p. 871). The extent and pace of climate change has now increased drastically such that the planet's average surface temperature has risen 1.4°F over the last thousand years, with the most extreme warming occurring over the last three decades (National Research Council, 2010). Although climate change is directly associated with a warming of the Earth's surface, it is also indirectly associated with a host of other significant environmental issues. These issues include: rising sea levels, loss of polar sea ice, melting of continental glaciers, changes in precipitation patterns, progressive shifting in the habitats of species and the boundaries of ecosystems, acidification of the oceans, population increases, loss of critical habitats, changes in the frequency and intensity of heat waves and droughts, ozone depletion, deforestation, decrease of oxygen in oceans, lakes, and rivers, contamination of the water supply, threats to a secure food supply, reduced fisheries, and an accelerated rate of extinction of nonhuman and plant species (IPCC, 2007a,b; Kazdin, 2009; National Research Council, 2010; Swim et al., 2011).

Recently, the IPCC reported they are 95% confident that the major cause of climate change is anthropogenic (Gibson, 2013). Humans primarily drive climate change by burning fossil fuels (e.g., coal, gas, oil) for energy (National Research Council, 2010), resulting in massive amounts of greenhouse gases being emitted into the atmosphere. Other environmentally destructive behaviors (e.g., overconsumption, littering, polluting air, water, and land) also contribute to climate change (Gifford, 2011; National Research Council, 2010; Swim, Clayton, & Howard, 2011). Such human contributions to climate change have resulted in a serious concern that is perhaps one of the greatest challenges facing humankind (Kazdin, 2009; Stern, 2011; Swim et al., 2011). What is more, much like its medical counterpart, climate change poses serious negative consequences to humans (e.g., it can negatively effect human physical and mental health; Doherty & Clayton, 2011; IPCC 2007a).

Investigating Climate Change: The Role of Social Science Research

Given the urgent and significant concern around climate change and the negative effects it poses, it is imperative that social scientific research investigates climate change. Although climate change has been researched for some time within the natural sciences (e.g., the process of climate change and its physical and biological effects on land and in waters; Swim et al., 2011), social science research is needed to gain a comprehensive understanding of how climate change can be mitigated. More specifically, given that the cause of climate change is largely anthropogenic, research that investigates how human behavioral change (e.g., promoting pro-environmental behaviors among individuals) can positively affect climate change is needed (American Psychological Association Task Force on the *Interface Between Psychology and Global Climate Change*, 2009). A science that focuses on the "human dimensions" of climate change (e.g., human behaviors that contribute to climate change, consequences of climate change that affect humans, and individual responses to climate change) has been developing over the last few decades. Some scholars suggest that the "human dimensions" are psychological, offering psychological research a significant opportunity in uncovering important insights into effective human responses to climate change (Swim et al., 2011).

Psychology and Climate Change Research

The notion that psychological research can play an important role in the human dimensions of climate change is not new; this research began to uncover important insights into the human understanding of and responses to climate change in the 1970s (Kazdin, 2009). During that time, research focused on developing and testing theories of pro-environmental behaviors (Stern, 2011). Since then, a plethora of studies that focused on fostering sustainable behaviors through psychological theories have surfaced (see Abrahamase, Steg, Vlek, & Rothengatter, 2005 for a review) and various journals have published a series of articles on this topic (see Kazdin [2009] for a list of these journals).

Despite these developments, psychology has only played a minor role in developing knowledge about the public's understanding of, and propensity to, address climate change (Weber & Stern, 2011). Thus, recent calls for psychologists to become more involved in climate change research have appeared. For example, in his APA presidential address, Alan Kazdin (2009) noted that "we know from our research a great deal on how to foster behavior change toward a sustainable environment. Yet, we need to do more, mobilize differently, and move to a scale that makes a difference" (p. 353). Further, many psychologists (e.g., Swim et al., 2011) are now encouraging their colleagues to become involved, arguing that they have an obligation to do so as set out in the APA's mission statement, vision statement, and ethical code, all of which indicate that psychologists are committed to using their expertise to benefit individuals and society, and to assist in the resolution of global challenges (Swim et al., 2011), including climate change. In short, psychologists believe that not only can the psychological community do more, but they also have an obligation to do so.

Psychologists are starting to answer these calls. For example, between 2008 and 2009, the APA Task Force on the *Interface Between Psychology and Global Climate Change* met to investigate the role of psychology in understanding and addressing efforts to mitigate and adapt to climate change. In doing so, the task force isolated relevant research questions and policy recommendations to help guide actions taken by psychologists, the APA, and other organizations. Additionally, the *American Psychologist* published a special issue, entitled "Psychology and Global Climate Change," in which several contributors outlined how psychologists and psychological research can begin to address the profound challenges associated with climate change (Swim et al., 2011). Although psychologists are taking initial steps, it is important that all psychologists, including those working in different subfields, such as industrial organizational (I-O) psychology and organizational behavior (OB), become involved in climate change research.

Organizational Behavior and Climate Change Research

Organizations are often cited to be amongst the largest contributors to climate change (Trudeau and Canada West Foundation, 2007); given this, expertise and knowledge from organizational scholars are needed if we are to mitigate climate change, prevent further environmental degradation, and foster a more sustainable environment. Supporting this assertion, several scholars (e.g., Andersson, Jackson, & Russell, 2013; Ones & Dilchert, 2012) suggest that OB scholars and I-O psychologists are uniquely positioned to shed light on how organizational greening activity can reduce organizations' environmental impact, redress ecological degradation, prevent further degradation, and ultimately, promote environmental sustainability.

Although some research has begun to investigate organizational greening activity, to date, much of this research has taken place at the macro level, in which the organization is the unit of analysis. As will become clear in several different chapters, parallel micro-level research that investigates employees' pro-environmental behaviors lags behind (Andersson et al., 2013; Ones & Dilchert, 2012; Russell & Griffiths, 2008). Several efforts to fill this gap and focus on employees' pro-environmental behaviors from an I-O psychology and OB research perspective have now emerged.

First, several annual conferences and consortiums have been devoted to and/or included organizational environmental sustainability themes. For example, the Society of Industrial and Organizational Psychology (SIOP) devoted one of its theme tracks at its 2009 annual meeting to corporate social responsibility. Different conference events focused on organizations' responsibility to the environment, and the role that organizational psychologists can play in meeting those responsibilities. Additionally, the Academy of Management chose "Green Management Matters" as its conference theme for 2010. During the 2011 annual meeting, SIOP dedicated a whole day of programming to the greening of organizations. More recently, the theme of SIOP's 2012 Leading Edge Consortium was "Environmental Sustainability at Work: Advancing Research, Enhancing Practice" (Ones & Dilchert, 2012).

Second, several journals have devoted special issues to the topic of climate change. The journal *Zeitschrift fur Personalforschung* (*German Journal of Research in Human Resource Management*) dedicated an issue to Green Human Resource Management (Jackson, Renwick, Jabbour, & Muller-Camen, 2011). The *Journal of Organizational Behavior* also published a special issue, "Greening Organizational Behavior," in which six articles, spanning various levels of analysis, provided a deeper insight into organizational greening activity (Andersson et al., 2013). Similarly, *Personnel Psychology* published a special issue that included a collection of four articles addressing corporate social responsibility topics, including environmental sustainability (Morgeson et al., 2013). Finally, several edited books, much like this one, have been published on this topic (e.g., Huffman & Klein [Eds.], 2013; Jackson, Ones, & Dilchert [Eds.], 2012).

Overview of Book

Given these recent developments, we feel it is a propitious moment to reflect on workplace pro-environmental behavior research evaluated within the fields of OB and I-O psychology. The goals of this book are to consolidate available knowledge on corporate environmental initiatives, stimulate future empirical research on this topic, and provide recommendations as to how organizations can promote workplace pro-environmental behaviors. To meet these goals, we have invited a number of researchers who are currently involved in studying different aspects of organizational environmental sustainability to take a retrospective and prospective orientation and review leading research in their domain, highlight practical implications of this research, and outline research questions that remain unexplored. In some chapters, case examples of environmentally sustainable organizations are explored to illustrate lessons gleaned from research.

The first section provides a conceptual, theoretical, and methodological foundation for research on workplace pro-environmental behaviors. Olivier Boiral, Pascal Paillé, and Nicolas Raineri integrate environmental management and I-O psychology literature (in chapter 2) to shed light on the conceptualization of workplace pro-environmental behaviors. These authors highlight the complexity, context-dependency, and multifaceted nature of the behaviors and provide a definition that best captures this concept. In chapter 3, Angela Ruepert, Linda Steg, and Kees Keizer review different theories of how general pro-environmental behaviors can be applied to the environmental context to increase our understanding of workplace environmental behavior determinants. These authors point out that contextual factors of the organization influence how different psychological factors explain workplace pro-environmental behaviors. The next two chapters focus on methodological approaches to researching workplace pro-environmental behaviors. In chapter 4, Timur Ozbilir and Kevin Kelloway provide an extensive review of the methodological bases (e.g., sample characteristics, research strategies and designs, data collection methods, and levels of analyses) of pro-environmental research by conducting a content analysis of 118 empirical articles drawn from 14 journals. In chapter 5, Megan Bissing-Olson, Kelly Fielding, and Aarti Iyer draw our attention to the value of one particular method, namely, diary methods, in the study of within-person variation in workplace pro-environmental behaviors.

The second section examines existing research on the role of individual-level variables in promoting general and workplace pro-environmental behaviors. Siu Hing Lo turns our attention to individual-level behavioral determinants of workplace pro-environmental beahviors (see chapter 6). Through her review on literature on workplace pro-environmental behaviors and pro-environmental behaviors in private or household contexts, Lo concludes that both cognitive and habitual or unconscious factors are associated with workplace pro-environmental behaviors. In chapter 7, Sally Russell and Elmar Friedrich explore the role of emotions in shaping pro-environmental behaviors. They introduce a multi-level framework of emotions in organizations as the basis for their review of research that has linked environmental issues to emotions at five levels of analysis, from the most micro, within-individual level, to a macro-organizational level of emotions. Jennifer Robertson and Julian Barling turn our attention to environmental leadership in chapter 8. They review different conceptualizations of environmental leadership, how environmental leaders influence corporate environmental initiatives, the characteristics of environmental leaders, and the leadership behaviors that influence subordinates' workplace pro-environmental behaviors. Robertson and Barling also provide a case example of environmental leadership at a Canadian brewery. In chapter 9, Mark Cleveland and Maria Kalamas apply locus of control theory to the environmental context, and introduce the concept of environmental locus of control. Cleveland and Kalamas show how internal and external environmental locus of control can positively and negatively impact employees' environmental initiatives.

The third section of this book turns to the role of organizations and contextual variables in promoting workplace pro-environmental behaviors. In chapter 10, Kerrie Unsworth suggests that organizations can encourage environmental initiatives by altering individual and psychological processes. To do so, Unsworth provides an overarching framework to help us understand how and why psychological interventions influence the goal-behavior process that affects workplace pro-environmental behaviors. Mathew Davis and Phillipa Coan discuss the link between organizational change theory and organizational environmental sustainability in chapter 11. Davis and Coan argue that organization-wide change can encourage a proactive approach to environmental performance. In chapter 12, Andrew Bratton and John Bratton highlight the role of human resource management (HRM) practices in encouraging what they refer to as low-carbon behaviors within organizations. They pose several questions about green HRM, and in doing so, provide a framework for examining the role of HRM in achieving environmentally sustainable organizations. Andrew Thatcher then examines ergonomics and human factors and how three theoretical approaches (namely, human factors and sustainable development, green ergonomics, and ergoecology) can increase sustainability in chapter 13. To conclude this section, Thormas Norton, Hannes Zacher, and Neal Ashkanasy define the concepts and outline the characteristics of pro-environmental organizational culture and climate. The authors then propose a conceptual framework of pro-environmental organizational culture and climate that seeks to explain how these two constructs can be integrated to influence employees' and organizations' environmental performance.

The fourth and last section concludes the book by exploring one organization that has successfully promoted employees environmental initiatives, namely, Interface. In this concluding chapter, Steve Kennedy, Gail Whiteman, and Amanda Williams present findings from their qualitative study to show how complex organizational and individual-level factors can be used to affect major changes in corporate environmental sustainability.

Conclusion

Concern about climate change and its potentially devastating consequences is widespread. As we noted at the outset of this chapter, humankind may be the culprit for causing climate change, but we also have the power to mitigate it and contribute to environmental preservation. As will become apparent from the different chapters, the theoretical and methodological traditions of I-O psychology and OB have much to offer our understanding of how human behavior in organizations is associated with environmental degradation, and even more so, how psychologically based interventions can be developed to positively affect climate change. It is on this notion that this book is based.

References

Abrahamse, W., Steg, L., Vlek, C., & Rothengatter, T. (2005). A review of intervention studies aimed at household energy conservation. *Journal of Environmental Psychology, 25*, 273–291.

American Psychological Association Task Force on the Interface Between Psychology and Global Climate Change. (2009). *Psychology and global climate change: Addressing a multi-faceted phenomenon and set of challenges*. Retrieved from http://www.apa.org/science/about/publications/climate-change.aspx on May 15, 2010.

Andersson, L., Jackson, S. E., & Russell, S. V. (2013). Greening organizational behaviour: An introduction to the special issue. *Journal of Organizational Behavior, 34*, 151–155.

Doherty, T. J., & Clayton, S. (2011). The psychological impacts of global climate change. *The American Psychologist, 66*, 265–276.

Gibson, M. (2013). UN Climate Panel: It's 95% certain that humans are the dominant cause of climate change. *Time*. Retrieved from http://world.time.com/2013/09/27/u-n-climate-panel-its-95-certain-that-humans-are-the-dominant-cause-of-climate-change/

Gifford, R. (2011). The dragons of inaction: Psychological barriers that limit climate change mitigation and adaptation. *American Psychologist, 66*, 290–302.

Huffman, A. H., & Klein, S. (Eds.) (2013). *Green organizations: Driving change with I-O psychology*. New York: Psychology Press/Routledge.

Intergovernmental Panel on Climate Change (2007a). *Climate change 2007: Impacts, adaptation, and vulnerability. Contribution of Working Group II to the Fourth Assessment Report of the Intergovernmental Panel on Climate Change* (M. L., Parry, O. F. Canziani, J. P. Palutikof, P. J. van der Linden, & C. E., Hanson, Eds.). New York: Cambridge University Press.

Intergovernmental Panel on Climate Change (2007b). *Climate change 2007: The psychical science basis. Contribution of Working Group I to the Fourth Assessment Report of the Intergovernmental Panel on Climate Change* (S. Solomon, D. Qin, M. Manning, Z. Chen, M. Marquis, K. B. Averyt, M. Tignor, & H. L. Miller, Eds.). New York: Cambridge University Press.

Jackson, E. S., Ones, D. S., & Dilchert, S. (Eds.). (2012). *Managing human resources for environmental sustainability*. San Francisco: Jossey-Bass/Wiley.

Jackson, S. E., Renwick, D. W. S., Jabbour, C. J. C., & Muller-Camen, M. (2011). State-of-the-art and future directions for green human resource management: Introduction to the special issue. *German Journal of Research in Human Resource Management, 25*, 99–116.

Kazdin, A. E. (2009). Psychological science's contributions to a sustainable environment: Extending our reach to a grand challenge of society. *American Psychologist, 64*, 339–356.

Morgeson, F. P., Aguinis, H., Walgman, D. A., & Siegel, D. S. (2013). Extending corporate social responsibility research to the human resource management and organizational behavior domains: A look to the future. *Personnel Psychology, 66*, 805–824.

National Research Council. (2010). *Advancing the science of climate change*. Washington, DC: National Academies Press.

Ones, D. S., & Dilchert, S. (2012). Environmental sustainability at work: A call to action. *Industrial and Organizational Psychology, 5*, 444–466.

Russell, S., & Griffiths, A. (2008). The role of emotions in driving workplace pro-environmental behaviors. *Research on Emotion in Organizations, 4*, 83–107.

Stern, P. C. (2011). Contributions of psychology to limiting climate change. *American Psychologist, 66*, 303–314.

Swim, J. K., Clayton, S., & Howard, G. S. (2011). Human behavioural contributions to climate change: Psychological and contextual drivers. *American Psychologist, 66*, 251–264.

Swim, J. K., Stern, P. C., Doherty, T. Y. J., Clayton, S., Reser, J. P., Weber, E. U., Gifford, R., & Howard, G. S. (2011). Psychology's contributions to understanding and addressing global climate change. *American Psychologist, 66*, 241–250.

Trudeau and Canada West Foundation. (2007). *Canadians look first to government to address climate change.* Retrieved from http:// www.trudeaufoundation.ca/community.igloo?r0=community&r0_script=/scripts/folder.html on September 15, 2008.

Weber, E. U., & Stern, P. C. (2011). Public understanding of climate change in the United States. *American Psychologist*, *66*, 315–328.

2 THE NATURE OF EMPLOYEES' PRO-ENVIRONMENTAL BEHAVIORS

Olivier Boiral, Pascal Paillé, and Nicolas Raineri

The main objective of this chapter is to shed light on the nature, scope, and definition of employees' pro-environmental behaviors. Such behaviors are inseparable from corporate greening initiatives and underlie most actions in this area. Many environmental initiatives, such as recycling waste materials or turning off lights and powering electronics down at the end of the day, rely almost entirely on employees' goodwill and individual behaviors. Even formal and organizational-level actions, such as the implementation of the ISO 14001 environmental management system, require employee participation and involvement to be successful (Boiral, 2007a; Kitazawa & Sarkis, 2000; Walley & Stubbs, 2000; Yin & Schmeidler, 2009). Therefore, the ISO 14001 standard can hardly be integrated in daily activities without pro-environmental behaviors in the workplace, which enable employees to identify environmental aspects, apply and update procedures, implement pollution prevention programs, and measure performance. Without employees' engagement in pro-environmental behaviors, organizational practices in this area will be reduced to symbolic, ceremonial, and unsubstantial activities (Boiral, 2007b; Christmann & Taylor, 2006). In this respect, the greening of organizations appears to result to a large extent from the aggregation of a multitude of green behaviors in the workplace (Boiral, 2005; Ruiz-Quintanilla, Bunge, Freeman-Gallant, & Cohen-Rosenthal, 1996; Walley & Stubbs, 2000). Paradoxically, although the importance of employee's pro-environmental behaviors is often emphasized in the literature, their nature and scope are not generally agreed upon and need to be better defined.

Generally speaking, pro-environmental behaviors in the workplace have been analyzed through two main perspectives. The first of those is based on established research in the field of environmental management, which since its beginnings has emphasized the critical role of employees' green behaviors (e.g., Hart, 1995; Schmidheiny, 1992; Shrivastava, 1995; Winter & Ewers, 1988). In this approach, such behaviors are most often considered as part of larger environmental practices and organizational change processes, whose effectiveness to a large extent relies on employee involvement (Boiral, 2005; Hanna, Newman, & Johnson, 2000; Kornbluh, Crowfoot, & Cohen-Rosenthal, 1985; Rothenberg, 2003). The second, more recent perspective is based on studies rooted in the industrial and organizational psychology literature. This burgeoning research has mostly focused on voluntary and individual initiatives in the workplace, which are generally considered as a new research area (Boiral & Paillé, 2012; Lamm, Tosti-Kharas, & Williams, 2013; Lülfs & Hahn, 2013; Ones & Dilchert, 2012a,b). For example, Ones and Dilchert (2012a) propose a comprehensive taxonomy of employee green behaviors based on five main categories: avoiding harm, conserving, working sustainably influencing others, and taking initiative.

Although these two streams of literature are complementary and focus on similar phenomena, they have developed quite separately. Furthermore, the definition of what constitutes employees' pro-environmental behaviors remains relatively unclear in the two approaches and the question has rarely been addressed directly (for an exception, see Ones & Dilchert, 2012a,b). As a result, workplace pro-environmental behaviors tend to be considered as something that is obvious, quite monolithic, and not requiring an explanation. Nevertheless, further exploration of this concept reveals its complexity, multifaceted nature, and context dependency. The nature of pro-environmental behaviors in the workplace is indeed eclectic and can depend on many factors, such as the type of organization, employee occupation, procedures in place, production process, clean technology, and so forth. Furthermore, because environmental actions can be socially sensitive, the concrete behaviors inside the workplace in this area are not necessarily transparent and easy to investigate. This difficulty can explain why the literature on environmental management has mostly focused on organizational-level and formal practices through large-scale quantitative studies instead of trying to systematically investigate what pro-environmental behaviors inside the workplace really are.

By exploring the "black box" of pro-environmental behaviors at work, this chapter aims to clarify the meaning of the concept and the reason why it is so essential for corporate greening. It also proposes a definition of employees' pro-environmental behaviors and explores existing taxonomies that have attempted to describe the applications of green initiatives in the workplace. In this, the chapter contributes to the integration of the rather scattered literature.

Nevertheless, it is not intended to describe the theoretical basis and determinants of environmental behaviors, which are explored in other chapters.

The remainder of the chapter is organized as follows. First, the literature on corporate greening and pro-environmental behaviors is explored. This exploration sheds more light on the complexity, diversity, and opacity of these behaviors. Second, the definitions and scope of pro-environmental behaviors are analyzed. A new stream of literature focused on the concept of organizational citizenship behaviors for the environment, which covers the majority of pro-environmental behaviors in organizational settings (Boiral & Paillé, 2012; Ones & Dilchert, 2012b), is also discussed. Last, the conclusion explores various avenues for further research in this area.

Corporate Greening through Pro-Environmental Behaviors

The role of individual behaviors in corporate greening has been highlighted in many environmental studies (e.g., Enander & Pannullo, 1990; Hart, 1995; Kornbluh et al., 1985; May & Flannery, 1995; Ruiz-Quintanilla et al., 1996). Empirical research in this area has demonstrated that the environmental performance of organizations depends, to a large extent, on employee involvement through various behaviors intended to reduce pollution, contribute to eco-innovations, and participate in recycling programs (Boiral, 2005; Bunge, Cohen-Rosenthal, & Ruiz-Quintanilla, 1996; Paillé, Chen, Boiral, & Jin, 2014; Ramus, 2001; Roy, Boiral, & Paillé, 2013). Generally speaking, the role of these pro-environmental behaviors has been associated in the literature with three main issues:

- Pollution prevention
- Internalization of environmental management practices
- Eco-innovations and knowledge management

Exploring these issues, which are interdependent and not mutually exclusive, makes it possible to explore the complex nature of environmental behaviors and the reasons why their definition and taxonomies are far from generally agreed upon.

Employees' Behaviors for Pollution Prevention

Pollution prevention is one of the main approaches aimed at improving the environmental performance of organizations (Boiral, 2005; Boiral & Sala, 1998;

Hart, 1995; Kleiner, 1991; Shrivastava, 1995). According to the Environmental Protection Agency (EPA), "pollution prevention is reducing or eliminating waste at the source by modifying production processes, promoting the use of non-toxic or less toxic substances, implementing conservation techniques, and re-using materials rather than putting them into the waste stream" (Munquía, Zavala, Marin, Moure-Eraso, & Velazquez, 2010, p. 325). Contrary to the palliative approach, which is characterized by the implementation of end-of-pipe technologies, pollution prevention most often involves significant changes in the production process and work habits at the source of contaminant discharges (Boiral, 2005; Hart, 1995). As emphasized by Hanna et al. (2000), this approach is far from new and has been promoted since the 1970s in the United States. Nevertheless, this change in attitude was not always clearly understood and taken into account inside organizations. In fact, until the late 1980s, most programs for pollution prevention focused on cleaner technologies. However, over the last 25 years, the focus has expanded to incorporate changes in working behaviors, which have been considered as essential for the success of pollution prevention programs by governments and organizations alike. As one example, in the early 1990s the EPA required that manufacturers report measures to promote pollution prevention through human resource management (Bunge et al., 1996). Similarly, between 1993 and 1996, the Danish Ministry of Environment developed a program called "Employee Participation in the Introduction of Cleaner Technologies," which was intended to better understand and promote pollution prevention behaviors in the workplace (Remmen & Lorentzen, 2000). In the same vein, most empirical studies on the implementation of pollution prevention initiatives inside organizations emphasize the role of employee involvement and behavioral changes (e.g., Boiral, 2005; Hanna et al., 2000; Kornbluh et al., 1985; May & Flannery, 1995; Theyel, 2000). For example, based on the EPA *Toxics Release Inventory* (TRI), Bunge, Ruiz-Quintanilla, and colleagues (Bunge et al., 1996; Ruiz-Quintanilla et al., 1996) showed that employee participation is one of the main drivers ensuring the success of pollution prevention and can result in a significant reduction in contaminant emissions. Hanna et al.'s (2000) study focused on 349 employees involved in team projects, and showed that pro-environmental behaviors play a key role in pollution prevention and environmental performance improvement.

Although the role of employee behaviors in pollution prevention is now well established, the specific nature of these behaviors seems to be overlooked in the literature. Most studies in this area are based on quantitative analyses in which employee behaviors tend to appear as quite monolithic and limited to a few specific measurable variables, which can hardly cover the diversity of these behaviors. Nevertheless, the exploration of employees' behaviors for pollution prevention through qualitative research has shed more light on their complexity, context-dependency, and multifaceted nature. For example, Boiral (2005) conducted 108 interviews on the role of employee involvement in pollution prevention at industrial facilities, and showed that such involvement cannot easily be dissociated from very technical aspects related to the production process, which differ from one facility to another. In one of the facilities studied, the microorganisms at the heart of the purification station were disrupted by the unforeseeable release of specific contaminants (furfural, caustic soda, ammonia) generated by various operations upstream the production process. The preventive measures implemented in this facility required various technical and human changes that cannot be classified under a specific type of behavior.

Generally speaking, the analysis of pollution prevention measures in manufacturing firms shows that the nature of pro-environmental behaviors depends on the type of organization (e.g., sector of activity, production process) and the activity of individuals, with the exception of quite simple and standardized behaviors related to deskwork.

Internalization of Environmental Management Practices

The role of pro-environmental behaviors has also been associated with the internalization of environmental management practices. Thus, the success of various managerial initiatives, such as the implementation of environmental policies, codes of conduct, and industrial ecology actions, largely depends on employees' pro-environmental behaviors (Boiral, 2007a; Shrivastava, 1995; Walley & Stubbs, 2000; Winter & Ewers, 1988). Since environmental management systems, such as the ISO 14001 standard was developed and launched in 1996, many studies have shown the importance of employee involvement in this area (e.g., Boiral & Sala, 1998; Christmann & Taylor, 2006; Yin & Schmeidler, 2009). These studies are often based on a neo-institutional perspective, according to which organizations face increasing institutional pressures to integrate environmental issues in their management practices. To respond to these pressures in implementing environmental management practices such as the ISO 14001 standard, organizations are mostly driven by the desire to improve their social legitimacy, rather than their environmental performance. As a result, these practices are often superficial, ceremonial, and do not necessarily translate into concrete pro-environmental behaviors in the workplace (Boiral, 2007b; Boiral & Henri, 2012; Christmann & Taylor, 2006). For example, in his case study among facilities certified to ISO 14001, Boiral (2007b) illustrated how the integration and implementation of this standard inside certified organizations is superficial, and what role of employees' behaviors play in improving its effectiveness. The ceremonial nature of the ISO standard integration in certain organizations was revealed by the employees' lack of knowledge of the standard and the superficial preparation for the certification audit, which tended to look like a school exam: last minute preparation, memorization of a few ISO procedures just before the audit, anticipation of questions raised by auditors, focus on documentation rather than substance, concealing non-conformity issues, and celebrations after certification (Boiral, 2007, 2012).

According to this stream of literature, it is generally the employees' pro-environmental behaviors that are responsible for either a ceremonial or a more substantial integration of environmental practices in daily activities. Nevertheless, the nature of such behaviors is rarely clearly defined and they appear to be identified with a variety of actions, such as the application of procedures, the involvement in environmental committees, and the initiatives for pollution prevention. Moreover, this literature highlights the opacity of environmental behaviors inside organizations by shedding light on the differences between the official rhetoric on this issue and actual practices (Boiral, 2007b; Jiang & Bansal, 2003). As a result, the study of pro-environmental behaviors in the workplace tends to be obscured by the social legitimacy and desirability bias associated with these issues.

Eco-Innovations and Knowledge Management

Employees' pro-environmental behaviors have also been analyzed in parallel with the development of innovations and knowledge management. Because of their complex, diverse, and interdisciplinary nature, environmental issues cannot be managed only through formal management systems and practices (Boiral, 2002, 2009; Lane & Robinson, 2009; Ramus & Killmer, 2007). They also require the active involvement of employees in problem solving, innovation development, and knowledge sharing. According to Ramus (2001), corporate greening depends on employees coming up with creative ideas and innovations. These eco-initiatives or eco-innovations (Ramus, 2001; Ramus & Killmer, 2007; Ramus & Steger, 2000) can be based, for instance, on behaviors intended to reduce environmental impacts, solve environmental problems, or develop more eco-efficient products or services. The study by Ramus (2001) sheds light on various employee-led environmental innovations such as the development of a new waste management program and innovative cleaner diesel fuel. Theyel (2000) also highlighted the role of employee suggestions and innovations in improving environmental practices and performance. These eco-innovations depend on the discretionary initiatives of environmental champions in the workplace studies (Andersson & Bateman, 2000; Gattiker & Carter, 2010; Zibarras & Ballinger,

2011). Those champions are able to challenge the status quo and inspire other employees through transformational leadership and environmental initiatives, which tend to be emulated inside the organization (Drumwright, 1994; Walley & Stubbs, 2000). Employee participation is necessary not only to develop innovations based on personal suggestions and initiatives. It is also vital for implementing cleaner technologies, which require changes in working behaviors and development of new knowledge (Remmen & Lorentzen, 2000).

In general, technical and human changes are inextricably linked and, consequently, corporate greening cannot be achieved without employee participation, which is not limited to environmental issues. This participation is intimately linked to knowledge management practices. Corporate greening thus encourages the development of specific skills and capabilities that can also improve the competitive advantage of the firm (Darnall & Edwards, 2006; Hart, 1995; Rothenberg, 2003). In a case study of industrial organizations, Boiral (2002) shows that these skills are largely based on employees' tacit knowledge, whose creation, transfer, and retention is largely discretionary. Employees can use this knowledge, resulting in particular from the close contact with the industrial processes and operations at the source of contaminants, to identify pollution sources, react quickly in emergency situations, or propose preventive solutions. As a result, some workplace pro-environmental behaviors are socially complex and causally ambiguous, and their actual impact is difficult to identify, measure, and foresee (Boiral, 2005). Nonetheless, their specificity makes them an intangible asset that is difficult to replicate for the competition, thereby contributing to the strategic capability of an organization (Hart, 1995).

Overall, studies on eco-innovations and knowledge management like those described in the preceding have shown that employee pro-environmental behaviors do not only depend on predictable routines and easy-to-describe actions, but also on tacit skills, creative ideas, and personal knowledge, which can be difficult to delineate.

Definition and Scope of Pro-Environmental Behaviors

Although environmental behaviors are considered essential for corporate greening, these behaviors are rarely clearly defined in the literature on environmental prevention, internalization of management practices, and eco-innovations (for exceptions, see Ramus, 2001; Ramus & Steger, 2000). Nevertheless, some recent studies have attempted to provide the definition and explain the nature and scope of these behaviors.

Defining an Umbrella and Multifaceted Concept

Pro-environmental behavior appears to be an umbrella concept describing a variety of actions directed toward the environment. This concept is by no means the only one used for describing environmental behaviors in the workplace. Similar concepts have been used in the literature, such as eco-initiatives (Ramus & Killmer, 2007; Ramus & Steger, 2000); eco-innovations (Ramus, 2001); individual environmental initiatives (Andersson & Bateman, 2000); environmental/pro-environmental behaviors (Boiral, 2009; Cantor, Morrow, & Montabon, 2012; Lülfs & Hahn, 2013; Mesmer-Magnus, Viswesvaran, & Wiernik, 2012; Zibarras & Ballinger, 2011); behaviors directed toward the environment (Boiral & Paillé, 2012; Daily, Bishop, & Govindarajulu, 2009; Lamm et al., 2013); green behaviors (Han, Hsu, & Lee, 2009; Ones & Dilchert, 2009, 2012a); eco-friendly behaviors (Rangarajan & Rahm, 2011); employees' environmental commitment/involvement (Boiral, 2005; Orecchini, 2000; Perez, Amichai-Hamburger, & Shterental, 2009); environmental sustainability at work (Muros, 2012; Ones & Dilchert, 2012b); behaviors toward sustainability in the workplace (Crosbie & Houghton, 2011); and environmentally responsible behaviors (Lee, Jan, & Yang, 2013; Rojšek, 2001; Smith & O'Sullivan, 2012; Tilley, 2000). In their study of the way in which psychological research contributes to a better understanding of environmental behaviors, Ones and Dilchert (2012b) identified more than a dozen similar concepts used in the literature, some of them different from those listed in the preceding, such as conservation behaviors and environmentally significant behaviors. Although all these concepts have been used by different studies and in different contexts, they all describe basically the same phenomenon.

The proliferation of concepts certainly illustrates the dynamic nature of research in this area, but also the absence of a clearly established definition of what a pro-environmental behavior within organizational settings is or should be. It confirms the lack of consensus in the research on employees' pro-environmental behaviors, and the emerging studies in this area tend to overlook established literature to claim ownership over a fairly old concept.

Only a few authors, notably Ones and Dilchert (2012a), Mesmer-Magnus et al. (2012), and Ramus and Steger (2000) have proposed a definition of environmental behaviors inside organizations. Although these definitions are not without limitations, they shed light on different aspects of a multifaceted concept. According to Ones and Dilchert (2012a, p. 87), "employee green behaviors are defined as scalable actions and behaviors that employees engage in that are linked with and contribute to or detract from environmental sustainability." Their study highlights four features associated with the definition: the focus on employees only, actions under their control, measurable actions, and the integration of both beneficial and harmful behaviors. As such, green behaviors can fall under both in-role and extra-role behaviors, including counterproductive ones (Ones & Dilchert, 2012b). Notwithstanding the value of the definition, such features both restrict and expand the nature and scope of these behaviors.

On the one hand, they only seem to account for behaviors that can be quantified, scaled, and compared at the employee level; on the other, they encompass behaviors that cause environmental harm. Many pro-environmental behaviors, such as participation in recycling programs or green committees, are subsumed in collective actions whose contribution to corporate greening cannot necessarily be traced back to individual actions and assessed at the individual level. Furthermore, many behaviors, such as the sharing of tacit knowledge are, socially complex and causally ambiguous, and cannot be easily measured. Similarly, mundane discretionary green behaviors, such as turning off the light when leaving a room, are by definition volitional and decentralized, and their contribution to the corporate environmental performance is best construed at the aggregate—group or organizational—level (Boiral, 2009; Lamm et al., 2013; Paillé et al., 2014). Last, although the inclusion of harmful behaviors is an interesting perspective to which attention should be drawn, it somehow contradicts the meaning of the concept of "green behavior." In fact, "employee 'ungreen' (or environmentally irresponsible) behaviors constitute a specific form of counterproductive work behaviors" (Ones & Dilchert, 2012b, p. 453), which need to be inhibited, and they can introduce further confusion in the definition of employees' pro-environmental behaviors and in fact create a conceptual oxymoron (i.e., employees' "contra-environmental behaviors" refer to a separate definitional framework).

Mesmer-Magnus et al. (2012) also propose a definition of workplace pro-environmental behaviors, which they describe as "all individual behaviors that contribute to environmental sustainability. Such behaviors are volitional, intentional, and entirely under the control of individual[s]" (p. 169). Although the first part of this definition seems inclusive, the focus in its second part is on behaviors that are intentional and under the full control of individuals is quite restrictive. Many environmental behaviors are not necessarily discretionary, as they depend on organizational practices and procedures. Mesmer-Magnus et al.'s (2012) definition tends to ignore the various prescribed and task-related environmental actions. With the development of environmental procedures, codes of conduct, and management systems, such as the ISO 14001 standard, an increasing number of environmental behaviors are prescribed by organizations, and employees' green behaviors should, therefore, not be limited only to individual and voluntary actions (Boiral, 2009; Ones & Dilchert, 2012b; Paillé & Boiral, 2013).

Another category of employees' green behaviors is highlighted in the concept of eco-initiatives. According to Ramus and Steger (2000), eco-initiative is a proxy for eco-innovation, which is defined as "any action taken by an employee that she or he thought would improve the environmental performance of the company" (p. 606). Interestingly, eco-innovations can occur at any organizational level, which suggests that all employees, from top management to line workers, can be eco-innovators. Ramus and Steger (2000) provide various examples, such as recycling, pollution prevention, reducing the need for hazardous waste disposal, and improving ecological efficiency to illustrate this definition. Although Ramus and Steger are among the pioneers in this area, the focus of their definition on the improvement of environmental performance of the company seems too restrictive. First, the concept of environmental performance is both vague and controversial (Boiral & Henri, 2012). Second, pro-environmental behaviors can have a nonmeasurable impact or may concern issues not directly related to the company activities, such as riding a bicycle to work instead of taking the car. Third, environmental behaviors can apply to individual actions that are not directly connected with performance, for example, representing the company at a conference or participating in an external meeting on environmental issues (Boiral & Paillé, 2012; Smith & O'Sullivan, 2012).

Drawing on these definitions and their limitations, we offer a definition of employees' pro-environmental behaviors that includes all types of voluntary or prescribed activity undertaken by individuals at work that aim to protect the natural environment or improve organizational practices in this area. This definition, which is relatively close to the one proposed by Ramus and Steger (2000), addresses the main limitations discussed in this section, as it avoids too narrow a view of a multifaceted concept and sheds light on two essential aspects of pro-environmental behaviors in work settings:

- Scope and diversity: Environmental behaviors are not necessarily restricted to employees' actions that are under their full control and can be measured or produce measurable results, and they can include various pro-environmental actions taken by employees and managers alike and focused on organizational practices or more informal initiatives.
- Voluntary or prescribed nature: Environmental behaviors can be based on discretionary, individual, and nonrewarded initiatives (organizational citizenship behaviors) or, conversely, on prescribed tasks and procedures.

Mapping the Diversity of Pro-Environmental Behaviors

Various taxonomies and models have been proposed to reflect the multifaceted nature of pro-environmental behaviors, and empirical studies have been conducted to describe them. The most comprehensive is probably the "green five taxonomy" by Ones and Dilchert (2012a). The development of this taxonomy was initially based on the analysis of 1,299 critical incidents related to various jobs, organizations, and industries. This analysis led to proposing various categories of behaviors with a negative or positive impact on the environment, which were then subjected to confirmation and cross-cultural generalizability analysis. Overall, this taxonomy is based on five main categories and 16 subcategories (Figure 2.1).

For most of these categories, Ones and Dilchert (2012a) provide examples of positive and negative behaviors. For example, a positive behavior for initiating programs and policies may consist in starting a new recycling program. Conversely, a negative behavior in this area may be discontinuing such a program for economic reasons. In our view, refraining from engaging in harmful behaviors does not belong to the same definitional framework as refraining from engaging in helpful behaviors. Nevertheless, this typology, which seems more broad than the definition of employee green behaviors proposed by the same authors (as it goes beyond scalable actions that can be measured and compared at the employee level), helps to better understand the broad scope and the elastic meaning of these behaviors.

Other taxonomies have been proposed based on the impacts, activities, or frequency of pro-environmental behaviors. For example, Smith and O'Sullivan's (2012) "classification of environmentally responsible workplace behavior" is based on two main dimensions that classify different types of behavior:

- Direct behavior (based on the individual's own actions, such as recycling cans) versus indirect behavior (actions to influence others, such as signing an environmental petition)

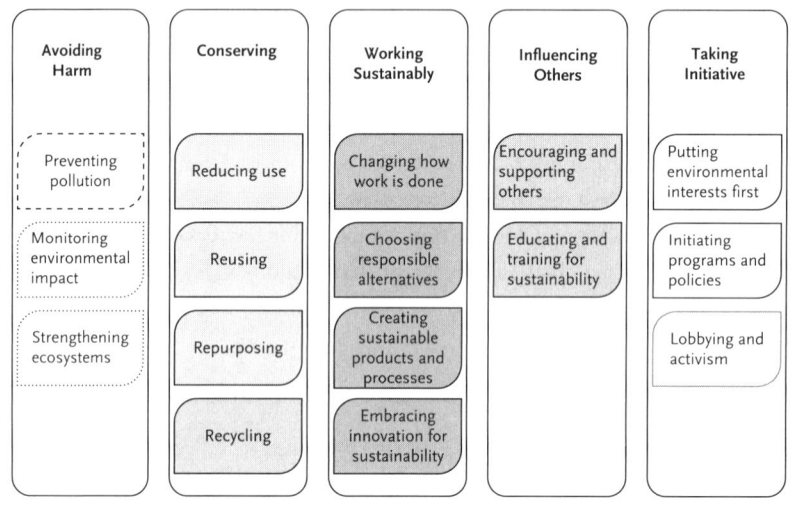

FIGURE 2.1 The "green five taxonomy."
Ones and Dilchert, 2012a, p. 92.

- Local impact (e.g., extending domestic behavior, such as switching off lights, to the work setting) versus wide impact (such as initiating new environmental management practices)

The model by Andersson and Bateman (2000) describes three types of "individual environmental initiatives" based on the nature of the "championing activity" performed in the workplace by employees who have played a key role in this area:

- Identifying environmental issues: "scanning behaviors" intended to acquire information on environmental issues inside or outside the organization
- Packaging environmental issues: behaviors focused on the framing and presentation of environmental issue to better influence the managers and the whole organization
- Selling environmental issues: behaviors intended to influence decision makers to adopt pro-environmental actions

Insights into environmental behaviors have also been based on descriptive studies conducted in the workplace. These studies are interesting in that they portray the relative importance of various types of environmental behaviors. For example, a survey based on a sample of 147 organizations in the United Kingdom (Zibarras & Ballinger, 2011) has shown that the most frequent initiatives are related to recycling and energy saving. Another survey based on a representative sample of 1,043 Australian employees (Crosbie & Houghton, 2011) produced similar results and identified two main categories of behaviors toward sustainability in the workplace. The first category covers behaviors that Australians claim to enact almost invariably, such as turning off the lights at night (71%), turning off computers and monitors at night (67%), and recycling paper (64%). The second category covers less frequent behaviors and areas requiring improvement, such as turning the monitor off when leaving the desk for a period of time, taking public transportation, and specifying environmental products (Figure 2.2). These behaviors are often based on discretionary and nonrewarded initiatives, otherwise known as organizational citizenship behaviors for the environment (Boiral, 2009; Boiral & Paillé, 2012; Daily et al., 2009; Lamm et al., 2013).

Exploring Organizational Citizenship Behaviors for the Environment

It is important to distinguish between voluntary and prescribed tasks involved in pro-environmental behaviors. This distinction is echoed in two streams of the literature that seem to otherwise ignore each other. The first of those is focused

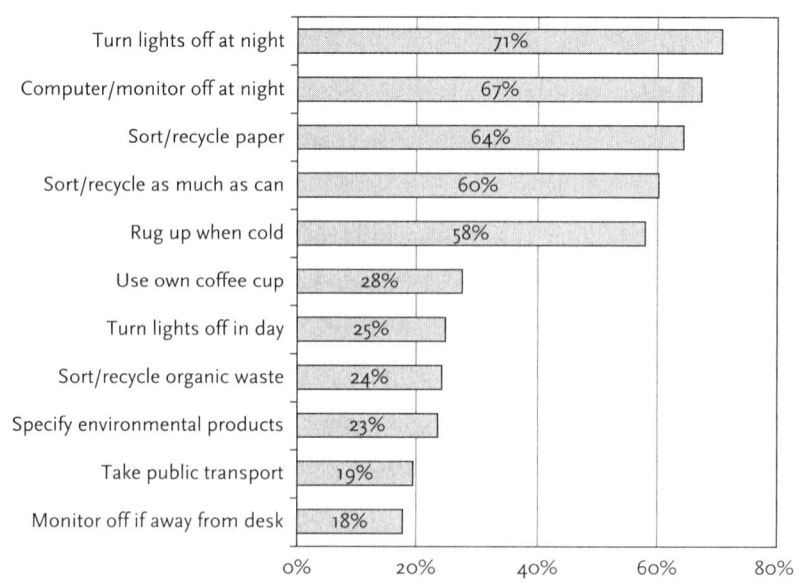

Behavior	Percentage
Turn lights off at night	71%
Computer/monitor off at night	67%
Sort/recycle paper	64%
Sort/recycle as much as can	60%
Rug up when cold	58%
Use own coffee cup	28%
Turn lights off in day	25%
Sort/recycle organic waste	24%
Specify environmental products	23%
Take public transport	19%
Monitor off if away from desk	18%

FIGURE 2.2 "Sustainable behaviors in the workplace."
Based on Crosbie and Houghton, 2011, $N = 1043$.

on environmental management. This more established and broader literature has essentially focused on formal and organizational-level practices, such as the implementation of an environmental management system, the definition of an environmental policy, the promotion of employee awareness and participation in environmental programs (Andersson & Bateman, 2000; Boiral, 2005; Boiral & Henri, 2012; Hart, 1995; Paillé, Boiral, & Chen, 2013; Roy et al., 2013). Although this managerial perspective has also repeatedly emphasized on the importance of individual and voluntary initiatives, it tends to focus more on organizational-level and prescribed environmental behaviors. The second stream of the literature is mostly rooted in the field of industrial and organizational psychology. Generally speaking, this literature is more recent and has given rise to an increasing number of studies on environmental behaviors (Boiral & Paillé, 2012; Lamm et al., 2013; Lülfs & Hahn, 2013; Mesmer-Magnus et al., 2012; Ones & Dilchert, 2009, 2012a; Paillé & Boiral, 2013). These studies mostly focus on individual-level and discretionary behaviors, although they sometimes state that environmental behaviors also can be prescribed.

The concept of organizational citizenship behavior for the environment (OCBE) is mostly rooted in the mentioned second stream of the literature, and has managerial implications. Organizational citizenship behaviors for the environment have been defined variously as "voluntary behaviors not specified in official job descriptions that, through the combined efforts of individual employees, help to make the organization and/or society more sustainable" (Lamm et al., 2013, p. 3), "discretionary acts by employees within the organization, not rewarded or required that are directed toward environmental improvement" (Daily et al., 2009, p. 246), or "individual and discretionary social behaviors that are not explicitly recognized by the formal reward system and that contribute to a more effective environmental management by organizations" (Boiral & Paillé, 2012, p. 431). Overall, all these definitions express the same idea: OCBEs are discretionary behaviors performed by employees whereby they demonstrate their willingness to cooperate with their company and its members by displaying workplace behaviors that benefit the natural environment. Following the classic proposition by Organ (1988), the concept of discretionary behaviors presupposes that individuals are free to act or not to act. Such actions cannot be assured, for example, through the stipulations of contract employment or the threat of punishment. In the particular context of green behavior, the term suggests that employees are able to take decisions at their own level without formal inducements. For employees, OCBEs reflect their willingness to cooperate with the company and its members by performing environmental behaviors in the workplace.

In their study of the main types of environmental behaviors, Ones and Dilchert (2012b, p. 456) suggested that "not all employee green behaviors are discretionary" and that "13-29% of employee green behaviors are required as part of job duties." If this estimate is correct, it means that a large majority—approximately 70% to 85%—of environmental behaviors can actually be considered as OCBEs. In this perspective, it is important to define more precisely what OCBEs really are. Although the literature in this area is in its infancy, some studies have explored the main types of OCBEs. Based on general research on organizational citizenship behaviors, Boiral (2009) proposed that we distinguish six possible forms of OCBEs: helping (collaboration and encouraging other workers to consider environmental issues), sportsmanship (positive attitude toward the inconveniences associated with environmental practices), organizational loyalty (support to the environmental policies and actions of the organization), organizational compliance (compliance with environmental practices and procedures), individual initiative (discretionary suggestions and initiatives in the workplace), and self-development (acquisition of environmental knowledge).

According to Lamm and colleagues (2013), this type of taxonomy is quite broad, and research needs to focus on more specific eco-initiatives. Therefore, Lamm et al. propose a list of 12 items describing typical OCBEs that includes: recycling bottles, using scrap paper for notes, printing double-sided, and turning off lights when leaving the office. These items are relevant and useful

Table 2.1 The Main Types of Organizational Citizenship Behavior for the Environment

	Eco-Initiatives	Eco-Civic Engagement	Eco-Helping
Definition	Discretionary behavior and suggestions to improve environmental practices	Voluntary participation in an organization's environmental programs and activities	Voluntarily helping colleagues to better integrate environmental concerns in the workplace
Main focus	Personal and direct initiatives in the workplace	Support for the commitments of the organization	Mutual support among employees, promotion of environmental concern
Relevance and usefulness	Improving internal practices Reducing environmental impacts Promoting green innovation and reducing costs Saving money (saving energy, water, waste disposal, etc.)	Achieving the environmental objectives of the organization. Improving the image of the organization Identifying environmental issues	Promoting discussion, cooperation and resolution of complex problems. Empowering new employees Influencing behaviors Encouraging and inspiring other employees
Examples	Making suggestions to reduce paper consumption Improving energy efficiency Establishing a ride-sharing program Placing recyclable materials in the proper containers Turning off lights and turning down heating before leaving the office	Participating in a green committee Meeting with stakeholders Becoming involved in the implementation of ISO 14001 Updating environmental procedures Contributing to the annual sustainability report	Helping the environmental service identify sources of pollution Explaining environmental procedures to new employees Asking colleagues to get involved in a new green committee Helping colleagues to clean up an accidental spill

Adapted from Boiral, O., & Paillé, P. (2012). Organizational citizenship behaviour for the environment: Measurement and validation. *Journal of Business Ethics, 109*, 431–445.

to measure certain types of OCBEs. Nevertheless, they are restrictive, essentially focus on daily deskwork. Therefore, they presuppose that regardless of the organizational and employee profile, OCBEs can be described through a small number of very specific behaviors that essentially seem to be an extension of environmental behaviors at home. Moreover, this list does not take into account important types of environmental behaviors, such as those intended to influence others and to support the environmental commitment of organizations (Andersson & Bateman, 2000; Boiral, 2009; Ones & Dilchert, 2012a; Smith & O'Sullivan, 2012).

Boiral and Paillé (2012) propose a more inclusive measurement scale based on three dimensions: eco-initiatives, eco-civic engagement, and eco-helping. The first dimension, eco-initiatives, is similar to the construct proposed by Lamm et al. (2013) and Smith and O'Sullivan's concept of direct behavior (2012). The eco-civic engagement (voluntary participation in an organization's environmental programs and activities) and eco-helping (voluntarily helping colleagues to better integrate environmental concerns) are essentially identical to the indirect behaviors described by Smith and O'Sullivan (2012) and the "championing activities" analyzed by Andersson and Bateman (2000). Table 2.1 summarizes these three main types of OCBEs and the manners in which they can be translated into practical measures.

Concluding Thoughts

Although research on employees' pro-environmental behaviors is far from new, the management and psychological literatures are still focused on providing a consensual or unified definition of the nature of these behaviors and creating provisional measurement instruments. Nevertheless, some important topics ought to be addressed to further our understanding of corporate greening, such as spillover effects between work and nonwork pro-environmental behaviors to shed more light on their constancy and underlying mechanisms (or lack thereof). Considering the communality between work and nonwork, green behaviors can help organizations, for instance, to implement sensitization campaigns or strategies that draw on the domestic and allegedly familiar behavioral patterns of the employees. Future research could also examine whether a directional relationship exists between the dual (e.g., specific vs. general; prescribed vs. voluntary) nature of some workplace green behaviors. For example, knowing that employees are motivated to bring their own reusable cups to work after participating in a collective environmental event (e.g., picking up trash in the parking lot of the company), or vice versa, would aid business practitioners to target the relevant category of so-called gateway behaviors.

This also means, in turn, that longitudinal studies are necessary for capturing temporal changes in employees' behaviors. A final promising avenue of research would consist of analyzing more systematically, in line with the suggestions by Ones and Dilchert (2012a,b), environmentally irresponsible behaviors at work about which we know little. Ungreen behaviors, such as the improper disposal of hazardous substances or the unnecessary use of nonrenewable resources are, by definition, detrimental to the organizational environmental performance. As such, they need to be addressed so that we can better understand how to successfully inhibit them and limit their consequences. Ultimately, there is perhaps as much to be learned, theoretically and empirically, from negative behaviors as from positive ones. Valuable contributions still need to be made, and academics from different theoretical streams must continue to support the development of greener organizations.

Future investigations could combine existing measurements of PEBs. Although scales developed by Paillé and Boiral (2013) seek to capture worker motivation concerning providing advice or encouragement to other individuals in the workplace to adopt direct PEBs, those provided by Lamm et al. (2013), focus on concrete gestures toward the environment (e.g., recycling). It would be useful to evaluate to what degree these scales overlap in order to assess if they capture different facets of PEBs. Future research might also examine the manners in which leaders could be a source of inspiration for the staff. Although the key role of leaders is often hypothesized in the environmental literature (e.g., Ramus, 2001), little research has been undertaken to examine to what extent employees are willing to perform PEBs when their leaders set an example by demonstrating their engagement toward the cause of sustainability in organizational context (for a notable exception see Boiral, Talbot, & Paillé, 2014).

Suggested Additional Readings

1. Boiral, O., Baron, C., & Gunnlaugson, O. (2013). Environmental leadership and consciousness development: A case study among Canadian SMEs. *Journal of Business Ethics*, doi: 10.1007/s10551-013-1845-5.
2. Boiral, O., Cayer, M., & Baron, C. (2009). The action logics of environmental leadership. A developmental perspective. *Journal of Business Ethics*, 85(4), 479–499.
3. Lamm, E., Tosti-Kharas, J., & King, C. E. (2014). Empowering employee sustainability: Perceived organizational support toward the environment. *Journal of Business Ethics*, doi: 10.1007/s10551-014-2093-z.
4. Paillé P., & Mejía Morelos, J. H. (2014). Antecedents of pro-environmental behaviours at work: The moderating influence of psychological contract breach. *Journal of Environmental Psychology*, 38, 124–131.

References

Andersson, L. M., & Bateman, T. S. (2000). Individual environmental initiative: Championing natural environmental issues in US business organizations. *Academy of Management Journal*, 43, 548–570.

Boiral, O. (2002). Tacit knowledge and environmental management. *Long Range Planning*, 35, 291–317.

Boiral, O. (2005). The impact of operator involvement in pollution reduction: Case studies in Canadian chemical companies. *Business Strategy and the Environment*, 14, 339–360.

Boiral, O. (2007a). *Environnement et gestion: De la prévention à la mobilisation*. Presses de l'Université Laval, Québec.

Boiral, O. (2007b). Corporate greening through ISO 14001: A rational myth? *Organization Science*, 18, 127–146.

Boiral, O. (2009). Greening the corporation through organizational citizenship behaviors. *Journal of Business Ethics*, 87, 221–236.

Boiral, O. (2012). ISO certificates as organizational degrees? Beyond the rational myths of the certification process. *Organization Studies*, 33, 633–654.

Boiral, O., & Henri, J. F. (2012). Modelling the impact of ISO 14001 on environmental performance: A comparative approach. *Journal of Environmental Management*, 99, 84–97.

Boiral, O., & Paillé, P. (2012). Organizational citizenship behaviour for the environment: Measurement and validation. *Journal of Business Ethics*, 109, 431–445.

Boiral, O., Talbot, D., & Paillé, P. (2014). Leading by example: A model of organizational citizenship behavior for the environment. *Business Strategy and the Environment*, doi: 10.1002/bse.1835.

Boiral, O., & Sala, J. M. (1998). Environmental management: Should industry adopt ISO 14001? *Business Horizons*, 41, 57–64.

Bunge, J., Cohen-Rosenthal, E., & Ruiz-Quintanilla, S. A. (1996). Employee participation in pollution reduction: Preliminary analysis of the Toxics Release Inventory. *Journal of Cleaner Production*, 4, 9–16.

Cantor, D. E., Morrow, P. C., & Montabon, F. (2012). Engagement in environmental behaviors among supply chain management employees: An organizational support theoretical perspective. *Journal of Supply Chain Management*, 48, 33–51.

Christmann, P., & Taylor, G. (2006). Firm self-regulation through international certifiable standards: Determinants of symbolic versus substantive implementation. *Journal of International Business Studies*, 37, 863–878.

Crosbie, T., & Houghton, M. (2011). Sustainability in the workplace: An analysis of the attitudes and behaviours of Australians to sustainability in the workplace and the home. *Sustainability at Work*, 2011, 1–16.

Daily, B. F., Bishop, J. W., & Govindarajulu, N. (2009). A conceptual model for organizational citizenship behavior directed toward the environment. *Business & Society*, 48, 243–256.

Darnall, N., & Edwards, D. (2006). Predicting the cost of environmental management system adoption: The role of capabilities, resources and ownership structure. *Strategic Management Journal, 27*, 301–320.

Drumwright, M. (1994). Socially responsible organizational buying: Environmental concern as a noneconomic buying criterion. *Journal of Marketing, 58*, 1–19.

Enander, R. T., & Pannullo, D. (1990). Employee involvement and pollution prevention. *The Journal for Quality and Participation*, 50–53.

Gattiker, T. F., & Carter, C. R. (2010). Understanding project champions' ability to gain intra-organizational commitment for environmental projects. *Journal of Operations Management, 28*, 72–85.

Han, H., Hsu, L. T. J., & Lee, J. S. (2009). Empirical investigation of the roles of attitudes toward green behaviors, overall image, gender, and age in hotel customers' eco-friendly decision-making process. *International Journal of Hospitality Management, 28*, 519–528.

Hanna, M. D., Newman, W. R., & Johnson, P. (2000). Linking operational and environmental improvement through employee involvement. *International Journal of Operations & Production Management, 20*, 148–165.

Hart, S. L. (1995). A natural-resource-based view of the firm. *The Academy of Management Review, 20*, 986–1014.

Jiang, R. J., & Bansal, P. (2003). Seeing the need for ISO 14001. *Journal of Management Studies, 40*, 1047–1067.

Kitazawa, S., & Sarkis, J. (2000). The relationship between ISO 14001 and continuous source reduction programs. *International Journal of Operations & Production Management, 20*, 225–248.

Kleiner, A. (1991). What does it mean to be green? *Harvard Business Review, 69*, 38–47.

Kornbluh, H., Crowfoot, J., & Cohen-Rosenthal, E. (1985). Worker participation in energy and natural resource conservation. *International Labour Review, 124*, 737–754.

Lamm, E., Tosti-Kharas, J., & Williams, E. G. (2013). Organizational citizenship behavior toward the environment. *Group & Organization Management, 38*, 163–197.

Lane, M. B., & Robinson, C. J. (2009). Institutional complexity and environmental management: The challenge of integration and the promise of large-scale collaboration. *Australasian Journal of Environmental Management, 16*, 16–24.

Lee, T. H., Jan, F. H., & Yang, C. C. (2013). Conceptualizing and measuring environmentally responsible behaviors from the perspective of community-based tourists. *Tourism Management, 36*, 454–468.

Lülfs, R., & Hahn, R. (2013). Corporate greening beyond formal programs, initiatives, and systems: A conceptual model for voluntary pro-environmental behavior of employees. *European Management Review, 10*, 83–98.

May, D. R., & Flannery, B. L. (1995). Cutting waste with employee involvement teams. *Business Horizons, 38*, 28–38.

Mesmer-Magnus, J., Viswesvaran, C., & Wiernik, B. M. (2012). The role of commitment in bridging the gap between organizational sustainability and environmental sustainability. In S. E. Jackson, D. S. Ones, & S. Dilchert (Eds.), *Managing HR for environmental sustainability* (pp. 155–186). San Francisco: Jossey-Bass/Wiley.

Munguía, N., Zavala, A., Marin, A., Moure-Eraso, R., & Velazquez, L. (2010). Identifying pollution prevention opportunities in the Mexican auto refinishing industry. *Management of Environmental Quality: An International Journal, 21*, 324–335.

Muros, J. P. (2012). Going after the green: Expanding industrial–organizational practice to include environmental sustainability. *Industrial and Organizational Psychology, 5*, 467–472.

Ones, D. S., & Dilchert, S. (2009). Green behaviors of workers: A taxonomy for the green economy. Paper presented at the annual meeting of the Academy of Management, Chicago.

Ones, D. S., & Dilchert, S. (2012a). Employee green behaviors. In S. E. Jackson, D. S. Ones, & S. Dilchert (Eds.), *Managing HR for environmental sustainability* (pp. 155–186). San Francisco: Jossey-Bass/Wiley.

Ones, D. S., & Dilchert, S. (2012b). Environmental sustainability at work: A call to action. *Industrial and Organizational Psychology, 5*, 444–466.

Orecchini, F. (2000). The ISO 14001 certification of a machine-process. *Journal of Cleaner Production, 8*, 61–68.

Organ, D. W. (1988). *Organizational citizenship behavior: The Good Soldier Syndrome*. Lexington, MA: Lexington Books.

Paillé, P., & Boiral, O. (2013). Pro-environmental behavior at work: Construct validity and determinants. *Journal of Environmental Psychology, 36*, 118–128.

Paillé, P., Boiral, O., & Chen, Y. (2013). Linking environmental management practices and organizational citizenship behavior for the environment: A social exchange perspective. *International Journal of Human Resource Management, 24*, 3552–3575.

Paillé, P., Chen, Y., Boiral, O., & Jin, J. (2014). The impact of human resource management on environmental performance: An employee-level study. *Journal of Business Ethics, 121*, 451–466.

Perez, O., Amichai-Hamburger, Y., & Shterental, T. (2009). The dynamic of corporate self-regulation: ISO 14001, environmental commitment, and organizational citizenship behavior. *Law & Society Review, 43*, 593–630.

Ramus, C. A. (2001). Organizational support for employees: Encouraging creative ideas for environmental sustainability. *California Management Review, 43*, 85–105.

Ramus, C. A., & Killmer, A. B. C. (2007). Corporate greening through prosocial extrarole behaviours: A conceptual framework for employee motivation. *Business Strategy and the Environment, 16*, 554–570.

Ramus, C. A., & Steger, U. (2000). The roles of supervisory support behaviors and environmental policy in employee "ecoinitiatives" at leading-edge European companies. *Academy of Management Journal, 43*(4), 605–626.

Rangarajan, N., & Rahm, D. (2011). Greening human resources: A survey of city-level initiatives. *Review of Public Personnel Administration, 31*, 227–247.

Remmen, A., & Lorentzen, B. (2000). Employee participation and cleaner technology: Learning processes in environmental teams. *Journal of Cleaner Production, 8*, 365–373.

Rojšek, I. (2001). From red to green: Towards the environmental management in the country in transition. *Journal of Business Ethics, 33*, 37–50.

Rothenberg, S. (2003). Knowledge content and worker participation in environmental management at NUMMI. *Journal of Management Studies, 40*, 1783–1802.

Roy, M. J., Boiral, O., & Paillé, P. (2013). Pursuing quality and environmental performance: Initiatives and supporting processes. *Business Process Management Journal, 19*, 30–53.

Ruiz-Quintanilla, S. A., Bunge, J., Freeman-Gallant, A., & Cohen-Rosenthal, E. (1996). Employee participation in pollution reduction: A socio-technical perspective. *Business Strategy and the Environment, 5*, 137–144.

Schmidheiny, S. (1992). *Changing course: Executive summary: A global business perspective on development and the environment*. Cambridge, MA: MIT Press.

Shrivastava, P. (1995). The role of corporations in achieving ecological sustainability. *Academy of Management Review, 20*, 936–960.

Smith, A. M., & O'Sullivan, T. (2012). Environmentally responsible behaviour in the workplace: An internal social marketing approach. *Journal of Marketing Management, 28*, 469–493.

Theyel, G. (2000). Management practices for environmental innovation and performance. *International Journal of Operations & Production Management, 20*, 249–266.

Tilley, F. (2000). Small firm environmental ethics: How deep do they go? *Business Ethics: A European Review, 9*, 31–41.

Walley, L., & Stubbs, M. (2000). Termites and champions: Case comparisons by metaphor. *Greener Management International, 29*, 41–54.

Winter, G., & Ewers, H. J. (1988). *Business and the environment: A handbook of industrial ecology with 22 checklists for practical use and a concrete example of the integrated system of environmentalist business management (the Winter Model)*. New York: McGraw-Hill.

Yin, H., & Schmeidler, P. J. (2009). Why do standardized ISO 14001 environmental management systems lead to heterogeneous environmental outcomes? *Business Strategy and the Environment, 18*, 469–486.

Zibarras, L., & Ballinger, C. (2011). Promoting environmental behaviour in the workplace: A survey of UK organisations. In D. Bartlett (dir.). *Going green: The psychology of sustainability in the workplace* (pp. 84–90). Leicester, UK: The British Psychological Society.

3 THEORETICAL BASIS FOR ORGANIZATIONAL PRO-ENVIRONMENTAL RESEARCH

Angela M. Ruepert, Linda Steg, and Kees Keizer

Environmental problems due to greenhouse gas, pollution, and the use of raw materials and energy are to a large extent caused by human behavior. Environmental behavior refers to any behavior that has an impact on the environment, both good and bad. Pro-environmental behavior (PEB) reflects behavior that harms the environment as little as possible or even benefits it (Steg & Vlek, 2009). Most of the research on understanding and encouraging PEB has been focused on psychological factors influencing individual behavior within the household or the community, like household energy use and travel behavior (e.g., Abrahamse & Steg, 2011; Kurz, Donaghue, & Walker, 2005; Poortinga, Steg, & Vlek, 2003). These studies revealed important insights as to which psychological factors affect environmental behavior. Yet, individual behavior does not solely depend on psychological factors (Guagnano, Stern, & Dietz, 1995; Ölander & Thøgersen, 1995; Steg & Vlek, 2009; Stern, Dietz, Abel, Guagnano, & Kalop, 1999; Thøgersen, 2005). Various contextual factors, such as the availability of recycling facilities, parking policies, work requirements, or culture can facilitate or constrain PEB and influence the extent to which psychological factors determine PEB (Steg & Vlek, 2009).

One specific context that is likely to have important implications for the likelihood of PEB is the workplace. Within a lifetime, most people spend a substantial part of their time at work, and their behavior at work is likely to significantly affect environmental quality. Yet little is known about workplace pro-environmental behaviors (WPEB), which individual and contextual factors motivate such behavior, and how these factors interact. This knowledge is necessary if we are to understand how WPEB can be encouraged. In this chapter, we review theoretical frameworks that can increase our understanding of workplace environmental behaviors (WEB). We propose that WEB is determined by similar psychological factors as private environmental behavior at home. Therefore, we first provide an overview of theories that proved to be successful in improving our understanding of private environmental behavior. More specifically, we discuss value theories, goal-framing theory, theories that assume that behavior results from cost-benefit analyses (including individual, social, normative, and hedonic costs and benefits), and theories on habits. In the second part of this chapter, we argue that the work setting has some specific (contextual) characteristics that have important implications for WEB, which determine the significance of various psychological factors for explaining such behavior. Thus, we consider the general focus of organizations on profit generation, the extent to which WPEB is autonomous, high levels of interactions between employees and formally shaped relationships, and reduced self-control when spending prolonged effort to fulfill tasks at work. Finally, we present the main conclusions and provide a research agenda to better understand and promote WPEB.

Theoretical Frameworks to Predict Pro-Environmental Behavior

In some situations we carefully and deliberately elaborate on costs and benefits of available behavioral options before we act. Yet, in other situations we are likely to habitually repeat behavior we have shown before, without deliberation. We first review theories that assume that we reason before we act. Various theories aim to provide insight into which aspects we are likely to consider in this respect, and the nature of the decision processes involved. We first describe two general overarching frameworks: value theory, which focuses on general determinants of behavior, and goal-framing theory, which provides an overarching framework on which factors we consider before we act. Values and goals determine which individual, social, normative, or affective consequences people focus on when considering whether to act pro-environmentally. Next, we describe prominent theoretical frameworks that focus on some of these consequences: the theory of planned behavior, the norm activation model, the value-belief-norm theory, identity theory, social norms theories, and the theory of material possessions. After that, we elaborate on habits.

Value Theories

Values are defined as "desirable goals, varying in importance, that serve as guiding principles in people's lives" (Schwartz, 1992, p. 21). Values have different key features that make them particularly important for understanding environmental behavior. First, values reflect beliefs about the (un)desirability of certain end-states, such as social justice, wealth, or unity with nature. Values reflect the extent to which a person believes that for example the quality of nature and the environment is an important aspect in life. Second, values are ordered in a priority system, which means that although people generally endorse the same values, the importance of different values is likely to differ across individuals. Values guide the selection and evaluation of various behavior-specific beliefs, attitudes, intentions, and ultimately behaviors. Third, values are abstract and transcend specific situations and behaviors, and are relatively stable over time.

Four types of values are particularly relevant to understand environmental behavior: hedonic, egoistic, altruistic, and biospheric values (e.g., De Groot & Steg, 2008; Steg, Perlaviciute, Van der Werff, & Lurvink, 2014b). People with strong hedonic values find pleasure or sensuous satisfaction for themselves particularly important as a guiding principle in their life, whereas people with strong egoistic values focus on individual costs and benefits when making choices (Steg et al., 2014b). Both hedonic and egoistic values reflect self-enhancement values, with a main focus on self-interests. People with strong altruistic values are especially concerned about the welfare of other people and society, whereas people with strong biospheric values base their behavioral decision on the costs and benefits for the environment (De Groot & Steg, 2008; De Groot, Steg, & Dicke, 2008). These two value types reflect self-transcendent values, in which people particularly consider consequences beyond their short-term self-interest.

People who strongly endorse values beyond their immediate own interests, that is biospheric and (to a lesser extent) altruistic values, are more likely to have strong pro-environmental beliefs and norms and engage in PEB (e.g., De Groot et al., 2008; De Groot & Steg, 2008; Honkanen & Verplanken, 2004). In contrast, pro-environmental beliefs, norms, and behaviors appear to be less likely among those with strong egoistic and hedonic values, probably because PEB often is rather costly in terms of money, effort, or comfort. For example, research has shown that car use has clear positive hedonic and egoistic consequences, and people with strong egoistic and hedonic values use their car more often (Steg et al., 2014b). Yet in some cases hedonic or egoistic values may concur with behaving pro-environmentally. For example, reducing energy consumption decreases energy costs as well, and for some people cycling is not only pro-environmental but also pleasurable.

Goal-Framing Theory

Values influence which goals are prominent in a given situation. People may not always act upon the values they strongly endorse, as the strength of one's goals also depends on situational cues, as we explain in the following (Steg, 2012; Steg, Bolderdijk, Keizer, & Perlaviciute, 2014). Goal-framing theory (Lindenberg & Steg, 2007) provides an overarching theoretical framework for understanding the influence of goals and their situational dependency. Goal-framing theory proposes that goals "frame" the way people process information and act upon it in a specific situation. What people attend to, what knowledge and attitudes become cognitively accessible, how people evaluate various aspects of the situation, and what behavioral alternatives are being considered all depend on which goals are dominant at a given moment (which depends on values strength and situational cues). Three overarching goals are distinguished: the gain goal that focuses people on guarding and improving their resources, the normative goal that focuses a person on other people and acting appropriately, and the hedonic goal that focuses someone at feeling better right now. These goals coincide with the values described in the preceding, with altruistic and biospheric values both affecting the strength of normative goals (focusing either on the goal to increase the welfare of others or the biosphere).

Goal-framing theory states that the goal that is strongest or "focal" is the goal frame, whereas other goals remain in the background and increase the strength of the goal frame when they are compatible or decrease its strength when they are in conflict. For example, when your normative goal is focal and you have to choose how to get to work, you will probably particularly consider the environmental consequences of transport modes, and consequently, be motivated to go by bicycle rather than by car (if the travel distance is not too long). This choice is even more likely when other goals in the background support the normative goal, for example, when you realize that cycling makes you feel better than driving and when cycling saves money. In contrast, you may be less likely to cycle when this normative action would threaten the fulfillment of other goals in the background, for example, when you realize that cycling is less comfortable (e.g., when it is raining) or is time consuming.

Many PEBs involve a conflict between normative goals on the one hand and gain and hedonic goals at the other hand. Indeed, acting pro-environmentally is generally perceived as the right thing to do, but often it is more costly in terms of money, effort, or comfort. This implies that PEBs will be most likely when normative goals are focal, and less likely when gain or hedonic goals are focal. However, in some cases, acting pro-environmentally can fulfill gain or hedonic goals as well (e.g., it can be financially attractive or pleasurable). An example is turning in bottles or cans at a designated location instead of throwing them in the trash because of the rebate. However, as soon as the price or the pleasurableness changes and the personal costs outweigh the benefits, people with strong gain and hedonic goals are likely to no longer act pro-environmentally. Thus gain and hedonic goals are a relatively fickle basis for consistent and prolonged PEBs. Normative goals generally provide a more solid basis for stable and prolonged PEBs, as acting pro-environmentally is generally the right thing to do in many different situations (De Groot & Steg, 2009a). So, how can normative goals be strengthened and be made focal?

As indicated, goals strength not only depends on values, but also on situational cues. Hence, the relative strength and influence of goals can differ across situations (in contrast to values, which are believed to be relatively stable across time). More specifically, goals can be strengthened by situational cues that activate or deactivate different values (Lindenberg & Steg, 2007; Steg et al., 2014). For example, normative goals are more likely to be focal among those with strong biospheric and altruistic values. Normative goals can be further strengthened by normative cues in the environment, such as objects that are associated with normative goals (e.g., posters of charity, clearly visible recycle bins) or the presence of significant others who do the right thing. (We elaborate on the influence of norms in the section on social norm theory.) On the other hand, normative goals can be weakened by cues in the environment that strengthen gain or hedonic goals. For example, seeing objects that are typical in business situations, such as business suits, can strengthen a gain goal, thereby weakening the normative goal (Kay, Wheeler, Bargh, & Ross, 2004). This implies that normative goals can be strengthened by increasing the relative importance and cognitive accessibility of biospheric or altruistic values in specific situations through environmental cues (De Groot & Steg, 2009a).

The relative strength of different goals determines which costs and benefits people consider when making choices. In the following, we discuss theories that focus on different goals, and describe which types of costs and benefits are considered in these different theories.

Theories Focusing on Gain Goals

When gain goals are strong, people particularly focus on costs and benefits in terms of scarce resources (Lindenberg & Steg, 2007). Both individual (e.g., money, time) and social (e.g., social approval, status) costs and benefits are likely to be considered. People prefer to choose options with highest benefits against lowest costs. In the following, we describe two theories that assume that individuals base their choices mainly on such individual and social considerations: the theory of planned behavior and social norm theory.

The Theory of Planned Behavior

The theory of planned behavior (TPB; Ajzen, 1991) assumes that individuals make reasoned choices based on weighing the expected (individual and social) costs and benefits of behavior. The TPB assumes that behavior results from one's intention that reflects how hard an individual is willing to try to perform a behavior. For example, the stronger a person's intention toward energy conservation, the more likely it is that person puts effort to conserve energy. The intention depends on three factors: attitudes, subjective norms, and perceived behavioral control.

Attitudes toward behavior reflect the extent to which performing the behavior is evaluated positively or negatively. For example, if a person has a positive attitude toward organic products, it is more likely that he or she will intend to buy organic food, whereas this person may have a negative attitude toward recycled paper, decreasing the intention to buy recycled toilet paper. Attitudes are based on beliefs about positive or negative consequences of the behavior, taking into account the importance of these costs and benefits. For example, a person might believe that organic products are healthy and tasty, and find these factors very important. At the same time this person can believe that organic products are more expensive and expire faster, but believe that these factors are not too important. In this case, weighing the costs and benefits with their importance results in an overall positive attitude toward organic products. Which costs and benefits are most relevant for people varies across behaviors, and needs to be established in a pilot study.

Subjective norms reflect social costs and benefits and refer to the perception of whether important others would approve or disapprove of behavior, taking into account one's motivation to comply with these expectations. For example, if your neighbors, whose opinion you value, expect you to put your garden waste in the designated bin, you would be motivated to comply with these expectations.

Perceived behavioral control reflects the appraisal of one's ability to perform the behavior, and depends on the perceived availability of the requisite opportunities and resources. For example, if you think that you do not have enough money to buy organic products, your perceived behavioral control will be low, and consequently you may not intend to buy organic products. Perceived behavioral control can affect behavior via intention, but also directly, for example, if you intend to buy organic products, but while shopping realize they are out of stock.

The TPB proposes that people choose options with highest benefits against lowest costs, taking into account individual and social costs and benefits. All other factors, such as values, general beliefs, and socio-demographic factors, are assumed to influence behavior indirectly via attitudes, subjective norms, and perceived behavioral control. The TPB has been successful in predicting a range of environmental intentions and behaviors in households, such as recycling, energy conservation, travel mode choice, or pro-environmental buying (e.g., Armitage & Conner, 2001; Bamberg & Möser, 2007; Tonglet, Phillips, & Bates, 2004), and the predictive power of attitudes, subjective norms, and perceived behavioral control appeared to be similar (Bamberg & Möser, 2007). There is some evidence that the TPB is successful in predicting WPEB. For example, positive attitudes toward pro-environmental treatment of hazardous wastewater, the perception that important others would approve of this behavior, and a feeling of perceived behavioral control over this behavior increased pro-environmental intentions among managers (Flannery & May, 2000), whereas positive attitudes toward recycling increased recycling among employees (Tudor, Barr, & Gilg, 2007).

Social Norms

Some theories specifically focus on the perceived social costs and benefits of behavior, for example, theories on the influence of social norms. The focus theory of normative conduct (Cialdini, 2003) proposes a distinction between two types of social norms: descriptive norms and injunctive norms. *Descriptive norms* refer to perceptions of the behavior commonly shown by others in a certain situation. Descriptive norms influence behavior by providing information on which behavior is likely to be effective and adaptive in a certain situation (Cialdini, Reno, & Kallgren, 1990). For example, being in an organization in which many people leave their computer on during their lunch break signals that this is effective behavior, thereby increasing the probability that others will do the same. Descriptive norms are most influential when people are not sure how to act or when the descriptive norm is (made) salient. A message on the organizations' well-read bulletin board that 75% of the employees switch of their office light when going home, will most likely increase the effect of this pro-environmental descriptive norm on the remaining 25%.

Injunctive norms refer to the behavior that is perceived to be commonly approved or disapproved by others. Injunctive norms influence behavior by indicating which behaviors might be met with (social) rewards or sanctions. This type of social norm is comparable to the subjective norm as proposed by the TPB. For example, in an organization in which the norm favors energy savings, people may turn your lights off when leaving their workplace because they want to avoid comments of disapproval from their colleagues or gain approval.

Even if people personally do not care about the environmental consequences of injunctive norm violations, they may act pro-environmentally because they care about the potential (dis)approval of others. Hence, injunctive norms are more influential when others are present (i.e., public setting) and can observe the behavior (Nettle, Harper, Kidson, Stone, Penton-Voak, & Bateson, 2013; Raihani & Bshary, 2012).

Like the impact of descriptive social norms, the impact of injunctive norms on environmental behavior also depends on the salience of these norms (Cialdini et al., 1990). For example, in an organization with a "reduce energy policy," the probability that an employee will conform to this injunctive norm increases when he or she observes a colleague engaging in energy-saving behavior. The impact of an injunctive norm is also influenced by the extent to which descriptive norms seem to support this injunctive norm. Therefore, a well-intended campaign telling people that they should join the "reduce energy policy" because the majority of the employees leave their lights on are likely to lead to an increase rather than a decrease in the likelihood that employees will join. As a result, the influence of an injunctive norm can be weakened by a conflicting descriptive norm (Cialdini, 2003).

Interestingly, the influence of injunctive norms is also inhibited when disrespect for other injunctive norms is observed, the so-called cross-norm inhibition effect (Keizer, Lindenberg, & Steg, 2008, 2013). For example, people are less likely to follow an injunctive anti-litter norm when they observe that other people violated another norm, such as spraying graffiti where this is not allowed (Keizer et al., 2008). The cross-norm inhibition effect is stronger when disrespect for norms is (made) more salient. This implies that making an injunctive norm salient can be counter-effective in a setting with a conflicting descriptive norm, as it (also) increases the salience of these injunctive norm violations. For example, placing an anti-litter prohibition sign in a littered setting increased rather than decreased littering (Keizer, Lindenberg, & Steg, 2011) as the sign focuses one's attention on the fact that others do not respect (anti-litter) norms. In the organizational context, the cross-norm inhibition effect implies that violations of an environmental organizational rule can spread among employees and also weaken compliance to other (environmental) rules. This effect can be explained on the basis of goal-framing theory: Being aware of norm violations of others weakens one's normative goals and increases the relative strength of one's hedonic and gain goals (Keizer et al., 2008; Lindenberg & Steg, 2007).

Theories Focusing on Normative Goals

When normative goals are strong, people particularly consider normative costs and benefits of behavior options, such as moral considerations. Theories and models that focus on moral considerations assume that caring about the environment is perceived as a moral issue and that acting pro-environmentally is the right thing to do, whereas not acting pro-environmentally is morally wrong. We discuss three theoretical frameworks that focus on normative considerations: the norm activation model, the value-believe norm theory, and identity theory.

The Norm Activation Model

The norm activation model (NAM; Schwartz, 1977; Schwartz & Howard, 1981) proposes that people are more likely to engage in PEB when they experience a personal norm to do so, that is, when they feel morally obliged to engage in a specific action. Personal norms particularly influence behavior when they are activated, which depends on four situational factors (Steg & De Groot, 2010). First, people must be aware of the adverse consequences of not acting pro-environmentally (awareness of consequences). Second, individuals should feel responsible for the negative consequences of not acting pro-environmentally (ascription of responsibility). Third, people should think they can help reduce environmental problems by acting pro-environmentally (outcome-efficacy). Outcome-efficacy is very relevant in the environmental domain, as typically, environmental problems are only solved when many people collaborate (Steg & Nordlund, 2012). Outcome efficacy is low if people do not believe that others will do their bit (Steg & De Groot, 2010). Fourth, people should think they are capable of engaging in specific PEB (self-efficacy); this is comparable to perceived behavioral control as included in the TPB. Research shows that some of these activating factors are causally related: The more people are aware of the environmental problems caused by their behavior, the more they feel responsible for these problems, and/or the more they will perceive their own actions to reduce these problems as worthwhile. This in turn activates personal norms, which increases the likelihood of PEB (Figure 3.1; Steg & De Groot, 2010). The NAM proved to be successful in predicting individual PEB, including reducing car use (Nordlund & Garvill, 2003), environmental activism (Steg & De Groot, 2010), and the acceptance of pro-environmental policies (De Groot & Steg, 2009b). Some factors included in the NAM predicted WPEB as well (e.g., personal norms: Scherbaum, Popovich, & Finlinson, 2008, awareness of consequences: Gadenne, Kennedy, & McKeiver, 2009).

The Value-Belief-Norm Theory of Environmentalism

The value-belief-norm (VBN) theory of environmentalism (Stern, 2000; Stern et al., 1999) extends the NAM by assuming that awareness of consequences is influenced by stable individual variables: values and ecological worldviews. More specifically, VBN theory proposes that values influence awareness of

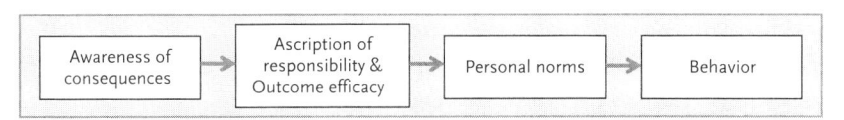

FIGURE 3.1 The norm activation model.

consequences via the strength of ecological worldviews as reflected in the New Environmental Paradigm (NEP; Dunlap, Van Liere, Mertig, & Jones, 2000). The NEP reflects fundamental beliefs about the relationship between human and nature and supports the idea of humankind as a part of nature, as opposed to the traditional social paradigm, which supports the idea that humankind was created to rule over the rest of nature (Dunlap et al., 2000). The degree of acceptance of the NEP depends on one's values. People with strong egoistic or hedonic values are less likely to define other living organisms within their notion of self and hence are less likely to support NEP. In contrast, strong altruistic and biospheric values are generally associated with seeing plants, animals, and other people as part of the self (Schultz, 2001), and hence, stronger support for the NEP.

The VBN theory has been empirically validated in a few studies on individual behavior (Jakovcevic & Steg, 2013; Steg, Dreijerink, & Abrahamse, 2005; Stern et al., 1999). To our knowledge, the VBN theory has not been tested systematically in organizations, although one study showed that stronger acceptance of the NEP increased energy-conservation behavior at work (Scherbaum et al., 2008). However, similar to research on private environmental behavior (e.g., Poortinga et al., 2003; Steg, De Groot, Dreijerink, Abrahamse, & Siero, 2011), this relationship was rather weak.

Environmental Self-Identity

The theories on normative considerations we discussed in the preceding focused on behavior-specific predictors of behavior, such as the personal norm to engage in that specific behavior. A more general type of normative consideration is environmental self-identity, which predicts a wide range of environmental intentions and behaviors (Van der Werff, Steg, & Keizer, 2013a,b, 2014a,b). Environmental self-identity reflects the extent to which people see themselves as people who act pro-environmentally (Van der Werff et al., 2013a). Individuals with a strong environmental self-identity will more strongly see themselves as people who act pro-environmentally and act accordingly (Manetti, Pierro, & Livi, 2004; Van der Werff et al., 2013a, 2014a,b). Research has shown that environmental self-identity depends on biospheric values and past behavior, which implies that the environmental self-identity has a stable core and is not highly susceptible to changes in different contexts, but can be enhanced to some extent by reminding people on their past PEB or weakened when people realize that they have not acted pro-environmentally in the past (Van der Werff et al., 2014a). Environmental self-identity is strengthened when an individual's previous PEBs were manifold, difficult, or unique (Van der Werff et al., 2014b). Environmental self-identity affects PEB via personal norms, suggesting that the environmental self-identity increases one's intrinsic motivation to act pro-environmentally (Van der Werff et al., 2013b).

The relationship between biospheric values and PEB on the one hand, and between past behavior and PEB on the other hand both appear to be mediated by the environmental self-identity (Van der Werff et al., 2014a), which implies that biospheric values as well as past environmental actions affect behavior because people are more likely to see themselves as a pro-environmental person. Hence, environmental self-identity not only reflects normative considerations, but also symbolic motivations, because behaving according to one's environmental self-identity signals to the self and others that you care for the environment (Noppers, Keizer, Bolderdijk, & Steg, 2014).

The significance of symbolic motivations for (environmental) behavior is also emphasized in the theory of material possession: People may engage in a particular behavior to show to the self or others who they are or aspire to be (Dittmar, 1992, 2004). Research has shown that people may indeed use or buy (pro-environmental) products to signify their self-identity, status, and group affiliations (e.g., Griskevicius, Tybur, & Van den Bergh, 2010; Steg, 2005; see Gatersleben & Steg, 2012, for a review). For example, buying an electric car can signal a concern for the environment or a personal innovativeness and thus fulfill symbolic functions (Noppers et al., 2014).

Hedonic Factors and Environmental Behavior

Many people believe that they act rationally and weigh relevant personal and moral costs and benefits of behavioral alternatives. However, this is not always the case (Zajonc, 1980). Affective motives can have a significant influence on environmental behavior, making people act upon their gut feelings rather than on conscious deliberations of pros and cons of actions. Also, people may act in a certain manner because it is more pleasant. *Affect* refers to experiences and feelings of emotions as a response to objects or events (Slovic, Finucane, Peters, & MacGregor, 2007). In general, if these feelings are pleasant, they influence attitudes positively and motivate behavior that reproduces these feelings; but if these feelings are unpleasant they influence attitudes negatively and motivate behavior that avoids the feelings. This means that the extent to which PEB results in a positive or negative affect (experienced affect), but also the extent to which people believe that behaving pro-environmentally will elicit positive or negative feelings (anticipated affect), can form a significant factor in predicting PEB (Fraj & Martinez, 2007; Gatersleben & Steg, 2012). For example, negative anticipated affect (e.g., if I would use public transport instead of the car I would feel angry, frustrated, unsatisfied, or sad) inhibited individual's desire to use public transportation to travel to work (Carrus, Passafaro, & Bonnes, 2008). Yet, people may also experience positive emotions when engaging in PEB, even though such behavior may not be that pleasurable, because it feels good to make a meaningful contribution to the collective good (Carrus et al., 2008; Venhoeven, Bolderdijk, & Steg, 2013). Anticipated affect may thus encourage PEBs as well.

Affect can strongly influence PEB and overrule cognitive considerations (personal and moral costs and benefits). Using an overall, readily available affective impression is much more efficient than weighing all the costs and benefits or retrieving many relevant examples from memory, especially when it comprises complex behavior and when cognitive resources are limited (Slovic et al., 2007).

Habits and Environmental Behavior

The theories we discussed in the preceding generally assume that PEB results from reasoned choices. Yet, everyday behavior is often habitual. In many cases people do not consider the implications and form no intentions before engaging in environmental behavior, but are guided by automatic cognitive structures. Habits are defined as "cognitive structures that automatically determine future behavior by linking specific situational cues to behavioral patterns" (Klöckner & Verplanken, 2012, p. 198). When people frequently behave in the same way in similar situations to reach a certain goal, situational cues will be mentally associated with that behavior. The more frequently this occurs, the stronger and more accessible the association becomes, and the more likely the behavior is repeated the next time these situational cues are encountered. Due to this, people do not need to think about everything they do, enabling a more efficient allocation of their scarce cognitive resources. Habits have four key features: They are performed frequently, there is a high degree of consistency in the context in which the specific behavior is performed, there is success in reaching a goal by performing the behavior, and the performance of behavior is without conscious control (Klöckner & Verplanken, 2012).

When habits are strong, people no longer make conscious choices. Indeed, research has shown that habits moderate the impact of factors such as intentions and personal norms on environmental behavior: Intentions and personal norms are particularly related to behavior when habits are weak (e.g., Klöckner & Matthies, 2004; Verplanken, Aarts, Van Knippenberg, & Van Knippenberg, 1994). Habits are generally considered to be barriers for PEB, assuming that many PEBs involve that people change existing routines. However, not all habits have a negative influence on the environment. People may habitually act pro-environmentally as well, for example, habitually separating their paper from other garbage or switch off the lights when they leave a room. Habitual behavior may involve misperceptions and selective attention: People tend to focus more on information that confirms their habits, and neglect information that is not compatible with their habitual behavior. This implies that habits are not easily broken; significant changes in a situation may be needed before people reconsider their habitual behavior.

Because habits form a direct and automatic link between situational cues and specific behavioral patterns, contextual factors or cues can be essential in the creation of good habits and the breaking of bad habits. More generally, contextual factors can have important influences on behavior. For example, the availability of facilities, rules, laws, or price regimes can determine the attractiveness of PEB or even form constraints for specific PEBs. This is particularly relevant for PEB in organizations, as the organizational context can affect the likelihood of WPEB in important ways. Contextual factors may affect WPEB in three different ways: They may affect behavior directly (e.g., you want to recycle your paper but realize that there is no paper recycle bin), they may moderate the relationship between goals and behavior (e.g., a normative goal may only result in a reduction in commuting by car when feasible alternatives are available), and they may determine which types of goals most strongly affect behavior (e.g., normative goals may be weakened when WPEB is very costly; see Steg & Vlek, 2009). In the next part of this chapter we focus on the latter and discuss relevant contextual factors in organizations that affect WPEB, which should be considered and targeted when trying to encourage WPEB.

Unique Characteristics of the Organizational Context That Determine the Importance of Factors Influencing Pro-Environmental Behavior

The theories discussed in the previous section are typically applied to predict PEB in the private sphere, and empirical evidence is mostly based on research on behavior in the private domain (e.g., in the household). But to what extent are these theories relevant for WPEB? This is a highly important question since most people spend a substantial part of their waking hours in a work setting. As indicated at the end of the previous section, we argue that the significance of factors influencing environmental behavior depends on the context in which choices are made. In this section, we discuss some key characteristics of the workplace context that may affect the significance of different factors for the likelihood of WPEB.

Organizations are social entities that possess values (which are often reflected in their mission statement), and a purpose for existence. The organizational mission and actions taken to accomplish that mission can affect employee behavior. Thus, within an organizational context, individual and organizational factors determine behavioral choices. We first discuss how the focus on profit-generation, which is prevalent in many organizations, may affect WPEB. Then we elaborate on the effects of high levels of social interaction typical for many workplace settings. Next, we discuss the effects of autonomy at work on environmental actions. Finally, we elaborate on how reduced levels of self-control after spending prolonged effort to fulfill tasks at work may affect WPEB.

The Organization as a Profit-Generating Context

Organizations can have different raisons d'être. In broad terms this can range from profit-generation to social services or more altruistic reasons. For commercial organizations, which are the most common types of organizations, a focus on profit-generation is evident, but an economic focus is also essential for nonprofit organizations to maintain their existence. In general, a focus on profit making is thus built into the system of the functioning of organizations. This profit-making goal of organizations, or of employees within organizations, can conflict with the goal to be pro-environmental, because WPEB is in general believed to be more financially costly (Wagner, Van Phu, Azomahou, & Wehrmeyer, 2002). However, WPEB can also involve cost savings for organizations. For example, saving energy saves money as well, and a pro-environmental image may have competitive advantages. Research has indeed shown that "green" organizations often benefit from pro-environmental decisions and behavior in the form of lower costs, fewer risks and liabilities, more efficient operations (Husted & Allen, 2007; Russo & Fouts, 1997), higher work motivation (Ellemers, Kingma, Van de Burgt, & Barreto, 2011), competitive advantages, preservation of resources and raw materials, and favorable corporate image (Rondinelli & Berry, 2000). Indeed, a meta-analysis revealed a positive relationship between corporate environmental performance and corporate financial performance across industries (Orlitzky, Schmidt, & Rynes, 2003). Although management may believe otherwise, pro-environmental decisions do not necessarily reduce profit generation. This may explain the growing interest in corporate social responsibility (CSR) and corporate environmental responsibility (CER) programs (Mueller, Hattrup, Spiess, & Lin-Hi, 2012).

Corporate social responsibility and corporate environmental responsibility imply that organizations aim to increase and optimally balance their economic, social, and environmental performance (Dahlsrud, 2008). The growing interest in CSR and CER indicates that besides profit generation, other goals such as the well-being of stakeholders and environmental impact play a role in organizational decision making too. Still, in general, environmental and social goals are not prioritized and mainly play a background role, whereas economic profitability is often the key concern in organizations (David, Bloom, & Hillman, 2007). There may be many cues in the organizational context suggesting that organizations are mainly concerned with economic profitability, such as reward systems on the basis of annual profitability, short- and long-term strategies focused on profit generation and outcomes measured in profit ratios. These are likely to strengthen employees' gain goals and inhibit WPEB (cf. Tudor, Barr, & Gilg, 2008). For example, research has shown that labeling a social dilemma game to coincide with the gain goal frame ("Wallstreet Game") as opposed to social or normative label ("Community Game") significantly increased the focus on profit making and therefore inhibited normative behavior (Liberman, Samuels, & Ross, 2004). From a goal-framing perspective, these results suggest that such cues strengthen gain goals of employees, thereby pushing their normative goals to the background (Lindenberg & Steg, 2013). Within organizational contexts, gain goals are likely to be constantly strengthened by situational cues indicating that profit making and competition play a central role, increasing the relative strength of gain goals. This implies that, in case of goal conflicts, decisions will likely mostly be decided in favor of profit making, as this goal is likely to be most salient (Lindenberg & Steg, 2013).

The economic focus of organizations can thus affect employees' WPEB and the levels of attention and resources directed toward WPEB (cf. Tudor et al., 2008). Based on the preceding and goal-framing theory, we argue that when gain goals are dominant, employees will engage in WPEB if it is mandatory or less costly. This implies that when WPEB is based on gain goals, there is no stable basis for WPEB, because employees will no longer perform the behavior when it is not mandatory or whenever the costs increase (De Groot & Steg, 2008). Yet, organizations with more embedded CER are likely to have developed a culture of environmental responsibility motivated by ethical and discretionary values and felt responsibility. In such cases, normative cues are likely to be present in the organizational context, which may increase the strength of employees' normative goals, which form a more stable basis for WPEB as it is less influenced by rules or costs (Pandey, Rupp, & Thornton, 2013; Werther & Chandler, 2011).

The Organization Can Limit Autonomy over Individual Pro-Environmental Behavior

Decision-making processes within organizations influence whether WEB is mandated or autonomous. Although in some organizations decisions are made bottom-up, with rules and procedures being initiated by employees, more often decisions are made top-down, with rules and procedures imposed by management. This affects employees' control over their WPEB. As discussed, environmental self-identity (the extent to which you see yourself as a type of person who acts pro-environmentally) is determined by values and past environmental behavior that signals who you are (Van der Werff et al., 2014b). Employees' environmental self-identity is most likely strengthened when they engage in autonomous WPEB, as in that case, the behavior clearly signals who they are. When management imposes rules and procedures, employees have limited control over their WPEB. As a consequence, employees may not believe that their WPEB is autonomous or unique and therefore their environmental self-identity will not be strengthened. Thus the organizational context can result in low autonomy, thereby decreasing the relative strength and influence of the environmental self-identity on behavior. This may have important implications, because, as argued, environmental self-identity is a stable predictor of a wide range of PEB. Even when WPEB is imposed by management, they likely not only aim to promote the enforced WPEB, but also other types of WPEB, thereby promoting positive spillover between behaviors. It is likely that the environmental self-identity promotes such positive spillover effects (Van der Werff et al., 2014b). Yet, when a specific WPEB is mandated, it will possibly promote that particular WPEB, but it will not strengthen employees' environmental self-identity, thereby limiting the likelihood of possible positive spillover effects to other WPEB.

The Organization as a Context with High Levels of Formally Shaped Social Interaction

Another key feature of the organizational context is the high level of interactions among employees. Employees have regular social interactions with one another and their behaviors are generally easily observed by their colleagues (Carrico & Riemer, 2011). As discussed, people form perceptions about which behavior is most commonly done (descriptive norms) and which behavior is perceived as most appropriate (injunctive norms) through social interactions and observing others (Cialdini et al., 1990; Keizer & Schultz, 2012). This implies that in a context in which social interactions are common, such as the workplace, social norms will probably be very salient and strongly influence environmental behavior. High levels of social interactions may also increase the likelihood of the cross-norm inhibition effect explained earlier. This implies that visible norm violations in organizations are likely to weaken employees' normative goals and strengthen their gain or hedonic goals, which probably inhibits WPEB. Importantly, this also implies that norm support cues, such as colleagues who act in line with pro-environmental norms, will strengthen employees' normative goals and encourage WPEB. Hence, social norms offer an important target for behavioral interventions at work.

Another important aspect of the organizational context is that many interactions and relationships in organizations are formally shaped in hierarchical relationships, which define the span of control of managers and supervisors. Although the degree to which and how interactions and relationships are formally shaped varies across organizations, typically those higher in the hierarchy such as managers are responsible for the introduction of company (environmental) policies. Research on the (cross-)norm inhibition effect reveals that specifically observed disrespect by these higher-ups decreases rule compliance by the lower echelon (Keizer, Lindenberg, Steg, Veldstra, & Hoekstra, forthcoming). This implies that it is important that managers conform to environmental rules and standards. Compliance with organizational norms or policies also depends on the perceived respect for these norms by fellow colleagues, as this conveys the descriptive norm that colleagues comply with these norms and policies. This is an important consideration, as many norms cannot be strictly enforced by sanctions and therefore depend on respect for norms. Hence, compliance by higher-ups is a prerequisite, but for durable respect for (environmental) norms and policies, it is of key importance that employees of the lower echelon observe that their fellow colleagues show respect for these norms and policies too.

The Organization as a Depleting Context

Another important characteristic of organizational context that is likely to affect WPEB is the high demands on self-control. Self-control entails individuals' effortful regulation of their thoughts and behaviors (Molden, Hui, Scholer, Meider, Noreen, D'Agostino, & Martin, 2012), which are governed by a limited resource consisting of the self's capacity or willingness to engage in self-regulation (Baumeister & Vohs, 2007). These acts of self-control can cause regulatory resource depletion, so-called ego depletion (Baumeister, Bratslavsky, Muraven, & Tice, 1998; Muraven & Baumeister, 2000; Vohs & Heatherton, 2000). Prolonged claims on self-control by high cognitive load due to work-related behavior can thus result in a temporary reduction in self-control. As WPEBs are generally more costly in the sense of comfort, effort, or money, individuals require a certain level of self-control to counter the impulse or urge to just aim for profit, easiness, or comfort. Therefore, ego depletion is likely to weaken normative goals, and strengthen hedonic and gain goals. Hence, when employees encounter reduced levels of self-control after a long workday or an effortful task, their normative goals are likely pushed to the background.

We might expect that low self-control is the rule rather than the exception for employees at work. This can further inhibit WPEB because of weaker normative goals. Yet, ego-depletion can sometimes promote WPEB. Research has shown that people with low levels of self-control are more likely to rely on habits and heuristics (simple decision-making rules) as quick guides to behavioral choices (e.g., Janssen, Fennis, Pruyn, & Vohs, 2008). This implies that employees with a strong environmental self-identity or strong biospheric values may act pro-environmentally even when self-control is low, as doing so may be habitual for them. In addition, people with low self-control are more likely to rely on heuristics such as social proofs (Salmon, Fennis, De Ridder, Adriaanse, & De Vet, 2013), and hence are more likely to base decisions on descriptive norms. This again suggests that descriptive norms will be influential in organizations, not only because the high level of social interactions, but also because of ego depletion. When colleagues act pro-environmentally, particularly depleted employees may follow this descriptive norm and act pro-environmentally too. Hence, lack of self-control may not always be a barrier to WPEB.

Conclusion and Research Agenda

This chapter provided an overview of relevant frameworks and theories on individual factors influencing environmental behavior. We first discussed theories that provide overarching frameworks for understanding and investigating factors influencing WPEB, notably, value theory and goal-framing theory. We argued that behavior is influenced by the strength of hedonic, gain, and normative goals in a particular situation, and that the strength of these goals depends on one's values and on situational cues that activate or deactivate these values. Second, we elaborated on theories that focus on gain, normative, and hedonic goals, respectively. We introduced the TPB and the social norm theory that focus on gain goals, and discussed the NAM, the VBN theory, and identity theory that focus on normative goals. We also indicated the significance of hedonic goals for environmental actions, and elaborated on habitual behavior. We indicated that these theories have mainly been applied to explain private environmental behavior. The question remains whether the theories are also applicable in an organizational context; this is an important topic for future research. Future research should also study communalities and differences between factors influencing behavior at work and at home.

Next, we argued that environmental behavior depends on both individual and contextual factors. The influence of contextual factors has hardly been examined in studies on environmental behavior, and is an important topic for future research. This is probably even more relevant for WEB, as the organizational context can substantially affect WPEB. We introduced four unique characteristics of the organizational context that are likely to affect the strength of normative, gain, and hedonic goals at work, thereby affecting the likelihood of WPEB. More specifically, we discussed implications of the general focus on profit generation, the possible limited autonomy of employees over individual WPEB, the high level of formally shaped interactions between employees, and lower levels of self-control due to high cognitive load. Importantly, we indicated that these four characteristics do not necessarily inhibit WPEB by strengthening (the influence of) gain and hedonic goals, but may also promote such behavior by strengthening (the influence of) normative goals. Future research is needed to examine under which circumstances organizational characteristics are most likely to strengthen normative goals and to encourage WPEB.

Environmental psychologists aim to study the interactions between humans and their environment. As such, they can play an important role in understanding and encouraging WPEB, by studying to what extent and how the interaction between individual and contextual factors affect WPEB. Such interactions between individual and contextual factors have hardly been conceptualized nor studied in environmental research, and are a key topic for future research. The organizational context offers unique opportunities to study such interactions.

To promote WPEB, organizations need to understand which factors are most influential for WEB, and how these factors can be effectively addressed via organizational changes and policies. This implies that we need to study to what extent interventions aimed to change individual and contextual factors are acceptable and effective in encouraging WPEB, and which factors are key to enhance these effects.

People spend a substantial proportion of their time at work, and behavior at work has important implications for environmental quality. This makes it highly important and timely to study factors encouraging WPEB, and to understand effective and acceptable ways to promote such behavior. We hope this chapter encourages researchers to take up the challenging research agenda and to enrich our understanding of factors influencing WEB.

Suggested Additional Readings

1. Kouchaki, M., & Smith, I. H. (2014). The morning morality effect: The influence of time of day on unethical behavior. *Psychological Science*, *25*(1), 95–102.
2. Lindenberg, S., & Steg, L. (2013). What makes organizations in market democracies adopt environmentally-friendly policies? In A. H. Huffman, & S. R. Klein (Eds.), *Green organizations. Driving change with I-O psychology*. New York: Routledge.
3. Steg, L., & Vlek, C. (2009). Encouraging pro-environmental behavior: An integrative review and research agenda. *Journal of Environmental Psychology*, *29*, 309–317.

References

Abrahamse, W., & Steg, L. (2011). Factors related to household energy use and intention to reduce it: The role of psychological and socio-demographic variables. *Human Ecological Review, 18*, 30–40.

Ajzen, I. (1991). The theory of planned behavior. *Organizational Behavior and Human Decision Processes, 50*, 179–211.

Armitage, C. J., & Conner, M. (2001). Efficacy of the theory of planned behavior: A meta-analytic review. *British Journal of Social Psychology, 40*, 471–499.

Bamberg, S., & Möser, G. (2007). Twenty years after Hines, Hungerford, and Tomera: A new meta-analysis of psycho-social determinants of pro-environmental behavior. *Journal of Environmental Psychology, 27*, 14–25.

Baumeister, R. F., Bratslavsky, E., Muraven, M., & Tice, D. M. (1998). Ego depletion: Is the active self a limited resource? *Journal of Personality and Social Psychology, 74*, 1252–1265.

Baumeister, R. F., & Vohs, K. D. (2007). Self-regulation, ego depletion, and motivation. *Social and Psychology Compass, 1*, 115–128.

Carrico, A. R., & Riemer, M. (2011). Motivating energy conservation in the workplace: An evaluation of the use of group-level feedback and peer education. *Journal of Environmental Psychology, 31*, 1–13.

Carrus, G., Passafaro, P., & Bonnes, M. (2008). Emotions, habits and rational choices in ecological behaviours: The case of recycling and use of public transportation. *Journal of Environmental Psychology, 28*, 51–62.

Cialdini, R. B. (2003). Crafting normative messages to protect the environment. *Current Directions in Psychological Science, 12*, 105–109.

Cialdini, R. B., Reno, R. R., & Kallgren, C. A. (1990). A focus theory of normative conduct: Recycling the concept of norms to reduce littering in public places. *Journal of Personality and Social Psychology, 58*, 1015–1026.

Dahlsrud, A. (2008). How corporate social responsibility is defined: An analysis of 37 definitions. *Corporate Social Responsibility and Environmental Management, 15*, 1–13.

David, P., Bloom, M., & Hillman, A. J. (2007). Investor activism, managerial responsiveness, and corporate social performance. *Strategic Management Journal, 28*, 91–100.

De Groot, J. I. M., & Steg, L. (2008). Value orientations to explain beliefs related to environmental significant behavior. How to measure egoistic, altruistic, and biospheric value orientations. *Environment and Behavior, 40*, 330–354.

De Groot, J. I. M., & Steg, L. (2009a). Mean or green: Which values can promote stable pro-environmental behavior? *Conservation Letters, 2*, 61–66.

De Groot, J. I. M., & Steg, L. (2009b). Morality and prosocial behavior: The role of awareness, responsibility and norms in the norm activation model. *The Journal of Social Psychology, 149*, 425–449.

De Groot, J. I. M., Steg, L., & Dicke, M. (2008). Transportation trends from a moral perspective: Value orientations, norms and reducing car use. In F. N. Gustavsson (Ed.), *New transportation research progress* (pp. 67–91). Hauppauge, NY: Nova Science Publishers.

Dittmar, H. (1992). *The social psychology of material possessions: To have is to be.* New York: St. Martin's Press.

Dittmar, H. (2004). Are you what you have? *The Psychologist, 17,* 206–210.

Dunlap, R. E., Van Liere, K. D., Mertig, A. G., & Jones, R. E. (2000). New trends in measuring environmental attitudes: Measuring endorsement of the New Ecological Paradigm: A revised NEP scale. *Journal of Social Issues, 56,* 425–442.

Ellemers, N., Kingma, L., van de Burgt, J., & Barreto, M. (2011). Corporate social responsibility as a source of organizational morality, employee commitment and satisfaction. *Journal of Organizational Moral Psychology, 1,* 97–124.

Flannery, B. L., & May, D. R. (2000). Environmental ethical decision making in the U.S. metal finishing industry. *Academy of Management Journal, 43,* 642–662.

Fraj, E., & Martinez, E. (2007). Ecological consumer behaviour: An empirical analysis. *International Journal of Consumer Studies, 31,* 26–33.

Gadenne, D. L., Kennedy, J., & McKeiver, C. (2009). An empirical study of environmental awareness and practices in SMEs. *Journal of Business Ethics, 84,* 45–63.

Gatersleben, B., & Steg, L. (2012). Affective and symbolic aspects of environmental behaviour. In L. Steg, A. E. van den Berg, & J. I. M. De Groot (Eds.), *Environmental psychology: An introduction* (pp. 165–174). Oxford, UK: John Wiley & Sons.

Griskevicius, V., Tybur, V., & Van den Bergh, B. (2010). Going green to be seen: Status, reputation, and conspicuous conservation. *Journal of Personality and Social Psychology, 98,* 392–404.

Guagnano, G. A., Stern, P. C., & Dietz, T. (1995). Influences on attitude-behavior relationships: A natural experiment with curbside recycling. *Environment and Behavior, 27,* 699–718.

Honkanen, P., & Verplanken, B. (2004). Understanding attitudes towards genetically modified food: The role of values and attitude strength. *Journal of Consumer Policy, 27,* 401–420.

Husted, B. W., & Allen, D. B. (2007). Strategic corporate social responsibility and value creation among large firms: Lessons from the Spanish experience. *Long Range Planning, 40,* 594–610.

Jakovcevic, A., & Steg, L. (2013). Sustainable transportation in Argentina: Values, beliefs, norms and car use reduction. *Transportation Research PartF: Traffic Psychology and Behaviour, 20,* 70–79.

Janssen, L., Fennis, B. M., Pruyn, A. T. H., & Vohs, K. D. (2008). The path of least resistance: Regulatory resource depletion and the effectiveness of social influence techniques. *Journal of Business Research, 61,* 1041–1045.

Kay, A. C., Wheeler, S. C., Bargh, J. A., & Ross, L. (2004). Material priming: The influence of mundane physical objects on situational construal and competitive behavioral choice. *Organizational Behavior and Human Decision Processes, 95,* 83–96.

Keizer, K., Lindenberg, S., & Steg, L. (2008). The spreading of disorder. *Science, 322,* 1681–1685.

Keizer, K., Lindenberg, S., & Steg, L. (2011). The reversal effect of prohibition signs. *Group Processes and Intergroup Relations, 14,* 681–688.

Keizer, K., Lindenberg, S., & Steg, L. (2013). The importance of demonstratively restoring order. *PLoS ONE, 8,* e65137.

Keizer, K., Lindenberg, S. M., Steg, L., Veldstra, J. L., & Hoekstra, E. (forthcoming). Higher-ups make especially influential norm violators.

Keizer, K., & Schultz, W. (2012). Social norms and pro-environmental behaviour. In L. Steg, A. E. Van den Berg, & J. I. M. De Groot (Eds.), *Environmental psychology. An introduction* (pp. 153–164). Oxford, UK: John Wiley & Sons.

Klöckner, C. A., & Matthies, E. (2004). How habits interfere with norm-directed behavior: A normative decision-making model for travel mode choice. *Journal of Environmental Psychology, 24,* 319–327.

Klöckner, C. A., & Verplanken, B. (2012). Yesterday's habits preventing change tomorrow? The influence of automaticity on environmental behaviour. In L. Steg, A. E. Van den Berg, & J. I. M. De Groot (Eds.), *Environmental psychology. An introduction* (pp. 197–210). Oxford, UK: John Wiley & Sons.

Kurz, T., Donaghue, N., & Walker, I. (2005). Utilizing a social-ecological framework to promote water and energy conservation: A field experiment. *Journal of Applied Social Psychology, 35,* 1281–1300.

Liberman, V., Samuels, S. M., & Ross, L. (2004). The name of game: Predictive power of reputations versus situational labels in determining prisoner's dilemma game moves. *Personality and Social Psychology Bulletin, 30,* 1175–1185.

Lindenberg, S., & Steg, L. (2007). Normative, gain and hedonic goal frames guiding environmental behavior. *Journal of Social Issues, 63,* 117–137.

Lindenberg, S., & Steg, L. (2013). What makes organizations in market democracies adopt environmentally-friendly policies? In A. H. Huffman, & S. R. Klein (Eds.), *Green organizations. Driving change with I-O Psychology* (pp. 93–114). New York: Routledge.

Manetti, L., Pierro, A., & Livi, S. (2004). Recycling: Planned and self-expressive behaviour. *Journal of Environmental Psychology, 24,* 227–236.

Molden, D. C., Hui, C. M., Scholer, A. A., Meier, B. P., Noreen, E. E., D'Agostino, P. R., & Martin, V. (2012). Motivational versus metabolic effects of carbohydrates on self-control. *Psychological Science, 23,* 1137–1144.

Mueller, K., Hattrup, K., Spiess, S., & Lin-Hi, N. (2012). The effects of corporate social responsibility on employees' affective commitment: A cross-cultural investigation. *Journal of Applied Psychology, 97,* 1186–1200.

Muraven, M., & Baumeister, R. F. (2000). Self-regulation and depletion of limited resources: Does self-control resemble a muscle? *Psychological Bulletin, 126,* 247–259.

Nettle, D., Harper, Z., Kidson, A., Stone, R., Penton-Voak, I. S., & Bateson, M. (2013). The watching eyes effect in the Dictator Game: It's not how much you give, it's being seen to give something. *Evolution and Human Behavior, 34*, 35–40.

Noppers, E. H., Keizer, K. E., Bolderdijk, J. W., & Steg, L. (2014). The adoption of sustainable innovations: Driven by symbolic and environmental motives. *Global Environmental Change, 25*, 52–62.

Nordlund, A. M., & Garvill, J. (2003). Effects of values, problem awareness, and personal norm on willingness to reduce personal car use. *Journal of Environmental Psychology, 23*, 339–347.

Ölander, F., & Thøgerson, J. (1995). Understanding of consumer behavior as a prerequisite for environmental protection. *Journal of Consumer Policy, 18*, 345–385.

Orlitzky, M., Schmidt, F. L., & Rynes, S. L. (2003). Corporate social and financial performance: A meta-analysis. *Organization Studies, 24*, 403–441.

Pandey, N., Rupp, D. E., & Thornton, M. A. (2013). The morality of corporate environmental sustainability: A psychological and philosophical perspective. In A. H. Huffman, & S. R. Klein (Eds.), *Green organizations. Driving change with I-O psychology* (pp. 69–92). New York: Routledge.

Poortinga, W., Steg, L., & Vlek, C. (2003). Myths of nature and environmental management strategies. A field study on energy savings in traffic and transport. In: G. Moser, E. Pol, Y. Bernard, M. Bonnes, J. A. Corraliza, & M. V. Giuliani (Eds.), *People, places and sustainability* (pp. 280–290). Seattle: Hogrefe & Huber Publishers.

Raihani, N. J., & Bshary, R. (2012). A positive effect of flowers rather than eye images in a large-scale, cross cultural Dictator Game. *Proceeding of the Royal Society B: Biological Sciences, 279*, 3556–3564.

Rondinelli, D. A., & Berry, M. A. (2000). Environmental citizenship in multinational corporations: Social responsibility and sustainable development. *European Management Journal, 18*, 70–84.

Russo, M. V., & Fouts, P. A. (1997). A resource-based perspective on corporate environmental performance and profitability. *Academy of Management, 40*, 534–559.

Salmon, S. J., Fennis, B. M., De Ridder, D. T. D., Adriaanse, M. A., & De Vet, E. (2013). Health on impulse: When low self-control promotes healthy food choices. *Health Psychology, 33*, 103–109.

Scherbaum, C. A., Popovich, P. M., & Finlinson, S. (2008). Exploring individual-level factors related to employee energy-conservation behaviors at work. *Journal of Applied Social Psychology, 38*, 818–835.

Schultz, W. P. (2001). The structure of environmental concern: concern for self, other people, and the biosphere. *Journal of Environmental Psychology, 21*, 327–339.

Schwartz, S. H. (1977). Normative influences on altruism. In L. Berkowitz (Ed.), *Advances in experimental social psychology* (Vol. 10, pp. 221–279). New York: Academic Press.

Schwartz, S. H. (1992). Universals in the content and structure of values: Theory and empirical tests in 20 countries. In M. Zanna (Ed.), *Advances in experimental social psychology* (Vol. 25, pp. 89–211). Hillsdale, NJ: Academic Press.

Schwartz, S. H., & Howard, J. A. (1981). A normative decision-making model of altruism. In. J. P. Rushton, & R. M. Sorrentino (Eds.), *Altruisim and helping behavior* (pp. 89–211). Hillsdale, NJ: Erlbaum.

Slovic, P., Finucane, M. L., Peters, E., & MacGregor, D. G. (2007). The affect heuristic. *European Journal of Operational Research, 177,* 1333–1352.

Steg, L. (2005). Car use: Lust and must. Instrumental, symbolic and affective motives for car use. *Transportation Research-A, 39,* 147–162.

Steg, L. (2012). *Niets duurt voort behalve verandering: De mens als sleutel tot duurzaamheid* [Nothing except change continues: Man as a key to sustainability]. Inaugural talk. University of Groningen, Faculty of Behavioural and Social Science [in Dutch].

Steg, L., Bolderdijk, J. W., Keizer K., & Perlaviciute G. (2014a). An integrated framework for encouraging pro-environmental behavior: The role of values, situational factors and goals. *Journal of Environmental Psychology, 38,* 104–115.

Steg, L., De Groot, J. I. M., Dreijerink, L., Abrahamse, W., & Siero, F. (2011). General antecedents of personal norms, policy acceptability, and intentions: The role of values, worldviews, and environmental concern. *Society and Natural Resources, 24,* 349–367.

Steg, L., Dreijerink, L., & Abrahamse, W. (2005). Factors influencing the acceptability of energy policies: Testing VBN theory. *Journal of Environmental Psychology, 25,* 415–425.

Steg, L., Perlaviciute, G., Van der Werff, E., & Lurvink, J. (2014b). The significance of hedonic values for environmentally relevant attitudes, preferences, and actions. *Environment and Behavior, 46,* 163–192.

Steg, L., & De Groot, J. (2010). Explaining prosocial intentions: Testing causal relationships in the norm activation model. *British Journal of Social Psychology, 49,* 725–743.

Steg, L., & Nordlund, A. (2012). Models to explain environmental behaviour. In L. Steg, A. E. Van den Berg, & J. I. M. De Groot (Eds.), *Environmental Psychology. An Introduction* (pp. 185–195). Oxford, UK: John Wiley & Sons.

Steg, L., & Vlek, C. (2009). Encouraging pro-environmental behavior: An integrative review and research agenda. *Journal of Environmental Psychology, 29,* 309–317.

Stern, P. C., Dietz, T., Abel, T., Guagnano, G. A., & Kalof, L. (1999). A value-belief-norm theory of support for social movements: The case of environmentalism. *Human Ecology Review, 6,* 81–97.

Stern, P. C. (2000). Toward a coherent theory of environmentally significant behavior. *Journal of Social Issues, 56,* 407–424.

Thøgersen, J. (2005). How many consumer policy empower consumer for sustainable lifestyles? *Journal of Consumer Policy, 28,* 143–178.

Tonglet, M., Phillips, P. S., & Bates, M. P. (2004). Determining the drivers for household pro-environmental behavior: Waste minimization compared to recycling. *Resources, Conservation and Recycling, 41,* 27–48.

Tudor, T. L., Barr, S. W., & Gilg, A. W. (2007). A tale of two locational settings: Is there a link between pro-environmental behavior at work and at home? *Local Environment: The International Journal of Justice and Sustainability, 12,* 409–421.

Tudor, T. L., Barr, S. W., & Gilg, A. W. (2008). A novel conceptual framework for examining environmental behavior in large organizations: A case study of the Cornwall National Health Service (NHS) in the United Kingdom. *Environment and Behavior, 40,* 426–450.

Van der Werff, E., Steg, L., & Keizer, K. (2013a). The value of environmental self-identity: The relationship between biospheric values, environmental self-identity and pro-environmental preferences, intentions and behaviour. *Journal of Environmental Psychology, 34,* 55–63.

Van der Werff, E., Steg, L., & Keizer, K. (2013b). It is a moral issue: The relationship between environmental self-identity, obligation-based intrinsic motivation and pro-environmental behaviour. *Global Environmental Change, 23,* 1258–1265.

Van der Werff, E., Steg, L., & Keizer, K. (2014a). I am what I am by looking past the present: The influence of biospheric values and past behaviour on environmental self-identity. *Environment and Behavior, 46,* 626–657.

Van der Werff, E., Steg, L., & Keizer, K. (2014b). Follow the signal: When past pro-environmental actions signal who you are, *Journal of Environmental Psychology, 40,* 273–282.

Venhoeven, L. A., Bolderdijk, J. W., & Steg, L. (2013). Explaining the paradox: How pro-environmental behaviour can both thwart and foster well-being. *Sustainability, 5,* 1372–1386.

Verplanken, B., Aarts, H., Van Knippenberg, A., & Van Knippenberg, C. (1994). Attitude versus general habit: Antecedents of travel mode choice. *Journal of Applied Social Psychology, 24,* 285–300.

Vohs, K. D., & Heatherton, T. F. (2000). Self-regulation failure: A resource-depletion approach. *Psychological Science, 11,* 249–254.

Wagner, M., Van Phu, N., Azomahou, T., & Wehrmeyer, W. (2002). The relationship between the environmental and economic performance of firms: An empirical analysis of the European paper industry. *Corporate Social Responsibility and Environmental Management, 9,* 133–146.

Werther, W. B., & Chandler, D. (2011). *Strategic corporate social responsibility: Stakeholders in a global environment* (2nd ed.). Thousand Oaks, CA: Sage.

Zajonc, R. B. (1980). Feeling and thinking: Preferences need no inferences. *American Psychologist, 35,* 151–175.

4 RESEARCH METHODS IN PRO-ENVIRONMENTAL RESEARCH

Timur Ozbilir and E. Kevin Kelloway

Over the past decade, environmental issues including climate change, environmental degradation, resource depletion, and pollution have become increasingly salient in the political, societal, and institutional domains (Banerjee, 2003; Child et al., 2007; Dahlman & Brammer, 2011; King, 2007). Growing concern about environmental issues has resulted in increased pressure on organizations to engage in responsible practices and to minimize their environmental impact, which has created significant managerial challenges for organizations (Brammer, Hoejmose, & Marchant, 2011). Research concerning organizations and the natural environment has been conducted within a diverse range of contexts and disciplines, including management, business, strategy, policy, psychology, marketing, and organizational behavior. In particular, researchers have investigated institutional pressures on organizations to engage in environmentally responsible practices (e.g., Christmann, 2004; Clark & Crawford, 2012; Roome & Wijen, 2006; Schaefer, 2007), shed light on determinants of improved environmental performance (e.g., Berrone, Cruz, Gomez-Mejia, & Larraza-Kintana, 2010; Kassinis & Vafeas, 2006; Lee & Lounsbury, 2011), explored the underlying mechanisms in the relationship between environmental performance and financial performance (e.g., Barnett & Salomon, 2012; Doh, Howton, Howton, & Siegel, 2010; Hull & Rothenberg, 2008; Orlitzky, Schmidt, & Rynes, 2003; Surroca, Tribo, & Waddock, 2010; Tang, Hull, & Rothenberg, 2012), studied the impact of environmental practices on employees (e.g., Evans & Davis, 2011; Mueller, Hattrup, Spiess, & Lin-Hi, 2012; Stites & Michael, 2011;), and tried to predict stakeholder behaviors by measuring their environmental perceptions and attitudes (e.g., Munoz, Bogner, Clement, & Carvalho, 2009; Tobler, Visschers, & Siegrist, 2012).

These efforts have resulted in an impressive body of work with important implications for both research and practice. At the same time, diverse perspectives have resulted in a fragmented literature (Etzion, 2007) including the use of diverse research methodologies. Our goal in this chapter is to review the methodological bases of pro-environmental research. To do so we report on a content analysis of 118 empirical articles drawn from 14 journals. The rest of the chapter is organized as follows. First, based on our content analysis, we focus on sample characteristics in pro-environmental research and highlight the need for more diverse samples. Second, we review research strategies and designs and address the divide between qualitative and quantitative approaches to research. Third, we provide an overview of the data collection methods and the different types of data used in pro-environmental research. Fourth, we address the need for multi-level studies by reviewing the work at the institutional, organizational, and individual levels. We end our chapter with suggestions for future research.

Scope of the Review

Our chapter is based on information from 118 journal articles. First, given the multidisciplinary nature of organization and environment research, we searched the following journals in the fields of management, business, organizational psychology, corporate social responsibility, and marketing: *Academy of Management Journal, Academy of Management Review, Administrative Science Quarterly, Business and Society, Journal of Applied Psychology, Journal of Management, Journal of Management Studies, Organization Studies, Strategic Management Journal, Journal of the Academy of Marketing Science, International Journal of Management Reviews, Journal of International Business Studies, Organization Science, Journal of Occupational and Organizational Psychology, Journal of Organizational Behavior,* and *Personnel Psychology.* These journals were selected based on previous reviews of organization and management research focusing on management (e.g., Bansal & Gao, 2006) and corporate social responsibility (Aguinis & Glavas, 2012), and research on high quality journals (Cohen, 2007; Podsakoff, MacKenzie, Podsakoff, & Bachrach, 2008). We also added the *Journal of Environmental Psychology,* which focuses on the transactions and interrelationships between people and their physical surroundings, including the natural environment. We limited our search to the years between January 1, 2002 and December 31, 2013. We did not include journals that focus on environmental issues that are technical in nature (as in the domains of design or manufacturing).

Table 4.1 Summary of Literature Search Results

Journal	Number of Empirical Articles
Academy of Management Journal	6
Academy of Management Review	–
Administrative Science Quarterly	3
Business and Society	30
Journal of Applied Psychology	1
Journal of Management	6
Journal of Management Studies	13
Organization Studies	7
Strategic Management Journal	23
Journal of the Academy of Marketing Science	6
International Journal of Management Reviews	–
Journal of International Business Studies	3
Organization Science	2
Journal of Occupational and Organizational Psychology	–
Journal of Organizational Behavior	5
Personnel Psychology	3
Journal of Environmental Psychology	11
Total	118

To access our targeted journals, we used the databases ABI/INFORM, EBSCOhost, ProQuest, and PsychInfo and searched for articles including the following keywords: ecological, environmental, environmental issues, environmental management, environmental performance, natural environment, corporate social responsibility, sustainable development, corporate social performance, climate change, toxic, pollution. As three of the journals we searched (i.e., *Academy of Management Review, International Journal of Management Reviews, Journal of Occupational and Organizational Psychology*) did not include any empirical articles, our review is based on a content analysis of 118 articles from 14 journals. See Table 4.1 for a summary of literature search results.

Research Methods in Pro-Environmental Research

Each empirical article in our review was content analyzed to assess sample characteristics, approach to research, research strategy, data collection methods, type of data, and the level of analysis.

Sample Characteristics in Pro-Environmental Research

To assess sample characteristics in pro-environmental research, we coded the articles for sample type (organizations, employees, or other), homogeneity versus heterogeneity of industries and jobs, geographical region represented, and sample source (database vs. non-database). Table 4.2 shows the results of our analysis.

Sixty-nine percent of the studies in our review used organizations as a sample; 21% used employees; and 10% used stakeholder resolutions, funds, acquisitions, or other units of analysis. Although the overwhelming majority (88%) of organizational samples were heterogeneous in industry, studies mostly focused on top polluting industries including the chemical, primary metal, and electric utilities industries (e.g., Bansal & Clelland, 2004; Christman, 2004; Kassinis,

Table 4.2 Descriptive Statistics for Different Sample Types

Characteristic	Number	%
Sample Type		
Firms	81	69
Homogeneous (industry)	10	12
Heterogeneous (industry)	71	88
Employees	25	21
Homogeneous (jobs)	12	48
Heterogeneous (jobs)	13	52
Other	12	10
Geographical region represented		
North America (US and Canada)	66	56
Latin America	1	1
Europe	25	21
Asia	4	3
Australia	5	4
South America	2	2
Africa	1	1
Worldwide	14	12
Sample Source		
Database	47 (of 81)	58
Non-database	34 (of 81)	42

2005). Furthermore, almost half (48%) of the samples consisting of individuals (i.e., employees, consumers) were homogeneous in occupation, for example, consisting of teachers (e.g., Munoz, Bogner, Clement, & Carvalho, 2009), farmers (e.g., Gosling & Williams, 2010), and environmental leaders (e.g., Frooman & Murrell, 2005). Although using homogenous samples may reduce irrelevant variance by keeping factors extraneous to the research question constant (Highhouse & Gillespie, 2008), it also limits the generalizability of the findings beyond the samples selected.

Sample size is an important determinant of statistical power (Cohen, 1988). Small sample sizes may increase the probability of failing to detect an effect when one genuinely exists (i.e., the probability of a Type II error), which may lead to inconsistent and biased findings and possible abandonment of a research area by researchers (Shen et al., 2011). Given the practical constraints researchers generally face in achieving large sample sizes, researchers in the articles we reviewed have been successful at recruiting large numbers of organizations and employees. Overall, the average sample size of the articles (excluding case studies) in our review was 239 (SD = 208) for organizations and 207 (SD = 140) for employees.[1] This is partly due to the commonly used data collection methodologies in pro-environmental research (i.e., document analysis, archival data) and the availability of databases, such as the Kinder, Lydenberg, Domini (KLD) database and Toxics Release Inventory (TRI), which store the environmental, social, governance (ESG) ratings of the world's leading companies. To identify such companies, researchers have used sources such as stock indexes and lists of companies compiled by business and finance publications. The most popular among these sources are Standard and Poor's 500, a stock market index based on the market capitalizations of 500 leading companies publicly traded in the United States, and the Fortune 500, a list compiled by Fortune magazine ranking the top 500 public corporations of the United States as measured by their gross revenue. Although these sources provide access to longitudinal databases of environmental responsiveness and other metrics pertaining to firms that leave a large environmental footprint (Dahlman & Brammer, 2011), the fact that small and medium-sized organizations are not included in these databases limits the generalizability of the research utilizing such databases.

Finally, the majority of samples (56%) were from North America and Europe (21%) with some representation of Asian samples (3%) and South American (2%) samples, and with 12% of studies using an international sample. The paucity of

---

1. Three outliers were deleted from organization samples; 4 outliers were deleted from employee samples.

Table 4.3 Summary of Research Approaches and Strategies Used in Content Analysis

Approach	Strategy	Number	%	Longitudinal Number(%)
Quantitative		96	81	4(4)
	Descriptive	2	2	
	Correlational (Cross sectional)	87	90	
	Experimental	7	7	
Qualitative		18	15	2(11)
	Grounded theory	5	28	
	Case study	13	72	
Both		4	3	

international samples limits our ability to make broader generalizations across cultures. Given the global nature of environmental issues, a wider perspective is necessary in order to develop more robust theories.

Research Approaches and Strategies in Pro-Environmental Research

In this section, we provide a summary of the research approaches and strategies commonly used in pro-environmental research. First we categorize research as qualitative versus quantitative, then we discuss common qualitative and quantitative research strategies. Table 4.3 provides an overview of the approaches and strategies used in the studies we content analyzed.

The decision to approach a study qualitatively or quantitatively depends on the research questions at hand, the state of the literature, and the contributions the researcher wishes to make (Edmondson & McManus, 2007). Often, a qualitative approach will be used to investigate new phenomena and test theories, whereas a quantitative approach will be taken to address questions of generalizability and calibration (Bluhm, Harman, Lee, & Mitchell, 2011; Lee, 1999).

Our review revealed that the majority (81%) of the articles in our content analysis used a quantitative approach. Of these, 90% used a correlational research strategy,[2] and 2% were descriptive. Both descriptive and correlational strategies

---
2. This number includes number of articles with differential designs.

are nonexperimental approaches to research that do not involve a manipulation of the variables by the researcher. The purpose of descriptive research, which involves measuring variables as they exist naturally, is to simply capture or summarize information (Gravetter & Forzano, 2003). For example, Kolk and Pinkse (2007) analyzed data from the *Carbon Disclosure Project*, which surveyed 117 firms from *Financial Times Global 500* to describe multinationals' political activities on climate change. The authors scanned the responses available on the internet and provided a summary of corporate political activities by country. In contrast, the goal of correlational research is to establish that a relationship exists between variables and to describe the nature of the relationship (Gravetter & Forzano, 2003). Christman (2004) used survey data from the chemical industry and found a positive relationship between external stakeholder pressure and the standardization of environmental policy dimensions by multinationals.

Both the descriptive and correlational strategies are useful when conducting preliminary research in areas that have not received a lot of research attention. Furthermore, the correlational strategy allows researchers an opportunity to investigate the relationship between variables that would be impossible or unethical to manipulate (Field & Hole, 2003). However, the correlational strategy is limited in that it cannot establish a direct relationship between variables (i.e., another variable may be responsible for the observed relation) or directionality (i.e., which variable is the cause and which is the effect). For instance, the possibility of reverse causality cannot be excluded in Christman's (2004) study. As the author acknowledges, it is plausible that multinational companies with environmental policies may have influenced external stakeholders to increase pressure in order to disadvantage competitors without policies.

A cause-and-effect relationship between two variables can be established through an experimental strategy. However, our review revealed that only 7% of the studies in our content analysis used this strategy. For example, Evans and Davis (2011) used an experimental design to study the relationship between corporate citizenship and job applicant attraction. The authors manipulated corporate citizenships through the use of vignettes, and randomly assigned participants to one of three corporate citizenship conditions (high-neutral-low). Similarly, Frooman, and Murrell (2005) used a series of vignettes to study the relationship between firm and stakeholder dependence and the choice of influence strategy.

Although the majority of the studies took a quantitative approach to pro-environmental research, only 18 (15%) of the studies in our content analysis employed qualitative methodologies. A qualitative approach can be a powerful tool that allows the researcher to discover new variables and relationships, reveal complex processes, and illustrate the influence of the social context (Shah

& Corley, 2006). In terms of theory advancement, qualitative research methodologies can be used in the generation, elaboration, testing, and challenging of theoretical assumptions (Lee et al., 1999). Theory generation refers to the generation of testable research propositions through qualitative creation of new theory. Theory elaboration occurs when the study draws on a pre-existing model and does not include formal hypotheses. Theory testing utilizes formal hypotheses from extant theory to inform study design. Critical theory is an attempt at inducing radical change through an overt political agenda (Lee et al., 1999). Five (27%) of the studies in our content analysis used a qualitative approach for the purpose of theory generation, 14 (77%) for theory elaboration, and only 2 (11%) for theory testing. None of the qualitative studies we content analyzed used critical theory. To serve one of these purposes, qualitative studies in our review have used a grounded theory or case study approach.

A grounded theory approach focuses on deriving theory grounded in systematically collected and analyzed data from the field (Straus & Corbin, 1998). Grounded theory rejects a priori theorizing (Locke, 2001); however, it requires the researcher to be familiar with existing theories (Shah & Corley, 2006). Data are collected through direct contact with the social world, usually through interviews with 20 to 30 individuals (Creswell, 2006). Researchers develop their interpretations through a strong coding mechanism and constant comparisons until they reach a "saturation" of categories (Glaser & Straus, 1967). The approach is best suited to research questions that explore phenomena in the early stages of development, address understudied phenomena and relations, or examine variables that cannot be studied via experimentation (Glaser & Straus, 1967; Straus, 1987; Yin, 2009). Five (28%) of the qualitative studies we content analyzed used grounded theory, for theory generation, theory elaboration, or theory testing. Jiang and Bansal (2003) used grounded theory for theory generation when investigating why firms certify for ISO 14001 in the Canadian pulp and paper industry. Closs, Speier, and Meacham (2011) used the approach for theory elaboration to better understand and further develop the phenomenon of sustainability in marketing. Hendry (2006) used it for theory testing to investigate why environmental nongovernmental organizations target particular firms.

Case study was the most popular qualitative approach (72%) in our content analysis, with all of the case studies elaborating theory (e.g., Child & Tsai, 2005; Doh & Guay, 2006; Kearins, Collins, & Tregidga, 2010). A case study allows the researcher to explore a phenomenon in-depth and within its context using a variety of data sources and through multiple lenses (Baxter & Jack, 2008; Creswell, 2006). According to Yin (2009), a case study design is appropriate when: (a) the focus of the study is to answer "how" and "why" questions, (b) it is not possible to manipulate behavior of those involved in the study, (c) contextual conditions are relevant to the phenomenon under study, or (d) the boundaries between the phenomenon and the context are not clear. Case studies can involve single- and multiple-case designs. A single case study requires a strong rationale for choosing a particular case and may raise questions regarding the unique conditions surrounding the case (e.g., conditions specific to a particular organization). Although conducting a multiple-case study may require more extensive resources and time (Yin, 2009), the evidence from multiple-case designs is considered more compelling, and the overall design is therefore regarded as being more robust (Herriott & Firestone, 1983). All of the case studies in our content analysis used a multiple-case design except Rothenberg (2003), who used a single case design to investigate the dynamics of worker participation in environmental management in United Motor Manufacturing, an automobile plant in the United States. In addition to analyzing the case as a whole to overcome the limitations of the single-case design, the author used the case cluster method in which parallel information on a number of environmental projects was collected and each project was treated as an individual observation.

In addition to a heavy reliance on cross-sectional research and case studies, our analysis revealed a dearth of longitudinal designs in pro-environmental research. Longitudinal designs would be especially useful in this research area, for instance, to investigate the short-term and long-term effects of regulatory conditions on strategic actions. Despite this benefit of longitudinal designs, however, only 4 (4%) of the quantitative studies in our content analysis were longitudinal. Tang, Hull, and Rothenberg (2012) investigated the relationship between corporate social responsibility and financial performance with longitudinal data collected from 130 firms from 1995 to 2007. With a longitudinal design, Dahlman and Brammer (2011) were able to explore the evolving pattern of environmental strategy within a large sample of US companies over the period 1997 to 2006. Only 2 (11%) of the qualitative studies in our content analysis used a longitudinal design. Bansal (2003) studied two organizations over the period of one year using a longitudinal multicase design to investigate the development of natural environmental issues. A longitudinal study allowed the researcher to make observations in real time, reducing bias around posthoc rationalization (Golden, 1992; Van de Ven, 1989). In a study exploring the adoption of environmental management systems in three companies in the UK water and sewerage industry, Schaefer (2007) used a longitudinal design to compare institutional and performance issues at two distinct periods of time, separated by five years.

Only a few (4%) in our review combined qualitative and quantitative methodologies. For example, in order to make sense of their large dataset, Lefsrud and Meyer (2012) quantified all qualitatively generated codes for further analyses when analyzing professionals' discursive construction of climate change science. In a study investigating stakeholder salience through content analysis of sustainability reports, Weber and Marley (2012) used quantitative measures of stakeholder power to ensure comparability across reports. Not surprisingly, research questions posed appear to dictate the type of method used in studies, with research focused at the macro level using more qualitative (especially case study) methodologies, whereas research at the individual level used more quantitative methodologies.

Data Collection Methods in Pro-Environmental Research

Several different data collection methods were used in the studies we content analyzed, including interviews, archival data, documentation, observation, and surveys (see Table 4.4 for summary of studies by data collection method). Among qualitative research, interviews were the most popular, used in 16 (88%) of the articles, followed by documentation in 10 (55%) of the articles, and observation in 3 (16%) of the articles. Of the qualitative studies, those adopting a grounded theory approach used only interviews, whereas half of the case studies used a single data collection method, and the other half used multiple methods. Among quantitative research, 71 (74%) used archival data, 42 (44%) used surveys, 7 (7%) used documentation, and 4 (4%) used interviews.

Interviews, documentation, and observation are commonly used in qualitative research; however, evidence from studies using these methods is more meaningful when they are implemented with longitudinal research designs, triangulation, and in-depth analysis (Bluhm, Harman, Lee, & Mitchell, 2011; Yin, 2009). For example, Bansal's (2003) article on the development of natural environmental issues in organizations sought to generate theory by examining models of issue flows in order to identify the factors that influence the scope,

Table 4.4 Summary of Studies by Data Collection Method

	Qualitative ($N = 18$) Number(%)	Quantitative ($N = 96$) Number(%)
Interviews	16(88)	4(4)
Archival Data	0	71(74)
Documentation	10(55)	7(7)
Observation	3(16)	0
Surveys	0	42(44)

Note. Percentages do not add up to 100%, as some studies use multiple data collection methods.

scale, and speed of organizational response to natural environmental issues. In a multiple-case design, the author tracked the development of natural environmental issues in two organizations in real time and over the course of one year with interviews, participant observations, informal discussions, and corporate document analysis. This iterative and in-depth analysis resulted in a new framework for issue flows in the development of environmental issues in organizations, which explains why some issues lead to organizational actions and some others do not. Only half (50%) of the qualitative studies we content analyzed used multiple methods of data collection, and only 4 (4%) of qualitative studies used longitudinal designs.

Two articles in our review used discourse analysis, which is different from content analysis in that it allows the researcher to study linguistic units to uncover particular uses of language. For example, Driscoll (2006) used discourse analysis to investigate organizational legitimating mechanisms in the Canadian forest sector and found that language was used to change definitions of social legitimacy with a view to enhance record of sustainable forest management practice.

Types of Data in Pro-Environmental Research

The data types we identified in our review were company self-report data, objective data, third-party assessment, stakeholder self-report data, and stakeholder assessment. We provide a brief explanation of each data type along with examples of research articles in Table 4.5.

Company Self-Report

Company self-report data may be collected through interviews, surveys, and documentation. Interviews and surveys tend to involve managers, whereas documentation involves annual reports, company reports, and websites. Company self-reports provide information about the company on institutional-level variables such as stakeholder pressures (e.g., Christman, 2004) and certification (Darnall, 2006), and organizational-level variables such as leadership (Waldman, Siegel, & Javidan, 2006) and strategy (Husted & Allen, 2006).

One of the most widely-used company self-reports is the *Toxics Release Inventory* (TRI) of the US Environmental Protection Agency. The TRI is a publicly available database containing information on toxic chemical releases and waste management activities in the United States, and is used in research as a proxy for environmental performance (e.g., Kassinis & Vafeas, 2006; Lee & Lounsbury, 2011). In addition to the usual concerns regarding accuracy and truthfulness, TRI has been criticized for focusing solely on the manufacturing processes, not accounting for greenhouse gases or environmental footprint, and

Table 4.5 Examples of Different Types of Data Used in Pro-Environmental Research

Type of Data	Variable	Source
Company self-report	*Stakeholder pressures*	
	Manager survey	Christmann, 2004
	Manager survey	Darnall, 2006
	Manager survey	Murillo-Luna, Garces-Ayerbe, & Rivera-Torres, 2008
	Environmental leadership strategy	
	Manager survey	Buysse & Verbeke, 2003
	Salience of CSR issues	
	Manager survey	Husted & Allen, 2006
	Pro-environmental marketing strategy	
	Manager survey	Baker & Sinkula, 2005
	Environmental performance	
	Toxic emissions (TRI)	Kassinis & Vafeas, 2006
Objective data	*Shareholder resolutions*	
	US Census Bureau data	Kassinis & Vafeas, 2006
	EthVest database	Lee & Lounsbury, 2011
	R&D intensity	
	R&D expenditure to total assets	Dahlman & Brammer, 2011
	Board composition	
	% of independent board directors	Post, Rahman, & Rubow, 2011
	Financial performance	
	Return on equity	Furrer, Hamprecht, & Hoffmann, 2012
Third-party assessment	*Environmental performance*	
	Dow Jones sustainability index	Furrer, Hamprecht, & Hoffmann, 2012
	EIRIS assessment	Dahlmanm & Brammer, 2011
	KLD	Deckop, Merriman, & Gupta, 2006; Neubaum & Zahra, 2006; de Villiers, Naiker, & van Staden; 2011
	Forbes Global 500	Overbeeke & Snizek, 2005
	Competition	
	IMD World Competitiveness Yearbook	Ioannou & Serafeim, 2012
	Corruption	
	World Bank Index	Ioannou & Serafeim, 2012

(Continued)

Table 4.5 (Continued)

Type of Data	Variable	Source
Stakeholder self-report	*Consumers' political affiliation* US consumer sensitivity survey *Connectedness to nature* Survey *Attitudes toward the environment* Consumer attitude survey	Meijer & Schuyt, 2005 Gosling & Williams, 2010 Tobler, Visschers, & Siegrist, 2012
Stakeholder assessment	*Policy implementation* Employee survey *Environmental performance* Employee survey	Ramus & Montiel, 2005 Mueller, Hattrup, Spiess, & Lin-Hi, 2012; Stites & Michael, 2011

ignoring issues like biodiversity and habitat protection; thus, offering a limited perspective on an organization's environmental performance (Etzion, 2007).

Objective Data

Objective data are usually collected through archival records. Examples include stakeholder pressure as indicated by the number of shareholder resolutions obtained from the US Census Bureau or the *EthVest Database*, run by the *Interfaith Center on Corporate Social Responsibility* to track the activities of faith-based and socially responsible investors (Kassinis & Vafeas, 2006; Lee & Lounsbury, 2011), research and development intensity as indicated by the ratio of R&D expenditure to total assets (Dahlman & Brammer, 2011), board composition as indicated by the percentage of independent board directors (Post, Rahman, & Rubow, 2011), financial performance as indicated by the company's return on equity (Furrer, Hamprecht, & Hoffmann, 2012), and the number of fines and penalties obtained from the Canadian Environmental Registry (Bansal, 2005).

Third Party Assessment

These refer to the environmental, social, and governance (ESG) ratings provided by screening and investment firms, such as KLD Research & Analytics, Dow

Jones, the Risk Metrics Group, Ethical Investment Research Service (EIRIS), and the Environmental Protection Agency (EPA) with the aim of providing investors and organizations with management tools to help them integrate ESG factors into their investment and strategic decisions.

The ratings provided by these firms and agencies focus on different aspects of environmental performance. For example, KLD analyzes seven strengths (beneficial environmental products and services; pollution prevention activities; recycling activities; use of alternative fuels; environmental communication; above-average environmental performance for its property, plant, and equipment; and other strengths) and seven concerns (hazardous waste, regulatory problems, ozone-depleting chemicals, substantial emissions, agricultural chemicals, climate change, and other concerns). The EPA's Enforcement and Compliance History Online allows users to find permit, inspection, violation, enforcement action, and penalty information (EPA, 2012). EIRIS provides data on environmental and climate change impacts (EIRIS, 2013), and the Dow Jones focuses on environmental sustainability criteria.

The KLD database has been the most commonly used index in environmental research to measure environmental performance (used by 20% of the studies in our review). Although the KLD provides the best environmental performance data currently available, its use in environmental research has been controversial. The common practice in environmental research, when using KLD, is to compile the total number of environmental strengths and environmental concerns, each between a minimum of 0 and a maximum of 7, and then subtract the concerns from the strengths. A negative number indicates poor performance (see Graves & Waddock, 1994; Griffin & Mahon, 1997; Waddock & Graves, 1997). This approach has been criticized for several reasons. First, research has demonstrated that the strengths and concerns measures in KLD data represent four distinct constructs and, therefore, should not be aggregated (Mattingly & Berman, 2006). Second, KLD strengths were found to be positively correlated with KLD concerns (Mattingly & Berman, 2006), as well as reporting scores (Delmas & Doctori-Blass, 2010), suggesting that companies that are better at reporting are also those with higher levels of toxic releases. Third, the aggregation method does not differentiate between companies with high or low scores on both dimensions (Delmas & Doctori-Blass, 2010, Mattingly & Berman, 2006). Researchers have taken different approaches to overcome the limitations of KLD. For example, some (e.g., Neubaum & Zahra, 2006; Sharfman & Fernando, 2008) have averaged the two KLD dimensions, whereas others (e.g., Berchicci, Dowell, & King, 2012; Chiu & Sharfman, 2011) have augmented the KLD measures with other scores from other databases.

Stakeholder Self-Report

Stakeholder self-report refers to data collected from shareholders, employees (including managers), consumers, suppliers, and investors regarding their perceptions, attitudes, and behaviors. This type of data is usually collected through interviews and surveys. Studies in our content analysis have used stakeholder self-reports to gather information on consumers' political affiliation (Meijer & Schuyt, 2005), connectedness to nature (Gosling & Williams, 2010), and attitudes toward to the environment (Tobler, Visschers, & Siegrist, 2012), among others.

Stakeholder Assessment

Stakeholder assessments refer to ratings of institutional and organizational level actions by shareholders, employees (including managers), consumers, suppliers, and investors. The articles in our content analysis used this type of data to measure policy implementation (Ramus & Montiel, 2005) and environmental performance (e.g., Mueller, Hattrup, Spiess, & Lin-Hi, 2012; Stites & Michael, 2011). Stakeholder assessment data is collected through surveys and interviews.

Level of Analysis

In the following sections, we first provide a brief summary of pro-environmental research at the institutional and organizational levels, and then turn our attention to the individual level. We organize our findings into predictors, outcomes, mediators, and moderators at each level of analysis and provide tables for the reader to easily locate articles.

Institutional Level of Analysis

Research in this category pertains to laws and standards, regulation, certification, as well as constructs that are influenced by society, consumers, and stakeholders external to the firm (Aguinis & Glavas, 2012; Scott, 2001).

Predictors

As shown in Table 4.6, one of the main reasons that organizations engage in pro-environmental activities is pressure from stakeholders. Stakeholders include governments (Christmann, 2004; Kassinis & Vafeas, 2006), industry participants (Christmann, 2004), legislative stakeholders (Kassinis & Vafeas, 2006), customers (Christmann, 2004), shareholders (Clark & Crawford, 2012; David, Bloom, & Hillman, 2007; Lee & Lounsbury, 2011), and the media (Bansal,

2005). In addition to pressure from stakeholders, organizations are increasingly aware of regulatory and market pressures (Darnall, 2006). These may be in the form of shareholder resolutions (Dahlman & Brammer, 2011) or information from social indices (Doh, Howton, Howton, & Siegel, 2010), which may increase suspicions about the organization's environmental actions. The industry and the country in which the organization operates are other important predictors of organizational and environmental outcomes.

Outcomes

Outcomes studied at the institutional level focus on the environmental performance of the organization (e.g., Berrone, Cruz, Gomez-Mejia, & Larraza-Kintana, 2010; de Villiers, Naiker, & van Staden; 2011; Kock, Santalo, & Diestre, 2012;), the impact of engaging in environmentally responsible activities on the organization's reputation (Brammer & Pavelin, 2006), and the impact of stakeholder and institutional pressures on the organization's activities (Darnall, 2006).

Mediators and Moderators

The predictor-outcome relationship at the institutional level is moderated by variables related to industry, stakeholders, and environmental performance. The industrial sector moderates the relationship between social/environmental performance and reputation (Brammer & Pavelin, 2006), whereas the positive relationship between long-term institutional owners' holdings and social/environmental performance grows stronger as institutional owners' activism increases (Neubaum & Zahra, 2006). Perceived honesty mediates the relationship between the congruency of communication regarding environmental engagement and consumer trust (Terwel, Harinck, Ellemers, & Daamen, 2009).

Organizational Level of Analysis

Forty-one percent of the articles included in our review focused on pro-environmental issues at the organizational level of analysis. (See Table 4.7 for a summary of empirical pro-environmental research at the organizational level of analysis.) Research on individuals when they are treated at a macro level (e.g., boards, senior management teams) is also included in this section (see Aguinis & Glavas, 2012).

Predictors

Predictors examined at the organizational level focused on governance and structure, legitimacy, strategy, and performance. Regarding governance and structure, board characteristics such as age, gender, and education level (Post,

Table 4.6 Summary of Empirical Pro-Environmental Research at the Institutional Level of Analysis

Predictors	Mediators and Moderators	Outcomes
Stakeholder pressures/resolutions/power (Christmann, 2004; Clark & Crawford, 2012; Dahlmann & Brammer, 2011; David, Bloom, & Hillman, 2007; Kassinis & Vafeas, 2006; Lee & Lounsbury, 2011; Roome & Wijen, 2006)	**Mediators**	*Global environmental policy standardization* (Christmann, 2004)
	Inferred motives (Terwel, Harinck, Ellemers, & Daamen, 2009)	*Consumer sensitivity to corporate social performance* (Meijer & Schuyt, 2005; Muller & Kolk, 2010; Waldman, Siegel, & Javidan, 2006)
Industry type/ visibility/ competitiveness (Bolivar, 2009; Chiu & Sharfman, 2011; Nikolaeva & Bicho, 2011; Ramus & Montiel, 2005; Weber & Marley, 2012)	*Perceived honesty* (Terwel, Harinck, Ellemers, & Daamen, 2009)	*Stakeholder influence strategy* (Frooman & Murrell, 2005)
	Moderators	
	Firm visibility to stakeholders (Chiu & Sharfman, 2011)	*NGO targeting of company/ pressure* (Hendry, 2006)
Legitimacy/legitimation (Driscoll, 2006)	*Industry affiliation* (Kassinis & Vafeas, 2006)	*ISO 14001 certification* (Darnall, 2006)
Institutional pressures/drivers (Darnall, 2006; Doh & Guay, 2006; Jiang & Bansal, 2003; Shaefer, 2007)	*Industry* (Brammer & Pavelin, 2006; Buysse & & Verbeke, 2003; Lee & Lounsbury, 2011; Reid & Toffel, 2009)	*Environmental performance* (Berrone, Cruz, Gomez-Mejia, & Larraza-Kintana, 2010; de Villiers, Naiker, & van Staden, 2011; Kearins, Collins, & Tregidga, 2010; Kock, Santalo, & Diestre, 2012; Lee & Lounsbury, 2011; Post, Rahman, & Rubow, 2011; Walls, Berrone, & Phan, 2012)
Country-specific variables (Ioannou & Serafeim, 2012; Munoz, Bogner, Clement, & Carvalho, 2009; Kolk & Pinske, 2007; Weber & Marley, 2012)		

Addition to/deletion from social index (Doh, Howton, Howton, & Siegel, 2010)

Deregulation (Delmas, Russo, & Montes-Sacho, 2007)

Media pressure (Bansal, 2005; Nikolaeva & Bicho, 2011)

Salience of environmental issues to customers (Christmann & Taylor, 2006)

Congruency of communication (Terwel, Harinck, Ellemers, & Daamen, 2009)

Environmental performance (Clark & Crawford, 2012)

Country (Mueller, Hattrup, Spiess, & Lin-Hi, 2012; Munoz, Bogner, Clement, & Carvalho, 2009)

Activism of owners of large investment funds (Neubaum & Zahra, 2006)

Environmental sensitivity (Delmas, Russo, & Montes-Sacho, 2007; Reid & Toffel, 2009)

Differentiation within industry (Hull & Rothenberg, 2008)

Stakeholder salience (Weber & Marley, 2012)

Corporate social performance (Chiu & Sharfman, 2011; David, Bloom, & Hillman, 2007; Deckop, Merriman, & Gupta, 2006; Ioannou & Serafeim, 2012; Neubaum & Zahra, 2006)

Reputation of firm (Brammer & Pavelin, 2006)

Perceived stakeholder impact (Buysse & Verbeke, 2003)

Environmental differentiation (Delmas, Russo, & Montes-Sacho, 2007)

Change in shareholder value (Godfrey, Merrill, & Hansen, 2009)

Corporate sustainable development (Bansal, 2005)

Policy implementation (Ramus & Montiel, 2005)

Consumer trust (Terwel, Harinck, Ellemers, & Daamen, 2009)

Table 4.7 Summary of Empirical Pro-Environmental Research at the Organizational Level of Analysis

Predictors	Mediators and Moderators	Outcomes
Legitimacy (Bansal & Clelland, 2004)	**Mediators**	*Unsystematic risk* (Bansal & Clelland, 2004)
R&D intensity (Dahlmann & Brammer, 2011)	*Intangible resources (innovation, reputation, human capital)* (Surroca, Tribo, & Waddock, 2010)	*Financial performance* (Barnett & Salomon, 2012; Barnett & Salomon, 2006; Doh, Howton, Howton, & Siegel, 2010; Hull & Rothenberg, 2008; Orlitzky, Schmidt, & Rynes, 2003; Surroca, Tribo, & Waddock, 2010; Tang, Hull, & Rothenberg, 2012)
Board composition (Dahlmann & Brammer, 2011; Post, Rahman, & Rubow, 2011)		
Organizational discourse (Caruana & Crane, 2008)	*Consolidation of emergent understandings* (Cegarra-Navarro, Eldridge, & Martinez-Martinez, 2010)	
Firm characteristics (Hendry, 2006)		*Organizational learning* (Moore & Beadle, 2006)
Perceived risk/uncertainty (Haigh & Griffiths, 2012)	**Moderators**	
Resource motivation (Lin, 2012)	*Size* (Bansal, 2005; Buysse & Verbeke, 2003; Furrer, Hamprecht, & Hoffmann, 2012; Lee & Lounsbury, 2011)	*Corporate environmental strategy* (Dahlmann & Brammer, 2011; Lin, 2012; Rothenberg & Levy, 2012)
CEO pay structure (Deckop, Merriman, & Gupta, 2006)		
Board characteristics (de Villiers, Naiker, & van Staden; 2011)	*Financial performance* (Bansal, 2005; Furrer, Hamprecht, & Hoffmann, 2012)	*Reporting/Disclosure* (Bolivar, 2009; Reid & Toffel, 2009)
Financial performance (Shaefer, 2007)	*Governance structure/firm ownership* (Berrone, Cruz, Gomez-Mejia, & Larraza-Kintana, 2010; Kassinis & Vafeas, 2006; Muller & Kolk, 2010)	*Political activity re: climate change* (Clark & Crawford, 2012; Kolk & Pinske, 2007)
Trade intensity (Muller & Kolk, 2010)		
Environmental leadership strategy (Buysse & Verbeke, 2003)	*Disclosures* (Bansal & Clelland, 2004)	*Climate strategy* (Furrer, Hamprecht, & Hoffmann, 2012)

Perceived performance (Branzei, Ursacki-Bryant, Vertinsky, & Zhang, 2004)

Social screening on mutual funds (Barnett & Salomon, 2006)

Corporate governance (Walls, Berrone, & Phan, 2012)

Environmental capabilities (Berchicci, Dowell, & King, 2012)

Capital management capabilities (Bansal 2005)

Enviropreneurial marketing (Baker & Sinkula, 2005)

Implementation of sustainability dimensions (Closs, Speier, & Meacham, 2011)

Strategic importance of CSR (Husted & Allen, 2006)

Perceptions of ISO 14001 certification (Boiral, 2007)

Expressions of commitment (Bansal & Clelland, 2004)

Subsidiary dependence (Christmann, 2004)

CSR task visibility (Jiang & Bansal, 2003)

Pace/consistency of CSR engagement (Tang, Hull, & Rothenberg, 2012)

MNE character (Buysse & Verbeke, 2003)

Opacity of firm environmental impact (Jiang & Bansal, 2003)

Innovation (Hull & Rothenberg, 2008)

Stakeholder influence capacity (Barnett & Salomon, 2012)

Environmental management systems (Darnall, 2006; Schaefer, 2007)

Cost of capital (Sharfman & Fernando, 2008)

Environmental proactivity (Murillo-Luna, Garces-Ayerbe, & Rivera-Torres, 2008)

Organizational responsiveness (Bansal, 2003)

Organizational strategy (Husted & Allen, 2006)

Competitiveness (Closs, Speier, & Meacham, 2011)

Reporting (Nikolaeva & Bicho, 2011)

New product development success (Baker & Sinkula, 2005)

Environmental knowledge (Cegarra-Navarro, Eldridge, & Martinez-Martinez, 2010)

Rahman, & Rubow, 2011), size of the board, the number of legal experts on the board, and the percentage of independent board directors were studied in relation to the implementation of environmental strategies and environmental performance (e.g., Dahlmanm & Brammer, 2011; de Villiers, Naiker, & van Staden, 2011). Regarding legitimacy, researchers investigated firm perceptions of certification (e.g., ISO 14001) and the firms' actual practices in the implementation of total quality programs (Boiral, 2007), and unsystematic stock market risk (Bansal & Clelland, 2004). Environmental marketing strategy was examined in relation to new product development (Baker & Sinkula, 2005) and regulatory pressures (Buysse & Verbeke, 2003). Finally, financial performance was studied as a determinant in the adoption of environmental strategies (Schaefer, 2007), and environmental performance as a predictor of adjustment in environmental strategies (Branzei, Ursacki-Bryant, Vertinsky, & Zhang, 2004).

Outcomes

Financial performance is still the most researched outcome at the organizational level of analysis (e.g., Barnett & Salomon, 2012; Orlitzky, Schmidt, & Rynes, 2003; Surroca, Tribo, & Waddock, 2010), whereas nonfinancial outcomes included corporate environmental strategy (e.g., Furrer, Hamprecht, & Hoffmann, 2012; Rothenberg & Levy, 2012), implementation of environmental management systems (Darnall, 2006; Schaefer, 2007), and environmental reporting (Bolivar, 2009; Nikolaeva & Bicho, 2011; Reid & Toffel, 2009).

Moderators and Mediators

Some researchers focused on company characteristics such as size (e.g., Bansal, 2005; Furrer, Hamprecht, & Hoffmann, 2012), firm ownership (e.g., Berrone, Cruz, Gomez-Mejia, & Larraza-Kintana, 2010; Muller & Kolk, 2010), and governance structure (Kassinis & Vafeas, 2006), whereas others focused on financial performance (Bansal, 2005; Furrer, Hamprecht, & Hoffmann, 2012), disclosures (Bansal & Clelland, 2004), and the pace and consistency of CSR engagement (Tang, Hull, & Rothenberg, 2012). Surroca, Tribo, and Waddock (2010) explored the mediating role of intangible resources in the relationship between social responsibility and financial performance.

Individual Level of Analysis

Studies focusing on variables at the individual level were surprisingly absent from major industrial/organizational journals such as *Journal of Applied Psychology, Journal of Occupational and Organizational Psychology, Journal of Organizational Behavior,* and *Personnel Psychology* until 2013, when both

Journal of Organizational Behavior, and *Personnel Psychology* published special issues on CSR. Still, only 18% of the articles in the remaining journals focused on pro-environmental issues at the individual level.

Predictors

Research at the individual level has focused on predictors related to leaders, employees, and consumers. Regarding leaders, researchers have found a recent change in CEO (Dahlmann & Brammer, 2011) and the leader's membership within a social movement organization (Sine & Lee, 2009) to be related to positive changes in environmental strategy, whereas the CEOs' political ideologies predict CSR engagement (Chin, Hambrick, & Trevino, 2013). Another focus concerning leaders has been on leadership style. For example, Waldman, Siegel, and Javidan (2006) found that transformational leadership, particularly intellectual stimulation, is associated with the propensity to engage in environmental CSR, whereas Robertson and Barling (2013) showed that environmentally-specific transformational leadership and leaders' pro-environmental behaviors predict employees' environmental behaviors.

Regarding employees, researchers have investigated employee perceptions and employee behavior. For example, positive employee perceptions of environmental CSR have been linked to higher levels of employee commitment (Stites & Michael, 2011). In an intervention study involving 352 employees, peer education resulted in higher reduction in electricity use than feedback via email (Carrico & Riemer, 2011). Some employee related predictors have been studied within specific groups of workers. For example Michel-Guillou and Moser (2006) examined the relationship between environment beliefs and representations and commitment to proenvironmental practices among farmers, whereas Munoz, Bogner, Clement, and Carvalho (2009) investigated the environmental attitudes of pre-service and in-service teachers in 16 countries.

Research involving consumer-related predictors has focused on consumer demographics, consumer behaviors, and consumer attitudes. In a study by Meijer and Schuyt (2005), having a left-wing political orientation, a higher level of education, being female, and being older have been associated with higher sensitivity to corporate social performance. Thogersen and Olander (2003) investigated the spillover of environment-friendly consumer behavior from one domain to another, and Tobler, Visschers, and Siegrist (2012) linked consumer attitudes to willingness to engage in environment-friendly behaviors.

Outcomes

Studies investigating outcomes at the individual level have mostly focused on employees. Evans and Davis (2011) found that perceptions of corporate citizenship attracted job applicants, whereas Gully et al. (2013) showed that social and environmentally responsible recruitment messages were related to job pursuit intentions through increased perceptions of person-organization fit. Several studies have linked employees' perceptions of environmental CSR with higher levels of commitment to the organization (Mueller, Hattrup, Spiess, & Lin-Hi, 2012; Stites & Michael, 2011) and organizational citizenship behaviors (Rupp, Shao, Thornton, & Skarlicki, 2013). Other studies (Robertson & Barling, 2013; Rothenberg, 2003) focused on employees' pro-environmental behaviors as outcomes. Another stream of research focused on managers. For example, in a study involving 360 Chinese firms, Branzei, Ursacki-Bryant, Vertinsky, and Zhang (2004) found that satisfactory environmental performance leads to higher manager commitment to environmental initiatives.

Mediators and Moderators

Only four studies investigated mediators at the individual level. (See Table 4.8 for a summary of empirical pro-environmental research at the individual level of analysis.) For example, Carrico and Riemer (2011) examined perceptions of norms and outcome expectancy as mediators of peer education and electricity consumption, whereas Gosling (2010) found that the relationship between connectedness to nature and management behaviors was mediated by the importance given to environmental benefits of vegetation management in a sample of farmers. Several variables were studied as moderators. For example, expectancy of success moderated the relationship between perceived performance and leader commitment to environmental initiatives (Branzei, Ursacki-Bryant, Vertinsky, & Zhang, 2004), ethical norms moderated the relationship between consumer attitudes and their willingness to engage in behaviors (Tobler, Visschers, & Siegrist, 2012), and moral identity moderated the relationship between perceptions of CSR and organizational citizenship behaviors (Rupp, Shao, Thornton, & Skarlicki, 2013).

In summary, despite the paucity of studies investigating environmental variables at the individual level of analysis, these few studies shed light on important issues regarding leaders, employees, and consumers. Leader style and involvement in environmental movements may influence corporate environmental engagement and strategy. Employees' perceptions of social responsibility may result in higher commitment to the organization. Consumers' pro-environmental behaviors in one domain may lead to similar behaviors in other domains. Several studies at this level of analysis have uncovered the underlying mechanisms by which environmental attitudes lead to environmental behaviors, whereas some others have expanded our knowledge regarding different populations of workers such as teachers and farmers.

Observations on Pro-Environmental Research and Directions for Future Research

In this chapter we presented a review of the research methodologies in pro-environmental research based on 118 articles from 14 journals. Specifically, we examined empirical research by sample characteristics, research approach, research strategy, data collection methods, types of data used, and level of analysis.

With databases such as Standard and Poor's 500 and TRI, which store ESG ratings of the world's leading companies, researchers have access to large amounts of data in pro-environmental research. Although sample sizes in studies we analyzed were promising, there are several issues worth noting regarding sample characteristics. First, the heavy reliance on these data sources has meant that most extant research is oriented to large, listed companies. Although large companies are clearly of interest due to their environmental impact, given the significance of small and medium sized companies in most developed economies (Brammer, Hoejmose, & Marchant, 2012), we believe their environmental impact warrants greater research attention. Second, although the majority of studies used organizational samples, almost half of the studies based on employee samples were homogeneous in occupation, raising concerns with regard to the generalizability of their findings. Finally, most of the research has been conducted on North American samples, which makes it difficult to make broader generalizations across cultures.

The majority (81%) of the articles in our sample took a quantitative approach. Ninety percent of these used a correlational strategy, which limits the ability to establish causal inferences. The abundance of correlational research may be reflective of the emergent nature of the field and the infeasibility of random assignment due to the macro-level variables that are often the topic of research on organizations and the natural environment. Furthermore, using archival data, which, by its nature, does not allow for random assignment, makes it difficult to establish causality. However, these limitations may be mitigated to a great extent through an approach that aims to establish causality by eliminating reverse causality and omitted variable bias, and ensuring the robustness of correlations across different samples and specifications (Cook & Campbell, 1979; Echambadi, Campbell, & Agarwall, 2006).

Researchers can also establish causality by providing evidence of clear temporal ordering of the variables through longitudinal data. Indeed, more longitudinal research is needed to answer important research questions at all levels of analysis, for example, the long-term effects of certification on corporate reputation at the institutional level, environmental strategy on financial performance at the organizational level, and perceptions of environmental performance on

Table 4.8 Summary of Empirical Pro-Environmental Research at the Individual Level of Analysis

Predictors	Mediators	Moderators	Outcomes
Consumer demographics (Meijer & Schuyt, 2005)	Perceptions of norms (Carrico & Riemer, 2011)	CSR education (Evans & Davis, 2011)	Organizational commitment (Mueller, Hattrup, Spiess, & Lin-Hi, 2012; Stites & Michael, 2011)
Political affiliation (Chin, Hambrick, & Trevino, 2013; Meijer & Schuyt, 2005)	Outcome expectancy (Carrico & Riemer, 2011)	Management commitment to ethics (Muller & Kolk, 2010)	Job applicant attraction (Evans & Davis, 2011; Rupp, Shao, Thornton, & Skarlicki, 2013)
Employee perceptions of CSR (Mueller, Hattrup, Spiess, & Lin-Hi, 2012; Stites & Michael, 2011)	Importance given to environmental benefits of vegetation managements (Gosling & Williams, 2010)	Expectancy of success (Branzei, Ursacki-Bryant, Vertinsky, & Zhang, 2004)	Worker participation in CSR (Rothenberg, 2003)
Social movement organization membership (Sine & Lee, 2009)	Employees' harmonious environmental passion (Robertson & Barling, 2013)	Goal attractiveness (Carrico & Riemer, 2011)	Leader commitment to environmental initiatives (Branzei, Ursacki-Bryant, Vertinsky, & Zhang, 2004)
CEO change/leadership (Dahlmann & Brammer, 2011; Robertson & Barling, 2013; Waldman, Siegel, & Javidan, 2006)	Interpersonal contacts (Delmas & Pekovic, 2013)	Ethical values/norms (Thogersen & Olander, 2003)	

Feedback/peer education re: energy consumption (Carrico & Riemer, 2011)

Connectedness to nature (Gosling, 2010) *Social representation of the environment* (Michel-Guillou & Moser, 2006)

Consumer attitudes/Behaviors (Thogersen & Olander, 2003; Tobler, Visschers, & Siegrist, 2012)

Pro-environmental interest/values (Michel-Guillou & Moser, 2006; Shepherd, Patzelt, & Baron, 2013)

Perceived cost/benefit (Tobler, Visschers, & Siegrist, 2012)

Entrepreneurial self-efficacy (Shepherd, Patzelt, & Baron, 2013)

CEO power (Chin, Hambrick, & Trevino, 2013)

Transformational leadership (Graves, Sarkis, & Zhu, 2013)

Pro-environmental attitude (Bissing-Olson, Iyer, Fielding, & Zacher, 2013)

Moral identity (Ormiston & Wong, 2013; Rupp, Shao, Thornton, & Skarlicki, 2013)

Distributive justice (Rupp, Shao, Thornton, & Skarlicki, 2013)

Management Behaviors (Gosling & Williams, 2010)

Environmental attitudes/Behaviors (Munoz, Bogner, Clement, & Carvalho, 2009; Tobler, Visschers, & Siegrist, 2012)

Climate change skepticism (Islam, Barnes, & Toma, 2013)

Pro-environmental Behaviors (Bissing-Olson, Iyer, Fielding, & Zacher, 2013; Graves, Sarkis, & Zhu, 2013; Robertson & Barling, 2013)

Organizational citizenship Behavior (Rupp, Shao, Thornton, & Skarlicki, 2013)

Perceived person-organization fit (Gully, Phillips, Castellano, & Kim, 2013) employee commitment at the individual level. The small number of experimental studies, on the other hand, have been used mainly to answer research questions at the individual level of analysis and been limited to the use of vignettes. Future studies would benefit from the use of vignette studies to investigate institutional- and organizational-level variables, as well as other methodologies, such as experience sampling and event studies, at all levels.

Despite the usefulness of a qualitative approach in emerging fields in terms of theory generation, theory elaboration, theory testing, and critical theory, it was used by less than a fifth of the studies in our content analysis. Of these studies, 72% used case studies to elaborate theory, which leads us to question (as did Bluhm et al., 2011, and Lee et al., 1999) the ability of qualitative researchers to produce good theory that will stand the test of time. At the same time, more research should apply the grounded theory approach to generate theory around research questions that haven't received a lot of research attention. The use of multi-case designs in most of the qualitative studies is promising; however, as is the case with quantitative research, the lack of longitudinal studies was noticeable. We recommend that qualitative researchers combine multi-case studies with longitudinal designs to provide the field with findings that are more compelling.

Both qualitative and quantitative approaches have strengths and weaknesses. Qualitative approaches allow the researcher to examine a new phenomenon in depth and generate theory (Yin, 2009), but it is often overly complex (Eisenhardt, 1991, Shah & Corley, 2006). Quantitative approaches, on the other hand, are simple and generalizable; however, the use of proxies to measure phenomena may result in reduced accuracy (Shah & Corley, 2006). Therefore, researchers may enhance their work by combining quantitative and qualitative approaches. A qualitative method may be used to develop a theoretical model, which may be tested using quantitative methods. Alternatively, qualitative methods may follow quantitative ones in order to explain unexpected findings or mechanisms that create unexpected patterns in the data (see Shah and Corley, 2006 for examples).

In terms of data collection methods, interviews, documentation, and observation were the most commonly used in qualitative studies, whereas archival data and surveys were the most commonly used in quantitative studies. Using these methods, researchers collected five different types of data: company self-reports, objective data, third-party assessments, stakeholder self-reports, and stakeholder assessments. Regarding these data collection methods and data types, we identified several shortcomings. First, less than half of the qualitative studies and almost none of the quantitative studies used multiple sources of data. Although some qualitative studies triangulated data sources, they used one primary method (usually, interviews) whereas the analysis of other sources was rarely described. Second, researchers relied heavily on archival data based on either company self-reports or third-party assessments. Limitations of using publicly available databases have been widely documented. For example, TRI is based on company self-reports and focuses only on the manufacturing process, failing to account for greenhouse gases or issues like biodiversity and habitat protection (Etzion, 2007). Furthermore, aggregating scores from the strengths and concerns dimensions of KLD, the most commonly used measure of environmental performance, may lead to inaccurate findings in research given the correlation between them (Mattingly & Berman, 2006) and evidence suggesting that the most advanced environmental practices are likely to be found at companies with higher levels of toxic releases and lower environmental compliance (Delmas & Doctori-Blass, 2010). To overcome these limitations, researchers have recommended using multiple databases (Berchicci, Dowell, & King, 2012; Chiu and Sharfman, 2011), favouring longitudinal designs, and the *Data Envelopment Methodology*, which allows the factoring of multiple scores into one efficiency score (Kuosmanen & Kortelainen, 2005). The third limitation we observed was the paucity of studies using novel data collection methods such as discourse analysis, conversation analysis, website analysis, experience sampling, and event studies. Bluhm et al. (2010) have stated that they view the use of novel and unfamiliar techniques as a sign of progress for research. We endorse their view and recommend that researchers continue to broaden the horizons of research by using novel data collection methods as well as data sources such as environmentally oriented venture capital funds and socially responsible investment funds (Etzion, 2007).

Similar to the literature on corporate social responsibility (see Aguinis & Glavas, 2012 for a review), pro-environmental research on organizations and the natural environment has been fragmented, with studies focusing mostly on one level of analysis, institutional, organizational, or, albeit fewer in number, individual. Although research at each of these levels has shed light on a number of important issues, research incorporating multiple levels of analysis is needed to better understand the interrelated nature of environmental issues in organizations. For example, multilevel designs may be used to answer questions related to the impact of institutional context on individual behavior and how employee values and attitudes impact the organization's environmental strategy. As such, methodologies commonly used at the institutional and organizational levels can inform the way researchers develop and explore research questions at the individual level, broadening the range of questions investigated at this level and preventing individual-level studies from relying too heavily on surveys. Furthermore, given that individuals operate within organizations and organizations operate within industries and countries, nested designs may be employed to reduce prediction errors stemming from ignoring the similarities among individuals within an organization or organizations within an industry or country (Hox, 2010).

In addition to the interactions between cross-level variables, researchers should explore mediators and moderators to gain a better understanding of the underlying mechanisms at different levels of analysis. More research is needed at the individual level to advance our knowledge regarding the psychological foundations of environmental attitudes and behaviors of employees, leaders and stakeholders.

Finally, we were surprised at the virtual absence of pro-environmental research in major industrial/organizational (I-O) journals, such as *Journal of Occupational and Organizational Psychology* and *Journal of Applied Psychology.* The special CSR issues of *Journal of Organizational Behavior* and *Personnel Psychology,* which included articles pertaining specifically to the natural environment, and the recent increase in the number of individual-level research articles are promising given the potential contributions I-O psychologist can make to the field, mainly in three areas. I-O psychologists can contribute to the field by (a) developing reliable and valid scales to measure environmental performance and stakeholder and employee attitudes and behaviors, (b) address the research gap at the individual level of analysis, and (c) conduct rigorous multilevel studies given their strong background in statistics and research design. At the same time, pro-environmental research provides I-O psychologists with a great opportunity to make contributions in a field that concerns both individuals and organizations.

Conclusion

Over the past ten years, topics pertaining to organizations and the natural environment have become more salient in research. Academics from different disciplines have attempted to answer important questions regarding key determinants and outcomes of pro-environmental engagement. In an effort to synthesize the work undertaken in all these different disciplines, we presented researchers with an overview of the research methodologies commonly used in pro-environmental research, highlighting the strengths and weaknesses of each methodology. We invite pro-environmental scholars everywhere to contribute to the advancement of our field by considering their role in improving research methods in pro-environmental research.

Suggested Additional Readings

1. Bansal, P., & Hoffman, A. J. (2011). *The Oxford handbook of business and the natural environment.* New York: Oxford University Press.
2. Etzion, D. (2007). Research on organizations and the natural environment, 1992–present: A review. *Journal of Management, 33*(4), 637–664.

3. Shah, S. K., & Corley, K. G. (2006). Building better theory by bridging the quantitative–qualitative divide. *Journal of Management Studies*, *43*(8), 1821–1835.

References

Aguinis, H., & Glavas, A. (2012). What we know and don't know about corporate social responsibility: A review and research agenda. *Journal of Management*, *38*, 932–968.

Baker, W., & Sinkula, J. (2005). Environmental marketing strategy and firm performance: Effects on new product performance and market share. *Journal of the Academy of Marketing Science*, *33*, 461–475.

Banerjee, S. (2003). Who sustains whose development? Sustainable development and the reinvention of nature. *Organization Studies*, *24*, 143–180.

Bansal, P. (2003). From issues to actions: The importance of individual concerns and organizational values in responding to natural environmental issues. *Organization Science*, *14*, 510–527.

Bansal, P. (2005). Evolving sustainably: A longitudinal study of corporate sustainable development. *Strategic Management Journal*, *26*, 197–218.

Bansal, P., & Clelland, I. (2004). Talking trash: Legitimacy, impression management, and unsystematic risk in the context of the natural environment. *Academy of Management Journal*, *47*, 93–103.

Bansal, P., & Gao, J. (2006). Building the future by looking to the past: Examining research published on organizations and environment. *Organization and Environment*, *19*, 458–478.

Barnett, M. L., & Salomon, R. M. (2006). Beyond dichotomy: The curvilinear relationship between social responsibility and financial performance. *Strategic Management Journal*, *27*, 1101–1122.

Barnett, M. L., & Salomon, R. M. (2012). Does it pay to be really good? Addressing the shape of the relationship between social and financial performance. *Strategic Management Journal*, *33*, 1304–1320.

Baxter, P., & Jack S. (2008). Qualitative case study methodology: study design and implementation for novice researchers. *Nurse Researcher*, *13*(1), 544–559.

Berchicci, L., Dowell, G., & King, A. A. (2012). Environmental capabilities and corporate strategy: Exploring acquisitions among us manufacturing firms. *Strategic Management Journal*, *33*, 1053–1071.

Berrone, P., Cruz, C., Gomez-Mejia, L. R., & Larraza-Kintana, M. (2010). Socioemotional wealth and corporate responses to institutional pressures: Do family-controlled firms pollute less? *Administrative Science Quarterly*, *55*, 82–113.

Bissing-Olson, M. J., Iyer, A., Fielding, K. S., & Zacher, H. (2013). Relationships between daily affect and pro-environmental behavior at work: The moderating role of pro-environmental attitude. *Journal of Organizational Behavior*, *34*, 156–175.

Bluhm, D. J., Harman, W., Lee, T. W., & Mitchell, T. R. (2011). Qualitative research in management: A decade of progress. *Journal of Management Studies, 48*, 1867–1891.

Boiral, O. (2007). Corporate greening through ISO 14001: A rational myth? *Organization Science, 18*, 127–146.

Bolivar, M. P. R. (2009). Evaluating corporate environmental reporting on the Internet. *Business & Society, 48*, 179–205.

Brammer, S., Hoejmose, S., & Marchant, K. (2011). Environmental management in SMEs in the UK: Practices, pressures and perceived benefits. *Business Strategy and the Environment, 21*, 423–434.

Brammer, S. J., & Pavelin, S. (2006). Corporate reputation and social performance: The importance of fit. *Journal of Management Studies, 43*, 435–455.

Branzei, O., Ursacki-Bryant, T. J., Vertinsky, I., & Zhang, W. (2004). The formation of green strategies in Chinese firms: matching corporate environmental responses and individual principles. *Strategic Management Journal, 25*, 1075–1095.

Buysse, K., & Verbeke, A. (2003). Proactive environmental strategies: a stakeholder management perspective. *Strategic Management Journal, 24*, 453–470.

Carrico, A. R., & Riemer, M. (2011). Motivating energy conservation in the workplace: An evaluation of the use of group-level feedback and peer education. *Journal of Environmental Psychology, 31*, 1–13.

Caruana, R., & Crane, A. (2008). Constructing consumer responsibility: Exploring the role of corporate communications. *Organization Studies, 29*, 1495–1519.

Cegarra-Navarro, J. G., Eldridge, S., & Martinez-Martinez, A. (2010). Managing environmental knowledge through unlearning in Spanish hospitality companies. *Journal of Environmental Psychology, 30*, 249–257.

Child, J., Lu, Y., & Tsai, T. (2007). Institutional entrepreneurship in building an environmental protection system for the People's Republic of China. *Organization Studies, 28*, 1013–1034.

Child, J., & Tsai, T. (2005). The dynamic between firms environmental strategies and institutional constraints in emerging economies: Evidence from China and Taiwan. *Journal of Management Studies, 42*, 95–125.

Chin, M. K., Hambrick, D. C., & Trevino, L. K. (2013). Political ideologies of CEOs: The influence of executives' values on corporate social responsibility. *Administrative Science Quarterly, 58*, 197–232.

Chiu, S., & Sharfman, M. (2011). Legitimacy, visibility, and the antecedents of corporate social performance: An investigation of the instrumental perspective. *Journal of Management, 37*, 1558–1585.

Christmann, P. (2004). Multinational companies and the natural environment: determinants of global environmental policy standardization. *Academy of Management Journal, 47*(5), 747–760.

Christmann, P., & Taylor, G. (2006). Firm self-regulation through international certifiable standards: Determinants of symbolic versus substantive implementation. *Journal of International Business Studies, 37*, 863–878.

Clark, C. E., & Crawford, E. P. (2012). Influencing climate change policy: The effect of shareholder pressure and firm environmental performance. *Business and Society*, *51*, 148–175.

Closs, D. J., Speier, C., & Meacham, N. (2011). Sustainability to support end-to-end value chains: the role of supply chain management. *Journal of the Academy of Marketing Science*, *39*, 101–116.

Cohen, B. (2007). Journal ratings and footprints: A North American perspective of organizations and the natural environment journal quality. *Business Strategy and the Environment*, *16*, 64–74.

Cook, T. D., & Campbell, D. T. (1979). Quasi-experimentation: Design and analysis issues for field settings. Boston: Houghton Mifflin.

Creswell, J. W. (2006). *Qualitative inquiry and research design: Choosing among five traditions*. CA: Sage Publications.

Dahlmann, F., & Brammer, S. (2011). Exploring and explaining patterns of adaptation and selection in corporate environmental strategy in the USA. *Organization Studies*, *32*, 527–553.

Darnall, N. (2006). Why firms mandate ISO 14001 certification. *Business & Society*, *45*, 354–382.

David, P., Bloom, M., & Hillman, A. (2007). Investor activism, managerial responsiveness, and corporate social performance. *Strategic Management Journal*, *28*, 91–100

Deckop, J. R., Merriman, K. K., & Gupta, S. (2006). The effects of CEO pay structure on corporate social performance. *Journal of Management*, *32*, 329–342.

Delmas, M., Russo, M., & Montes-Sancho, M. (2007). Deregulation and environmental differentiation in the electric utility industry. *Strategic Management Journal*, *28*, 189–209.

Delmas, M., & Doctori-Blass, V. (2010). Measuring corporate environmental performance: the trade-offs of sustainability ratings. *Business Strategy and the Environment*, *19*, 245–260.

Delmas, M. A., & Pekovic, S. (2013). Environmental standards and labor productivity: Understanding the mechanisms that sustain sustainability. *Journal of Organizational Behavior*, *34*, 230–252.

de, V. C., Naiker, V., & van, S. C. (2011). The effect of board characteristics on firm environmental performance. *Journal of Management*, *37*, 1636–1663.

Doh, J. P., & Guay, T. R. (2006). Corporate social responsibility, public policy, and NGO activism in Europe and the United States: An institutional-stakeholder perspective. *Journal of Management Studies*, *43*, 1, 47–73.

Doh, J. P., Howton, S. D., Howton, S. W., & Siegel, D. S. (2010). Does the market respond to endorsement of social responsibility? The role of institutions, information, and legitimacy. *Journal of Management*, *36*, 1461–1485.

Driscoll, C. (2006). The not so clear-cut nature of organizational legitimating mechanisms in the Canadian forest sector. *Business & Society*, *45*, 322–353.

Echambadi, R., Campbell, B., & Agarwal, R. (2006). Encouraging best practice in quantitative management research: an incomplete list of opportunities. *Journal of Management Studies, 43*, 1803–1822.

Edmondson, A. C., & McManus, S. E. (2007). Methodological fit in management field research. *Academy of Management Review, 32*, 1155–1179.

Eisenhardt, K. M. (1991). Better stories and better constructs – the case for rigor and comparative logic. *Academy of Management Review, 16*, 620–627.

Etzion, D. (2007). Research on organizations and the natural environment, 1992–present: A review. *Journal of Management, 33*, 637–664.

Evans, R. W., & Davis, W. (2011). An examination of perceived corporate citizenship, job applicant attraction, and CSR work role definition. *Business & Society, 50*, 456–480.

Field, A., & Hole, G. (2003). *How to design and report experiments*. CA: Sage Publications.

Frooman, J., & Murrell, A. (2005). Stakeholder influence strategies: The roles of structural and demographic determinants. *Business & Society, 44*, 3–31.

Furrer, B., Hamprecht, J., & Hoffmann, V. H. (2012). Much ado about nothing? How banks respond to climate change. *Business and Society, 51*, 62–88.

Godfrey, P. C., Merrill, C. B., & Hansen, J. M. (2009). The relationship between corporate social responsibility and shareholder value: an empirical test of the risk management hypothesis. *Strategic Management Journal, 30*, 425–445.

Golden, B. R. (1992). The past is the past – Or is it? The use of retrospective accounts as indicators of past strategy. *Academy of Management Journal*, 848–860.

Gosling, E., & Williams, K. J. H.(2010). Connectedness to nature, place attachment and conservation behaviour: Testing connectedness theory among farmers. *Journal of Environmental Psychology, 30*, 298–304.

Graves, L. M., Sarkis, J., & Zhu, Q. (2013). How transformational leadership and employee motivation combine to predict employee pro-environmental behaviors in China. *Journal of Environmental Psychology, 35*, 81–91.

Gravetter, F. J., & Forzano, L. B. (2003). *Research methods for behavioural sciences*. Belmont, CA: Wadsworth.

Gully, S. M., Phillips, J. M., Castellano, W. G., Han, K., & Kim, A. (2013). A mediated moderation model of recruiting socially and environmentally responsible job applicants. *Personnel Psychology, 66*, 935–973.

Haigh, N., & Griffiths, A. (2012). Surprise as a catalyst for including climatic change in the strategic environment. *Business and Society, 51*, 89–120.

Hendry, J. (2006). Taking aim at business. *Business & Society, 45*, 47–86.

Herriott, R. E., & Firestone, W. A. (1983). Multisite qualitative policy research: Optimizing description and generalizability. *Educational Researcher, 12*(2), 14–19.

Highhouse, S., & Gillespie, J. Z. (2008). Do samples really matter that much? In C. E. Lance & R. J. Vandenberg (Eds.), *Statistical and methodological myths and urban legends: Doctrine, verity, and fable in the organizational and social sciences* (pp. 249–267). Mahwah, NJ: Lawrence Erlbaum.

Hox, J. J. (2010). *Multilevel analysis: Techniques and applications*. London: Lawrence Erlbaum Associates.

Hull, C. E., & Rothenberg, S. (2008). Firm performance: the interactions of corporate social performance with innovation and industry differentiation. *Strategic Management Journal, 29*, 781–789.

Husted, B. W., & Allen, D. B. (2006). Corporate social responsibility in the multinational enterprise: strategic and institutional approaches. *Journal of International Business Studies, 37*, 838–849.

Ioannou, I., & Serafeim, G. (2012). What drives corporate social performance? The role of nation-level institutions. *Journal of International Business Studies, 43*, 834–864.

Islam, M. M., Barnes, A., & Toma, L. (2013). An investigation into climate change scepticism among farmers. *Journal of Environmental Psychology, 34*, 137–150.

Jiang, R. J., & Bansal, P. (2003). Seeing the need for ISO 14001. *Journal of Management Studies, 40*, 1047–1067.

Kassinis, G., & Vafeas, N. (2006). Stakeholder pressures and environmental performance. *Academy of Management Journal, 49*, 145–159.

Kearins, K., Collins, E., & Tregidga, H. (2010). Beyond corporate environmental management to a consideration of nature in visionary small enterprise. *Business & Society, 49*, 512–547.

King, A. (2007). Cooperation between corporations and environmental groups: A transaction cost perspective. *Academy of Management Review, 32*, 889–900.

Kock, C. J., Santalo, J., & Diestre, L. (2012). Corporate governance and the environment: what type of governance creates greener companies? *Journal of Management Studies, 49*, 492–514.

Kolk, A., & Pinkse, J. (2007). Multinationals' political activities on climate change. *Business & Society, 46*(2), 201–228.

Kuosmanen, T., & Kortelainen, M. (2005). Measuring eco-efficiency of production with data envelopment analysis. *Journal of Industrial Ecology, 9*(4), 59–72.

Lee, M. D., & Lounsbury, M. (2011). Domesticating radical rant and rage: An exploration of the consequences of environmental shareholder resolutions on corporate environmental performance. *Business & Society, 50*, 155–188.

Lee, T. W. (1999). *Using qualitative methods in organizational research*. Thousand Oaks, CA: Sage.

Lefsrud, L. M., & Meyer, R. E. (2012). Science or science fiction? Professionals' discursive construction of climate change. *Organization Studies, 33*, 1477–1506.

Lin, H. (2012). Strategic alliances for environmental improvements. *Business and Society, 51*, 335–348.

Locke, K. D. (2001). *Grounded theory in management research*. CA: Sage Publications.

Mattingly, J. E., & Berman, S. L. (2006). Measurement of corporate social action: Discovering taxonomy in the Kinder, Lydenburg, Domini ratings data. *Business & Society, 45,* 20–46.

Meijer, M. and Schuyt, T. (2005). Corporate social performance as a bottom line for consumers. *Business and Society, 44,* 442–461.

Michel-Guillou, E., & Moser, G. (2006). Commitment of farmers to environmental protection: From social pressure to environmental conscience. *Journal of Environmental Psychology, 26,* 227–235.

Moore, G., & Beadle, R. (2006). In search of organizational virtue in business: agents, goods, practices, institutions and environments. *Organization Studies, 27*(3), 369–389.

Mueller, K., Hattrup, K., Spiess, S. O., & Lin-Hi, N. (2012). The effects of corporate social responsibility on employees' affective commitment: a cross-cultural investigation. *The Journal of Applied Psychology, 97,* 1186–200.

Muller, A., & Kolk, A. (2010). Extrinsic and intrinsic drivers of corporate social performance: evidence from foreign and domestic firms in Mexico. *Journal of Management Studies, 47,* 1–26.

Munoz, F., Bogner, F., Clement, P., & Carvalho, G. S. (2009). Teachers' conceptions of nature and environment in 16 countries. *Journal of Environmental Psychology, 29,* 407–413.

Murrillo-Luna, J., Garcés-Ayerbe, C., & Rivera-Torres, P. (2008). Why do patterns of environmental responses differ? A stakeholders' pressure approach. *Strategic Management Journal, 29,* 1225–1240.

Neubaum, D. O., & Zahra, S. A. (2006). Institutional ownership and corporate social performance: The moderating effects of investment horizon, activism, and coordination. *Journal of Management, 32,* 108.

Nikolaeva, R., & Bicho, M. (2011). The role of institutional and reputational factors in the voluntary adoption of corporate social responsibility reporting standards. *Journal of the Academy of Marketing Science, 39,* 136–157.

Orlitzky, M., Schmidt, F., & Rynes, S. (2003). Corporate social and financial performance: A meta-analysis. *Organization Studies, 24,* 403–441.

Ormiston, M. E., & Wong, E. M. (2013). License to Ill: The effects of corporate social responsibility and CEO moral identity on corporate social irresponsibility. *Personnel Psychology, 66,* 861–893.

Overbeeke, M., & Snizek, W. E. (2005). Websites and corporate culture: A research agenda. Business and Society, *44,* 346–356.

Podsakoff, P. M., MacKenzie, S. B., Podsakoff, N. P., & Bachrach, D. G. (2008). Scholarly influence in the field of management: A bibliometric analysis of the determinants of university and author impact in the management literature in the past quarter century. *Journal of Management, 34,* 641–720.

Post, C., Rahman, N., & Rubow, E. (2011). Green governance: Boards of directors' composition and environmental corporate social responsibility. *Business & Society, 50*, 189–223.

Ramus, C., & Montiel, I. (2005). When are corporate environmental policies a form of greenwashing?. *Business & Society, 44*, 377–414.

Reid, E. M., & Toffel, M. W. (2009). Responding to public and private politics: corporate disclosure of climate change strategies. *Strategic Management Journal, 30*, 1157–1178.

Robertson, J. L., & Barling, J. (2013). Greening organizations through leaders' influence on employees' pro-environmental behaviors. *Journal of Organizational Behavior, 34*, 176–194.

Roome, N., & Wijen, F. (2006). Stakeholder power and organizational learning in corporate environmental management. *Organization Studies, 27*, 235–263.

Rothenberg, S., & Levy, D. L. (2012). Corporate perceptions of climate science: The role of corporate environmental scientists. *Business and Society, 51*, 31–61.

Rothenberg, S. (2003). Knowledge content and worker participation in environmental management at NUMMI. *Journal of Management Studies, 40*, 1783–1802.

Rupp, D. E., Shao, R., Thornton, M. A., & Skarlicki, D. P. (2013). Applicants' and employees' reactions to corporate social responsibility: The moderating effects of first-party justice perceptions and moral identity. *Personnel Psychology, 66*, 895–933.

Schaefer, A. (2007). Contrasting institutional and performance accounts of environmental management systems: Three case studies in the UK Water & Sewerage Industry. *Journal of Management Studies, 44*, 506–535.

Scott, W. R. (2001). *Institutions and organizations*. CA: Sage Publications.

Shah, S. K., & Corley, K. G. (2006). Building better theory by bridging the quantitative–qualitative divide. *Journal of Management Studies, 43*, 1821–1835

Sharfman, M., & Fernando, C. (2008). Environmental risk management and the cost of capital. *Strategic Management Journal, 296*, 569–592.

Shen, W., Kiger, T. B., Davies, S. E., Rasch, R. L., Simon, K. M., & Ones, D. S. (2011). Samples in applied psychology: over a decade of research in review. *The Journal of Applied Psychology, 96*, 1055–1064.

Shepherd, D. A., Patzelt, H., & Baron, R. A. (October 21, 2013). "I care about nature, but . . .": Disengaging values in assessing opportunities that cause harm. *Academy of Management Journal, 56*(5), 1251–1273.

Sine, W. D., & Lee, B. H. (2009). Tilting at windmills? The environmental movement and the emergence of the US wind energy sector. *Administrative Science Quarterly, 54*, 123–155.

Stites, J., & Michael, J. (2011). Organizational commitment in manufacturing employees: relationships with corporate social performance. *Business & Society, 50*, 50–70.

Surroca, J., Tribo, J. A., & Waddock, S. (2010). Corporate responsibility and financial performance: The role of intangible resources. *Strategic Management Journal*, *31*, 463–490.

Tang, Z., Hull, C. E., & Rothenberg, S. (2012). How corporate social responsibility engagement strategy moderates the CSR-financial performance relationship. *Journal of Management Studies*, *49*(7), 1274–1303.

Terwel, B. W., Harinck, F., Ellemers, N., & Daamen, D. D. L. (2009). How organizational motives and communications affect public trust in organizations: The case of carbon dioxide capture and storage. *Journal of Environmental Psychology*, *29*, 290–299.

Thøgersen, J., & Ölander, F. (2003). Spillover of environment-friendly consumer behaviour. *Journal of Environmental Psychology*, *23*, 225–236.

Tobler, C., Visschers, V. H. M., & Siegrist, M. (2012). Addressing climate change: Determinants of consumers' willingness to act and to support policy measures. *Journal of Environmental Psychology*, *32*, 197–207.

Van de Ven, A. H. (1989). 'Nothing is quite so practical as a good theory'. *Academy of Management Review*, *14*, 486–489.

Waldman, D. A., Siegel, D. S., & Javidan, M. (2006). Components of CEO transformational leadership and corporate social responsibility. *Journal of Management Studies*, *43*, 1703–1725.

Walls, J. L., Berrone, P., & Phan, P. H. (2012). Corporate governance and environmental performance: Is there really a link? *Strategic Management Journal*, *33*, 885–913.

Weber, J., & Marley, K. A. (2012). In search of stakeholder salience: exploring corporate social and sustainability reports. *Business and Society*, *51*, 626–649.

Yin, R. K. (2009). *Case study research: Design and methods*. CA: Sage Publications.

5 DIARY METHODS AND WORKPLACE PRO-ENVIRONMENTAL BEHAVIORS

Megan J. Bissing-Olson, Kelly S. Fielding, and Aarti Iyer

Research on workplace pro-environmental behaviors has generally used conventional methods such as cross-sectional surveys or interventions administered over a period of weeks or months (see chapter 4). This research has created a solid foundation of knowledge on important principles, ranging from documenting the different types of workplace pro-environmental behaviors that employees engage in (Boiral & Paillé, 2012; Lamm, Tosti-Kharas, & Williams, 2013; Ones & Dilchert, 2012) to the types of interventions that can increase these behaviors (Carrico & Riemer, 2011; Daamen, Staats, Wilke, & Engelen, 2001) and the strategies leading to successful environmental championing within organizations (Andersson & Bateman, 2000). These traditional methods share the general assumption that workplace pro-environmental behaviors and their antecedent factors are stable across contexts and time. Even studies that investigate the impact of interventions assume that individuals' behavior was stable prior to their exposure to the intervention, and that the change in behavior triggered by the intervention will remain stable in the future (although the possibility that behavior will revert back to previous patterns is also acknowledged). Mean scores of both predictor and outcome variables are compared among employees (or work groups) in order to draw conclusions about the predictors of workplace pro-environmental behaviors. In other words, traditional methods generally conceptualize workplace pro-environmental behaviors as *between-person* variables: employees' engagement in pro-environmental behaviors is seen as culminating from a set of stable individual characteristics (e.g., employees' general positive or negative attitude toward the behaviors) or stable features of the work context (e.g., degree of perceived organizational support for the behaviors).

What traditional methods are not able to capture is *within-person* differences or changes in behavior. Within-person variation in behavior refers to fluctuations in behavior within employees over short time periods (e.g., hourly, daily, or weekly) in different contexts. Central to the examination of such short-term variation in employee behavior is the use of diary methods (Bolger, Davis, & Rafaeli, 2003; Mehl & Conner, 2012; Ohly, Sonnentag, Niessen, & Zapf, 2010). In contrast with traditional methods, diary methods allow an examination of workplace pro-environmental behaviors as varying within a person between different contexts and time points. An employee may engage in pro-environmental behaviors at work on one day but not on another day, depending on factors such as daily stressors at work, resources, or job satisfaction. Diary methods can be used to address this within-person variation in behavior and, in doing so, can contribute to a greater understanding of workplace pro-environmental behaviors and the factors that predict more or less engagement in these actions.

In this chapter, we focus on the value of diary methods in organizational research, particularly for the study of workplace pro-environmental behaviors. Although a number of reviews exist that introduce diary methods in general (Bolger et al., 2003; Mehl & Conner, 2012; Reis & Gable, 2000) as well as in reference to organizational research (Alliger & Williams, 1993; Beal & Weiss, 2003; Fisher & To, 2012; Ohly et al., 2010), in this chapter we discuss how diary methods can be applied to the study of workplace pro-environmental behaviors specifically, and suggest a variety of avenues for future research (see also Bissing-Olson, Zacher, Fielding, & Iyer, 2012). We first present an overview of diary methods and give recommendations for the practical application of diary methods to the study of workplace pro-environmental behaviors. Second, we offer an agenda for future research, focusing on three main topics that can be addressed through diary methods: identifying different types of workplace pro-environmental behaviors, and examining how employees' psychological states influence within-person variation in workplace pro-environmental behaviors, and the role of job characteristics in influencing within-person variation in workplace pro-environmental behaviors. Within each of these sections, we offer suggestions for future research on workplace pro-environmental behaviors that may be addressed through the use of diary methods.

Diary Methods: An Overview and Recommendations for Practice

Diary methods involve the measurement of key variables (e.g., workplace pro-environmental behaviors, antecedents, and/or consequences) taken at multiple time points from the same people over a set period (Bolger et al., 2003;

Mehl & Conner, 2012; Reis & Gable, 2000). This is in comparison with traditional methods (Figure 5.1), which are concerned with employees' general levels of pro-environmental behaviors (e.g., over the past week, although a time frame is typically not specified in many surveys). Diary methods allow researchers to

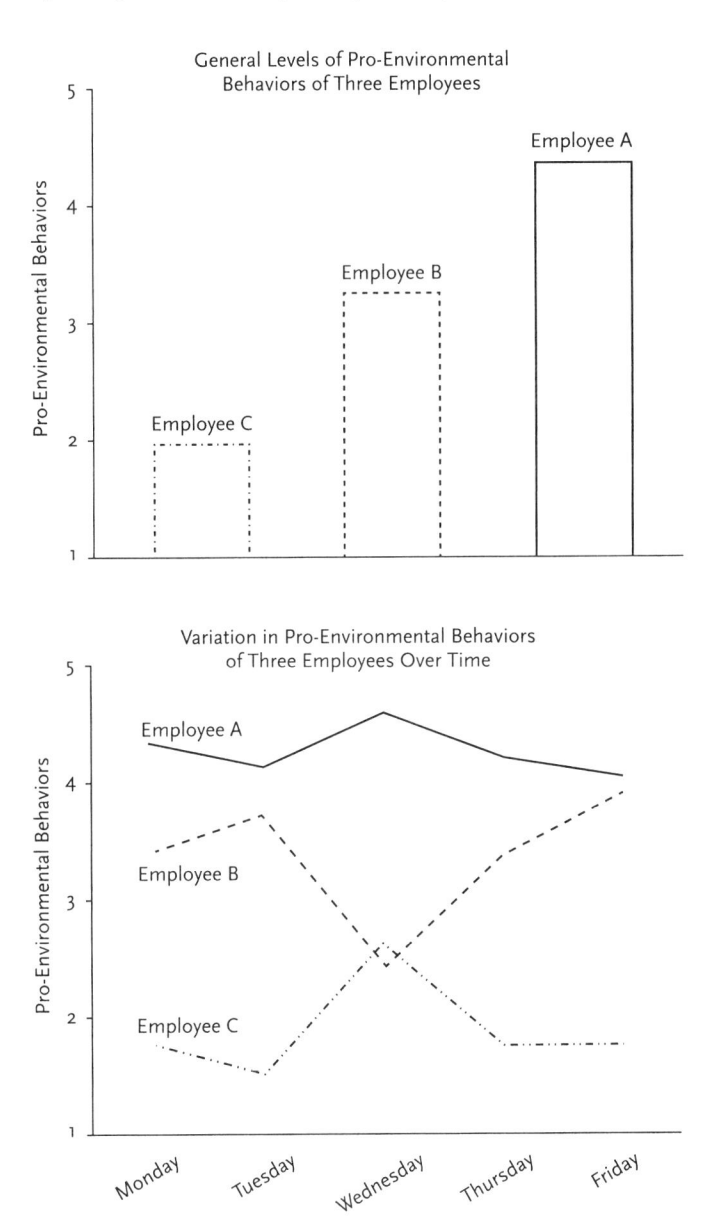

FIGURE 5.1 Comparison between general measures of pro-environmental workplace behaviors (*top*) and repeated measures of pro-environmental workplace behaviors (*bottom*).

gain access to dynamic experiences and behaviors within the workplace that are only accessible to and observable by participants. Repeated measurement of key variables enables researchers to examine experiences and processes in naturally occurring settings in (close to) real time while reducing retrospection bias.

When using diary methods, researchers typically collect data through standardized, quantitative surveys as opposed to open-ended, qualitative entries in a journal-like format (e.g., Poppleton, Briner, & Kiefer, 2008). These quantitative surveys can be administered through paper-and-pencil booklets, handheld electronic devices, or links to online surveys. Depending on the research question at hand, measurements are usually taken between one and ten times daily over a period of days or weeks (Conner & Lehman, 2012). There are three different methodological schemes for using diary methods in research (Table 5.1): experience sampling, daily diaries, and event sampling.

Experience Sampling

Experience sampling taps into ongoing experiences by having employees provide reports multiple times throughout the day. For example, experience sampling has been used to examine the daily relationships among job control, social support, learning, and well-being (positive affect) at work through employees reporting on measures of these variables up to four times a day for five working days (Daniels, Boocock, Glover, Hartley, & Holland, 2009). When using the experience-sampling methodology, researchers can adopt one of two types of sampling strategies (Conner & Lehman, 2012): variable time–based or fixed time–based. When using a *variable time–based strategy*, researchers direct participants to complete a report usually between four and ten times a day at semi-random times. At a random point during a specified time interval, the researcher contacts participants (e.g., via a text message) to signal that they should complete a report. The *fixed time–based strategy* also takes reports multiple times throughout the day, but here the reporting times are on a fixed schedule known to the participant. For example, in Daniels et al.'s (2009) study, participants completed daily measures of job control, social support, learning, and well-being (positive affect) at fixed times (i.e., 10:30 a.m., 12:30 p.m., 2:30 p.m., and 4:30 p.m.). Participants were instructed to report on the first three variables as they experienced them during the hour previous to assessment and to report on their well-being at the moment of assessment. Experience sampling and the more specific variable time–based and fixed time–based strategies are suited to studying phenomena that are ongoing (e.g., conscious awareness of environmental problems) or that could be affected by retrospective memory bias (e.g., actual engagement in workplace pro-environmental behaviors throughout the day). These strategies allow

Table 5.1 Research Methods for Conducting Diary Studies

Type of Method	Description of Method	Advantages	Disadvantages	Research Questions
Experience sampling	Participants provide multiple responses at semi-random (variable time–based sampling) or fixed time intervals (fixed time–based sampling) throughout the day	Taps into ongoing experiences and reduces memory bias	May be burdensome for participants to provide such frequent reports	Best suited to answer RQs about relationships between affect or stress and work PEB; the daily chronology of work PEB; work PEB that may not be recalled after a short period of time
Daily diaries	Participants report on behaviors and/or experiences once a day at a fixed time	Less burdensome than multiple reports. High compliance rates	Some degree of retrospection (e.g., recall of only key instances of pro-environmental behavior from the day)	Best suited to answer RQs about work PEB and other variables that may be easily recalled at the end of the day and work PEB that occur only once daily at a typical time of the day (e.g., end-of-day closing activities)
Event sampling	Participants report on behaviors and/or experiences only after a predefined event (e.g., purchasing decision) occurs	Can measure infrequent, discrete events and processes related to them. Retrospection greatly reduced	The participant needs to remember to fill out surveys at fitting times. Requesting reports of only negative aspects of an event may increase participant reactivity	Best suited to answer RQs about specific, predefined events, behaviors, or thoughts that may occur infrequently (e.g., events, behaviors, or thoughts related to ecopreneurial activity)

PEB, Pro-environmental behavior; RQ, research question.

Adapted from Conner, T. S., & Lehman, B. J. (2012). Getting started: Launching a study in daily life. In M. R. Mehl & T. S. Conner (Eds.), *Handbook of research methods for studying daily life* (pp. 89–107). New York: Guilford Press.

Supplemented with information from Gunthert and Wenze (2012), Moskowitz and Sadikaj (2012), Mehl and Robbins (2012), and Goodwin (2012).

participants to report on workplace pro-environmental behaviors and associated variables that are occurring at the moment of assessment or that have occurred since the previous assessment.

Daily Diaries

Daily diaries are used to collect employees' reports on behaviors and/or experiences once or twice a day at a fixed time, usually at the beginning or end of the workday. They are used to assess experiences and processes that occur during the day (e.g., the amount of time pressure felt that day). Daily diaries are less burdensome than multiple reports within a single day and may have higher compliance rates, particularly when collecting data for longer periods (e.g., for more than a few days; Gunthert & Wenze, 2012). However, in comparison to experience sampling methods that ask for reports more frequently, the once- or twice-daily reports collected through daily diaries may introduce some degree of retrospection bias (Schwarz, 2012). For example, when participants are asked frequently to report on their affect, they may be more likely to report minor incidents of experienced affect as opposed to reporting only major incidents. This could apply to workplace pro-environmental behaviors as well, with participants recalling more minor behaviors when asked to complete more frequent reports. For example, employees may not report behaviors that occurred in the morning or were easily forgotten (e.g., using scrap paper for notes) when asked at the end of the day to recall how often they engaged to pro-environmental behaviors at work. Thus, daily diaries may be best suited to examining specific behaviors that are more easily recalled or that occur at the end of the day (e.g., turning off computers and lights).

Event Sampling

Event sampling is used when researchers are interested in relatively rare or discrete events and processes related to them. With this method, participants provide reports on behaviors and/or experiences only after a predefined event has occurred. This strategy greatly reduces retrospection when compared with cross-sectional study designs. Event sampling may be optimal for examining the processes underpinning phenomena such as ecopreneurship (Pichel, 2008; Ramus & Steger, 2000), which is employees' proactive engagement in creating environmentally friendly changes within an organization (Pichel, 2008; Ramus & Steger, 2000). As ecopreneurial activities stem from employee initiatives that go beyond required work duties, it can be expected that they do not occur very often (see the section on different types of workplace pro-environmental behaviors for a more detailed description). Thus, event sampling may be well-suited for studying ecopreneurship, as employees could complete reports only when they have engaged in or intended to engage in a behavior that could be considered ecopreneurial.

Researchers' choice of sampling strategy depends on the research question under investigation. When studying workplace pro-environmental behaviors and associated factors that occur throughout the day experience sampling may be most appropriate, whereas when investigating phenomena that take place less frequently or that may be experienced more intensely, event sampling or a daily diary strategy may be more suitable. In addition, researchers may be interested in other types of research questions, such as the chronology of the workday (e.g., at what times of the workday do different types of workplace pro-environmental behaviors take place?). Experience sampling with either a fixed– or variable time–based sampling strategy may be the best approach to address this type of question.

Methodological Issues and Practical Constraints

Although the diary methods presented here have advantages over traditional methods (e.g., reduced retrospection and increased ecological validity), there are also methodological issues and practical constraints that need to be taken into account. The three most important limitations and issues that need to be addressed are: (a) participant burden, (b) data collection devices, and (c) sample recruitment. First, a general consideration when using diary methodology is the amount of burden and effort participants experience when completing such frequent reports. For all sampling strategies, therefore, long questionnaires should be avoided in order to reduce participant burden and increase response rates. Preferably, surveys should take no longer than five to seven minutes (Reis & Gable, 2000). This means that abbreviated and adapted scales along with one-item measures should be used (Ohly et al., 2010). It is important to carefully test the reliability and validity of such measures (Bolger et al., 2003).

Second, consideration needs to be given to how data are collected. This could take the form of paper booklets, handheld electronic devices, or web-based surveys. Paper booklets, which contain all diary surveys for all required reporting times, have the advantage of being accessible to all participants. A disadvantage of paper-and-pencil approaches is that participants may complete surveys at unscheduled times (e.g., going back and retrospectively filling out a missed survey). Researchers have no way to verify whether or not a report was completed at the correct time. The use of either handheld electronic devices or web-based surveys avoids this problem (i.e., timing of responses can be automatically recorded);

however, both require some computer knowledge, which some potential participants may not have. In addition, participants' access to the Internet (e.g., during the day or at night) may be limited, affecting reporting times (Ohly et al., 2010). The number of handheld devices available for the researcher to distribute may also be limited, which would extend the data collection period for the researcher. Overall, researchers' choice of data collection device will depend on study design and the available resources as well as characteristics of the sample (e.g., whether or not they are computer literate).

A third issue is sample recruitment. To gain access to employees, it may be necessary to first contact and convince organizational leaders (Ohly et al., 2010). This may be a challenge, as diary studies, particularly experience sampling studies that require participants to complete questionnaires multiple times a day, might be distracting or disruptive during a normal workday. To persuade organizational leaders, researchers could examine variables that organizational leaders may be interested in improving, such as employees' well-being and performance. Researchers could also offer to provide useful feedback for the organization (e.g., perhaps there are daily routines that place too much stress on employees). In addition, because reports are collected in real-world, working conditions, diary studies allow more precise and valid measurements of study variables (Ohly et al., 2010). This could result in more practical recommendations, which may be appealing to organizational leaders. Once access to potential participants is granted, it is important to establish good researcher–participant rapport to keep participants motivated and reduce attrition (Green, Rafaeli, Bolger, Shrout, & Reis, 2006). This means fostering an environment of collaboration with participants in which they feel committed to the project. Researchers can offer to inform participants of the outcomes of the study, keep lines of communication open by encouraging questions and feedback to the researcher, and offer to remind participants of reporting deadlines to help keep them on track.

In sum, researchers can apply different types of diary method strategies to the study of workplace pro-environmental behaviors. These approaches include experience sampling with either variable– or fixed time–based strategies, daily diary, or event sampling. The choice of strategy depends on the research question under investigation. For all diary method strategies, there are limitations and issues to address, including participant burden, choice of data collection device, and participant recruitment.

An Agenda for Future Research

To date, *within-person* processes of workplace pro-environmental behavior have been neglected within organizational research. As noted, *within-person processes* refer to how people vary in the frequency with which they carry out workplace pro-environmental behaviors on an everyday basis and how different types of real-world, workplace-specific contextual factors influence this variation. Diary methods are the most fitting approach to address research questions about these within-person processes. In this section, we present a broad framework for identifying variables that may be studied in relation to workplace pro-environmental behaviors using diary methods. We then describe three general research topics that may be particularly pertinent to the study of within-person processes of workplace pro-environmental behaviors.

To help determine what type of variables may be important to consider in investigating within-person variability in pro-environmental behaviors at work, we propose a broad conceptual framework with two key dimensions. The first dimension refers to the extent to which variables change over time (i.e., whether they are fluctuating or stable). The second dimension refers to potential sources of variability (i.e., employee or work context). Table 5.2 depicts this 2 (fluctuating, stable) × 2 (employee, work context) framework, including examples of variables that fit within each category. We acknowledge that stability is not a static characteristic of a given construct: It will vary depending on the time frame under consideration or the specific conceptualization of the construct. For example, employee-focused variables such as attitudes and beliefs are relatively stable traits over the short term (e.g., days and weeks), but may fluctuate over longer time periods (e.g., months or years; Cattell, 1957; Rajecki, 1990). Organizational climate and culture may change, but that can take several years (Schneider, Ehrhart, & Macey, 2013). On the other hand, affect (an employee-focused variable) and

Table 5.2 Conceptual Framework of Predictors of Workplace Pro-environmental Behaviors

Source of Factor	Variability of Factor	
	Fluctuating	**Stable**
Employee	Affect	Personality
	Job satisfaction	Attitudes
	Self-efficacy	Personal norms
Work context	Daily work events	Pro-environmental organizational climate and culture
	Daily job goals and demands	Physical infrastructure
	Organizational constraints	Industry laws and regulations

daily events at work (a work context-focused variable) can fluctuate greatly during the day.

Drawing from this framework, we identify three broad types of information organizational researchers and practitioners can gather about workplace pro-environmental behaviors by applying diary methods. These include (a) insights into the variation in different types of workplace pro-environmental behaviors, (b) the role of daily employee characteristics as predictors of daily behavior, and (c) the influence of different job characteristics on daily behavior. In the following sections, we elaborate on these topics and discuss how they might be investigated using diary methods.

Variation in Different Types of Workplace Pro-Environmental Behaviors

In contrast to the static "snapshots" of workplace pro-environmental behaviors that traditional methods (e.g., cross-sectional surveys) have captured (Bolger et al., 2003; Mehl & Conner, 2012), diary methods can offer organizational researchers and practitioners dynamic "films" of workplace pro-environmental behaviors. This allows researchers to observe whether—and how—employees might vary in the frequency of their pro-environmental behaviors at work. Importantly, diary methods can help quantify such variation and identify the predictors of the variation. A greater understanding of workplace pro-environmental behaviors and the factors that predict engagement in these actions as they occur daily at work could help organizational researchers and practitioners create more effective strategies for increasing these behaviors.

When conceptualizing workplace pro-environmental behaviors, two important dimensions suggested by the organizational literature to consider are maximum and typical performance. Maximum performance can be described as what a person is generally capable of doing. Typical performance is what a person actually will do or does (Sackett, 2007; Sackett, Sheldon, & Fogli, 1988; Totterdell, Wood, & Wall, 2005). Applying these concepts to within-person differences in workplace pro-environmental behaviors (Dilchert & Ones, 2012), it is likely that workplace pro-environmental behaviors will have the strongest impact when levels of "typical" performance are high and sustained—close to "maximum" performance. In reality, some employees habitually have low levels of workplace pro-environmental behaviors and, for others, it is likely that variation in daily or weekly pro-environmental behaviors at work means that they sometimes engage in pro-environmental behaviors far below their level of capability (due to lack of motivation or extrinsic factors, for example). Using daily diary or experience sampling strategies (i.e., employees report on their behavior at least once a day), researchers could determine what factors distinguish those who achieve sustained maximum performance from those who fluctuate in their performance of workplace pro-environmental behaviors or habitually perform these at low levels.

The extent to which employees are able to maintain maximum performance of a workplace pro-environmental behavior is likely to depend on the characteristics of the behavior. In the literature on workplace pro-environmental behaviors, different types of workplace pro-environmental behaviors have been identified (Bissing-Olson, Iyer, Fielding, & Zacher, 2013; Boiral & Paillé, 2012; Ones & Dilchert, 2012). Different typologies of workplace pro-environmental behaviors have been developed that are based on, for example, content of the action (e.g., conserving behaviors vs. decision-making behaviors) as well as the amount of proactivity needed to engage in the action (e.g., recycling when recycling bins are available vs. proposing and implementing a system for recycling). Some workplace pro-environmental behaviors take place every day or multiple times a day (e.g., turning lights off when not needed), whereas as others are infrequent (e.g., installing a more efficient air conditioning system).

In general, frequently occurring (e.g., daily) workplace pro-environmental behaviors may be best studied using experience sampling or daily diaries. These behaviors could include common conserving behaviors such as reducing use (e.g., printing double-sided), reusing (reusing disposable plastic products), and recycling (e.g., recycling bottles and paper) (Ones & Dilchert, 2012). It may also be expected that discretionary pro-environmental behaviors that directly stem from required work tasks, which Bissing-Olson and colleagues (2013) conceptualize under the term *task-related pro-environmental behavior*, may be carried out frequently. As these behaviors most likely occur daily or multiple times per day, it may be most fitting for researchers to collect behavioral reports once or multiple times a day using daily diary or experience sampling strategies, respectively.

For those behaviors that occur less frequently, such as those requiring high personal initiative, event sampling may be the best study design. In workplace pro-environmental behavior research, such behaviors have been referred to as *proactive pro-environmental* behaviors (Bissing-Olson et al., 2013), *ecopreneurial* behaviors (Pichel, 2008), or as those that require *taking initiative* (Ones & Dilchert, 2012). Employees who take initiative may be taking a personal risk to challenge the status quo (Ones & Dilchert, 2012). These employees put environmental interests first (e.g., turn down an environmentally unfriendly project), initiate programs and policies (e.g., start a new environmental program), and engage in lobbying and activism (e.g., pushing the organization to disclose its environmental record). Such activities may not be carried out very often, which means that it may be more practical to ask participants to report on engagement in these behaviors only when they occur (i.e., event sampling). It may also be enlightening to collect reports of related concepts or experiences (e.g., thoughts about taking initiative to engage in pro-environmental behaviors at work) to examine which situational circumstances or psychological states trigger proactive pro-environmental behaviors at work.

The Role of Psychological States on Workplace Pro-Environmental Behaviors

There is a range of potential predictors of within-person variation in workplace pro-environmental behaviors (see Table 5.2), including stable characteristics of the person and the environment (e.g., pro-environmental attitude, pro-environmental climate), as well as fluctuating factors such as psychological states and daily events and requirements at work (e.g., affect, motivation, and job demands). In this section, we focus on the relationship between employees' psychological states and engagement in workplace pro-environmental behaviors. These psychological states could include—but are not limited to—affect, self-regulation, and motivation.

Affect was one of the first topics to be studied using diary methods in the workplace (Csikszentmihalyi & LeFevre, 1989). It has become an important topic in organizational research with researchers investigating, for example, temporal patterns of affective experience (Beal & Ghandour, 2011; Trougakos, Beal, Green, & Weiss, 2008; Weiss, Nicholas, & Daus, 1999), influence of events on affect (Beal & Ghandour, 2011; Miner, Glomb, & Hulin, 2005), and the relationships between affect and job satisfaction (Ilies & Judge, 2002; Judge & Ilies, 2004) and organizational citizenship behaviors (Ilies, Scott, & Judge, 2006). Affect could also play an important role in shaping workplace pro-environmental behaviors. Increased knowledge about relationships between affect and workplace pro-environmental behaviors could provide information to practitioners about how to incorporate affective elements into interventions to more successfully increase workplace pro-environmental behaviors.

Currently, we know of only one study examining the relationship between affect and workplace pro-environmental behaviors. Bissing-Olson and colleagues (2013) applied diary methods to investigate the link between pro-environmental behaviors and positive transient emotions at work. The study drew on broaden-and-build theory (Fredrickson, 1998, 2001), which postulates that positive emotions expand a person's range of thoughts and actions and build personal resources. Specifically, Bissing-Olson et al. (2013) examined relationships between employees' daily positive affect, pro-environmental attitude, and engagement in two types of daily pro-environmental behavior: task-related (i.e., completing required work tasks in environmentally friendly ways), and proactive (i.e., showing personal initiative when acting in environmentally friendly ways at work). Participants included 56 employees working in small businesses, who completed a baseline survey (measuring pro-environmental attitude) and two daily surveys (measuring daily affect at noon and daily pro-environmental behaviors at the end of the workday). Participants filled out the daily surveys over 10 workdays. The findings revealed that daily unactivated positive affect (e.g., feeling calm) and pro-environmental attitude were positively related to daily task-related pro-environmental behaviors. Daily activated positive affect (e.g., feeling enthusiastic) was also positively related to daily proactive pro-environmental behaviors, but only for employees with a less positive pro-environmental attitude. No relationship was found between activated positive affect and proactive pro-environmental behaviors for employees with a more positive pro-environmental attitude, possibly because employees who already feel a sense of responsibility or respect toward the environment do not need the extra initiative that activated positive emotions trigger. Taken together, the results show how incidental emotions (i.e., those not specifically related to environmental issues) may help shape workplace pro-environmental behaviors. This study demonstrates the potential that diary methods have to uncover novel information about workplace pro-environmental behaviors.

Although positive emotions seem to be linked with more pro-environmental behaviors at work (Bissing-Olson et al., 2013), it is also possible that certain negative emotions, such as guilt, will also increase workplace pro-environmental behaviors. Research on how guilt and other similar emotions relate to workplace pro-environmental behaviors on a daily basis would complement the limited existing literature on guilt and pro-environmental behaviors (e.g., Kals & Müller, 2012). Past pro-environmental research has shown that feelings of moral responsibility (or personal obligation), which are related to guilt, have been linked with greater engagement in pro-environmental behaviors in general (e.g., Bamberg, Hunecke, & Blöbaum, 2007). The application of experience sampling methods to this topic could provide an in-depth and nuanced understanding of employees' emotional and cognitive responses that are related to guilt as they happen or close to when they happen. For example, employees may experience guilt from failing to engage in workplace pro-environmental behaviors at one point in time and try to compensate for their lack of action by engaging in more positive pro-environmental actions at a later point. Alternatively, employees may protect themselves from the effects of guilt through rationalizing their behavior. Experience sampling methods could also be used to explore whether responses (i.e., guilt or rationalization) vary as a result of factors such as organizational culture or environmental attitudes or values.

In addition to affect, changes in self-regulation may be related to workplace pro-environmental behavior. According to the limited-resource model of self-control (Baumeister, Bratslavsky, Muraven, & Tice, 1998; Vohs et al., 2008), whenever we exert effort to regulate our behavior, our willpower is drained, resulting in *ego depletion*. Ego depletion is defined as a personal resource loss that occurs after the exertion of self-control (Muraven, 2007). Following from this, at the end of the workday when employees are potentially ego-depleted, they may be less likely to engage in workplace pro-environmental behaviors, especially if these behaviors are difficult or require significant cognitive or physical resources. Hence, it could be that there are daily cycles of workplace pro-environmental behaviors that map on to the extent to which employees are ego-depleted, especially in workplaces that do not have established procedures or opportunities to encourage pro-environmental engagement. A daily diary or experience sampling approach, in which employees report on their workplace pro-environmental behaviors in the morning and at the end of the workday (or more frequently), could be used to investigate this potential cycle.

Motivation to engage in pro-environmental behaviors at work may also fluctuate depending on a variety of factors. In the broader literature on workplace behaviors, it has been shown that daily recovery during leisure time is positively related to work engagement and proactive behavior at work (e.g., personal initiative) during the following workday (Sonnentag, 2003). Xanthopoulou and colleagues have shown that day-level coaching from supervisors (Xanthopoulou, Bakker, Demerouti, & Schaufeli, 2009) as well as colleague support (Xanthopoulou, Bakker, Heuven, Demerouti, & Schaufeli, 2008) are positively related with daily work engagement. Drawing on these examples, it is possible that the same factors that impact general engagement at work could be linked to employees' motivation to engage in pro-environmental behaviors at work as well. If employees are well recovered from the previous workday, they may have more personal resources available to engage in workplace pro-environmental behaviors, particularly if the behaviors require personal initiative.

For example, employees with more personal resources may be more likely than employees with less personal resources to think of switching lights off where they are not needed (in some workplaces, this may be something that is not common practice) or to initiate conversations about environmentally friendly changes to workplace policies and procedures. Similarly, daily support from supervisors or colleagues may increase motivation to engage in pro-environmental behaviors at work, particularly if the support is directly focused on engaging in green behaviors. Daily diary designs are most suited to examining these types of research questions. For instance, employees could complete end-of-day reports on their pro-environmental behavior and the amount of support they received from colleagues and supervisors during that day. To examine recovery during leisure time and its relationship to engagement in next-day workplace pro-environmental behaviors, reports on daily recovery may be best completed before bed, whereas reports on pro-environmental behaviors should be completed at the end of the workday.

In summary, fluctuating psychological states of employees may impact employees' engagement in workplace pro-environmental behaviors. Positive affect has been linked with increased pro-environmental behaviors at work (Bissing-Olson et al., 2013); however, negative emotions, such as guilt, could also play a role. Ego-depletion may be related to workplace pro-environmental behaviors as well, particularly if the behaviors require more effort or self-control to carry out. Finally, motivation to act in environmentally friendly ways at work may fluctuate, impacting on engagement in such actions.

The Role of Job Characteristics on Workplace Pro-Environmental Behaviors

Although within-person variation in workplace pro-environmental behaviors could be influenced by fluctuating psychological states of employees, job characteristics could also play a role. According to the job characteristics model (Hackman & Oldham, 1976), the five key job characteristics are skill variety, task identity, task significance, autonomy, and feedback. In the following, we briefly describe these and suggest how diary methods may be used to examine the influence of different job characteristics on within-person variation in workplace pro-environmental behaviors. Job characteristics most likely serve as moderating variables on the relationships of this variation with other within-person predictors.

Skill variety refers to the amount of diversity in the activities required in a job. A greater variety of tasks would potentially lead to more opportunities to engage in different types of workplace pro-environmental behaviors. This could result in more within-person variability in behaviors, as employees may use their discretion in deciding how and when to act in pro-environmental ways. Employees with jobs requiring low skill variety may have fewer opportunities to engage in different types of environmentally friendly behaviors. In addition, when employees carry out a smaller range of activities at work, they may be more likely to follow established routines for task-related pro-environmental behaviors (i.e., those pro-environmental behaviors that directly stem from work tasks). As a result, employees in low skill variety jobs may have lower within-person variability in their work behaviors. For example, an employee in a grocery store, who only works on the cash register, will have fewer types of work activities—and therefore fewer types of pro-environmental behaviors to engage in—than an employee who rotates across positions (e.g., stocking shelves, receiving deliveries, working behind a deli counter). Thus, to examine variation in workplace pro-environmental behaviors in jobs high in skill variety, it may be most fitting to apply experience sampling methods. In contrast, daily diary study designs may be best to study variation in pro-environmental behavior in job with low skill variety.

Task identity refers to the degree that a job requires an employee to complete a project or piece of work from start to finish (Hackman & Oldham, 1975). For jobs with high task identity, the meaningfulness of the work for the employee should be higher than for jobs with low task identity. This should be true of jobs with high compared with low task significance as well. Task significance is the degree to which a job affects other people's lives and work (Hackman & Oldham, 1975). According to the job characteristics model (Hackman & Oldham, 1976), the three job characteristics, skill variety, task identity, and task significance all serve to increase the experienced meaningfulness of the work for the employee. Thus, these job characteristics may interact with psychological states of the employee to influence within-person variation in workplace pro-environmental behaviors. For example, employees with strong pro-environmental attitudes could be expected to experience increased sense of awareness and responsiveness to opportunities to engage in workplace pro-environmental behaviors, especially if the meaningfulness of their work is high. For the environmentally committed employee, meaningful work provides an important opportunity to express their environmental values or act in value-consistent ways (Kristof, 1996).

Following from this, the use of daily diary or experience sampling methods may be best suited to examine variation in pro-environmental behavior in jobs that are high in task identity and task significance. In such jobs, employees may be more engaged at work and motivated to express any pro-environmental leanings they may have, resulting in more frequent and more varied displays of pro-environmental behavior. In addition, event sampling study designs may be specifically useful for jobs high in task identity in order to study pro-environmental engagement at different stages of work on a project. That is, as employees work through each stage of a project from start to finish, they may develop in-depth knowledge of their work activities allowing them to take initiative to act in environmentally friendly ways (e.g., make a pro-environmental change to a procedure). Event sampling could be used to examine this type of pro-environmental engagement as it occurs.

Autonomy reflects the amount of control a job provides in decisions about when and how employees carry out their job tasks. Autonomy (job control) has been shown to moderate within-person relationships between daily creativity and daily negative affect, daily situational constraints, and daily time pressure (Binnewies & Wörnlein, 2011). It is possible that daily time pressure is associated with daily workplace pro-environmental behaviors and that, following the example given in the preceding, job control serves as a moderator to this relationship. In general, employees in jobs high in autonomy should feel a sense of responsibility for the outcomes of their work. Furthermore, when employees have more control over work processes, they should have more opportunities as well as efficacy to engage in pro-environmental behaviors. In particular, jobs high in autonomy should also allow greater engagement in pro-environmental behaviors that require higher personal initiative. That is, when employees have more control over their work processes and are environmentally conscious, they may be more likely to make environmentally friendly changes or improvements to the way they carry out their work (e.g., taking more time to search for environmentally friendly alternatives) as opposed to acting only with already available resources (e.g., recycling only when bins are available). To investigate these types of proactive pro-environmental behaviors, daily diary or event sampling study designs are most appropriate. Such behaviors may be more easily remembered at the end of the day (as opposed to minor behaviors, such as recycling small pieces of paper), which supports a daily diary approach. Proactive behaviors may also be relatively infrequent or occur in clusters (e.g., a conversation about an environmentally friendly change may lead to a number of actions in close sequence). As a result, an event sampling design would capture this type of behavior best as participants would report on the behavior shortly after it occurs as opposed to hours later.

Feedback refers to the amount of clear and direct information employees receive about their performance. Increased feedback should result in increased knowledge about the actual outcomes of employees' work tasks. Although feedback in the broader literature generally generally focuses on the effectiveness of employees' job performance (e.g., quality and quantity) (Hackman & Oldham, 1976; Morgeson & Humphrey, 2006), it is possible that employees could receive feedback regarding the ecological sustainability of their work. The latter type of feedback could serve as encouragement to engage in pro-environmental behaviors at work or to make environmentally friendly changes to how they carry out their work tasks. The former type of feedback, referring to job performance more narrowly, may have the opposite effect. Potentially, feedback on job performance may restrict employees' focus to their required work tasks, so that attention to environmental behaviors decreases (Unsworth, Dmitrieva, & Adriasola, 2013). Event sampling study designs, in which employees complete a survey after a predefined event has occurred (e.g., after receiving feedback from a supervisor), could be used to gain insight into the relationship between different types of performance feedback and workplace pro-environmental behaviors.

Conclusion

Diary methods allow researchers and practitioners to answer theoretical and practical questions about workplace pro-environmental behaviors that are not easily addressed using other methods. In this chapter we illustrated the use of the diary method by highlighting how these methods could be used to address questions about variation in different types of workplace pro-environmental behaviors, the impact of psychological states on these behaviors, as well as the impact of job characteristics. The questions that we have advanced throughout this chapter are just a sampling of the possible research questions that can be addressed by applying diary methods to the study of workplace pro-environmental behaviors. To date, the application of diary methods to the study of workplace pro-environmental behaviors is extremely limited. Thus, we hope that the examples we provide serve as an impetus for organizational researchers and practitioners interested in within-person processes related to workplace pro-environmental behaviors. Diary methods can help shed light on factors and processes related to within-person variation in these behaviors, extending theory and providing important practical information for organizations wishing to increase employee engagement in pro-environmental behavior at work.

Suggested Additional Readings

1. Mehl, M. R., & Conner, T. S. (Eds.). (2012). *Handbook of research methods for studying daily life*. New York: Guilford Press.
2. Nezlek, J. B. (2012). *Diary methods*. Thousand Oaks, CA: Sage.
3. Hektner, J. M., Schmidt, J. A., & Csikszentmihalyi, M. (2007). *Experience sampling method: Measuring the quality of everyday life*. Thousand Oaks, CA: Sage.

References

Alliger, G. M., & Williams, K. J. (1993). Using signal-contingent experience sampling methodology to study work in the field: A discussion and illustration examining task perceptions and mood. *Personnel Psychology, 46*, 525–549.

Andersson, L., & Bateman, T. S. (2000). Individual environmental initiative: Championing natural environmental issues in U.S. business organizations. *Academy of Management Journal, 43*, 548–570.

Bamberg, S., Hunecke, M., & Blöbaum, A. (2007). Social context, personal norms and the use of public transportation: Two field studies. *Journal of Environmental Psychology, 27,* 190–203.

Baumeister, R. F., Bratslavsky, E., Muraven, M., & Tice, D. M. (1998). Ego depletion: Is the active self a limited resource? *Journal of Personality and Social Psychology, 74,* 1252–1265.

Beal, D. J., & Ghandour, L. (2011). Stability, change, and the stability of change in daily workplace affect. *Journal of Organizational Behavior, 32,* 526–546.

Beal, D. J., & Weiss, H. M. (2003). Methods of ecological momentary assessment in organizational research. *Organizational Research Methods, 6,* 440–464.

Binnewies, C., & Wörnlein, S. C. (2011). What makes a creative day? A diary study on the interplay between affect, job stressors, and job control. *Journal of Organizational Behavior, 32,* 589–607

Bissing-Olson, M. J., Iyer, A., Fielding, K. S., & Zacher, H. (2013). Relationships between daily affect and pro-environmental behavior at work: The moderating role of pro-environmental attitude. *Journal of Organizational Behavior, 34,* 151–171.

Bissing-Olson, M. J., Zacher, H., Fielding, K. S., & Iyer, A. (2012). An intraindividual perspective on pro-environmental behaviors at work. *Industrial and Organizational Psychology: Perspectives on Science and Practice, 5,* 500–502.

Boiral, O., & Paillé, P. (2012). Organizational citizenship behaviour for the environment: Measurement and validation. *Journal of Business Ethics, 109,* 431–445.

Bolger, N., Davis, A., & Rafaeli, E. (2003). Diary methods: Capturing life as it is lived. *Annual Review of Psychology, 54,* 579–616.

Carrico, A. R., & Riemer, M. (2011). Motivating energy conservation in the workplace: An evaluation of the use of group-level feedback and peer education. *Journal of Environmental Psychology, 31,* 1–13.

Cattell, R. B. (1957). *Personality and motivation structure and measurement.* Oxford, UK: World Book Co.

Conner, T. S., & Lehman, B. J. (2012). Getting started: Launching a study in daily life. In M. R. Mehl & T. S. Conner (Eds.), *Handbook of research methods for studying daily life* (pp. 89–107). New York: Guilford Press.

Csikszentmihalyi, M., & LeFevre, J. (1989). Optimal experience in work and leisure. *Journal of Personality and Social Psychology, 56,* 815–822.

Daamen, D. D. L., Staats, H., Wilke, H. A. M., & Engelen, M. (2001). Improving environmental behavior in companies: The effectiveness of tailored versus nontailored interventions. *Environment and Behavior, 33,* 229–248.

Daniels, K., Boocock, G., Glover, J., Hartley, R., & Holland, J. (2009). An experience sampling study of learning, affect, and the demands control support model. *Journal of Applied Psychology, 94,* 1003–1017.

Dilchert, S., & Ones, D. S. (2012). Environmental sustainability in and of organizations. *Industrial and Organizational Psychology: Perspectives on Science and Practice, 5,* 503–511.

Fisher, C. D., & To, M. L. (2012). Using experience sampling methodology in organizational behavior. *Journal of Organizational Behavior, 33*, 865–877. doi: 10.1002/job.1803

Fredrickson, B. L. (1998). What good are positive emotions? *Review of General Psychology, 2*, 300–319.

Fredrickson, B. L. (2001). The role of positive emotions in positive psychology: The broaden-and-build theory of positive emotions. *American Psychologist, 56*, 218–226.

Goodwin, M. S. (2012). Passive telemetric monitoring: Novel methods for real-world behavioral assessment. In M. R. Mehl & T. S. Conner (Eds.), *Handbook of research methods for studying daily life* (pp. 251–266). New York: Guilford Press.

Green, A. S., Rafaeli, E., Bolger, N., Shrout, P. E., & Reis, H. T. (2006). Paper or plastic? Data equivalence in paper and electronic diaries. *Psychological Methods, 11*, 87–105.

Gunthert, K. C., & Wenze, S. J. (2012). Daily diary methods. In M. R. Mehl & T. S. Conner (Eds.), *Handbook of research methods for studying daily life* (pp. 144–159). New York: Guilford Press.

Hackman, J. R., & Oldham, G. R. (1975). Development of the job diagnostic survey. *Journal of Applied Psychology, 60*, 159–170.

Hackman, J. R., & Oldham, G. R. (1976). Motivation through the design of work: Test of a theory. *Organizational Behavior and Human Performance, 16*, 250–279.

Ilies, R., & Judge, T. A. (2002). Understanding the dynamic relationships among personality, mood, and job satisfaction: A field experience sampling study. *Organizational Behavior and Human Decision Processes, 89*, 1119–1139.

Ilies, R., Scott, B. A., & Judge, T. A. (2006). The interactive effects of personal traits and experienced states on intraindividual patterns of organizational citizenship behavior. *Academy of Management Journal, 49*, 561–575.

Judge, T. A., & Ilies, R. (2004). Affect and job satisfaction: A study of their relationship at work and at home. *Journal of Applied Psychology, 89*, 661–673.

Kals, E., & Müller, M. M. (2012). Emotions and environment. In S. D. Clayton (Ed.), *The Oxford handbook of environmental and conservation psychology* (pp. 128–147). New York: Oxford University Press.

Kristof, A. L. (1996). Person-organization fit: An integrative review of its conceptualizations, measurement, and implications. *Personnel Psychology, 49*, 1–49.

Lamm, E., Tosti-Kharas, J., & Williams, E. G. (2013). Read this article, but don't print it: Organizational citizenship behavior toward the environment. *Group & Organization Management*. doi: 10.1177/1059601112475210.

Mehl, M. R., & Conner, T. S. (Eds.). (2012). *Handbook of research methods for studying daily life*. New York: Guilford Press.

Mehl, M. R., & Robbins, M. L. (2012). Naturalistic observation sampling: The electronically activated ear (EAR). In M. R. Mehl, & T. S. Conner (Eds.), *Handbook of research methods for studying daily life* (pp. 176–192). New York: Guilford Press.

Miner, A. G., Glomb, T. M., & Hulin, C. (2005). Experience sampling mood and its correlates at work. *Journal of Occupational and Organizational Psychology, 78,* 171–193.

Morgeson, F. P., & Humphrey, S. E. (2006). The Work Design Questionnaire (WDQ): Developing and validating a comprehensive measure for assessing job design and the nature of work. *Journal of Applied Psychology, 91,* 1321–1339.

Moskowitz, D. S., & Sadikaj, G. (2012). Event-contingent sampling. In M. R. Mehl, & T. S. Conner (Eds.), *Handbook of research methods for studying daily life* (pp. 160–175). New York: Guilford Press.

Muraven, M. (2007). Ego depletion. In R. F. Baumeister, & K. D. Vohs (Eds.), *Encyclopedia of social psychology* (pp. 279–281). Thousand Oaks, CA: Sage.

Ohly, S., Sonnentag, S., Niessen, C., & Zapf, D. (2010). Diary studies in organizational research: An introduction and some practical recommendations. *Journal of Personnel Psychology, 9,* 79–93.

Ones, D. S., & Dilchert, S. (2012). Employee green behaviors. In S. E. Jackson, D. S. Ones, & S. Dilchert (Eds.), *Managing human resources for environmental sustainability* (pp. 85–116). San Francisco: Jossey-Bass/Wiley.

Pichel, K. (2008). Enhancing ecopreneurship through an environmental management system: A longitudinal analysis for factors leading to proactive environmental behaviour. In R. Wüstenhagen, J. Hamschmidt & S. Sharma (Eds.), *Sustainable innovation and entrepreneurship* (pp. 141–196). Cheltenham, UK: Edward Elgar.

Poppleton, S., Briner, R. B., & Kiefer, T. (2008). The roles of context and everyday experience in understanding work-non-work relationships: A qualitative diary study of white- and blue-collar workers. *Journal of Occupational and Organizational Psychology, 81,* 481–502.

Rajecki, D. W. (1990). *Attitudes*. Sunderland, MA: Sinauer Associates.

Ramus, C. A., & Steger, U. (2000). The roles of supervisory support behaviors and environmental policy in employee 'ecoinitiatives' at leading-edge European companies. *Academy of Management Journal, 43,* 605–626.

Reis, H. T., & Gable, S. L. (2000). Event-sampling and other methods for studying everyday experience. In H. T. Reis, & C. M. Judd (Eds.), *Handbook of research methods in social and personality psychology* (pp. 190–222). New York: Cambridge University Press.

Sackett, P. R. (2007). Revisiting the origins of the typical-maximum performance distinction. *Human Performance, 20,* 179–185.

Sackett, P. R., Sheldon, Z., & Fogli, L. (1988). Relations between measures of typical and maximum job performance. *Journal of Applied Psychology, 73,* 482–486.

Schneider, B., Ehrhart, M. G., & Macey, W. H. (2013). Organizational climate and culture. *Annual Review of Psychology, 64,* 361–388.

Schwarz, N. (2012). Why researchers should think "real-time": A cognitive rationale. In M. R. Mehl, & T. S. Conner (Eds.), *Handbook of research methods for studying daily life* (pp. 22–42). New York: Guilford Press.

Sonnentag, S. (2003). Recovery, work engagement, and proactive behavior: A new look at the interface between nonwork and work. *Journal of Applied Psychology*, *88*, 518–528.

Totterdell, P., Wood, S., & Wall, T. (2005). An intra-individual test of the demands–control model: A weekly diary study of psychological strain in portfolio workers. *Journal of Occupational and Organizational Psychology*, *79*, 63–84.

Trougakos, J. P., Beal, D. J., Green, S. G., & Weiss, H. M. (2008). Making the break count: An episodic examination of recovery activities, emotional experiences, and positive affective displays. *Academy of Management Journal*, *51*, 131–146.

Unsworth, K., Dmitrieva, A., & Adriasola, E. (2013). Changing behaviour: Increasing the effectiveness of workplace interventions in creating pro-environmental behaviour change. *Journal of Organizational Behavior*, *34*, 211–229.

Vohs, K. D., Baumeister, R. F., Schmeichel, B. J., Twenge, J. M., Nelson, N. M., & Tice, D. M. (2008). Making choices impairs subsequent self-control: A limited-resource account of decision making, self-regulation, and active initiative. *Journal of Personality and Social Psychology*, *94*, 883–898.

Weiss, H. M., Nicholas, J. P., & Daus, C. S. (1999). An examination of the joint effects of affective experiences and job beliefs on job satisfaction and variations in affective experiences over time. *Organizational Behavior and Human Decision Processes*, *78*, 1–24.

Xanthopoulou, D., Bakker, A. B., Demerouti, E., & Schaufeli, W. B. (2009). Work engagement and financial returns: A diary study on the role of job and personal resources. *Journal of Occupational and Organizational Psychology*, *82*, 183–200.

Xanthopoulou, D., Bakker, A. B., Heuven, E., Demerouti, E., & Schaufeli, W. B. (2008). Working in the sky: A diary study on work engagement among flight attendants. *Journal of Occupational Health Psychology*, *13*, 345–356.

THE ROLE OF INDIVIDUALS IN PROMOTING WORKPLACE PRO-ENVIRONMENTAL BEHAVIORS

6 INDIVIDUAL DETERMINANTS OF WORKPLACE PRO-ENVIRONMENTAL BEHAVIORS

Siu Hing Lo

Most research on organizations and the natural environment has either implicitly or explicitly endorsed the view that features of the organizational unit or external, industry-level and societal-level factors are the most relevant factors for its environmental sustainability performance. Previous studies have mainly examined the role of organizational characteristics and external factors in organizational engagement with environmental sustainability (Etzion, 2007). Organizational characteristics include obvious factors such as the fit between the organization's environmental sustainability strategy with its general strategy and employee involvement, but also its size, slack, research and development activity, and international scope. Some of these factors, such as business strategies, organizational change, and organizational culture are extensively discussed in chapters 11, 12, 14, 15, respectively. The industry to which the organization belongs and external stakeholders, such as regulators, the media, activists, consumers and investors, are also examples of external factors previously examined. However, as we saw in chapter 4, relatively few studies have examined workplace pro-environmental behaviors at the individual, behavioral level of analysis (Bansal & Gao, 2006; Lo, Peters, & Kok, 2012b). Most of these individual-level studies have exclusively focused on organizational members who are responsible for environmental engagement of the organization as a whole, such as directors and corporate sustainability managers (e.g., Walls & Hoffman, 2013; Wright, Nyberg, & Grant, 2012).

Although organizational-level engagement is certainly important to the overall impact of the organization on the natural environment, the actions of individual employees can also contribute to or thwart the organization's pro-environmental goals. National-level estimates suggest that meaningful energy consumption reductions are feasible (Dietz, Gardner, Gilligan, Stern, & Vandenbergh, 2009). However, mixed evidence from workplace pro-environmental behavior change interventions casts doubt on achieving this potential without a more refined understanding of how organizational-level measures impact and interact with individual employees' psychology and behavior (Lo et al., 2012b; Unsworth, Dmitrieva, & Adriasola, 2013).

In this chapter, I will first define workplace pro-environmental behaviors and provide a "taxonomy" of these behaviors. Characteristics of pro-environmental behaviors determine to a large extent what influences each specific workplace pro-environmental behavior. I will use the term *individual determinants* for individual-level influences on behavior in the remainder of this chapter. I will then review studies of individual determinants of workplace pro-environmental behaviors and supplement this evidence base with insights derived from studies conducted in other, non-organizational contexts and on other types of behaviors. Psychological models of pro-environmental behaviors and proposed additions to these models will be discussed. In contrast to workplace pro-environmental behaviors, private and household pro-environmental behaviors have been extensively studied (for reviews see Abrahamse, Steg, Vlek, & Rothengatter, 2005; Bamberg & Moser, 2007). Many of the theoretical insights and empirical evidence reviewed in this chapter will draw on this literature. One limitation of this body of work, however, is its focus on beliefs and related constructs to explain pro-environmental behaviors. This potentially overlooks other individual determinants that are unconscious and therefore not accessible in the form of explicit beliefs. To redress this limitation, research findings from other behavioral domains will be used to identify other relevant individual determinants. In particular, we will look at the role of habits and unconscious influences and more distal predictors such as person characteristics.

Workplace Pro-Environmental Behaviors

There is considerable heterogeneity between pro-environmental behaviors, be it in the workplace or in other contexts. It is therefore important to first establish that the study of these behaviors as one category is meaningful. One justification is the common aim—environmental sustainability—of all these behaviors. On a conceptual level, it could also be argued that pro-environmental behaviors can all be, and probably are, motivated by a combination of self-interest and concern for the environment. Environmental issues are typically long-term concerns that frequently clash with people's personal, short-term interests. If this is compounded by a (perceived) lack of cooperation from other people, it might lead to a "tragedy of the commons" (Hardin, 1968; Weber, 2006), which results from individuals knowingly overexploiting shared resources because the short-term gain directly benefits the exploiter, whereas the long-term costs are borne by all. Not surprisingly, therefore, awareness of environmental problems may not lead to behavioral change (e.g. Staats, Wit, & Midden, 1996). However, the similarity among pro-environmental behaviors does suggest that beliefs about how to treat common resources and related beliefs could be relevant to many if not all pro-environmental behaviors.

Another question is how pro-environmental behaviors can be divided into useful subcategories. One important feature of behaviors is their frequency, which falls on a continuum between one-off (e.g., investment decisions) and oft-repeated (e.g., daily routines) behaviors (Uitdenbogerd, Egmond, Jonkers, & Kok, 2007). Frequency is an important feature because the determinants of habitual and less ingrained behaviors differ (Aarts & Dijksterhuis, 2000; Wood, Tam, & Guerrero Witt, 2005). As a consequence, the effectiveness of interventions also varies depending on the repetitiveness and habit strength of specific behaviors (Verplanken & Orbell, 2003). Change methods for cognitive determinants (e.g., attitudes, self-efficacy) differ from those used to target habits (Bartholomew, Parcel, Kok, Gottlieb, & Fernández, 2011).

Another important feature of pro-environmental behaviors is the degree of effort or "sacrifice," or behavioral difficulty, they entail. Especially in the presence of conflicting interests, this could influence whether people can reconcile common and personal interests. Low-cost or "easy" behaviors may require different change strategies than high-cost or "difficult" behaviors. The relative impact of various psychosocial determinants on behavior may vary depending on behavioral difficulty (Corraliza & Berenguer, 2000; Kaiser & Schultz, 2009). All things considered, it seems clear that behavioral difficulty should be taken into account in any efforts to understand divergent or convergent empirical findings between studies on pro-environmental behaviors. For example, perceived behavioral control or self-efficacy could be more relevant to difficult behaviors than easy behaviors. Similarly, attitude strength might matter more if performance of a behavior would compromise competing interests.

The view that all pro-environmental behaviors are prone to a "tragedy of the commons" logic obscures the fact that, especially in the workplace, the responsibility for and execution of pro-environmental behaviors can be shared. First, if the behavior involves common facilities, individuals may not have full control over the successful execution of a given pro-environmental behavior. For example, turning the heating or air-conditioning down may quickly be reversed if a colleague in the office disagrees with this course of action (Lo, Peters, & Kok, 2012a). Another possible influence is diffusion of responsibility for pro-environmental behaviors that involve shared facilities (Latane, Williams, & Harkins, 1979), although some workplace pro-environmental behaviors (e.g., switching off computers and monitors) remain largely an individual choice. Second, some workplace pro-environmental behaviors and choices may be under the control of and/or the responsibility of a select few within the organization. Examples include the technical settings of physical facilities and organizational policies impacting environmentally relevant behaviors (Lo, et al., 2012a). The degree to which a behavior is perceived as one's personal responsibility, and whether others play a role, could influence which individual determinants are most relevant to any given workplace pro-environmental behavior.

Theoretical Perspectives on Pro-Environmental Behaviors

Research on pro-environmental behavior has generally focused on the concept of environmental concern itself, the individual determinants of pro-environmental behavior, or the effectiveness of pro-environmental behavior change interventions. From a practical point of view, these research topics complement each other. Environmental concern is an obvious candidate as a relevant (though not necessarily the most important) determinant of pro-environmental behavior (Dunlap, Van Liere, Mertig, & Jones, 2000). Together with an understanding of environmental concern, identification of relevant individual determinants can inform the design of behavior change interventions and help illuminate the mechanisms underlying their (lack of) effectiveness.

Various psychosocial theories of human social behavior have been applied to the study of individual determinants of pro-environmental behavior. The choice of a particular theory often depends on whether self-interest or concern for others and nature are the prime motivation for pro-environmental actions. The theory of planned behavior (TPB) and its precursor the theory of reasoned action (TRA) have typically been used when emphasizing rational, self-interested motivations behind pro-environmental behavior (Ajzen, 1991; Fishbein & Ajzen, 1975). In contrast, the norm activation model (NAM) and its successor in the environmental domain, the value-belief-norm theory (VBN), have been widely used to examine the role of norms and values (Schwartz, 1973; Stern, Dietz, Abel, & Guagnano, 1999). Viewing pro-environmental behavior as motivated by a combination of self-interest and wider environmental concern, some researchers have also integrated the TPB/TRA and NAM/VBN. An overview of each theory is offered in the following.

Reasoned Action

Reasoned action (RA) is a general social psychological framework that has been used to explain a wide range of social behaviors (Ajzen, 1991; Fishbein & Ajzen, 1975, 2010), including a range of household pro-environmental behaviors such as recycling (e.g., Boldero, 1995), travel mode choice (e.g., Bamberg, Ajzen, & Schmidt, 2003) and pro-environmental behavior in general (e.g., Kaiser & Gutscher, 2003). A central tenet of the model is that (behavioral) intention is the most important immediate antecedent of behavior. Intention itself is determined by attitude, perceived norm, and perceived behavioral control (PBC). Perceived behavioral control is also postulated to have a direct effect on behavior, although empirical support for this hypothesis is mixed. To apply the RA framework to specific pro-environmental behaviors, it is important to first identify salient behavioral, normative and control beliefs that inform attitude, perceived norm, and perceived behavioral control, respectively.

Attitude refers to an individual's general evaluation of a behavior, which is informed by relevant behavioral beliefs. It comprises both instrumental attitude, which is concerned with the outcome of a behavior, and experiential attitude, which refers to the experience of engaging in a behavior. For example, I might believe that traveling by train to a client meeting is better for the environment (i.e., instrumental attitude) and more comfortable (i.e., experiential attitude) than driving.

Perceived norm—also known as the *social norm* or *subjective norm*—reflects the perception of what other (relevant) people think and do. Normative beliefs are the basis of the overall perceived norm, which can be subdivided into injunctive norms, the perception of other (relevant) people's (dis)approval of one's own behavior, and descriptive norms, the perception of others people's behavior. As an example, my company's sustainability awards might lead me to believe that pro-environmental initiatives are well-regarded by management (i.e., injunctive norm) and that my colleagues have initiated green campaigns (i.e., descriptive norms).

Perceived behavioral control, which is similar to Bandura's self-efficacy, is the perceived ability to perform a behavior or carry out a certain course of action and is based on control beliefs (Bandura, 1997). There are capacity and autonomy components to PBC. *Capacity* refers to the (inherent) ability to perform a behavior, whereas *autonomy* is the (situational) control an individual has over whether to act or not. For example, I know how to print double-sided documents (i.e., capacity) with the printer in my office, which has a double-sided printing option (i.e., autonomy).

The small number of available studies suggest TPB predictors are also relevant to workplace pro-environmental behaviors. In a survey study on recycling among university staff, attitudes and perceived norms predicted recycling intention and behavior; PBC was not examined in this study (Jones, 1990). Results of two studies on environmental decision making in organizations replicated the relevance of TPB predictors (Cordano & Frieze, 2000; Flannery & May, 2000). Other factors, such as financial cost (Flannery & May, 2000) and past organizational activity (Cordano & Frieze, 2000), independently predicted pro-environmental decision making in the organizations examined. Furthermore, the relevance of TPB predictors interacted with contextual factors, such as the magnitude of consequences for the natural environment (Flannery & May, 2000).

As mentioned earlier, reasoned action does not specify which beliefs are relevant to the behavior(s) of interest and relies on pilot work to identify these beliefs. In the context of organizational sustainability and corporate social responsibility, Thomas and Lamm (2012) proposed that attitudes and perceived norms both have three dimensions that are relevant to what they coined *legitimacy* (overall evaluation in reasoned action) of organizational sustainability. First, the pragmatic dimension refers to the extent to which it is believed that there is a business case for engaging in action. The second dimension is a moral evaluation of the proposed action, that is, is it perceived to be the right thing to do? Third, the cognitive dimension relates to the difficulty of a proposed action in relation to an individual's job.

Normative Theories of Pro-Environmental Behavior

Although reasoned action takes the behavior itself as a starting point for investigating pro-environmental behavior, other theorists have focused on the role of environmental beliefs, norms, and worldviews.

Viewing environmental degradation from a broader political and cultural perspective, researchers initially aimed to better understand concern for the environment in general. The New Ecological Paradigm (NEP), and its precursor the New Environmental Paradigm, was developed for this purpose and provided the most widely used scale of pro-environmental orientation (Dunlap & Van Liere, 1978; Dunlap, et al., 2000), its key objective being to measure endorsement of a general ecological worldview. More specifically, it was designed to assess fundamental beliefs about the ability of humans to upset the balance of nature, the existence of limits to economic growth, humanity's right to rule over nature, and acceptance of the constraints of nature.

The scale reliably distinguished environmentalists from the general public and was positively associated with a liberal political orientation, younger age, and higher education (Jones & Dunlap, 1992). Many studies have indeed reported significant associations between the NEP scale and specific, pro-environmental behavioral intentions and behaviors (e.g., O'Connor, Bord, & Fisher, 1999; Vining & Ebreo, 1992). It should be noted, however, that the relationship between the NEP score and specific behaviors is not expected to be consistent due to barriers and opportunities in the specific implementation context of pro-environmental behaviors. As such, one limitation of NEP research is its lack of specificity with respect to the link between environmental concern and pro-environmental behavior.

Another line of normatively focused research examined the link between environmental norms and pro-environmental behaviors. The NAM was originally proposed as a normative explanation of prosocial behavior (Schwartz, 1977). Thus, this model is geared toward understanding a more specific behavioral domain—in this case, prosocial behavior—than reasoned action, which aims to explain human social behavior in general. Pro-environmental behaviors have often been perceived as similar to prosocial behavior because of the lack of obvious, short-term personal gains for both types of behaviors. The NAM has been extensively applied to the study of many household pro-environmental behaviors, including recycling, travel mode choice and economical use of water (e.g., Harland, Staats, & Wilke, 2007; Hopper & Nielsen, 1991; Hunecke, Blobaum, Matthies, & Hoger, 2001).

A key assumption of the NAM is that personal norms—the moral obligation felt by an individual to perform a behavior—is an important proximal antecedent of behavior. As a result, personal norms are sometimes viewed as conceptually similar to intention, albeit only in the context of prosocial behavior (Fishbein & Ajzen, 2010). Others have suggested that personal norms are antecedents of attitudes or intentions (Kaiser, 2006; Parker, Manstead, & Stradling, 1995). Other distinguishing features of the NAM include the role that awareness of consequences and ascription of responsibility play in explaining prosocial behavior. Awareness of consequences refers to awareness of the consequences of one's behavior for the welfare of others and is thus conceptually similar to a subset of Fishbein and Ajzen's behavioral beliefs that inform instrumental attitude (i.e., those that refer to the welfare of others). Ascription of responsibility reflects the belief that one is responsible and capable of controlling actions affecting others, and therefore overlaps with the constructs instrumental attitude and perceived behavioral control in the TRA.

The VBN theory integrated research on personal values, Dunlap and Van Liere's NEP, and Schwartz's NAM to explain support for environmentalism (Stern, 2000; Stern et al., 1999). Since its publication, it has been extensively applied to various private and household pro-environmental behaviors, such as personal car use (Nordlund & Garvill, 2003), the acceptance of environmental policies (Steg, Dreijerink, & Abrahamse, 2005) and the adoption of alternative fuel vehicles (Jansson, Marell, & Nordlund, 2011).

In the VBN theory, personal values are less domain-specific than in the NEP. Altruism toward other humans and altruism toward other species and the biosphere are the main values expected to positively predict environmentalism. In contrast, egoistic values are the main type of values theorized to be negatively associated with environmentalism. The main contribution of VBN theory was to clarify the link between distal determinants—personal values and environmental concern—to that of the more proximal NAM determinants of behavior.

A few studies in organizational settings have also used the VBN theory. One study on office energy-conservation behaviors showed that—as predicted by VBN theory—ecological worldview influenced personal norms, which in turn had a direct effect on energy-conservation intentions and behaviors (Scherbaum, Popovich, & Finlinson, 2008). However, a study on acceptance of climate change policy measures in organizations showed that the hypothesized links between values, norms, and acceptance were supported by data derived from public sector decision-makers, but not private sector decision makers (Nilsson, von Borgstede, & Biel, 2004). Results of a study on supervisor behaviors indicating support for ecological sustainability were also less promising (Andersson, Shivarajan, & Blau, 2005). Only the perceived corporate commitment to ecological sustainability (i.e., the organizational equivalent of ecological worldviews) predicted supervisor support behaviors, whereas beliefs and norms—theoretically more proximal antecedents of behavior—did not. Although these results could be due to the operationalization of the VBN framework within this specific study, it still raises the question of generalizability of the framework across contexts.

Reasoned Action versus Value-Belief-Norm: Integrative Models and Beyond

In studies comparing RA against VBN, RA has been shown to account for more variance in pro-environmental behaviors than VBN across various populations and a range of pro-environmental behaviors, including pro-environmental conservation behaviors (del Carmen Aguilar-Luzon, Angel Garcia-Martinez, Calvo-Salguero, & Maria Salinas, 2012; Kaiser, Hubner, & Bogner, 2005; Oreg & Katz-Gerro, 2006) and willingness to pay for the environment (Lopez-Mosquera & Sanchez, 2012). However, this should not be seen as conclusive proof for the superiority of the RA framework because comparative studies have not fully accounted for several caveats.

As noted earlier, RA and VBN theory differ in their degree of specificity. This has implications for the comparability of the models. Because RA is a generic model of social behavior, its relative success to account for behavior is heavily dependent on whether the relevant beliefs have been identified through pilot work. When comparing RA to VBN, the superiority of one over the other can only be established if it is reasonable to assume that all important relevant beliefs have been measured. This is often not the case for RA-based research (Fishbein & Ajzen, 2010). Similarly, correct measurement is also a concern for VBN, although the theory does provide more specific guidelines than RA.

In contrast to its lack of specificity about what beliefs should be measured, RA emphasizes the importance of measuring psychosocial determinants of behavior in relation to the specific behavior(s) of interest (Fishbein & Ajzen, 2010). When comparing the two models, the level of correspondence between the predictors and behavior must be considered. Although linking generic values to pro-environmental behavior is an explicit aim of the VBN theory, there should be a similar level of correspondence between personal norms (i.e., the most immediate antecedent of behavior in the model) and the pro-environmental behavior for the two models to be comparable.

When comparing the two models it is also important to consider that studies using RA assume that the primary motivation for people to engage with pro-environmental behaviors is self-interest, whereas VBN-based studies have emphasized moral motivations. However, RA is not inherently a self-interest model and is generic enough to incorporate other motivations (Fishbein & Ajzen, 2010).

Because pro-environmental behaviors are unlikely to be exclusively motivated by self-interest or moral concerns, some researchers have attempted to integrate the two models. Because the TPB is the most general framework, attempts to integrate the models have expanded the TPB by including personal norms—sometimes referred to as *moral norms*—as an additional variable in the model. Results of such endeavors are mixed. Some studies have shown this approach to add to our understanding (Abrahamse, Steg, Gifford, & Vlek, 2009; Bamberg, Hunecke, & Blobaum, 2007; Harland et al., 2007), but other studies failed to do so, possibly because moral norms seemed to be reflected in people's attitudes (Kaiser & Scheuthle, 2003).

Closer inspection of the attitude measures used in the studies that found personal norm to be an independent significant predictor showed that these were general (e.g., bad—good) or experiential attitude measures (e.g., unpleasant—pleasant). Although the distinction between experiential and instrumental attitude may not always be clear, the measures used in these studies only refer to the personal consequences of performing pro-environmental behaviors. In contrast, attitude measures in the study that found moral norm to be reflected in attitudes also contained measures that could be interpreted as normative (e.g., inappropriate—appropriate). Thus, it seems that depending on the composition of attitudinal measures, personal norm could be a component of attitude or an independent predictor. What all the studies discussed have in common is that environmental concern, or moral concern, was a relevant determinant of pro-environmental behavior.

Both RA and VBN are cognitive models of behavior, which postulate that pro-environmental behaviors are determined by an individual's beliefs about the behavior itself or its consequences. Similar to subjective expected utility models in the field of economics, the underlying assumption is that humans are rational—in the broad sense of acting according to the beliefs they hold—and fully conscious of the forces driving their own behavior. However, researchers have increasingly been interested in the role of non-deliberative or even unconscious influences on behavior. The next sections of this chapter will provide an overview of research on the role of habits, emotions, personality traits, identity, and socio-demographics in workplace pro-environmental behaviors.

Habit and Unconscious Influences

When behaviors are repeatedly performed, they require less deliberative thought and eventually become habits. Cognitive models of behavior such as reasoned action acknowledge this but contest the validity of habit as an explanatory construct (Fishbein & Ajzen, 2010). Most existing studies that have examined the role of habits in pro-environmental behavior have either asked people to self-report their own habits (Knussen, Yule, MacKenzie, & Wells, 2004) or used self-reported past behavior as a proxy of habit strength (Bamberg, et al., 2003; Carrus, Passafaro, & Bonnes, 2008). Findings from these studies suggest that habit or past behavior—under relatively stable circumstances—independently predict pro-environmental behavior over-and-above social-cognitive predictors. Proponents of cognitive models have argued that these measures beg the question why people behave the way they do (Ajzen, 2011). Nevertheless, the fact that (self-reported) habit predicts behavior over-and-above social-cognitive variables suggests that existing cognitive models do not fully account for pro-environmental and other social behaviors.

To avoid equating habit with past behavior, some have suggested that habit should be conceptually separated from behavioral frequency (Verplanken & Orbell, 2003). Although behavioral repetition is seen as necessary for habit formation to occur, the degree of habit strength could vary, depending on factors such as task complexity and contextual stability (Verplanken, 2006). Defining features of habitual behaviors are their automaticity and the lack of conscious thought and emotion (Wood, Quinn, & Kashy, 2002). However, this raises another problem with using self-report measures of habit. If habits are automatic and characterized by no or little conscious thought, are people able to accurately report their own habits?

Related to potential limitations of self-report measures of habit is whether people are aware of influences on their own behavior more generally. An increasing number of studies suggest that social behavior is influenced by both conscious and unconscious factors (Aarts & Dijksterhuis, 2000; Bargh & Morsella, 2008; Hassin, Bargh, & Zimerman, 2009). Contextual cues, for example, have been postulated to influence behavior through conscious as well as unconscious processes (Kremers, 2010). In the case of habitual behaviors, contextual cues (e.g., time, place) play a more prominent role in determining behavior than social-cognitive variables (Wood et al., 2005).

In the context of repetitive workplace pro-environmental behaviors, the physical environment (i.e., arrangement and availability of organizational facilities) is an obvious source of contextual cues. Previous studies have shown that changes in organizational facilities strongly influence employee office recycling behavior (Brothers, Krantz, & McClannahan, 1994; Humphrey, Bord, Hammond, & Mann, 1977). However, little research has examined the role of habit and unconscious influences in producing these substantial effects caused by differences in the physical environment. Furthermore, the impact of less obvious contextual cues has been understudied. Qualitative research has shown that employees believe that facilities in the office environment heavily influence their workplace energy-saving behaviors (Lo et al., 2012a). However, employees are not necessarily able to identify contextual influences. One example comes from an employee's struggle to explain why she left the lights on at work but not at home: "... I think it is a habit ... because you always see lights burning everywhere ... At my place it's dark except where I am ... I think that's the reason why, I never really thought about it" (Lo et al., 2012a, p. 237). Moreover, organizational context directly affects workplace pro-environmental behaviors, which are not mediated by cognitive factors in the case of habitual pro-environmental behaviors (Lo, Peters, van Breukelen, & Kok, 2014). In sum, the scarce evidence available to date suggests that although some contextual factors affect employees' conscious beliefs about workplace pro-environmental behaviors, it is likely that unconscious factors also influence these behaviors.

Emotions

Until recently, little attention was paid to emotions as a determinant of pro-environmental behavior (Carrus et al., 2008; Vining & Ebreo, 2002).

The role of emotions in workplace pro-environmental behavior is discussed in more detail in chapter 7; the discussion here is limited to their role in cognitive models of pro-environmental behaviors discussed earlier in this chapter.

Existing cognitive models, such as reasoned action and VBN theory can incorporate emotional influences on behavior in the form of beliefs about the emotional consequences of performing behaviors. Although this does not explain the origins of relevant emotions, it does contribute to a more comprehensive explanation of workplace pro-environmental behaviors. The RA construct that most easily accommodates emotional motivators of behavior is experiential attitude, or affective attitude (Bamberg & Schmidt, 2003), and some progress has been made in incorporating the role of emotions more explicitly in the basic RA framework. The model of goal-directed behavior (MGB) was proposed as an extension of the RA framework and introduced the constructs of anticipated emotions, desire (as an immediate antecedent of intention), and past behavior (Carrus et al., 2008). It remains for future research to examine whether the MGB or other extensions of RA can avoid some of the theoretical and methodological pitfalls discussed in the preceding section on habits and unconscious influences. Another interesting hypothesis worth examining further in this context is the protective effect of pro-environmental attitudes on affective barriers to engage with pro-environmental behavior. One recent study showed that employees with stronger pro-environmental attitudes were more likely to consistently perform some workplace pro-environmental behaviors, despite mood fluctuations (Bissing-Olson, Iyer, Fielding, & Zacher, 2013).

Person Characteristics

So far, we have discussed individual determinants that are directly linked to environmental sustainability. Some of the previously discussed literature on general environmental concern and values has also raised the question whether certain broader values (e.g., altruism, political values) and other person characteristics (e.g., socio-demographics) are relevant to environmental concern, and ultimately, pro-environmental behavior. In one study, a liberal (vs. conservative) political orientation, higher education, urban living, employment outside of primary industries, and young age were positively associated with environmental concern (Jones & Dunlap, 1992). In another study, egoistic values were negatively related to pro-environmental behavior but openness to change values were unrelated (Stern, Dietz, & Guagnano, 1998).

Political orientation has been related to pro-environmental attitude (McCright & Dunlap, 2011). Rather unsurprisingly, the best-known politicians (e.g., Al Gore) who have supported the environmental movement have typically been Democrats. What is more, support for environmental sustainability is commonly perceived as a political act. The political nature of the discourse has often resulted in a polarization of opinions regarding environmental policies. However, considering that environmental degradation has the potential to affect everyone's quality of life, environmental attitudes are not inherently polarized. A recent study showed that changing the rhetoric by appealing to different types of moral concerns greatly reduces the difference between liberals' and conservatives' pro-environmental attitudes (Feinberg & Willer, 2013). Pro-environmental attitudes did not differ between liberals and conservatives after they had read a persuasive message with pictures of environmental pollution and contamination—assumed to appeal to concern for purity/sanctity and its inverse, disgust. However, when presented with pictures of barren landscapes and seascapes—assumed to appeal to moral values related to harm and care—liberals had significantly higher pro-environmental attitude scores than conservatives.

Perhaps the most widely examined category of person characteristics are socio-demographics. In marketing, socio-demographics have been used extensively to 'profile' green consumers. Socio-demographic variables are appealing as possible predictors of pro-environmental behaviors because of their accessibility. However, results have generally been mixed and of limited predictive value (Diamantopoulos, Schlegelmilch, Sinkovics, & Bohlen, 2003). Although the relationship between various socio-demographics and environmental attitudes are consistent, they are also weak. Women and younger people report stronger environmental attitudes than men and older people respectively (Diamantopoulos et al., 2003; Jones & Dunlap, 1992; Zelezny, Chua, & Aldrich, 2000). The link between socio-demographics and pro-environmental behaviors is even less clear (Diamantopoulos et al., 2003), with the exception of household income, which has a strong, positive association with total energy consumption levels, most likely due to increased opportunity to consume (Moll et al., 2005). Still, this relationship does not help understand *why* people make different choices under similar circumstances.

In contrast to socio-demographics and values, personality traits have not received much attention in the context of pro-environmental behavior. One notable exception is a study that examined the relationship between personality traits and waste management behaviors (Swami, Chamorro-Premuzic, Snelgar, & Furnham, 2011). Both conscientiousness and agreeableness were hypothesized to be positively related to waste management. Conscientiousness was indeed significantly related to waste management behaviors, but agreeableness was not. Although it is premature to draw conclusions about the role of personality traits in workplace pro-environmental behavior, these findings raise interesting questions. For example, are more conscientious employees more likely to enact pro-environmental behaviors? Is openness to experience related to willingness to engage with new pro-environmental initiatives in the organization? A better understanding of personality differences might improve interventions that use personal tailoring techniques to address each individual. From a management perspective, an understanding of personality differences could also be useful to select organizational members that could take on a more active role in implementing pro-environmental initiatives.

Identity

The individual determinants of workplace pro-environmental behavior discussed thus far in this chapter have been predominantly examined in quantitative survey research and intervention studies. One limitation of quantitative research, and especially cross-sectional studies, is that it mainly looks for linear associations between predictors and outcome variables rather than person-environment dynamics. Qualitative research, on the other hand, is generally more suited to acknowledge these—often intricate—dynamics, and can shed light on the rich human experiences of dealing with environmental issues in the workplace (see chapter 4 for a more detailed discussion of the different research methodologies). Personal identity has been of particular interest to qualitative researchers in this field. Most research in this area has focused on key organizational actors (e.g., directors, senior managers, or sustainability managers) who are covered in more detail in chapter 8, so only a brief discussion of how this research might benefit our understanding of individual determinants of workplace pro-environmental behaviors is presented here.

In a recent study on sustainability managers and consultants, Wright and colleagues (2012) concluded that context influenced their identities. For example, in the presence of senior managers they might present and perceive themselves as rational managers, but take on the role of green change agents among like-minded colleagues. Although others have reported relatively uniform views of the self among managers (Fineman, 1997), Wright and colleagues depict more variation, with individuals resolving tensions and contradictions between their various roles in different ways. Another key insight from the Wright study is that epiphany or critical events led interviewees to reassess their priorities and identities. These findings suggest that research should pay more attention to how cognitive dissonance or internal conflicts are resolved and possible nonlinear relationships between individual determinants and behaviors.

The Dynamics between Individual Determinants

So far, I have discussed many an array of individual determinants of workplace pro-environmental behaviors. I offered a tentative taxonomy of workplace pro-environmental behaviors at the beginning of this chapter because not all individual determinants are equally relevant to all behaviors within this broad class of behaviors. Yet there is little empirical evidence comparing the relative importance of individual determinants for different pro-environmental behaviors. Another related empirical question is how the organizational environment influences the relevance of individual determinants. In one recent study, the degree to which habit predicted everyday office energy-saving behaviors varied considerably between different types of workplace pro-environmental behaviors (Lo et al., 2014). Switching off lights and monitors were much more strongly associated with habit than printing two or more pages on one side and refraining from printing e-mails. Furthermore, the results showed that the relationships among habit, intention, and behavior for each behavior could also differ between organizations.

In a recently proposed model of workplace pro-environmental interventions, a combination of organizational factors and personal beliefs was hypothesized to determine the extent of goal adoption (Unsworth et al., 2013). This model postulates that the efficacy and attractiveness of a workplace intervention and the level of self-concordance (i.e., in line with the employee's stable interests and values) interact to affect short-term behavior change. Further along the path, conflicting goals and the extent to which the environmental goal is perceived to have been achieved should determine whether behavior change is sustained and spillover to related behaviors occurs.

Future Research

As discussed earlier in this chapter, considerable efforts have been made to integrate commonly used models of individual determinants of pro-environmental behaviors. Although these efforts are to be applauded, a limitation of these models is their focus on cognitive determinants of pro-environmental behaviors; some influences on behavior may not be reflected in people's reported beliefs about pro-environmental behaviors. Future research should examine whether, and if so, to what extent such influences can be incorporated into existing, cognitive models. Alternatively, novel theoretical frameworks could be developed that provide a more comprehensive understanding of pro-environmental behaviors than the existing models.

I have also outlined differences between general pro-environmental behaviors and features specific to workplace pro-environmental behaviors that could impact the relevance of specific individual determinants, and discussed some recent studies which have examined this question. A more systematic investigation and a theoretical framework of the conditions under which specific individual determinants are relevant to a given workplace pro-environmental behavior would be a welcome addition to this body of research.

Another area in need of further study is possible interactions between individual determinants of pro-environmental behaviors. Unsworth and colleagues' (2013) recent model of workplace pro-environmental interventions suggests that it is the combination of relevant beliefs related to the intervention and employees' personal interests and values which determines the outcome. Future studies should focus on examining such interactions and furthering our conceptual understanding of individual determinants of workplace pro-environmental behaviors.

Conclusion

The study of individual determinants of workplace pro-environmental behaviors draws on a rich psychological literature, which has previously been applied to many private and household pro-environmental behaviors and other social behaviors. However, it is not always clear how these general theoretical insights can serve to understand workplace pro-environmental behaviors. One challenge is the fragmented state of the theoretical literature. Many competing, but overlapping and not necessarily mutually exclusive models of individual determinants of pro-environmental behavior have been proposed over the past few decades. More recently, some headway has been made towards integrating various theoretical strands. Another issue is the dearth of research examining the interaction between individual determinants and organizational-level factors relevant to workplace environmental behaviors. A systematic examination of the role of individual determinants in workplace pro-environmental behaviors would therefore be a challenging but worthwhile aim for future research.

Suggested Additional Readings

1. Clayton, S. D. (Ed.) (2012). *The Oxford handbook of environmental and conservation psychology*. Oxford: Oxford University Press.
2. Zibarras, L., & Ballinger, C. (2010). Promoting environmental behaviour in the workplace: A survey of UK organisations. British Psychological Society Division of Occupational Psychology: Going Green Working Group Report.

3. Zibarras, L., Judson, H., & Barnes, C. (2012), Promoting environmental behaviour in the workplace: A survey of UK organisations. Available at: http://greenedge.co.za/files/Downloads-Pro-environmental-behaviour-in-the-workplace-UK-survey-2012.pdf

References

Aarts, H., & Dijksterhuis, A. (2000). The automatic activation of goal-directed behaviour: The case of travel habit. *Journal of Environmental Psychology, 20*, 75–82.

Abrahamse, W., Steg, L., Gifford, R., & Vlek, C. (2009). Factors influencing car use for commuting and the intention to reduce it: A question of self-interest or morality? *Transportation Research Part F-Traffic Psychology and Behaviour, 12*, 317–324.

Abrahamse, W., Steg, L., Vlek, C., & Rothengatter, T. (2005). A review of intervention studies aimed at household energy conservation. *Journal of Environmental Psychology, 25*, 273–291.

Ajzen, I. (1991). The theory of planned behavior. *Organizational Behavior and Human Decision Processes, 50*, 179–211.

Ajzen, I. (2011). The theory of planned behaviour: Reactions and reflections. *Psychology & Health, 26*, 1113–1127. doi: 10.1080/08870446.2011.613995

Andersson, L., Shivarajan, S., & Blau, G. (2005). Enacting ecological sustainability in the MNC: A test of an adapted value-belief-norm framework. *Journal of Business Ethics, 59*, 295–305.

Bamberg, S., Ajzen, I., & Schmidt, P. (2003). Choice of travel mode in the theory of planned behavior: The roles of past behavior, habit, and reasoned action. *Basic and Applied Social Psychology, 25*, 175–187.

Bamberg, S., Hunecke, M., & Blobaum, A. (2007). Social context, personal norms and the use of public transportation: Two field studies. *Journal of Environmental Psychology, 27*, 190–203.

Bamberg, S., & Moser, G. (2007). Twenty years after Hines, Hungerford, and Tomera: A new meta-analysis of psycho-social determinants of pro-environmental behaviour. *Journal of Environmental Psychology, 27*, 14–25.

Bamberg, S., & Schmidt, P. (2003). Incentives, morality, or habit? Predicting students' car use for university routes with the models of Ajzen, Schwartz, and Triandis. *Environment and Behavior, 35*, 264–285. doi: 10.1177/0013916502250134

Bandura, A. (1997). *Self-efficacy: The exercise of control*. New York: Worth Publishers.

Bansal, P., & Gao, J. J. (2006). Building the future by looking to the past: Examining research published on organizations and environment. *Organization & Environment, 19*, 458–478.

Bargh, J. A., & Morsella, E. (2008). The unconscious mind. *Perspectives on Psychological Science, 3*, 73–79.

Bartholomew, L. K., Parcel, G. S., Kok, G., Gottlieb, N., & Fernández, M. E. (2011). *Planning health promotion programs: An intervention mapping approach* (3rd ed.). San Francisco: Jossey-Bass.

Bissing-Olson, M. J., Iyer, A., Fielding, K. S., & Zacher, H. (2013). Relationships between daily affect and proenvironmental behavior at work: The moderating role of pro-environmental attitude. *Journal of Organizational Behavior, 34*, 156–175.

Boldero, J. (1995). The prediction of household recycling of newspapers: The role of attitudes, intentions, and situational factors. *Journal of Applied Social Psychology, 25*, 440–462.

Brothers, K. J., Krantz, P. J., & McClannahan, L. E. (1994). Office paper recycling: A function of container proximity. *Journal of Applied Behavior Analysis, 27*, 153–160.

Carrus, G., Passafaro, P., & Bonnes, M. (2008). Emotions, habits and rational choices in ecological behaviours: The case of recycling and use of public transportation. *Journal of Environmental Psychology, 28*, 51–62.

Cordano, M., & Frieze, I. H. (2000). Pollution reduction preferences of US environmental managers: Applying Ajzen's theory of planned behavior. *Academy of Management Journal, 43*, 627–641.

Corraliza, J. A., & Berenguer, J. (2000). Environmental values, beliefs, and actions: A situational approach. *Environment and Behavior, 32*, 832–848.

del Carmen Aguilar-Luzon, M., Angel Garcia-Martinez, J. M., Calvo-Salguero, A., & Maria Salinas, J. (2012). Comparative study between the theory of planned behavior and the value-belief-norm model regarding the environment, on spanish housewives' recycling behavior. *Journal of Applied Social Psychology, 42*, 2797–2833. doi: 10.1111/j.1559-1816.2012.00962.x

Diamantopoulos, A., Schlegelmilch, B. B., Sinkovics, R. R., & Bohlen, G. M. (2003). Can socio-demographics still play a role in profiling green consumers? A review of the evidence and an empirical investigation. *Journal of Business Research, 56*, 465–480. doi: 10.1016/s0148-2963(01)00241-7

Dietz, T., Gardner, G. T., Gilligan, J., Stern, P. C., & Vandenbergh, M. P. (2009). Household actions can provide a behavioral wedge to rapidly reduce US carbon emissions. *Proceedings of the National Academy of Sciences of the United States of America, 106*, 18452–18456.

Dunlap, R. E., & Van Liere, K. D. (1978). The "new environmental paradigm": A proposed measuring instrument and preliminary results. *Journal of Environmental Education, 9*, 10–19.

Dunlap, R. E., Van Liere, K. D., Mertig, A. G., & Jones, R. E. (2000). Measuring endorsement of the new ecological paradigm: A revised NEP scale. *Journal of Social Issues, 56*, 425–442.

Etzion, D. (2007). Research on organizations and the natural environment, 1992-present: A review. *Journal of Management, 33*, 637–664.

Feinberg, M., & Willer, R. (2013). The moral roots of environmental attitudes. *Psychological Science, 24*, 56–62. doi: 10.1177/0956797612449177

Fineman, S. (1997). Constructing the green manager. *British Journal of Management, 8*, 31–38.

Fishbein, M., & Ajzen, I. (1975). *Belief, attitude, intention, and behavior: an introduction to theory and research*. Reading, MA: Addison-Wesley.

Fishbein, M., & Ajzen, I. (2010). *Predicting and changing behavior: The reasoned action approach*. New York: Taylor & Francis Group.

Flannery, B. L., & May, D. R. (2000). Environmental ethical decision making in the US metal-finishing industry. *Academy of Management Journal, 43*, 642–662.

Hardin, G. (1968). The tragedy of the commons. *Science, 162*, 1243–1248.

Harland, P., Staats, H., & Wilke, H. A. M. (2007). Situational and personality factors as direct or personal norm mediated predictors of pro-environmental behavior: Questions derived from norm-activation theory. *Basic and Applied Social Psychology, 29*, 323–334.

Hassin, R. R., Bargh, J. A., & Zimerman, S. (2009). Automatic and flexible: The case of nonconscious goal pursuit. *Social Cognition, 27*, 20–36.

Hopper, J. R., & Nielsen, J. M. (1991). Recycling as altruistic behavior: Normative and behavioral strategies to expand participation in a community recycling program. *Environment and Behavior, 23*, 195–220.

Humphrey, C.-R., Bord, R.-J., Hammond, M.-M., & Mann, S.-H. (1977). Attitudes and conditions for cooperation in a paper recycling program. *Environment and Behavior, 9*, 107–124.

Hunecke, M., Blobaum, A., Matthies, E., & Hoger, R. (2001). Responsibility and environment: Ecological norm orientation and external factors in the domain of travel mode choice behavior. *Environment and Behavior, 33*, 830–852. doi: 10.1177/00139160121973269

Jansson, J., Marell, A., & Nordlund, A. (2011). Exploring consumer adoption of a high involvement eco-innovation using value-belief-norm theory. *Journal of Consumer Behaviour, 10*, 51–60. doi: 10.1002/cb.346

Jones, R. E. (1990). Understanding paper recycling in an institutionally supportive setting: An application of the theory of reasoned action. *Journal of Environmental Systems, 19*, 307–321.

Jones, R. E., & Dunlap, R. E. (1992). The social bases of environmental concern: Have they changed over time? *Rural Sociology, 57*, 28–47.

Kaiser, F. G. (2006). A moral extension of the theory of planned behavior: Norms and anticipated feelings of regret in conservationism. *Personality and Individual Differences, 41*, 71–81.

Kaiser, F. G., & Gutscher, H. (2003). The proposition of a general version of the theory of planned behavior: Predicting ecological behavior. *Journal of Applied Social Psychology, 33*, 586–603.

Kaiser, F. G., Hubner, G., & Bogner, F. X. (2005). Contrasting the theory of planned behavior with the value-belief-norm model in explaining conservation behavior. *Journal of Applied Social Psychology, 35*, 2150–2170.

Kaiser, F. G., & Scheuthle, H. (2003). Two challenges to a moral extension of the theory of planned behavior: Moral norms and just world beliefs in conservationism. *Personality and Individual Differences, 35*, 1033–1048.

Kaiser, F. G., & Schultz, P. W. (2009). The attitude-behavior relationship: A test of three models of the moderating role of behavioral difficulty. *Journal of Applied Social Psychology, 39*, 186–207.

Knussen, C., Yule, F., MacKenzie, J., & Wells, M. (2004). An analysis of intentions to recycle household waste: The roles of past behaviour, perceived habit, and perceived lack of facilities. *Journal of Environmental Psychology, 24*, 237–246.

Kremers, S. P. J. (2010). Theory and practice in the study of influences on energy balance-related behaviors. *Patient Education and Counseling, 79*, 291–298. doi: 10.1016/j.pec.2010.03.002

Latane, B., Williams, K., & Harkins, S. (1979). Many hands make light the work: Causes and consequences of social loafing. *Journal of Personality and Social Psychology, 37*, 822–832. doi: 10.1037//0022-3514.37.6.822

Lo, S. H., Peters, G. J., van Breukelen, G. J. P., & Kok, G. (2014). Only reasoned action? An interorganizational study of energy-saving behaviors in office buildings. *Energy Efficiency, 7*, 761–775, doi: 10.1007/s12053-014-9254-x.

Lo, S. H., Peters, G. Y., & Kok, G. (2012a). Energy-related behaviors in office buildings: A qualitative study on individual and organizational determinants. *Applied Psychology: an International Review, 61*, 227–249. doi: 10.1111/j.1464-0597.2011.00464.x

Lo, S. H., Peters, G. Y., & Kok, G. (2012b). A review of determinants of and interventions for proenvironmental behaviors in organizations. *Journal of Applied Social Psychology, 42*, 2933–2967. doi: 0.1111/j.1559-1816.2012.00969.x

Lopez-Mosquera, N., & Sanchez, M. (2012). Theory of planned behavior and the value-belief-norm theory explaining willingness to pay for a suburban park. *Journal of Environmental Management, 113*, 251–262. doi: 10.1016/j.jenvman.2012.08.029

McCright, A. M., & Dunlap, R. E. (2011). The politicization of climate change and polarization in the american public's views of global warming, 2001-2010. *Sociological Quarterly, 52*, 155–194. doi: 10.1111/j.1533-8525.2011.01198.x

Moll, H. C., Noorman, K. J., Kok, R., Engstrom, R., Throne-Holst, H., & Clark, C. (2005). Pursuing more sustainable consumption by analyzing household metabolism in European countries and cities. *Journal of Industrial Ecology, 9*, 259–275.

Nilsson, A., von Borgstede, C., & Biel, A. (2004). Willingness to accept climate change strategies: The effect of values and norms. *Journal of Environmental Psychology, 24*, 267–277. doi: 10.1016/j.jenvp.2004.06.002

Nordlund, A. M., & Garvill, J. (2003). Effects of values, problem awareness, and personal norm on willingness to reduce personal car use. *Journal of Environmental Psychology, 23*, 339–347. doi: 10.1016/s0272-4944(03)00037-9

O'Connor, R. E., Bord, R. J., & Fisher, A. (1999). Risk perceptions, general environmental beliefs, and willingness to address climate change. *Risk Analysis, 19*, 461–471.

Oreg, S., & Katz-Gerro, T. (2006). Predicting proenvironmental behavior cross-nationally: Values, the theory of planned behavior, and value-belief-norm theory. *Environment and Behavior, 38*, 462–483.

Parker, D., Manstead, A. S. R., & Stradling, S. G. (1995). Extending the theory of planned behavior: The role of personal norm. *British Journal of Social Psychology, 34*, 127–137.

Scherbaum, C. A., Popovich, P. M., & Finlinson, S. (2008). Exploring individual-level factors related to employee energy-conservation behaviors at work. *Journal of Applied Social Psychology, 38*, 818–835.

Schwartz, S. H. (1973). Normative explanations of helping behavior: A critique, proposal, and empirical test. *Journal of Experimental Social Psychology, 9*, 349–364.

Schwartz, S. H. (1977). Normative influences on altruism. In L. Berkowitz (Ed.), *Advances in experimental social psychology* (Vol. 10, pp. 221–279). New York: Academic Press.

Staats, H. J., Wit, A. P., & Midden, C. Y. (1996). Communicating the greenhouse effect to the public: Evaluation of a mass media campaign from a social dilemma perspective. *Journal of Environmental Management, 46*, 189–203.

Steg, L., Dreijerink, L., & Abrahamse, W. (2005). Factors influencing the acceptability of energy policies: A test of VBN theory. *Journal of Environmental Psychology, 25*, 415–425.

Stern, P. C. (2000). Toward a coherent theory of environmentally significant behavior. *Journal of Social Issues, 56*, 407–424.

Stern, P. C., Dietz, T., Abel, T., & Guagnano, G. (1999). A value-belief-norm theory of support for social movements: The case of environmentalism *Human Ecology Review, 6*, 81–97.

Stern, P. C., Dietz, T., & Guagnano, G. A. (1998). A brief inventory of values. *Educational and Psychological Measurement, 58*, 984–1001.

Swami, V., Chamorro-Premuzic, T., Snelgar, R., & Furnham, A. (2011). Personality, individual differences, and demographic antecedents of self-reported household waste management behaviours. *Journal of Environmental Psychology, 31*, 21–26. doi: 10.1016/j.jenvp.2010.08.001

Thomas, T. E., & Lamm, E. (2012). Legitimacy and organizational sustainability. *Journal of Business Ethics, 110*, 191–203. doi: 10.1007/s10551-012-1421-4

Uitdenbogerd, D., Egmond, C., Jonkers, R., & Kok, G. (2007). Energy-related intervention success factors: a literature review. Paper presented at the ECEEE Summer Studies of the European Council for an Energy Efficient Economy.

Unsworth, K. L., Dmitrieva, A., & Adriasola, E. (2013). Changing behaviour: Increasing the effectiveness of workplace interventions in creating pro-environmental behaviour change. *Journal of Organizational Behavior, 34*, 211–229. doi: 10.1002/job.1837

Verplanken, B. (2006). Beyond frequency: Habit as mental construct. *British Journal of Social Psychology, 45*, 639–656.

Verplanken, B., & Orbell, S. (2003). Reflections on past behavior: A self-report index of habit strength. *Journal of Applied Social Psychology, 33*, 1313–1330.

Vining, J., & Ebreo, A. (1992). Predicting recycling behavior from global and specific environmental attitudes and changes in recycling opportunities. *Journal of Applied Social Psychology, 22*, 1580–1607. doi: 10.1111/j.1559-1816.1992.tb01758.x

Vining, J., & Ebreo, A. (2002). Emerging theoretical and methodological perspective on conservation behaviour. In R. Bechtel, & A. Churchman (Eds.), *Handbook of environmental psychology* (pp. 541–558). New York: Wiley.

Walls, J. L., & Hoffman, A. J. (2013). Exceptional boards: Environmental experience and positive deviance from institutional norms. *Journal of Organizational Behavior, 34*, 253–271. doi: 10.1002/job.1813

Weber, E. U. (2006). Experience-based and description-based perceptions of long-term risk: Why global warming does not scare us (yet). *Climatic Change, 77*, 103–120.

Wood, W., Quinn, J. M., & Kashy, D. A. (2002). Habits in everyday life: Thought, emotion, and action. *Journal of Personality and Social Psychology, 83*, 1281–1297. doi: 10.1037//0022-3514.83.6.1281

Wood, W., Tam, L., & Guerrero Witt, M. (2005). Changing circumstances, disrupting habits. *Journal of Personality and Social Psychology, 88*, 918–933.

Wright, C., Nyberg, D., & Grant, D. (2012). "Hippies on the third floor": Climate change, narrative identity and the micro-politics of corporate environmentalism. *Organization Studies, 33*, 1451–1475. doi: 10.1177/0170840612463316

Zelezny, L. C., Chua, P. P., & Aldrich, C. (2000). Elaborating on gender differences in environmentalism. *Journal of Social Issues, 56*, 443–457.

7 THE RELATIONSHIP BETWEEN EMOTIONS AND WORKPLACE PRO-ENVIRONMENTAL BEHAVIORS

Sally Russell and Elmar Friedrich

In this chapter we argue that the role of emotion in greening organizations deserves further attention and is a fruitful area for further research. Research in the broader management literature has clearly demonstrated how organizations are inherently emotional places (Ashkanasy & Ashton-James, 2005; Elfenbein, 2007; Voronov & Vince, 2012), yet far fewer studies have examined the relationship between emotions and organizational greening (Russell & Griffiths, 2008). Scholars such as Fineman (1996, 1997) and Pratt and Dutton (2000) have suggested that environmental issues are likely to be more emotional than other types of issues within organizations. Yet the relative lack of emotion-based research has meant that research in organizational greening may not have kept pace with theoretical and empirical developments in the wider organizational literature (Ashforth & Humphrey, 1995; Barsade, Brief, & Spataro, 2003). In this chapter we review what research has been conducted to date with the aim of setting an agenda for future research in this burgeoning area.

For the purposes of setting a clear research agenda, we use Ashkanasy's (2003) integrated multi-level framework of emotions in organizations as a starting point to review relevant research and literature. Ashkanasy suggests that emotions in the workplace can be categorized according to the five levels at which they occur. The most micro-level of the model focuses on within-person emotions, followed by emotions at the individual level. The levels then proceed through the meso-level, including interpersonal and group-level emotions, and finally the macro-level perspective of organizational level emotions. We argue that this framework provides a useful foundation for our chapter and it allows us to examine current research as it relates to each level of analysis. In the following section we set the context of the chapter by first defining emotion. We then review current research that examines emotion at each level of analysis and identify the relevance of the level to the study of pro-environmental behavior in general and then specifically to the organizational context. In the final section of the chapter we outline the challenges and opportunities of studying emotion as it relates to the psychology of greening organizations and in doing so we aim to set an agenda for future research that is both innovative and impactful.

Defining Emotion

Throughout this chapter we use the term *emotion* to describe an intense reaction to an event (Frijda, 1986; Scherer, 2000, p. 152). Although there is ongoing debate on how emotion should be defined, this definition captures the predominant scholarly point of view that emotions are a reaction to an event, and are strong in intensity (Briner & Kiefer, 2005; Frijda, 1993; Izard, 1991). Throughout the chapter we predominantly use the term *emotion* rather than other affective constructs, such as mood, or affect, as it is the object specificity of emotion that is of most relevance when discussing emotion and environmental issues. In contrast to emotion, *moods* are diffuse, lack object specificity, and are generally less intense (Forgas, 1994; Scherer, 2000). Moods can be described as operating ". . . more in the background, with lower intensity" (Briner & Kiefer, 2005, p. 286). Alternatively, *affect* is commonly used as an umbrella term for all affective phenomena (Briner & Kiefer, 2005; Elfenbein, 2007) and therefore lacks the specificity that is implied by the term *emotion*.

Elfenbein (2007) describes the emotional experience as a process that begins when an individual is exposed to an emotion-eliciting stimulus. The individual then registers the stimulus for meaning, leading to the experience of a feeling state as well as physiological changes. Elfenbein argues that this process of experiencing emotion has consequences for attitudes, behaviors, and cognitions, as well as for facial expressions and other emotionally expressive cues. The relationships that Elfenbein describes between emotional experiences, cognition, and behavior are particularly important in the context of greening organizations.

Scholars have suggested that emotions activate and prioritize behaviors by signaling action readiness—a concept that links different emotions with different behavioral responses (e.g., to run away in fear, or to fight in anger) (see Frijda, 1986; Izard, 1991). Lazarus (1991) suggests that emotional experiences trigger specific automatic responses that lead to a state of action readiness. These behavioral tendencies have a strong adaptive function, helping the individual to adjust to or shape the changing environment (Elfenbein, 2007; Frijda, 1986; Lazarus, 1991).

Cognition is another important component of emotion (Elfenbein, 2007). The most widespread view is that emotions result from cognitive appraisals made following an event that is of major importance to the individual (Lazarus, 1991; Scherer, 2000). Lazarus (1991) and Scherer (2000) suggest that events are appraised in relation to different dimensions that may include an individual's personal values, goals, or social norms. These appraisals serve as an information processing mechanism that helps distinguish the relevance and importance of events or information (Scherer, 2000).

Level 1: Within-Person Emotions

The first level of Ashkanasy's (2003) multi-level model is the *within*-person level. Individuals' emotions have been shown to fluctuate over time (To, Fisher, Ashkanasy, & Rowe, 2012; Weiss & Cropanzano, 1996), with day-to-day as well as moment-to-moment fluctuations. By including this level of analysis, Ashkanasy takes account of the dynamic nature of emotion and the fluctuations that occur *within* individuals. We agree with Ashkanasy and suggest that it is important to consider variations at the within-person level of analysis and the subsequent impacts that these fluctuations may have on behavior. Indeed, as noted in our introduction, emotional reactions to environmental issues can take many forms and they may differ depending on the cognitive appraisals that individuals ascribe to specific issues.

More recent theories of emotion take account of within person fluctuations in emotion, including affective events theory (AET; Weiss & Cropanzano, 1996) and the affect infusion model (Forgas, 1995). Affective events theory posits that emotional states at work are determined by the daily hassles and uplifts that are experienced in working life. These experiences generate specific emotional reactions that are hypothesized to influence subsequent behaviors and actions. The affect infusion model is focused more specifically on positive emotions. Fredrickson (2003) suggests that the experience of positive emotion broadens an individual's scope of thoughts and possible actions and builds his or her personal resources. It is posited that the result of this process leads individuals to demonstrate greater engagement in alternative and positive workplace behaviors.

The work of Bissing-Olson, Iyer, Fielding, and Zacher (2013) is the first study of which we are aware that has sought to specifically examine within-person fluctuations in emotion and their effect on pro-environmental behavior. This study is an important development in the field and clearly demonstrates how fluctuations in emotion can influence individual pro-environmental behavior. Using a diary-based method, Bissing-Olson et al. (2013) were able to capture fluctuations in emotional expressions over the course of 10 days. The authors challenge the assumption of previous research that individuals are consistent from day to day in their emotional expressions and their propensity to perform pro-environmental behaviors. Bissing-Olson and colleagues examined the degree to which daily positive affect and pro-environmental attitude predicted two different types of pro-environmental workplace behavior. Their results revealed that employees were more likely to carry out their required work tasks in environmentally friendly ways when they felt calm, relaxed, and content, providing evidence that emotional states do indeed influence pro-environmental behavior at work. Another unique and interesting conclusion from this study is that the emotions that predicted environmentally friendly behavior need not be directed toward environmental issues; rather, incidental emotion about any target can influence pro-environmental behaviors in the workplace.

Based on the research on within-person emotions it is clear that emotions vary from day to day and even from moment to moment (Bissing-Olson et al., 2013; To et al., 2012). Indeed, at one moment we may experience sadness and the very next moment we may feel joy or hope or elation (Ashkanasy, 2003). Although research to date has demonstrated that there is variation at this level, little is known about how these variations may affect pro-environmental behavior in general and in the workplace specifically. Bissing-Olson and colleagues (2013) extend our understanding of this phenomenon, but more needs to be done. Indeed, there is little known about how negative emotions affect pro-environmental behavior, nor is it clear how discrete emotions at the within-person level may affect subsequent behaviors and decision making.

Level 2: Emotions Between Persons

Although emotions have been shown to fluctuate within individuals, Ashkanasy (2003) notes that there are some elements of emotion that can be described at the between-person level. Emotions at this level of analysis can also be described as individual differences. Traits are one example, whereby individuals demonstrate trait emotion as a general personal disposition to be in a long-term positive or negative affective state. Past research has shown that trait affect plays a small role in determining personal outcomes in organizational settings (Fox & Spector, 2000; Staw & Barsade, 1993). Within the pro-environmental literature much work has been conducted on between-person variables, or traits, and their influence on behavior; however, the focus of these studies has tended to be dominated by attitudinal and cognitive variables rather than the affective determinants of behavior (e.g., Bamberg & Möser, 2007; Steg & Vlek, 2009). However, there are some notable exceptions.

First, Kals, Schumacher, and Montada (1999) found that pro-environmental behavior, or nature protective behavior as they term it, could not be sufficiently explained using a purely rational-cognitive approach; rather, they found that both positive and negative emotions serve as predictors of nature protective behaviors. Pooley and O'Connor (2000) also examined emotion as an antecedent of motivation and found that the inclusion of both cognitive and affective variables as antecedents for environmental attitudes greatly improved the strength of their model predicting pro-environmental behavior.

Other researchers have considered more specific discrete emotion experiences. For example Bamberg, Hunecke, and Blöbaum (2007) examined the role of guilt in the formation of personal norms and subsequent public transport use. In a large-scale field survey, they found that feelings of guilt were caused by an awareness of the negative environmental impacts of car use. This emotion then led to an obligation (or personal norm) to use public transport, a more "environmentally friendly" mode of transport. Contrary to their expectations, however, they also found a direct, negative relationship between guilt and behavior. They suggested a possible explanation of the direct effect could be that feelings of guilt may paralyze the ability to act. The evidence suggests, however, that paralysis is subverted in the presence of strong personal norms (Bamberg et al., 2007).

Within a workplace context, Giacalone and his colleagues (Andersson, Giacalone, & Jurkiewicz, 2007; Giacalone, Paul, & Jurkiewics, 2005) have also demonstrated the importance of emotion. In these studies, Giacalone et al. (2005) and Andersson et al. (2007) demonstrated that the emotions of hope and gratitude had a significant impact on self-reported corporate social responsibility (CSR). Although not measuring pro-environmental behavior per se, the measures of CSR used in these two studies integrate pro-environmental behaviors as a dimension of CSR. The results from these studies showed that respondents who reported greater levels of hope and gratitude also reported a greater sense of responsibility for employee and societal issues. If CSR is taken as an approximation of pro-environmental behavior, these findings suggest that positive emotions can lead to greater engagement in pro-environmental behavior, a finding congruent with results at the within-person level of analysis (Bissing-Olson et al., 2013).

Emotions have also been shown to be important in determining a career choice in organizational greening. Vining (1992), for example, showed that positive emotional affinity for nature was a strong motivational force for individuals who entered careers in environmental and resource management. Similarly,

Kearins and Sharma (2007) also found emotion to be an important factor in driving sustainability careers.

Another aspect of the between-persons level is the trait of emotional intelligence (2003). Although the trait of emotion intelligence is yet to be studied in depth in relation to organizational greening, it may be important in understanding greening behavior. Defined as an individual's capacity to deal with emotions in everyday life (Ashkanasy, 2003, p. 24), emotional intelligence is a relevant variable that can impact behavior, but it is not a direct measurement of emotional expressions or experiences.

Research studies by Egri and Herman (2000) and Andersson and Bateman (2000) hint at the importance of emotional intelligence for those individuals who are involved in organizational greening. Egri and Herman (2000) investigated the concept of *emotional maturity*, rather than emotional intelligence, although the two constructs do have similarities. What Egri and Herman found was that emotional maturity was a significant factor in predicting the environmental leadership success of not-for-profit organizations, but not for-profit organizations.

The work of Andersson and Bateman (2000) may also suggest that emotional intelligence is important in determining the success of environmental champions. In their study of environmental championing behavior, Andersson and Bateman found that the most successful champions were those that were able to sell environmental issues in a way that was aligned with the organizational context or paradigm. In other words, those individuals who were most successful in selling environmental issues were also those who were aware of the emotional climate of the organization and were able to sell their environmental issues accordingly.

The studies described in this section demonstrate the importance of emotion as a driver of pro-environmental behavior. Research has shown that both positive and negative emotions are important (Kals et al., 1999; Pooley & O'Connor, 2000) and that discrete emotions can lead to differential effects on pro-environmental behavior (Andersson et al., 2007; Bamberg et al., 2007; Giacalone et al., 2005). Although these studies certainly add to knowledge of the role of between-person emotions and pro-environmental behavior, more research is needed. Vining and Ebreo (2002), for example, suggest that additional research on self-conscious emotions such as pride, shame, and guilt, may be particularly important for future research.

The evidence of emotion at this level also shows that emotional intelligence may be important in determining the success of environmental champions (Andersson & Bateman, 2000; Egri & Herman, 2000). This suggests that the most successful environmental champions may be those who have higher emotional intelligence. Without strong empirical data to support this proposition, however, this relationship remains speculative. Therefore, future research that examines the relationship between emotional intelligence and championing success would be valuable in advancing this area of research.

Level 3: Interpersonal Interactions and Emotions

The third level includes the emotions of interpersonal interactions, and this involves the communication of emotion. At this level of analysis emotions can be considered a relational phenomenon and they are therefore the central tenants of literature on emotions in organizations. Ashkanasy (2003) suggests that emotions at this level of analysis serve as the links between Levels 1 and 2 (at the micro-level) and Levels 4 and 5 (at the group and organizational levels). As such, Level 3 of the model can be considered a meso-level construct (Rousseau, 1985).

Emotion is an essential element of communication and it has been shown to be an important signal of message importance or relevance (Clore, 1994). Nonverbal emotions that are displayed via facial expressions, voice tone, and body language also have been shown to indicate the importance of a message (Ekman, 1982). Thus the communicative function of emotion is critically important (Ashkanasy, 2003).

Evidence from environmental psychology suggests that valence and intensity of emotion in communication has an impact on pro-environmental actions. For example, Lord (1994) grouped emotions according to their valence (either positive or negative), and demonstrated that both positive and negative messages have a significant impact on pro-environmental action and attitudes. In his experimental study of recycling behavior, he found that those messages that were positively framed tended to engender positive attitudes, belief in the recycling message, and inducement of pro-environmental action. However, contrary to his hypotheses, he found that negatively framed appeals were also an effective means of increasing recycling behavior. Such findings suggest that both positive and negative emotions can be inducements of pro-environmental action.

Vining (1987) has also conducted experimental research using variables of emotional communication. In this case, however, she did not test the valence of emotion, but, rather, the intensity. In her study she presented scenarios in which participants were forced to decide for or against a development application based on the environmental information they were given. Vining found that individuals presented with information using a "hot" emotional style were more likely to be make a pro-preservation decision, compared to those who received information that was less emotive, or "cool." Based on these findings, it is possible that the intensity of emotion (hot or cool) is likely to impact the pro-environmental actions of individuals.

More recent work has tended to focus on climate change communication. O'Neill and Nicholson-Cole (2009), for example, demonstrated that fear-inducing representations of climate change were effective in attracting attention; however, they were ineffective in motivating genuine personal engagement in pro-environmental behaviors. Rather, they found that nonthreatening imagery that links to individuals' everyday emotions and concerns tended to be most engaging.

Wright and Nyberg (2012) researched the responses to climate change from another interpersonal perspective. Their study focused on the role of corporate sustainability specialists as intermediaries, or "emotionology workers," acting between the social discourse and organizational contexts (Wright & Nyberg, 2012). Wright and Nyberg drew on the work of Stearns and Stearns (1985, p. 813) in describing emotionologies as the "attitudes or standards that a society, or a definable group within a society, maintains towards basic emotions and their appropriate expression" and the "ways that institutions reflect and encouraged these attitudes in human conduct" (Wright & Nyberg, 2012, p. 1562). Wright and Nyberg found that sustainability professionals are key agents in the design and implementation of a positive emotionology toward an environmental issue.

Opotow and Weiss (2000) also studied the development of emotions in response to an environmental challenge. With respect to the threat of global warming, they showed how individuals avoid being informed about an inconvenient issue. They noted that the "denial of self-involvement minimizes the extent to which an environmental dispute is relevant to one's self or one's group . . . By casting themselves as 'clean' and insignificant contributors to pollution, they assert their nonrelevance to environmental controversy" (Opotow & Weiss, 2000, p. 485). Opotow and Weiss showed how an emotional reaction, the denial of self-involvement, can influence the perception of an environmental threat within a (sub)group of individuals, leading to neglecting the appropriate and socially demanded group response.

At this level of analysis we note a tendency for researchers to examine emotions according to either positive or negative valence, with the very few exceptions (cf., O'Neill & Nicholson-Cole, 2009; Wright & Nyberg, 2012). Contemporary emotions scholars (Briner & Kiefer, 2005; Elfenbein, 2007; Gooty, Ashkanasy, & Gavin, 2009; Seo, Feldman Barrett, & Jin, 2008) have made the point that it is no longer sufficient to study emotion in terms of just positive and negative affective valence. This is because discrete emotions with a particular affective valance (e.g., anger and sadness are both examples of negative affect) may have differential effects. We argue that the study of discrete emotions is of utmost importance in understanding the effect of emotion on behavior across all levels of analysis, but particularly in relation to communication, which has to date been dominated by research on positive or negative emotions. Indeed, although the research we have described has demonstrated that emotional communications can influence pro-environmental behavior, much less is understood about the differential effects of discrete emotions.

Level 4: Group-Level Emotions

Groups can be defined as "a collection of two or more people who work with one another regularly to achieve common goals" (Schermerhorn, Hunt, & Osborn, 2001, p. 174). Although groups interact on a dyadic and collective basis, they also add an additional layer of complexity to relationships and emotions. Ashkanasy (2003) therefore considers groups as a separate level to the dyadic interactions described at Level 3. Research on emotions and organizational greening often explores individual-level emotions with relatively little attention paid to phenomena at the more macro-levels of the group or organization. Indeed, our literature search returned a distinct lack of research that was particularly relevant at the group level of analysis. Yet, as noted in Ashkanasy's model (2003), emotions at the group and organizational level are also an important focus for research in this domain.

There is, however, some research to suggest the importance of groups for sustainability issues, particularly in relation to how groups or subcultures can affect the depth and diffusion of pro-environmental change within organizations. For example, Howard-Grenville (2006) found that subcultures can influence how organizational members interpret problems and set agendas and strategies for resolving them. Similarly, Linnenluecke, Russell, and Griffiths (2009) showed that the dominance of bureaucratic subcultures within an organization led to a focus on economic dimensions of sustainability. This research demonstrates how members of a subculture understand and enact sustainability within their organization in line with the dominant subculture of the organization. Although these studies do not directly measure emotion, they do demonstrate how the collective understanding of a group can influence the course of action taken in response to environmental- or sustainability-related issues.

Although research on organizational greening at the group level is scant, there is one study that is particularly relevant. Welcomer, Gioia, and Kilduff (2000) demonstrated how emotion affected two groups in their negotiation of a significant environmental problem. Welcomer et al. (2000) studied communications between the developers of a hazardous waste facility and the community that would be located near the facility. In their analysis of positive and negative emotions of stakeholder groups they found that emotionality was an important dimension in the discourse between communities and corporations. They found that the dominant negative emotionality expressed in the community's discourse clashed with the rational discourse of the developers, resulting in poor communication outcomes. This study highlights how the emotionality of an environmental issue can cause communication between groups to break down, ultimately leading to the disruption and breakdown of communication between two groups.

Although research at the group level was scant, the evidence does suggest that group-level emotions play an important role in the collective understanding of sustainability and the depth and degree of uptake of pro-environmental behaviors. Furthermore, Welcomer et al. (2000) showed that emotions are an important part of the collective understanding of environmental issues. Research tells us that emotions are contagious and spread among group members (Barsade, 2002), yet there is a lack of knowledge about how emotional responses to environmental issues spread within groups. Emotions at a group level can influence individuals from the bottom up or top down (Barsade & Gibson, 1998). Yet little is known about how to manage emotions that arise in response to issues like climate change. For example, climate change may prompt strong and divergent emotions for group members, and these different responses may lead to conflict. As emotional responses intensify, such conflict becomes more difficult to manage. Further research at this level will be important in exploring the relationships among individual-, group-, and organizational-level emotions.

Level 5: Organization-Wide Emotions

The fifth and final level of Ashkanasy's (2003) multi-level model of emotions is the organizational level. This level of analysis is different from the other levels in that at the lower levels of analysis organizational policies and practices can be interpreted in the context of interactions between individuals and groups. In dealing with the organization-wide or macro view, however, the situation becomes much less clear. Although some interactions may indicate emotion at the organizational level, it is much less explicit. Rather, at this level of analysis it is necessary to deal with the emotional climate of the organization; defined by De Rivera (1992, p. 197) as "an objective group phenomenon that can be palpably sensed—as when one enters a party or a city and feels an attitude of gaiety or depression, openness or fear." The concept of the emotional climate is quite separate from organizational culture in that the organizational climate is essentially an emotional phenomenon, whereas culture can be considered more stable and rooted in beliefs, values, and embedded assumptions (Ashkanasy, 2003; Ashkanasy, Wilderom, & Peterson, 2000).

Research of emotions at the organization level is a relatively new but growing area within organization theory (Campbell, White, & Johnson, 2003; Madlock, 2008; Voronov & Vince, 2012). One reason for the lack of research at this level is that members of organizations may perceive emotions in a professional context as irrational, leading to subjective and potentially unfavorable outcomes that lack legitimacy (Fineman, 2000, 2003). Yet as shown by Fineman (2000) and Ashkanasy (2003), emotions and rationality are not exclusive but intertwined. They frame, for example, the interpersonal interactions within organizations (Ashkanasy, 2003), how an issue is interpreted (Sharma, 2000), or how an organization reacts to change in its organizational field (Voronov & Vince, 2012).

Norgaard's (2011) work provides evidence of individual- and organizational-level emotional reactions in discourse around climate change. Her work demonstrates that some organizations have strong emotional responses in their organizational climates. These emotional responses, however, depend largely on the values and beliefs that are collectively shared within the organization's culture (Norgaard, 2011). Research by Wright and Nyberg (2012) has also demonstrated the emotionality of climate change at the organizational level. In their research of large corporations, Wright and Nyberg investigated how organizations define their response to the emotionology surrounding the public discourse on climate change.

Unpredictable environmental events such as the BP oil spill in the Gulf of Mexico in 2010 or the nuclear incident in Fukushima in 2011 can have a significant impact on an organization and trigger a collective emotional response. In organizations, such events can lead to anxiety as members experience disrupted work routines and operations (Pearson & Clair, 1998). Such crises can trigger emotions such as anger at those who caused events, guilt for those at fault, and hopelessness and despair at acts of nature, or grief for what has been lost (James, Wooten, & Dushek, 2011).

In broader sustainability-related contexts, the effect of emotions is illustrated in issues of renewable energies (Sherry-Brennan, Devine-Wright, & Devine-Wright, 2010), sustainable management practices (Branzei, Vertinsky, & Zietsma, 2000; Sekerka & Stimel, 2012), as well is in relation to climate change (Norgaard, 2011; Wright & Nyberg, 2012). The emotional climate that develops in response to an environmental issue can influence how the organization addresses such important issues. Sharma (2000) and Hoffman (1997) for instance, argue that the options considered by an organization in response to a sustainability-driven change can be limited by the emotional interpretation of it. Furthermore, Wright, Nyberg, and Grant (2012) state that the emotionology that develops within an organization in response to an environmental issue like climate change has an influence on its strategic response. Indeed, they noted that the discourses of "profitability" and "shareholder value" competed with the broader social discourse around "climate change." The competition between the organizational and broader social discourses influenced the emotionality of the issue (Wright & Nyberg, 2012). The work of Hulme (2009) has extended this notion from the organizational to societal level by suggesting that cognitive and behavioral barriers prevent society as a whole from meaningfully responding to climate change.

Fineman (1996) has also conducted research that is relevant to emotions at the organizational level. Fineman (1996, 1998) investigated greening behaviors in organizations and found that both positive and negative emotions played a strategic role in the adoption of pro-environmental behaviors within organizations. In the more environmentally proactive organizations he studied, he found that managers spoke of positive emotions in relation to commitment to environmental issues, citing emotions such as belonging, respect, awe, and loyalty. However, he also found that negative emotions, such as fear and embarrassment also played a role. In explaining these findings he suggests that the most proactive organizations, and those with the highest public profile, had the most to fear from public embarrassment. The managers in these organizations had "invested their image and reputation in claims for environmental care, loss of face could be a blow to role identity, to professional status within the company and to corporate image" (Fineman, 1996, p. 491).

Managers from less environmentally committed supermarkets did not display the same level of fear of embarrassment. Fineman (1996) suggested that these organizations and their managers had, in effect, less to lose. As they did not claim to be going beyond minimum levels of environmental compliance, they had no environmental reputation to defend, and therefore believed they could not be significantly embarrassed by public criticism (Fineman, 1996). Particularly, the role of fear as described by Fineman suggests that managers' displays of emotion were based on their organization's environmental paradigm and commitment.

Although there is increasingly more research at this level of analysis, there is a lack of understanding of the role and effect of emotions at the organization level (Bell & Taylor, 2011; Huy, 2012; Kangasharju & Nikko, 2009; Smollan & Sayers, 2009). It is clear that emotions affect decision making (Bechara, Damasio, & Damasio, 2000), and given the importance of organizational decisions to create and resolve environmental issues, it is imperative that academics and managers gain a better understanding of emotions at the organizational level as they relate to organizational greening. We know that emotions influence how an organization interprets an environmental issue (Sharma, 2000), that environmental agents play a key role in defining an organization's emotionology around climate change (Wright & Nyberg, 2012), and how emotions in response to an event that significantly distresses an organization can affect its members (Pearson & Clair, 1998); yet more remains to be done. We identify three key areas as priorities for research at this level of analysis. First, research is needed to examine how emotions become part of the organizational climate; second, how emotions influence the identity and culture of an organization; and third, how emotions affect an organization's response to environmental issues. A deeper knowledge of these processes is necessary to understand the potentially critical role that organizational-level emotions play in determining an organization's culture, identity, and environmental strategy. Furthermore, we suggest that one opportunity to respond to this call is the application of individual-level psychological theories to the organization-level in order to enhance our understanding of organizational emotions (Bowman, 1982; Shimizu, 2007; Staw, Sandelands, & Dutton, 1981).

The work cited in the preceding paragraph highlights a tension at the organizational level of analysis. Indeed, although the level of analysis is at the organizational level there is also a capturing of expressions of emotions at the individual level. Hence, the tension arises among the micro-, meso-, and macro-levels of analysis. In the final section of this chapter we outline these issues and offer a future agenda for research that may shed light on the interrelationships among these levels and enhance understanding of how emotion operates at all levels of analysis and can both enhance and impede organizational greening efforts.

Cross-Level Emotions

In this chapter we have examined research from the most micro-level of emotional experience through to the macro-view of emotions within organizational climate. A recurring theme throughout our review, however, is the interconnectedness among levels of analysis. In this section we highlight those studies that explicitly examine cross-level emotions and effects. These studies illustrate the dynamic nature of emotions and the interrelatedness of emotional variables across all levels of analysis (Ashkanasy, 2003).

The findings from Bissing-Olson et al. (2013) demonstrate the importance of considering multiple levels of analysis. Indeed, what Bissing-Olson et al. found was that it was the relationship between fluctuations in emotion at the within-person level (Level 1) in conjunction with individual differences at the between-person level (Level 2) that explained pro-environmental behavior within the workplace. More specifically, they found that daily unactivated positive affect and pro-environmental attitude positively predicted task-related pro-environmental behavior. Furthermore, daily activated positive affect positively predicted daily proactive pro-environmental behavior but only among employees with a less positive pro-environmental attitude. These findings show that the emotions at the within-person level have an important role to play as a driver of behavior at the individual level.

Wright and Nyberg (2012) have also demonstrated cross-level emotion effects. Their research showed how sustainability professionals were key agents in the design and implementation of a positive emotionology toward an environmental issue, thus connecting the individual (Level 2) with the collective emotionology and within the group (Level 4) and the organization (Level 5).

The work of Norgaard (2006) connects individual (Level 2), interpersonal (Level 3), and group-level (Level 4) phenomena. She studied the reasons for climate change denial by analyzing the reactions of individuals in a remote village in Norway in response to climate change impacts. Her study outlines how an individual's perception of an issue is self-reinforced through interpersonal interaction and can lead to collectively shared emotions and group-level reactions. She "attempts to highlight the importance of these dimensions in a way that bridges the troublesome, yet nevertheless artificial, gap between micro- and macro social processes" (Norgaard, 2006, p. 364). In this way, Norgaard highlights how emotions can span levels of analysis and she notes the somewhat false sense that our research can be categorized within one level.

Although Bissing-Olson et al. (2013) and Norgaard (2006) show how emotions flow from the micro- to the macro-level, Fineman's (1996, 1998) work highlights processes in the opposite direction. Indeed, what he found was that the type of organization (proactive or reactive) (Level 5) helped to determine the sorts of emotional expressions he observed when interviewing managers (Level 2) within those organizations. Andersson and Bateman (2000) have also shown how the organizational climate (Level 5) can influence how environmental champions go about selling environmental issues within their organizations (Level 2).

A Future Research Agenda

In this chapter, we have examined the role of emotion in organizational greening from the most micro-level of emotional experience to the macro-view of emotions as they relate to organizational climate and culture. In this final section we aim to emphasize three key themes that have come out of this review with the aim of setting a research agenda for future work in this area. In particular, we emphasize the need for future research to develop further in the exploration of emotions at macro-level analyses, the examination of relationships across multiple levels of analysis, and the exploration of emotion as a longitudinal process. We address each of these implications for research in turn and conclude the chapter by outlining some of the key implications for practice.

Implications for Research

A key area for future research is the need to study emotions at more macro levels of analysis. We note that there were far fewer studies at Levels 4 and 5 and this warrants further attention. Indeed, although research on emotions in an organizational context has gained more attention in recent years, studies examining the effect of emotions on an organizational level remain scarce (Kangasharju & Nikko, 2009; Voronov & Vince, 2012). In particular, we encourage future researchers to develop a better understanding of the role of emotions at the organizational level (Huy, 2012; Kangasharju & Nikko, 2009). There remains a lack of research on the processes leading to collectively shared emotions and their respective effects on an organization's culture, strategy, or identity. Therefore, we suggest that research that examines how emotions progress from the individual to the organization and vice versa will be important in advancing understanding of how emotions affect organizational greening.

One of the significant challenges in examining emotions at the macro-level of analysis is that it remains difficult to measure. It is more difficult to gather data that validates the evolution of an emotional climate within an organization than it is to gather data at the individual level. Although psychologists have developed a number of methods and tools to observe emotions on an individual level, as indicated in the literature we cite in Levels 1, 2, and 3, the gathering of data mirroring emotions that are collectively shared at the organizational level presents a challenge for organizational researchers. We suggest that the development and application of a set of tools to measure emotions on an organization level would allow a more comprehensive understanding of the role of emotions in organizations in the context of organizational greening. This could enhance understanding of the role of emotions in the development of environmental strategies, the perception and evaluation of sustainability-related risks, or the formulation of strategic responses to green challenges.

The research we have described in the preceding sections shows that organizations are inherently emotional places (Ashkanasy & Ashton-James, 2005; Elfenbein, 2007; Voronov & Vince, 2012). We note, however, that most of these studies focus on emotion states at one point in time. Although such research helps to further understanding of the important role and effects that emotions can and do have in a management context, these studies largely do not acknowledge the astatic nature of emotions.

Medical studies draw a much more sophisticated picture of emotional reactions as a process, rather than a state. Indeed, many of these types of studies investigate the process of emotional change over time in relation to a specific issue or event. Kübler-Ross (1969), for example, showed that in grief an individual goes through a process of emotions, including denial, anger, bargaining, depression, and acceptance. Zell (2003) argued that this process also applies to organizational change and thus demonstrates that emotions can form a process rather than a state.

Especially with regard to organizational greening, a field in which public, governmental, and corporate perceptions and responses significantly change over time, there is a need to gain a better understanding of the role of emotions as they change. Senge et al. (2006) noted that, "as people become more committed to sustainability work, they will gain a deeper understanding of their own emotional energy and their ability for contemplation." Ashkanasy (2003) also recognized the dynamic nature of emotion, yet to date we have not observed research that takes a longitudinal perspective to examine the evolution of emotions over time as they relate to organizational greening. We therefore call for further research investigating how emotions evolve and their respective role in environmental change processes.

Finally, we suggest that research that crosses levels of analyses would be of benefit in advancing knowledge in this area. A recurring theme throughout our chapter is the interrelatedness of variables across all of the levels of analysis. Indeed, although we have attempted to categorized the research studies into each of the levels of Ashkanasy's (2003) multi-level model, this categorization is somewhat false in that many of the articles could be considered to span multiple levels. We have attempted to highlight specifically when this occurs. For example, research by Bissing-Olson et al. (2013) spans both the within-person level of analysis (Level 1) and the between-person level of analysis (Level 2). Similarly, Norgaard's (2011) work on climate change discourses moves between the level of communication (Level 3), groups (Level 4), and organizations (Level 5). These scholars highlight the complexity of studying emotion and the interrelationships that occur between levels of analysis. We would encourage further research that examines emotion both within and across all five levels of analysis.

In summary, we argue that stronger integration of emotional theories is needed in organizational greening research across all levels of analysis (Voronov & Vince, 2012). We argue that this is particularly important when considering environmental issues, which have been demonstrated to be more emotional than other issues within organizations (Fineman, 1996, 1997; Pratt, 2000). Battilana and D'Aunno (2009) state that organizational research has the two boundaries of a "rational choice model of agency on one side and structural determinism on the other" (Battilana & D'Aunno, 2009, p. 73). Voronov and Vince (2012), however, note that this determination neglects the importance of emotions and "their complicity with domination, and their contribution to both reproducing and transforming the institutional order" (Voronov & Vince, 2012, p. 73). The two are closely intertwined, yet despite their impact on an organization level they have not received much attention by organizational scholars (Madlock, 2008). We argue that a much stronger consideration and integration of emotional theories in organization studies is needed particularly in the consideration of environmental issues in general, and climate change in particular.

Implications for Practice

In this chapter we have used Ashkanasy's (2003) framework to illustrate how emotions in organizational greening occur at all levels of analysis, from the most fundamental level that includes fluctuations in day-to-day emotions of all employees, through to the shared emotional experiences of organizational members that make up the emotional climate of the organization. Research results to date show that emotions are important determinants of pro-environmental behavior. Indeed, there is evidence to suggest that the arousal of positive emotions is a significant determinant of workplace pro-environmental behaviors (Bissing-Olson et al., 2013) and corporate social responsibility (Andersson et al., 2007; Giacalone et al., 2005). These findings at the micro-level suggest that there may be some efficacy in promoting positive emotions when encouraging employees to engage in pro-environmental behavior. This could be facilitated, for example, by facilitating positive work events (Weiss & Cropanzano, 1996). Future research that tests this proposition would be beneficial in advancing the practical relevance of this research and enhancing future intervention design.

There is also evidence to suggest that emotions are important in determining career choice in organizational greening (Kearins & Sharma, 2007; Vining, 1992). Once in a greening-related career, it is also possible that emotional intelligence skills may be important for future success (Andersson & Bateman, 2000; Egri & Herman, 2000). It is therefore possible that the success of environmental champions or change agents might be improved by training in emotional competencies. Future research that further examines the relationship between emotional intelligence and organizational greening success would be of particular benefit to change agents and environmental champions.

Conclusion

In conclusion, the research we have described in this chapter demonstrates the beginnings of a valuable stream of study in emotions and organizational greening. There are many questions that remain unanswered and many opportunities for scholars in this area to make a unique contribution to research and practice. Our aim in this chapter was to review current research in emotions and organizational greening and to set an agenda for future research in this burgeoning area. Organizational psychologists and organizational behavior researchers have an important role to play in further developing understanding of how individuals and organizations can most effectively respond to environmental issues. We hope that by setting this agenda we will encourage more scholars to pursue research in this area and that their results have a positive impact on the future practice of organizational greening.

Acknowledgment

The authors gratefully acknowledge the feedback and suggestions provided by Judith Walls on an earlier version of this chapter.

Suggested Additional Readings

1. Senge, P., Laur, J., Schley, S., & Smith, B. (2006). *Learning for sustainability*. Cambridge, MA: The Society for Organizational Learning.
2. Goleman, D. (2009). *Ecological intelligence: Knowing the hidden impacts of what we buy*. New York: Penguin.
3. Tolle, E. (2006). *A new earth*. New York: Penguin.

References

Andersson, L. M., & Bateman, T. S. (2000). Individual environmental initiative: Championing natural environmental issues in U.S. business organizations. *Academy of Management Journal, 43*, 548–570.

Andersson, L. M., Giacalone, R. A., & Jurkiewicz, C. (2007). On the relationship of hope and gratitude to corporate social responsibility. *Journal of Business Ethics, 70*, 401–409.

Ashforth, B. E., & Humphrey, R. H. (1995). Emotion in the workplace: A reappraisal. *Human Relations, 48*, 97–125.

Ashkanasy, N. M. (2003). Emotions in organizations: A multi-level perspective. In F. Dansereau, & F. J. Yammarino (Eds.), *Multi-level issues in organizational behavior and strategy* (pp. 9–54). Amsterdam: JAI.

Ashkanasy, N. M., & Ashton-James, C. E. (2005). Emotion in organizations: A neglected topic in I/O psychology, but with a bright future. In G. P. Hodgkinson, & J. K. Ford (Eds.), *International review of industrial and organizational psychology* (Vol. 20, pp. 221–268). Chichester, UK: Wiley.

Ashkanasy, N. M., Wilderom, C. P. M., & Peterson, M. F. (2000). *Handbook of Organizational Culture & Climate*. Thousand Oaks, CA: Sage.

Bamberg, S., Hunecke, M., & Blöbaum, A. (2007). Social context, personal norms and the use of public transportation: Two field studies. *Journal of Environmental Psychology, 27*, 190–203.

Bamberg, S., & Möser, G. (2007). Twenty years after Hines, Hungerford, and Tomera: A new meta-analysis of psycho-social determinants of pro-environmental behavior. *Journal of Environmental Psychology, 27*, 14–25.

Barsade, S. G. (2002). The ripple effect: Emotional contagion and its influence on group behavior. *Administrative Science Quarterly, 47*, 644–675.

Barsade, S. G., Brief, A. P., & Spataro, S. E. (2003). The affective revolution in organizational behavior: The emergence of a paradigm. In J. Greenberg (Ed.), *Organizational behavior: State of the science* (2nd ed., pp. 3–50). Mahwah, NJ: Lawrence Erlbaum.

Barsade, S. G., & Gibson, D. E. (1998). Group emotion: A view from top and bottom. In D. Gruenfeld, M. Neale, & E. Mannix (Eds.), *Research on managing in groups and teams* (Vol. 1, pp. 81–102). Greenwich, CT: JAI Press.

Battilana, J., & D'Aunno, T. (2009). Institutional work and the paradox of embedded agency. In T. B. Lawrence, R. Suddaby, & B. Leca (Eds.), *Institutional work: Actors and agency in institutional studies of organizations* (pp. 31–58). Cambridge, UK: Cambridge University Press.

Bechara, A., Damasio, H., & Damasio, A. R. (2000). Emotion, decision making and the orbitofrontal cortex. *Cerebral Cortex, 10*(3), 295–307.

Bell, E., & Taylor, S. (2011). Beyond letting go and moving on: New perspectives on organizational death, loss and grief. *Scandinavian Journal of Management, 27*, 1–10.

Bissing-Olson, M., Iyer, A., Fielding, K., & Zacher, H. (2013). Relationships between daily affect and pro-environmental behavior at work: The moderating role of pro-environmental attitude. *Journal of Organizational Behavior, 34*, 156–175.

Bowman, E. H. (1982). Risk seeking by troubled firms. *Sloan Management Review, 23*, 33–42.

Branzei, O., Vertinsky, I., & Zietsma, C. (2000). From green-blindness to the pursuit of eco-sustainability: An empirical investigation of leader cognitions and corporate environmental strategy choices. *Academy of Management Proceedings, 2000*, 1.

Briner, R. B., & Kiefer, T. (2005). Psychological research into the experience of emotion at work: Definitely older, but are we any wiser? In N. M. Ashkanasy,

C. E. J. Härtel, & W. J. Zerbe (Eds.), *The effect of affect in organizational settings* (Vol. 1, pp. 281–307). Amsterdam: Elsevier JAI.

Campbell, K. S., White, C. D., & Johnson, D. E. (2003). Leader-member relations as a function of rapport management. *Journal of Business Communication, 40*, 170–194.

Clore, G. C. (1994). Why emotions are felt. In P. Ekman, & R. J. Davidson (Eds.), *The nature of emotions* (pp. 103–111). New York: Oxford University Press.

De Rivera, J. (1992). Emotional climate: Social structure and emotional dynamics. *International Review of Studies of Emotion, 2*, 197–218.

Egri, C. P., & Herman, S. (2000). Leadership in the North American environmental sector: Values, leadership styles, and contexts of environmental leaders and their organizations. *Academy of Management Journal, 43*, 571–604.

Ekman, P. (1982). *Emotion in the human face* (2nd ed.). Cambridge, UK: Cambridge University Press.

Elfenbein, H. A. (2007). Emotion in organizations: A review and theoretical integration. *The Academy of Management Annals, 1*, 315–386.

Fineman, S. (1996). Emotional subtexts in corporate greening. *Organization Studies, 17*, 479–500.

Fineman, S. (1997). Constructing the green manager. *British Journal of Management, 8*, 31–38.

Fineman, S. (1998). Street-level bureaucrats and the social construction of environmental control. *Organization Studies, 19*, 953–974.

Fineman, S. (2000). *Emotion in organizations* (2nd ed.). London: Sage.

Fineman, S. (2003). *Understanding emotion at work*. London: Sage.

Forgas, J. P. (1994). The role of emotion in social judgements: An introductory review and an Affect Infusion Model (AIM). *European Journal of Social Psychology, 24*, 1–24.

Forgas, J. P. (1995). Mood and judgment: The affect infusion model (AIM). *Psychological Bulletin, 117*, 39–66.

Fox, S., & Spector, P. E. (2000). Relations of emotional intelligence, practical intelligence, general intelligence, and trait affectivity with interview outcomes: It's not all just "G." *Journal of Organizational Behavior, 21*, 203–220.

Fredrickson, B. L. (2003). Positive emotions and upward spirals in organizations. In K. S. Cameron, J. E. Dutton, & R. E. Quinn (Eds.), *Positive organizational scholarship: Foundations of a new discipline* (pp. 163–176). San Francisco: Berrett-Koehler.

Frijda, N. H. (1986). *The emotions*. Cambridge, UK: Cambridge University Press.

Frijda, N. H. (1993). Moods, emotion episodes and emotions. In M. Lewis, & J. Haviland (Eds.), *Handbook of emotions* (pp. 381–403). New York: Guilford Press.

Giacalone, R. A., Paul, K., & Jurkiewics, C. L. (2005). A preliminary investigation into the role of positive psychology in consumer sensitivity to corporate social performance. *Journal of Business Ethics, 58*, 295–305.

Gooty, J., Ashkanasy, N. M., & Gavin, M. (2009). Emotions research in OB: The challenges that lie ahead. *Journal of Organizational Behavior, 30,* 833–838.

Hoffman, A. J. (1997). *From heresy to dogma: An institutional history of corporate environmentalism.* San Francisco: New Lexington Press.

Howard-Grenville, J. A. (2006). Inside the "black box": How organizational culture and subcultures inform interpretations and actions on environmental issues. *Organization & Environment, 19,* 46–73.

Hulme, M. (2009). *Why we disagree about climate change: Understanding controversy, inaction and opportunity.* Cambridge, UK: Cambridge University Press.

Huy, Q. N. (2012). Emotions in strategic organization: Opportunities for impactful research. *Strategic Organization, 10,* 240–247.

Izard, C. E. (1991). *The psychology of emotions.* New York: Plenum Press.

James, E. H., Wooten, L. P., & Dushek, K. (2011). Crisis management: Informing a new leadership research agenda. *The Academy of Management Annals, 5,* 455–493.

Kals, E., Schumacher, D., & Montada, L. (1999). Emotional affinity toward nature as a basis to protect nature. *Environment and Behavior, 31,* 178–202.

Kangasharju, H., & Nikko, T. (2009). Emotions in organizations. *Journal of Business Communication, 46,* 100–119.

Kearins, K., & Sharma, A. (2007). *The passion that drives sustainability careers. The yellow brick road to doing well by doing good: Finding our brain, heart, and courage.* Philadelphia: Academy of Management.

Kübler-Ross, E. (1969). *On death and dying.* New York: Macmillan.

Lazarus, R. S. (1991). *Emotion and adaptation.* New York: Oxford University Press.

Linnenluecke, M. K., Russell, S. V., & Griffiths, A. (2009). Subcultures and sustainability practices: The impact on understanding corporate sustainability. *Business Strategy and the Environment, 18,* 432–452.

Lord, K. R. (1994). Motivating recycling behavior: A quasiexperimental investigation of message and source strategies. *Psychology & Marketing, 11,* 341–358.

Madlock, P. E. (2008). The link between leadership style, communication competence, and employee satisfaction. *Journal of Business Communication, 45,* 61–78.

Norgaard, K. M. (2006). "We don't really want to know": Environmental justice and socially organized denial of global warming in Norway. *Organization & Environment, 19,* 347–370.

Norgaard, K. M. (2011). *Living in denial: Climate change, emotions and everyday life.* Cambridge, MA: MIT Press.

O'Neill, S., & Nicholson-Cole, S. (2009). "Fear won't do it": Promoting positive engagement with climate change through visual and iconic representations. *Science Communication, 30,* 355–379.

Opotow, S., & Weiss, L. (2000). Denial and the process of moral exclusion in environmental conflict. *Journal of Social Issues, 56,* 475–490.

Pearson, C. M., & Clair, J. A. (1998). Reframing crisis management. *Academy of Management Review, 23,* 59–76.

Pooley, J. A., & O'Connor, M. (2000). Environmental education and attitudes: Emotions and beliefs are what is needed. *Environment and Behavior*, *32*, 711–723.

Pratt, M. G. (2000). The good, the bad, and the ambivalent: Managing identification among Amway distributors. *Administrative Science Quarterly*, *45*, 456–493.

Rousseau, D. M. (1985). Issues of level in organizational research: Multi-level and cross-level perspectives. *Research in Organizational Behavior*, *7*, 1–37.

Russell, S., & Griffiths, A. (2008). The role of emotions in driving workplace pro-environmental behaviors. In W. Zerbe, N. M. Ashkanasy, & C. E. J. Härtel (Eds.), *Managing emotions in the workplace* (pp. 83–107). New York: M. E. Sharpe.

Scherer, K. R. (2000). Emotion. In M. Hewstone, & W. Stroebe (Eds.), *Introduction to social psychology: A European perspective* (3rd ed., pp. 151–191). Oxford, UK: Blackwell.

Schermerhorn, R. R., Jr., Hunt, J. G., & Osborn, R. N. (2001). *Organizational behavior* (7th ed.). New York: Wiley.

Sekerka, L. E., & Stimel, D. (2012). Environmental sustainability decision-making: clearing a path to change. *Journal of Public Affairs*, *12*, 195–205.

Senge, P., Laur, J., Schley, S., & Smith, B. (2006). *Learning for sustainability*. Cambridge, MA: The Society for Organizational Learning.

Seo, M.-G., Feldman Barrett, L., & Jin, S. (2008). The structure of affect: History, theory, and implications for emotion research in organizations. In N. M. Ashkanasy, & C. L. Cooper (Eds.), *Research companion to emotions in organizations* (pp. 17–44). Cheltenham, UK: Edwin Elgar.

Sharma, S. (2000). Managerial interpretations and organizational context as predictors of corporate choice of environmental strategy. *Academy of Management Journal*, *43*, 681–697.

Sherry-Brennan, F., Devine-Wright, H., & Devine-Wright, P. (2010). Public understanding of hydrogen energy: A theoretical approach. *Energy Policy*, *38*, 5311–5319.

Shimizu, K. (2007). Prospect theory, behavioral theory, and the threat-rigidity thesis: Combinative effects on organizational decisions to divest formerly acquired units. *Academy of Management Journal*, *50*, 1495–1514.

Smollan, R. K., & Sayers, J. G. (2009). Organizational culture, change and emotions: A qualitative study. *Journal of Change Management*, *9*, 435–457.

Staw, B. M., & Barsade, S. G. (1993). Affect and managerial performance: A test of the sadder-but-wiser vs. happier-and-smarter hypotheses. *Administrative Science Quarterly*, *38*, 304–328.

Staw, B. M., Sandelands, L. E., & Dutton, J. E. (1981). Threat-rigidity effects in organizational behavior: A multilevel analysis. *Administrative Science Quarterly*, *26*, 501–524.

Stearns, P. N., & Stearns, C. Z. (1985). Emotionology: Clarifying the history of emotions and emotional standards. *The American Historical Review*, *90*, 813–836.

Steg, L., & Vlek, C. (2009). Encouraging pro-environmental behaviour: An integrative review and research agenda. *Journal of Environmental Psychology*, *29*, 309–317.

To, M. L., Fisher, C. D., Ashkanasy, N. M., & Rowe, P. A. (2012). Within-person relationships between mood and creativity. *Journal of Applied Psychology*, *97*, 599–612.

Vining, J. (1987). Environmental decisions: The interaction of emotions, information, and decision context. *Journal of Environmental Psychology*, *7*, 13–30.

Vining, J. (1992). Environmental emotions and decisions: A comparison of the responses and expectations of forest managers, an environmental group, and the public. *Environment and Behavior*, *24*, 3–34.

Vining, J., & Ebreo, A. (2002). Emerging theoretical and methodological perspectives on conservation behavior. In R. B. Bechtel, & A. Churchman (Eds.), *Handbook of environmental psychology* (pp. 541–558). New York: John Wiley & Sons.

Voronov, M., & Vince, R. (2012). Integrating emotions into the analysis of institutional work. *Academy of Management Review*, *37*, 58–81.

Weiss, H. M., & Cropanzano, R. (1996). Affective events theory: A theoretical discussion of the structure, causes and consequences of affective experiences at work. *Research in Organizational Behavior*, *18*, 1–74.

Welcomer, S. A., Gioia, D. A., & Kilduff, M. (2000). Resisting the discourse of modernity: Rationality versus emotion in hazardous waste siting. *Human Relations*, *53*, 1175–1205.

Wright, C., & Nyberg, D. (2012). Working with passion: Emotionology, corporate environmentalism and climate change. *Human Relations*, *65*, 1561–1587.

Wright, C., Nyberg, D., & Grant, D. (2012). "Hippies on the third floor": Climate change, narrative identity and the micro-politics of corporate environmentalism. *Organization Studies*, *33*, 1451–1475.

Zell, D. (2003). Organizational change as a process of death, dying, and rebirth. *The Journal of Applied Behavioral Science*, *39*, 73–96.

8 THE ROLE OF LEADERSHIP IN PROMOTING WORKPLACE PRO-ENVIRONMENTAL BEHAVIORS

Jennifer L. Robertson and Julian Barling

We are exposed to people in leadership roles (e.g., parents, teachers, sports coaches, organizational leaders), both personally and professionally, across our entire lives. From birth, our parents' behaviors exert widespread and profound influence over us. As we develop, we encounter parents, grandparents, teachers, sport coaches, and other nonparental role models who influence our attitudes, beliefs, and behaviors. From our earliest exposure to part-time teenage employment, and extending for decades through our working lives, the organizational leaders we encounter become an important part of our everyday lives.

It is not surprising then, that in what might be deemed something of an understatement, leadership is considered to be "one of the more foundational topics in organizational behavior" (Judge, Fluegge-Woolf, Hurst, & Livingston, 2008, p. 334) that has long attracted scholarly attention. Although the focus of this attention has varied, much of it has been on leaders' influence over both traditional individual-level outcomes (e.g., organizational commitment, individual performance, job satisfaction, satisfaction with the leader, organizational citizenship behaviors; Barling, Christie, & Hoption, 2010; Judge & Piccolo, 2004; Piccolo & Colquitt, 2006), as well as less frequently studied outcomes such as creativity, ingenuity (Shin & Zhou, 2003), psychological safety (Deter & Burris, 2007), and safety-related behaviors and injuries (Barling, Loughlin, & Kelloway, 2002; Mullen, Kelloway, & Teed, 2011). Suffice it to say, a substantial body of literature has highlighted the importance of leadership in driving and shaping organizational life (Barling, 2014). Most recently, researchers have begun to respond to calls for organizations to be more environmentally responsible, and have extended the leadership literature to investigate whether and how leaders' might influence individuals' pro-environmental behaviors, and organizations' environmental performance.

As is apparent in chapter 1, organizations' impact on the environment has been increasingly scrutinized by environmental activists, the media, and individuals involved in setting public policy. As a result, corporations worldwide are beginning to embrace environmental sustainability (Robertson & Barling, 2013). The success of corporate environmental initiatives rests, in some part, on those who lead these companies. Indeed, leaders are now recognizing environmental sustainability as a critical concern and many are implementing environmental governance issues into their business strategy (Accenture & United Nations Global Compact, 2010; Ones & Dilchert, 2012). The recognition of and response to environmental degradation has sparked considerable scholarly interest, and a growing body of literature recognizing the importance of leadership to both organizational and individual-level environmental performance has emerged (e.g., Boiral, Cayer, & Baron, 2009; Egri & Herman, 2000; Ramus & Steger, 2000; Robertson & Barling, 2013).

The focus of this chapter is on how leaders can influence subordinates' workplace pro-environmental attitudes and behaviors. We first explore the conceptualization of environmental leadership, the processes through which it positively affects corporate environmental issues, and the characteristics of these leaders. We then review and synthesize the empirical evidence linking leaders' transformational leadership and supervisory supportive behaviors to a variety of employees' pro-environmental initiatives. After that, we examine environmental leadership at *Steam Whistle Brewing Company*, which is located in Ontario, Canada. We conclude by providing some thoughts for future research on ways in which organizational leadership might influence employees' pro-environmental behavior.

Before embarking on our review, we acknowledge that environmental leadership takes place in an array of diverse settings (e.g., individual homes, classrooms, sports teams, government, and community and professional associations). Consistent with the goal of this book, however, we limit our focus to leadership in nonprofit and for-profit organizations. As well, we adopt Ramus and Steger's (2000) definition of workplace pro-environmental activities as "any action taken by employees that . . . [they] . . . thought would improve the environmental performance of the company" (p. 606), and include several types of activities (e.g., eco-initiatives, workplace pro-environmental behaviors, environmental organizational citizenship behaviors) within this definition.

Environmental Leadership: What and How?

As leaders become concerned with corporate environmental issues, and greater numbers of leaders take an active role in addressing them, researchers have begun to examine what it means to be an environmental leader, and the processes through which their leadership behaviors can shape their organizations' environmental impact. Not surprisingly, therefore, scholars have turned their attention to defining and conceptualizing "environmental leadership," and over the last two decades several definitions of environmental leadership have been offered.

Early work delineated eco-centric management as a form of leadership, in which the values of ecology and the preservation of nature were at the forefront of organizational and managerial concern (Shirvasta, 1994). Extending this conceptualization, Egri and Herman (2000) later noted that environmental leaders are guided by their value of and identification with nature, as a result of which they enact eco-centric values in their relationships, activities, and organizational processes. Thus, they defined environmental leadership as "the ability to influence individuals and mobilize organizations to realize a vision of long-term ecological sustainability" (p. 572). This definition dominated the environmental management literature until Gallagher (2012) argued for including the urgent need to confront environmental issues. She defined environmental leadership as "a process by which Earth's inhabitants apply interpersonal influence and engage in collective action to protect the planet's natural resources and its inhabitants from further harm" (p. 5). Although this approach includes environmental leaders outside of organizations, both Gallagher's and Egri and Herman's definitions highlight the importance of leaders' micro-level (e.g., individual, interpersonal influence) and macro-level (e.g., organization, collective action) social influence in achieving positive environmental change. Thus, we conclude that organizational environmental leadership is best conceptualized as a process in which, inspired by their own personal values, leaders strive to influence others at all levels of the organization in an effort to benefit the natural environment.

Portugal and Yukl's (1994) framework for environmental leadership highlights the role of leaders' influence in dealing with environmental concerns. They suggest that environmental leaders affect their organization's environmental performance through two *levels* of influence (individual and organizational) and two *types* of influence relationships (internal and external). At the individual level of influence, environmental leaders use their interactions to influence single or small groups of individuals, whereas at the organizational level, environmental leaders use their actions to directly influence a larger group of people. At this level, leaders can also change organizational policies, structure, and culture to indirectly influence individuals. Looking to the types of influence within Portugal and Yukl's model, internal influence involves persuading individuals within the organization (i.e., colleagues, subordinates, upper management), whereas external influence involves motivating outsiders (e.g., governments, other organizations, customers, environmental groups), both of which can take place at the individual and organizational level. For example, at the individual level, environmental leaders' internal influence may involve encouraging organizational members' commitment to environmental policies, whereas at the organizational level, internal influence may involve implementing an environmental management system. On the other hand, leaders' external influence at the individual level could include meeting with an elected official to affect environmental regulations; at the organizational level it may include forming alliances with other organizations to collectively solve an environmental problem. Although recognizing the importance of both levels, and both types of influence outlined by Portugal and Yukl, our focus in this chapter is on individual internal influence, and the ways in which environmental leaders influence their subordinates' pro-environmental initiatives.

Characteristics of Environmental Leaders

Gaining a full understanding of the effects of environmental leadership requires that we first appreciate who these leaders are. To do so, we first turn our attention to research findings describing the values, attitudes, and perceptions typically held by environmental leaders. We then consider the leadership behaviors enacted by these leaders and their effects on subordinates' workplace pro-environmental activities.

Values

Research findings consistently point to the significance of values that extend beyond self-interest in predicting individual pro-environmental behaviors (Steg & Vlek, 2009). To a large extent, environmental leaders hold similar values. The importance of values to environmental leadership is well recognized in theoretical work, and findings from both qualitative and quantitative research have identified various values environmental leaders typically hold (e.g., Egri & Herrman, 2000; Shirvastava, 1994).

First, Egri and Herman (2000) identified several personal values held by environmental leaders. They found that environmental leaders were more to open to change, self-transcendent and eco-centric. Supporting these findings, research conducted on two samples of Chinese managers found that eco-centric values influenced the propensity to engage in different forms of pro-environmental initiatives (Fryxell & Lo, 2003). Second, investigating somewhat different values, Bansal and Roth (2000) isolated individual concern for the natural environment as an important factor in leaders' corporate ecological initiatives. Third, although the environmental leadership model (ELM) developed by Flannery and May (1993) posited that leaders' hold personal values surrounding the belief that the organization, rather than the government, is primarily responsible for environmental protection, empirical evidence has failed to support this hypothesis. For example, one case study showed that a "shared responsibility" approach between organizations and the government to environmental issues characterizes leaders' values (Flannery & May, 1994), whereas a feeling of moral obligation (i.e., personal feeling of responsibility to address environmental issues) did not predict environmental decision making among a sample of managers in the metal-finishing industry (Flannery & May, 2000).

Attitudes

Scholars began to appreciate the importance of environmental attitudes to environmental leadership approximately 20 years ago (e.g., Ashford, 1993; Dieleman & de Hoo, 1993; Flannery & May, 1993). However, most research investigating attitudes as an antecedent of pro-environmental behaviors emerged a full decade later. This research drew upon the theory of reasoned action (Fishbein & Ajzen, 1975) and the theory of planned behavior (Ajzen, 1985, 1987, 1991) to highlight the salience of leaders' environmental attitudes as predictors of environmental responsibility. These two theories suggest that individuals' attitudes toward a specific behavior are positively associated with their behavioral intentions to engage in that behavior. In the context of environmental leadership, managers' intentions to formulate, engage in, and implement corporate environmental initiatives increases as their attitudes toward the natural environment become more favorable. Supporting this assertion, empirical data from several studies across a variety of industries have demonstrated that pro-environmental attitudes are indeed antecedents of managers' pro-environmental behavioral intentions (e.g., Cordano & Frieze, 2000; Flannery & May, 1994, 2000; Marshall, Cordano, & Silverman, 2005).

Perceptions

In addition to values and attitudes, research has also examined links between leaders' perceptions and their environmental leadership behaviors, with three types of perceptions being identified. Again, drawing on the theory of reasoned action (Fishbein & Ajzen, 1975) and the theory of planned behavior (Ajzen, 1985, 1987, 1991), researchers investigated the effects of subjective norms on leaders' environmental tendencies. Subjective norms refer to individuals' perception of social pressure to perform or not perform a specific behavior (Ajzen, 1991). Findings across several studies suggest that as leaders' beliefs that important others favor environmental initiatives become stronger, so do their intentions to engage in behaviors that will improve their organizations' environmental performance (e.g., Cordano & Frieze, 2000; Flannery & May, 1994, 2000; Marshall et al., 2005).

Descriptive norms (i.e., perceptions that most others engage in pro-environmental behaviors) are also associated with environmental leadership. In our own research (Robertson & Barling, 2013), we showed that higher levels of leaders' environmental descriptive norms predicted their own environmentally-specific transformational leadership (described in the following), as well as their workplace pro-environmental behaviors.

Other research has shown that whether leaders think that environmental issues are threats or opportunities will predict their environmental leadership behaviors (e.g., Fernandez, Junquera, & Ordiz, 2003; Sharma, 2000). For example, when managers employed in the oil and gas industry perceived environmental issues as opportunities, rather than threats, they were more likely to implement voluntary environmental strategies that go beyond compliance to regulation and common industry practices (e.g., habitat protection, voluntary repair of environmental damage, substitution of nonrenewable to renewable materials; Sharma, 2000).

In sum, pro-environmental leaders are more likely to (a) hold personal values that go beyond self-interest, (b) have favorable attitudes toward the natural environment, (c) perceive social pressure (in the form of subjective and descriptive norms) to support environmental initiatives, and (d) view environmental issues as opportunities for their organizations. But of at least equal interest and importance are the ways in which these leaders behave in attempting to influence the pro-environmental attitudes and behaviors of their employees, and we now turn our attention to these behaviors.

Leadership Behaviors

The different types of leadership behaviors enacted in organizations have long captivated scholarly attention. Countless different theories have been offered, some of which have been subjected to considerable empirical scrutiny, resulting in several substantive reviews (e.g., Barling, 2014; Judge et al., 2008) and meta-analyses (e.g., Bono & Judge, 2004; Dirks & Ferrin, 2002; Judge & Piccolo,

2004). Parallel interest in the types of leadership behaviors enacted by environmental leaders, however, has only recently begun to surface. Despite this "late blooming," empirical findings have identified several different leadership behaviors enacted by environmental leaders and the effects they have on employees' environmental initiatives.

Supervisory Supportive Behaviors

First, leaders' supportive behaviors have been shown to be an important component of environmental leadership. In their conceptual framework, Ramus and Killmer (2007) consider both general and environmentally-specific (Ramus & Steger, 2000) supervisory supportive behaviors as a dominant factor that influence employee's environmental initiatives. Likewise, Daily, Bishop, and Govindarajulu (2009) drew on the norm of reciprocity and social exchange theory to posit that supervisors' support for environmental initiatives is positively related to employees' environmental organizational citizenship behaviors (OCBE; discretionary pro-environmental behaviors that are not explicitly recognized by the formal reward system; Boiral, 2009). Daily et al. suggest that even though OCBEs are not formally recognized or rewarded, employees are motivated to enact these voluntary behaviors in exchange for the attention and consideration that results when employees engage in behaviors valued by their leaders/supervisors.

Supporting these theoretical claims, findings across several empirical studies consistently demonstrate that leaders' supportive behaviors do matter in the context of influencing workplace pro-environmental behaviors. Early work conducted by Ramus (Ramus, 2001, 2002; Ramus & Steger, 2000) pointed to six types of supervisory supportive behaviors exhibited by leaders in firms with a record of supporting employees' environmental initiatives. These behaviors include innovation (fostering employees' initiatives, ideas, and learning) competence building (supporting training and education initiatives), communication (encouraging employees to bring forth their ideas and critiques), information dissemination (sharing corporate information), rewards and recognition (praising and rewarding employees in an effort to support and reinforce desired behaviors), and management of goals and responsibilities (disseminating performance goals and responsibilities by using quantitative and qualitative measures; see Ramus, 2002). At about the same time, Ramus and Steger (2000) showed that employees who experienced general and environmentally-specific support from their managers were more likely to promote an environmental initiative (i.e., eco-initiative). Importantly, findings from this research demonstrated that general supportive behaviors were not as effective in promoting eco-initiatives as environmentally-supportive behaviors. That is, only three of the general types of behaviors were significantly related to eco-initiatives, compared with five of the environmental supportive behaviors, and all environmental supportive behaviors had stronger effects. These findings led Ramus and Steger (2000) to conclude that environmental leaders are more successful in their endeavors if they enact supportive behaviors targeted at employees' environmental activities specifically. Other research has shown that "backing up" subordinates' enhances their decision to participate in environmental programs (Howard-Grenville, Nash, & Coglianese, 2008).

Not all findings, however, have yielded such positive effects. Paille, Boiral, and Chen (2013) recently showed that perceived supervisory support was negatively related to employees' OCBEs, suggesting that supportive managers might deter subordinates from enacting pro-environmental behaviors. Although these results are surprising, Paille et al. suggest that despite supervisors valuing and caring for their subordinates, they themselves need to feel supported for the social exchange with their own subordinates to be effective. When this does not occur, supervisors may not reciprocate by supporting the environmental initiatives of their subordinates. This would be consistent with recent research focused on other leadership behaviors showing that supervisors' own leadership behaviors are affected by the way in which they themselves are treated at work and at home (e.g., Aryee, Chen, Sun, & Debrah, 2007; Mawritz, Mayer, Hoobler, Wayne, & Marinova, 2012). To all of this we add an additional possibility: Earlier research on supportive behaviors suggested that both the level and source of any supervisory support might affect subsequent employee behavior (Barling, MacEwen, & Pratt, 1988). For example, very high levels of emotional support might in fact be demotivating, and the source, type, and level of support needs to be considered in interpreting its effects.

Taken together, most of the available research findings suggest that supervisory support in general, and environmentally-specific support in particular, are associated with subordinates' workplace pro-environmental behaviors. However, research has also shown that leaders' negative actions toward sustainability efforts, and thus unsupportive behaviors, can stifle employees' efforts. Based on semi-structure interviews with 44 executives and managers at several organizations, Harris and Crane (2002) reported that one manager believed that a CEO's overt hostility toward environmental initiatives had more of a negative effect on developing environmental consciousness within his firm than any other positive action taken by the organization. Such findings demonstrate the importance of preventing negative leadership behaviors at the organizational level in any effort to promote sustainability within the company.

Transformational Leadership

Thus far, we have seen that environmental leaders' supportiveness can influence employees' environmental actions, but the specific leadership behaviors they enact also have profound effects. To date, several leadership types have been linked to positive environmental initiatives (e.g., instrumental, strategic, and interactive; Bossink, 2007; transactional; Egri & Herman, 2000; authentic and ethical; see Metcalf & Benn, 2013; participatory; Siebenhuner & Arnold, 2007; command control, administrative, distributive, collaborative, and unifying leadership; Walker & Daniels, 2012). As is the case with the literature on general leadership, transformational leadership is currently the dominant theory applied to understanding environmental leadership. Early work boldly stated that organizational greening activity requires transformational leadership (Gladwin, 1993). More recently, Graves and Sarkis (2012) noted that the values-based inspiration associated with transformational leadership is well-suited to stimulate changes in employees' pro-environmental behaviors.

Transformational leadership involves four behaviors: idealized influence (sharing of ethical values to act as role models), inspirational motivation (elevating employees' motivation), intellectual stimulation (helping employees think about issues in new and innovative ways), and individualized consideration (demonstrating concern for individuals' needs) to inspire subordinates to achieve extraordinary outcomes and develop their own leadership abilities (Bass, 1998; Bass & Riggio, 2006). Each of these behaviors offers important insights into the nature and challenge of environmental leadership. For example, Portugal and Yukl (1994) highlight "articulating an appealing vision with environmental elements (inspirational motivation), changing perceptions about environmental issues (intellectual stimulation), and taking symbolic actions to demonstrate personal commitment to environmental issues" (idealized influence; p. 274) as relevant behaviors for environmental leadership. Similarly, Graves and Sarkis (2012) point to the importance of these leadership behaviors to environmental leadership, but extend their focus to include individualized consideration (e.g., recognizing each individual's ability to address environmental problems and provide tailored learning opportunities based on these abilities) as an important component.

Supporting these claims, empirical research has linked transformational leadership behaviors to environmental leadership. In one of the earliest empirical studies on this topic, Egri and Herman (2000) showed that in addition to transactional leadership, environmental leaders exhibit transformational leadership behaviors. Likewise, through interviews with 40 ecopreneurs (i.e., ". . . a specific group of entrepreneurs who focus on achieving environmental sustainability,"

p. 173), Gilstrap and Gilstrap (2012) found that ecopreneurs recognize the importance of creating a vision, leading by exampling and motivating others, and suggest that ecorpreneurial leadership fits within the transformational leadership typology.

Other research has shown that transformational leadership positively influences organizations' and individuals' environmental performance. For example, based on a case study of eight ISO 14001 certified factories involving interviews with the environmental manager and the human resource manager of each company, Del Brio, Junquera, and Ordiz (2008) concluded that managers' transformational leadership behaviors are critical in factories' environmental performance. In a different survey-based study, business students who scored high on transformational leadership were supportive of environmentally sustainable business practices (Ng & Burke, 2010).

Most recently, Metcalf and Benn (2013) dismissed the notion that environmental leaders exhibit any one leadership style, and suggested instead that environmentally sustainable leaders are extraordinary leaders who can manage complex issues and problems, involve employees in organizational change that is both dynamic and adaptive, and effectively handle emotions. In an attempt to integrate all these different perspectives, scholars have extended transformational leadership theory to the environmental context, and offered the notion of environmentally-specific transformational leadership.

Environmentally-Specific Transformational Leadership

About a decade ago, Barling and his colleagues introduced the notion of safety-specific transformational leadership (Barling et al., 2002), which refers to leadership that is characterized by the four components of transformational leadership but is targeted at influencing positive safety practices. Subsequently, they and others (e.g., Conchie & Donald, 2009; Conchie, Taylor, & Donald, 2012; Kelloway, Mullen, & Francis, 2006; Mullen & Kelloway, 2009; Mullen et al., 2011), have shown that target-specific transformational leadership (i.e., transformational leadership in which the behaviors that are expressed focus on influencing a specific outcome) is an important predictor of specific targeted behaviors. Barling and colleagues recent research has also demonstrated the validity of another type of target-specific transformational leadership, namely, transformational teaching—an approach in which teachers were successfully taught the central tenets of transformational leadership (Beauchamp, Barling, & Morton, 2011). Extending the focus of target-specific transformational leadership, we recently proposed environmentally-specific transformational leadership, and defined it as "a manifestation of transformational leadership in which the content of the leadership behaviors is all focused on encouraging pro-environmental initiatives" (Robertson & Barling, 2013, p. 177). In doing so, we suggest that through the enactment of the four transformational leadership behaviors, environmentally-specific transformational leaders use their relationship with subordinates to intentionally influence and encourage their subordinates to engage in workplace pro-environmental behaviors.

In manifesting idealized influence, environmentally-specific transformational leaders are guided by and demonstrate a moral commitment to an environmentally sustainable planet (the collective good), by encouraging and enacting behaviors that will benefit the natural environment. By doing so, environmentally-specific transformational leaders become role models for subordinates, who are then more likely to engage in these behaviors themselves. Leaders high in inspirational motivation encourage their employees through their own passion and optimism to overcome psychological setbacks and external obstacles, and to go beyond what is good for themselves by engaging in behaviors that benefit the natural environment. Intellectually stimulating leaders remain open to subordinates' ideas to improve the organizations' environmental performance. They encourage subordinates to think about environmental issues for themselves, question long-held assumptions about their own and their organization's environmental practices, and address environmental problems in an innovative manner. Finally, leaders who exhibit individualized consideration establish close relationships with followers within which they can transmit their environmental values, model their environmental behaviors, and raise questions about environmental assumptions and priorities. Table 8.1 provides examples of each of the four behaviors that comprise environmentally-specific transformational leadership. In short, environmentally-specific transformational leaders are driven by their own values to engage in these behaviors to enhance their organizations' environmental performance through their influence on subordinates. Recent research has shown that they are successful in this endeavor.

Based on a sample of leader–subordinate dyads working in different organizations in the United States and Canada, we showed that environmentally-specific transformational leadership indirectly influences subordinates' workplace pro-environmental behaviors, by first evoking employees' passion for the environment. In addition, it was not only formal leadership behaviors that influenced subordinates' pro-environmental attitudes and behaviors. Providing some support for a modeling effect, leaders' own behaviors influenced their subordinates' behaviors. Specifically, leaders' workplace pro-environmental behaviors directly and indirectly (through employees' environmental passion) predicted subordinates' pro-environmental behaviors (Robertson & Barling, 2013).

Table 8.1 Examples of Environmentally Specific Transformational Leadership Behaviors

Dimension	Example of Behaviors
Idealized influence	Leaders are guided by and demonstrate their moral commitment to the natural environment. In doing so, they serve as role models who share their environmental values and choose to do what is right by taking actions that serve to protect the environment.
Inspirational motivation	Leaders motivate employees through passion and optimism to overcome psychological setbacks and external obstacles, and to go beyond what is good for themselves by engaging in behaviors that benefit the natural environment.
Intellectual stimulation	Leaders encourage subordinates to think about environmental issues in new and innovative ways, question long-held assumptions about their own and their organization's environmental practices, and address environmental problems in an innovative manner.
Individualized consideration	Leaders establish close individualized relationships with followers within which they help each employee to develop his or her skills and abilities to protect the natural environment. To do so, leaders transmit their environmental values, model their environmental behaviors, and raise questions about environmental assumptions and priorities.

Confidence in these findings is enhanced, as similar effects have emerged in research with Chinese leaders. Graves, Sarkis, and Zhu (2013) reported that Chinese employees' rating of their managers' environmentally-specific transformational leadership both directly and indirectly (through employees' autonomous motivation) influenced their own workplace pro-environmental behaviors. Extending the way in which environmentally-specific transformational leadership exerts any effects, Graves et al. (2013) also demonstrated that employees' external motivation and workplace pro-environmental behaviors were positively correlated when environmentally-specific transformational leadership was high, but negatively correlated when environmentally-specific transformational leadership was low.

Integrating all these findings, we develop a model (see figure 8.1 below) to explain how different aspects of environmental leadership affect employees' environmental

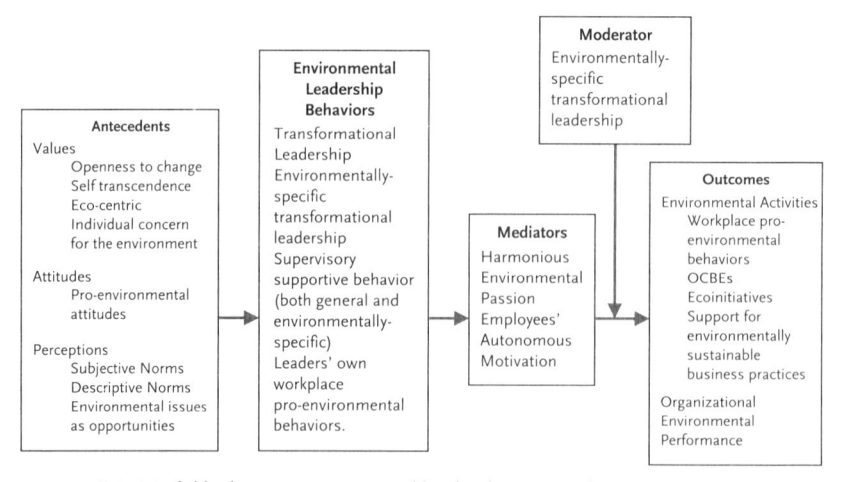

FIGURE 8.1 Model linking environmental leadership research.

performance. Whereas most research and theorizing emphasizes leadership outcomes, our model offers several antecedents to environmental leadership (namely, several types of pro-environmental values, attitudes, and perceptions), and shows that the transformational leadership and pro-environmental behaviors enacted by environmental leaders influence employees' pro-environmental initiatives directly, and indirectly, because they raise employees' passion for the environment and their autonomous motivation.

Case Example of Environmental Leadership

Although there are numerous case examples of environmental leaders and environmental leadership, we focus on one example in this chapter, namely, environmental leadership at Steam Whistle Brewing. We have selected Steam Whistle Brewing as a fitting example of environmentally-specific transformational leadership behaviors enacted by members of the management team in a private sector organization. First, we provide some background information about this organization.

Steam Whistle Brewing is a craft brewery located in Toronto, Ontario, Canada, that was founded by three friends, Greg Taylor, Cam Heaps, and Greg Cromwell, in 1998. The company focuses on making one beer, a premium Pilsner that is brewed from all-natural, GMO-free ingredients. Steam Whistle Brewing's beer is packaged in custom-made green glass bottles comprising 30% more glass than other beer bottles on the market, making it reusable approximately 45 to 50 times. The company produces an average of 110,000 bottles of beer a day, which are sold across four Canadian provinces, Ontario, Manitoba, Alberta, and British Columbia. Steam Whistle Brewing has received numerous accolades for its beer, business success, contributions to communities, and of interest to this chapter, its environmental performance. Environmental awards won by this company include the *Minister's Award for Environmental Excellence*, the *Green Toronto Award* and the *Excellence in Corporate Responsibility* award. As well, Steam Whistle Brewing has been recognized as one of *Canada's Clean 50 Companies* and one of *Canada's Greenest Employers* (Steamwhistle.ca, 2013).[1]

The success of Steam Whistle's environmental initiatives can be attributed largely to the environmental leadership provided by its co-owners, Greg Taylor and Cam Heaps, and its director of communications, Sybil Taylor (wife of co-founder, Greg Taylor, and the brewery's first employee), all of whom embody the four behaviors associated with environmentally-specific transformational leadership. First, the co-founders display idealized influence by strongly believing in, and doing the right thing, which extends to include doing what is right for the natural environment. For example, the co-founders' decisions to implement various environmental initiatives at the operations level (e.g., using GMO-free ingredients and renewable electricity from Bullfrog Power, painting labels on bottles to save trees and eliminate waste, and supporting sustainable organizations and events; Steamwhistle.ca, 2013) demonstrate their commitment to environmental sustainability. This in turn, enables the co-founders to act as role models whose support for environmental initiatives can be emulated by all employees. Recently, the co-founders have acted as environmental role models by approving funds to be spent on the implementation of showers, bike racks and a public bike maintenance station, in an effort to encourage employees' to travel to and from work in an environmentally sustainable manner. This initiative has been well received by the biking community within the organization (personal communication, November 21, 2013).

Second, in terms of inspirational motivation, Steam Whistle Brewing's top management team influences its employees by communicating to employees' their vision of the environmental practices they wish to implement, showing support for these practices, and encouraging employees to help develop and carry out these practices. This in turn influences employees to go out on their own and suggest further ideas for environmentally sustainable practices. For example, one of the co-founders told the company's electrical engineer that management wanted to audit the amount of electricity being used in an attempt to conserve the organization's energy use. This initial communication about and support for conservation practices motivated the engineer to go further and develop his own

---

1. All information on Steam Whistle Brewing comes from an interview conducted by Jennifer Robertson on November 21, 2013 with Sybil Taylor, taken from the SWB website, http://www.steamwhistle.ca, and press releases posted to the company's website.

energy conservation practice (i.e., installing motion sensors in low traffic areas of the organization; personal communication, November 21, 2013).

The co-founders also influence their employees through the company's environmental committee. Feedback and information are given to managers about areas in which the company can improve its environmental performance, and all staff are trained in environmentally friendly work practices (Lopez-Pacheco, 2011). By doing so, this committee, founded by Sybil Traylor, displays confidence and optimism that each employee can go beyond what is good for themselves by working in an environmentally responsible manner.

Third, the co-founders engage in intellectual stimulation by giving employees the opportunity to question the company's current practices, and being open to staff ideas as to how the company can change their practices to be more environmentally friendly (personal communication, November 21, 2013). Moreover, the management team at Steam Whistle Brewing deliberately creates an atmosphere that encourages and rewards creativity ("Steam Whistle Brewing Named One of Greater Toronto's Better Employers," 2009), which extends to the ways in which employees think about environmental sustainability. As one example, co-founder Greg Taylor noted during an interview with the *Business News Network* (2010) that many of Steam Whistle's environmental practices originate from employees' innovative ideas that are communicated upward to the co-founders, who then implemented them (www.watch.bnn.ca/#clip281302).

Finally, by encouraging dialogue with employees, listening to each individual employees' ideas, acting upon these ideas immediately, training employees to work in a more environmentally friendly manner, retaining a close-knit family atmosphere, creating a flat organizational structure, and practicing "management by walking around" (personal communication, November 21, 2013; Wilkinson-Latham, 2010, p. 47), Steam Whistle's management develops close relationships with employees through which they can further transmit their environmental values and model their environmental behaviors. Perhaps more importantly, it is within the trusting relationship that results that the co-founders' values and beliefs and the challenges they raise about environmental assumptions and priorities are most likely to be accepted. In sum, by invoking the behaviors associated with environmentally-specific transformational leadership, the management team at Steam Whistle Brewing has meaningfully influenced their company's environmental performance.

Future Research

Despite receiving initial scholarly interest, and empirical support, research investigating the effects of environmental leadership on organizational environmental issues is still in its infancy. Given this, the potential for future research in this area is virtually unlimited, and we conclude this chapter by exploring several avenues for future research.

First, given that relatively little research has focused on the *antecedents* of environmental leadership, with most research investigating its *consequences*, much more needs to be known about why environmental leaders choose to behave the way they do. Researchers could investigate what motivating factors differentiate between nonleaders, general leaders, and environmental leaders. Pro-environmental values, attitudes, and perceptions may very well differentiate these three groups.

Second, although a growing body of research suggests that different leadership behaviors matter in the context of corporate environmental issues, there is no research suggesting that leaders who enact specific leadership behaviors are more successful in influencing organizations' and individuals' environmental performance. Ramus and Killmer (2007) contend that supervisors' support may be the key factor in employees' motivation to engage in pro-environmental initiatives. Future research should examine whether this argument holds true by investigating the relative effects of these behaviors and other leadership behaviors (e.g., environmentally-specific transformational leadership behaviors) on organizations' and employees' environmental performance.

Like other areas (e.g., occupational health and safety), research has focused on the effects of general and target-specific leadership behaviors on specific targeted outcomes. Although both have shown to exert positive effects, research now needs to understand which is more effective. More specific to this chapter, research should examine whether general or environmentally-specific transformational leadership evokes higher levels of employees' workplace pro-environmental behaviors and investigate why one might exert greater effects. We suggest that environmentally-specific transformational leaders may evoke higher levels of employees' workplace pro-environmental behaviors because it is clear to employees that corporate environmental sustainability is a priority to these leaders.

We also suggest that future research tease out the relative effects of general and target-specific leadership behaviors, which would most appropriately be conducted in an experimental context. Conducting such a study could help isolate which leadership behaviors (general or target specific; supportive or transformational) are the best predictors of employees' environmental performance, thereby providing organizations with important information as to which behaviors they should train amongst their managers and encourage them to enact.

Finally, future research should seek to answer the questions of why and how environmental leadership affects employees' environmental performance, and under what circumstances any such effects are enhanced or minimized.

Extending Robertson and Barling's (2013) research that identified employees' harmonious environmental passion as a mediating variable, future research could investigate other organizational variables as potential mediators. One such variable of considerable interest is organizational pro-environmental climate (Norton, Zacher, & Ashkanasy, 2013; Russell & Griffiths, 2008). Previous research on occupational health and safety demonstrates that leaders play a large role in shaping group members' safety climate perceptions, which in turn affect their safety-related behaviors (e.g., Neal & Griffin, 2004; Zohar, 1980; Zohar & Luria, 2005). Extending this to an environmental context may suggest that environmental leadership behaviors are important in determining employees' pro-environmental climate perceptions. With respect to moderating variables, future research could examine both individual difference variables and organizational contextual variables. For example, future research could investigate whether employees' materialistic values (Richins & Dawson, 1992) affect the relationship between environmental leadership behaviors and employees' environmental performance, or whether the implementation of an environmental management system and/or green human resource management practices (see Renwick, Redman, & Maguire, 2013 for a review) strengthens this relationship.

Conclusion

Two decades ago, Portugal and Yukl (1994) argued that environmental leadership would become more important in the twenty-first century than it was in the previous century; emerging research on environmental leadership suggests that they were correct. Because of this research, we now know that leaders influence employees' and their organizations' environmental performance, but much more needs to be understood about how these effects occur. As researchers answer these questions, a more complete picture of the nature, antecedents, and outcomes of environmental leadership will be developed, with potentially profound consequences for employees, the organizations that employ them, and the planet we all inhabit.

Suggested Additional Readings

1. Gallager, D. R. (2012). *Environmental leadership: A reference handbook.* Thousand Oaks, CA: Sage.
2. Barling, J. (2014). *The science of leadership: Lessons from research for organizational leaders.* New York: Oxford University Press.
3. Redekop, B. W. (2010). *Leadership for environmental sustainabilitiy.* New York: Routledge.

References

Accenture & United Nations Global Compact. (2010). *A new era of sustainability: UN global compact-accenture CEO Study 2010.*

Ajzen, I. (1985). From intentions to actions: A theory of planned behavior. In J. Kuhl, & J. Beckmann (Eds.), *Action control: From cognition to behavior* (pp. 11–39). New York: Springer-Verlag.

Ajzen, I. (1987). Attitudes, traits, and actions: A theory of planned behavior. In L. Berkowitz (Ed.), *Advances in experimental social psychology* (pp. 1–63). New York: Academy Press.

Ajzen, I. (1991). The theory of planned behavior. *Organization Behavior and Human Decision Processes*, *50*, 179–211.

Ashford, N. A. (1993). Understanding technological responses of industrial firms to environmental problems: Implications for government policy. In J. Schot, & K. Fisher (Eds.), *Environmental strategies for industry: International perspective on research needs and policy implications* (pp. 277–310). Washington, DC: Island Press.

Aryee, S., Chen, Z. X., Sun, L., & Debrah, Y. A. (2007). Antecedents and outcomes of abusive supervision: Test of a trickle-down model. *Journal of Applied Psychology*, *92*, 191–201.

Bansal, P., & Roth, K. (2000). Why companies go green: A model of ecological responsiveness. *The Academy of Management Journal*, *43*, 717–736.

Barling, J. (2014). *The science of leadership: Lessons from research for organizational leaders*. New York: Oxford University Press.

Barling, J., Christie, A., & Hoption, A. (2010). Leadership. In S. Zedeck et al. (Eds.), *Handbook of industrial and organizational psychology* (pp. 183–240). Washington, DC: American Psychological Association.

Barling, J., Loughlin, C., & Kelloway, E. K. (2002). Development and test of a model linking safety-specific transformational leadership and occupational safety. *Journal of Applied Psychology*, *87*, 488–496.

Barling, J., MacEwen, K. E., & Pratt, L. (1988). Manipulating the type and source of social support: An experimental investigation. *Canadian Journal of Behavioural Science*, *20*, 140–154.

Bass, B. M. (1998). *Transformational leadership: Industry, military and educational impact*. Mahwah, NJ: Lawrence Erlbaum.

Bass, B. M., & Riggio, R. E. (2006). *Transformational leadership* (2nd ed.). Mahwah, NJ: Lawrence Erlbaum.

Beauchamp, M. R., Barling, J., & Morton, K. (2011). Transformational teaching and adolescent self-determined motivation, self-efficacy, and intentions to engage in leisure time physical activity: A randomized controlled pilot trial. *Applied Psychology: Health and Well-Being*, *3*, 127–150.

Boiral, O. (2009). Greening the corporation through organizational citizenship behaviors. *Journal of Business Ethics*, *87*, 221–236.

Boiral, O., Cayer, M., & Baron, C. M. (2009). The action logics of environmental leadership: A developmental perspective. *Journal of Business Ethics, 85*, 479–499.

Bono, J. E., & Judge, T. A. (2004). Personality and transformational and transactional leadership: A meta-analysis. *Journal of Applied Psychology, 89*, 901–910.

Bossink, B. A. G. (2007). Leadership for sustainable innovation. *International Journal of Technology Management & Sustainable Development, 6*, 135–149.

Business News Network. (Producer). (2010*). Business of green special: Steam Whistle Brewery [Video Broadcast].* Available from http://watch.bnn.ca/#clip281302

Cordano, M., & Frieze, I. H. (2000). Pollution reduction preferences of U.S. environmental managers: Applying Ajzen's theory of planned behavior. *The Academy of Management Journal, 43*, 627–641.

Conchie, S. M., & Donald, I. J. (2009). The moderating role of safety-specific trust on the relation between safety-specific leadership and safety citizenship behaviors. *Journal of Occupational Health Psychology, 14*, 137–147.

Conchie, S. M., Taylor, P. J., & Donald, I. J. (2012). Promoting safety voice with safety-specific transformational leadership: The mediating role of two dimensions of trust. *Journal of Occupational Health Psychology, 17*, 105–115.

Daily, B. F., Bishop, J. W., & Govindarajulu, N. (2009). A conceptual model for organizational citizenship behavior directed toward the environment. *Business & Society, 48*, 243–256.

del Brío, J. A, Junquera, B., & Ordiz, M. (2008). Human resources in advanced environmental approaches—a case analysis. *International Journal of Production Research, 46*, 6029–6053.

Deter, J. R., & Burris, E. R. (2007). Leadership behaviors and employee voice: Is the door really open? *Academy of Management Journal, 50*, 869–884.

Dieleman, H., & de Hoo, S. (1993). Toward a tailor-made process of pollution prevention and cleaner production: Results and implications of the PRISMA project. In J. Schot, & K. Fisher (Eds.), *Environmental strategies for industry: International perspective on research needs and policy implications* (pp. 277–310). Washington, DC: Island Press.

Dirks, K. T., & Ferrin, D. L. (2002). Trust in leadership: Meta-analytic findings and implications for research and practice. *Journal of Applied Psychology, 87*, 611–628.

Egri, C. P., & Herman, S. (2000). Leadership in the North American environmental sector: Values, leadership styles, and contexts of environmental leaders and their organizations. *Academy of Management Journal, 43*, 571–604.

Fernández, E., Junquera, B., & Ordiz, M. (2003). Organizational culture and human resources in the environmental issue: A review of the literature. *The International Journal of Human Resource Management, 14*, 634–656.

Fishbein, M., & Ajzen, I. (1975). *Belief, attitude, intention, and behavior: An introduction to theory and research.* Reading, MA: Addison-Wesley.

Flannery, B. L., & May, D. R. (1993). Organizations and pro-environmental behaviors: A model for future research. In M. Schnake (Ed.), *Southern Management*

Association Proceedings (pp. 453–455). Valdostra, GA: Southern Management Association.

Flannery, B. L., & May, D. R. (1994). Prominent factors influencing environmental activities: Application of the environmental leadership model (ELM). *The Leadership Quarterly, 5*, 201–221.

Flannery, B. L., & May, D. R. (2000). Environmental ethical decision making in the U.S. metal-finishing industry. *The Academy of Management Journal, 43*, 642–662.

Fryxell, G. E., & Lo, C. W. H. (2003). The influence of environmental knowledge and values on managerial behaviours on behalf of the environment: An empirical examination of managers in china. *Journal of Business Ethics, 46*, 45–69.

Gallagher, D. L. (2012). Why environmental leadership? In D. R. Gallagher (Ed.), *Environmental leadership: A reference handbook* (pp. 3–10). Thousand Oaks, CA: Sage.

Gilstrap, C. A., & Gilstrap, C. M. (2012). Ecopreneurial leaders and transformational leadership. In D. R. Gallagher (Ed.), *Environmental leadership: A reference handbook* (pp. 172–180). Thousand Oaks, CA: Sage.

Gladwin, T. N. (1993). The meaning of greening: A plea for organizational theory. In K. Fischer, & J. Schot (Eds.), *Environmental strategies for industry: International perspectives on research needs and policy implications* (pp. 37–62). Washington, DC: Island Press.

Graves, L. M., & Sarkis, J. (2012). Fostering employees pro-environmental behavior: The impact of leadership and motivation. In D. R. Gallagher (Ed.), *Environmental leadership: A reference handbook* (pp. 3–10). Thousand Oaks, CA: Sage.

Graves, L. M., Sarkis, J., & Zhu, Q. (2013). How transformational leadership and employee motivation combine to predict employee proenvironmental behaviors in China. *Journal of Environmental Psychology, 35*, 81–91.

Harris, L. C., & Crane, A. (2002). The greening of organizational culture. *Journal of Organizational Change Management, 15*, 214–234.

Howard-Grenvill, J., Nash, J., & Coglianese, C. (2008). Constructing the license to operate: Internal factors and their influence on corporate environmental decisions. *Law & Policy, 30*, 73–107.

Judge, T. A., Fluegge-Woolf, E., Hurst, C., & Livingston, B. (2008). Leadership. In J. Barling & C. L. Cooper (Eds.), *The SAGE handbook of organizational behaviors. Volume 1: Micro approaches* (pp. 334–352). London: Sage.

Judge, T. A., & Piccolo, R. F. (2004). Transformational and transactional leadership: A meta analytic test of their relative validity. *Journal of Applied Psychology, 89*, 755–768.

Kelloway, E. K., Mullen, J., & Francis, L. (2006). Divergent effects of transformational and passive leadership on employee safety. *Journal of Occupational Health Psychology, 11*, 76–86.

Lopez-Pacheco, A. (August 25, 2011). Raising a glass to green. *Financial Post.* Retrieved from http://business.financialpost.com/2011/08/25/raising-a-glass-to-green/.

Marshall, R. S., Cordano, M., & Silverman, M. (2005). Exploring individual and institutional drivers of proactive environmentalism in the US wine industry. *Business Strategy and the Environment, 14,* 92–109.

Mawritz, M. B., Mayer, D. M., Hoobler, J. M., Wayne, S. J., & Marinova, S. V. (2012). A trickle-down model of abusive supervision. *Personnel Psychology, 65,* 325–357.

Metcalf, L., & Benn, S. (2013). Leadership for sustainability: An evolution of leadership ability. *Journal of Business Ethics, 112,* 369–384.

Mullen, J. E., & Kelloway, E. K. (2009). Safety leadership: A longitudinal study of the effects of transformational leadership on safety outcomes. *Journal of Occupational and Organizational Psychology, 82,* 253–272.

Mullen, J. E., Kelloway, E. K., & Teed, M. (2011). Inconsistent style of leadership as a predictor of safety behavior. *Work and Stress, 25,* 41–54.

Ng, E., & Burke, R. (2010). Predictor of business students' attitudes toward sustainable business practices. *Journal of Business Ethics, 95,* 603–615.

Norton, T.A., Zacher, H., & Ashkanasy, N.M. (2012). On the importance of pro-environmental organizational climate for employee green behavior. *Industrial and Organizational Psychology, 5,* 497–500.

Neal., A., & Griffin, M. A. (2004). Safety climate and safety at work. In J. Barling, & M. R. Frone (Eds.), *The psychology of workplace safety* (pp. 15–34). Washington, DC: American Psychological Association.

Ones, D. S., & Dilchert, S. (2012). Environmental sustainability at work: A call to action. *Industrial and Organizational Psychology, 5,* 444–466.

Paille, P., Boiral, O., & Chen, Y. (2013). Linking environmental management practices and organizational citizenship behavior for the environment: A social exchange perspective. *The International Journal of Human Resource Management, 24,* 3553–3575.

Piccolo, R. F., & Colquitt, J. A. (2006). Transformational leadership and job behaviors: The mediating role of core job characteristics. *Academy of Management Journal, 49,* 327–340.

Portugal, E., & Yukl, G. (1994). Perspective on environmental leadership. *Leadership Quarterly, 5,* 271–276.

Ramus, C. A. (2001). Organizational support for employees: Encouraging creative ideas for environmental sustainability. *California Management Review, 43,* 85–105.

Ramus, C. A. (2002). Encouraging innovative environmental actions: What companies and managers must do. *Journal of World Business, 37,* 151–164.

Ramus, C. A., & Killmer, A. B. C. (2007). Corporate greening through prosocial extrarole behaviors—a conceptual framework for employee motivation. *Business Strategy and the Environment, 16,* 554–570.

Ramus, C. A., & Steger, U. (2000). The roles of supervisory support behaviors and environmental policy in employee eco-initiatives at leading-edge European companies. *Academy of Management Journal, 43*, 605–626.

Renwick, D. W. S., Redman, T., & Maguire, S. (2013). Green human resource management: A review and research agenda. *International Journal of Management Reviews, 15*, 1–14.

Richins, M. L., & Dawson, S. (1992). A consumer values orientation for materialism and its measurement: Scale development and validation. *Journal of Consumer Research, 19*, 303–316.

Robertson, J. L., & Barling, J. (2013). Greening organizations through leaders' influence on employees' pro-environmental behaviors. *Journal of Organizational Behavior, 34*, 176–194.

Russell, S., & Griffiths, A. (2008). The role of emotions in driving workplace pro-environmental behaviors. *Research on Emotion in Organizations, 4*, 83–107.

Sharma, S. (2000). Managerial interpretations and organizational context as predictors of corporate choice of environmental strategy. *The Academy of Management Journal, 43*, 681–697.

Shin, S. J., & Zhou, J. (2003). Transformational leadership, conservation, and creativity: Evidence from Korea. *Academy of Management Journal, 46*, 703–714.

Shrivastava, P. (1994). Ecocentric leadership in the 21st century. *The Leadership Quarterly, 5*, 223–226.

Siebenhüner, B., & Arnold, M. (2007). Organizational learning to manage sustainable development. *Business Strategy and the Environment, 16*, 339–353.

Steamwhislte.ca (2013). Information retrieved from www.steamwhistle.ca. Steam Whistle Brewing named one of Greater Toronto's better employers. (2009, October 20). *HR.com*. Retrieved from http://www.hr.com/SITEFORUM?&t=/Default/gateway&i=1116423256281&application=story&active=no&ParentID=1119278002800&StoryID=1256152316045&xref=http%3A//www.google.ca/url%3Fsa%3Dt%26rct%3Dj%26q%3D%26esrc%3Ds%26source%3Dweb%26cd%3D5%26ved%3D0CE0QFjAE%26url%3Dhttp%253A%252F%252Fwww.hr.com%252Fhr%252Fcommunities%252Fsteam_whistle_brewing_named_one_of__greater_toronto_s_better_employers_eng.html%26ei%3DxrhBUvWdE8afqwH_roCYCQ%26usg%3DAFQjCNEuQ_T-9A44IA-gdchK7F7ROt7wrw%26sig2%3DnQpVrtBy-H0-EvIOmLlLzw%26bvm%3Dbv.52434380%2Cd.aWM

Steg, L., & Vlek, C. (2009). Encouraging pro-envirnmental behavior: An integrative review and research agenda. *Journal of Environmental Psychology, 29*, 309–317.

Walker, G. B., & Daniels, S. E. (2012). The nature and role of agency leadership: Building and sustaining collaboration in natural resource management and environmental policy decision making. In D. R. Gallagher (Ed.), *Environmental leadership: A reference handbook* (pp. 148–157). Thousand Oaks, CA: Sage.

Wilkinson-Latham, E. (2010). Whistle while you work. *The Journal of Porter Airlines*, 9, 45–47.

Zohar, D. (1980). Safety climate in industrial organizations: Theoretical and applied implications. *Journal of Applied Psychology*, 65, 96–102.

Zohar, D., & Luria, G. (2005). A multilevel model of safety climate: Cross-level relationships between organization and group-level climates. *Journal of Applied Psychology*, 90, 616–628.

9 ENVIRONMENTAL LOCUS OF CONTROL

Mark Cleveland and Maria Kalamas

'I think we have two groups of [environmental] extremists. There are, of course those people on one side who would pave the country over in the name of progress. There is an extremist group on the other extreme that wouldn't let you build a house unless it looked like a bird's nest. Now, I think there has to be a commonsense in-between that recognizes that people are ecology, too.'

—RONALD REAGAN, *August 1976, c.f. Adler & Adler, 1998, p. 96–97*

The division of labor, free markets, and productivity characterizing capitalism are embodied in Adam Smith's (1776) *The Wealth of Nations*. Smith theorized that each person, autonomously pursuing self-interest activities that maximize personal benefit, will in due course yield the best outcome for society as a whole. In his seminal rebuttal, *The Tragedy of the Commons*, Garrett Hardin (1968) invoked the depletion of a finite, shared resource that occurs when individuals independently and rationally conclude that it is to each one's self-advantage to extract more, even with the knowledge that this will ultimately be deleterious to the welfare of the group.

Employees and managers of firms are similarly faced with the tensions ensuing between environmentally-appropriate versus economically suitable behaviors. The implementation of workplace ecoinitiatives can clash with short-term, profit-maximizing objectives. Some researchers state that the additional expenses incurred by socially-responsible firms puts them at a financial disadvantage; others contend that the supplementary costs are often minimal, and are more than offset by improved employee morale and thus enhanced productivity (Cronin et al., 2011), to say nothing of the increased goodwill generated from the firm's customers and other stakeholders. Should these ecoinitiatives not increase short-term profits, cost savings may still accrue in the long run, which along with heightened stakeholder commitment may provide a competitive advantage. Although it may prove difficult to have employees and other concerned parties buy into a firm's green initiatives, the task is not insurmountable.

An ecologically-concerned person might see little benefit in engaging in pro-environmental behaviors (hereafter, PEBs) because such activities are futile unless others take part. Individuals are loath to incur the expense and effort if they believe that others will freeload; particularly with awareness of the widespread environmental degradation committed by powerful others in society (e.g., corporations, abetted by political/economic policies, both at home and abroad). The benefits of pro-environmentalism accrue to society—perhaps not evidenced until an indeterminate point in the future—yet the costs are largely borne by the individual person or firm (Cleveland et al., 2012; Heiskanen et al., 2010); conjuring a social dilemma likened to a 'reverse commons' (Hardin, 1968). Because encouragement (i.e., appeals to public/ecological welfare) and voluntary compliance are necessary, yet insufficient to bring about real change (Hardin, 1968), it is up to firms to fully invest in and manage their own green movements. As complex entities, firms can choose the extent to which they support a green outlook and ensuing ecoinitiatives.

The sustainability of private behavior is not only the product of individual decisions. Three superordinate groups shape and thus shoulder responsibility for the sustainability of economic activity: individuals, corporations, and governments (Thøgersen, 2005). In his influential paper on the psychological factors relevant to environmental change, Stern (1992) highlighted the need for organizational research at the level of the individual, stating that "[a] neglected, but potentially important area for psychological research concerns the role of individuals in determining what firms, communities, and governments do to the global environment" (pp. 285-286). Firm behavior—including resource use—is the intricate product of myriad executive, managerial, and employee actions over time; which in turn are influenced by stakeholders such as shareholders, suppliers, and customers; as well as by the actions of competitors and their stakeholders; all operating within the greater framework of the economic, political, and regulatory environments, and moreover the fluctuating opinions of the general public across numerous cultures and markets.

Many companies have integrated environmental objectives into their mission statements and policies, and have put pressure on channel members to do likewise (Englis & Phillips, 2013). However, the contexts are too numerous and the dilemmas are too complex to ever completely codify environmentally-conscious behavior. At the individual level, the literature demonstrates that pro-environmental consciousness is an indispensable yet inadequate mental state for sustaining PEBs. This chapter argues that without consideration of peoples' ascriptions of accountability for and capabilities in achieving ecological outcomes, "green creeds are unlikely to translate into green deeds" (Cleveland et al., 2012, p. 294). It is therefore appropriate to conceive environmental dispositions and behaviors from a locus of control perspective.

Against this backdrop of shared environmental responsibility, governments, firms, and individuals all bear the ecological burden. By ascribing responsibility to different ecological players, the concept of environmental locus of control (ELOC) is applicable in different contexts, including the organizational domain. Although it was developed in marketing, there are numerous reasons why ELOC applies equally to organizational contexts. First, employees and other organizational stakeholders are also consumers, and thus their internal dispositions and responses to social and situational influences are highly relevant when performing either role. Furthermore, roughly half of the waking hours of employed adults are spent at their vocation (Ones & Dilchert, 2012). Second, the broader foundational concept, locus of control (LOC), derives from psychology and has a rich history of application in organizational contexts. Locus of control has been investigated across many workplace settings, including behavioral orientation, well-being, motivation, leadership, job satisfaction, job performance, turnover, style of supervision, and role strain (see Judge & Bono, 2001; Ng et al., 2006; Phares, 1976; Spector, 1982 for comprehensive reviews). Third, the economic activities of organizations collectively rank as the largest source of greenhouse gas emissions (Stern 1992; Tilly, 2000). Solutions to environmental degradation must include the organizational sphere and all its constituent actors. Fourth, ELOC shares theoretical linkages with numerous core organizational topics, including motivation and task performance, recruitment and retention, as well as leadership and organizational citizenship behaviors. Thus, ELOC informs to organizational behavior issues. Finally, from a corporate sustainability perspective, ELOC is relevant to the legal and competitive/strategic spheres.

Theoretical Background

The Environmental Attitude-Behavior Gap

Four decades ago, Maloney and Ward (1973) characterized the environmental predicament as "... a crisis of maladaptive behavior. Thus, the problem falls squarely in the domain of psychology ... [and] ultimately, the solution lies with the sciences that deal with changing behavior" (p. 583). Survey upon survey shows that the majority of individuals express ecological concerns (Urien & Kilbourne, 2011); however, for the most part these apprehensions have not translated into behavioral changes (Shrum et al., 1995; Thøgersen, 2005). This shirking was amply demonstrated in Bickman's (1972) study, which reported that although

94% of research participants believed that it was everyone's responsibility to pick up litter, only 2% actually picked up the trash laid out by the researcher.

Along with economic impediments, one explanation for this gap is that environmental attitudes are multilayered and differentially salient (Biswas et al., 2000). Pro-environmental behavior, like behavior in general, is a more complex function of psychological, social, and situational factors (Stern, 1992) and less foretold by simple demographic indicators (Cleveland et al., 2012; Straughn & Roberts, 1999). Researchers have offered methodological reasons for the tenuous environmental attitude-behavior (A-B) link. The predictive power of general measures conceived at a high level of abstraction (e.g., environmental concern) when applied to particular contexts and specific behaviors are typically poor, especially when assessed in uncontrolled settings (McCarty & Shrum, 2001). To improve prediction, the alleged cause and effect variables require measurement at the same level of specificity (Fishbein & Ajzen, 2010; Cleveland et al., 2005). Pro-environmental behaviors are myriad—in the public versus private spheres, reactive versus proactive, and so forth—and each may be predicted by different antecedents (Cleveland et al., 2005; 2012; Urien & Kilbourne, 2011). The A-B correspondence further increases when actual (vs. self-report) behaviors are gauged (Hines et al., 1987), when the time lag between measuring attitudes and behavior is kept short (Englis & Phillips, 2013), and when normative influences are invoked and other situational constraints are considered (Fishbein & Ajzen, 2010). Situational constraints include behavioral influences perceived to impact volitional control. Injunctive norms comprise individuals' beliefs about morally acceptable or reproachable behaviors (Cialdini et al., 1990). The threat of castigation from one's reference groups may be as strong a motivator for engaging in certain PEBs or desisting from detrimental actions as material penalties are for others.

Numerous psychographic constructs have been proposed to explain and help predict pro-environmental A-B relationships. Examples include consumer values and beliefs (e.g., Collins et al., 2007), altruism (Schwartz, 1977; Stern, 2000), attribution (Bamberg & Moser, 2007), self-efficacy (e.g., Bandura, 1997), and locus of control (Guagnano, 1995; Rotter, 1966).

Drawing from Schwartz's (1977) moral norm activation theory, the enactment of PEBs requires focusing beyond oneself, being aware of and caring enough about the potential negative consequences to others in society, and accepting personal responsibility for thwarting these outcomes (Guagnano, 1995). Stern's (2000) value-belief-norm theory similarly states that as the individual becomes cognizant of environmental issues and develops beliefs about the consequences of (in)action, a moral predisposition regarding personal responsibility for performing pro-environmental actions is formed, ultimately leading to PEBs. Attributions consist of assigning causality to events that occurred in the past (Bradley & Sparks, 2002). Self-efficacy and locus of control are concerned with future events. Temporality matters because anticipated control beliefs and attitudes fundamentally regulate behavior whereas retroactive beliefs chiefly affect interpretations (e.g., success or failure) of the aftermath (Skinner, 1996). Self-efficacy represents expectations of control over behavioral consequences, whereas LOC denotes actual control beliefs (Bradley & Sparks, 2002). Improving upon the theory of reasoned action (Fishbein & Ajzen, 1975), the theory of planned behavior (TPB: Azjen, 1985) incorporates individuals' assessments of their capacity to behave in a certain way, as well as their perceptions about how significant others want them to perform (or avoid) a certain behavior. A major component of the TPB, perceived behavioral control, has corresponding constructs in the environmental literature; namely perceived environmental control (PCE: Smith-Sebasto, 1992), perceived consumer effectiveness (Roberts, 1996), ascription of responsibility to self (AR: Stern, 2000), and environmental locus of control (ELOC: Cleveland et al., 2005, 2012; Kalamas et al., 2014). Explicitly including external ascriptions of responsibility (i.e., to other people or entities), ELOC goes beyond the TBP, PCE, AR, and similar constructs, which only consider individual responsibility and personal control beliefs. The next sections summarize the literature on LOC, specifically its dimensionality and application to organizational contexts; and elucidate a domain-specific operationalization of LOC to environmental contexts (ELOC).

Locus of Control: Concept and Dimensionality

Locus of control ranks among the most enduring and diagnostic of personality constructs (Judge & Bono, 2001; Spector, 1982). Derived from the Latin word for "place" or "location," a person's locus is primarily internal or external. According to Julian Rotter (1966; 1990), who is credited with the concept, LOC is a fairly stable tendency to see the world in a particular way, regarding general views about the underlying causes of rewards and punishments. Individuals who believe that they have command over events occurring during their lives are internals, whereas externals suppose that their decisions and lives are primarily the result of external forces for which they cannot influence. To date, Rotter's original (1966) publication has received over 17,000 citations.[1] Inspired by Rotter's work, myriad domain-particular LOC constructs have been formulated for psychology, economics, management, as well as marketing; these

---

1. http://scholar.google.ca/scholar?cites=7735167492908987910&as_sdt=2005&sciodt=0,5&hl=en (Accessed January 17, 2014)

include constructs specific to health (Wallston et al., 1976), savings and investments (Furnham, 1986), work (Spector, 1988), sales performance (Chung & Ding, 2002), consumer behavior (Busseri et al., 1998), and services (Bradley & Sparks, 2002).

Synopsizing the early studies on LOC, Phares (1976) reported that internals—compared to externals—took greater initiative and attempted to assert control over their work environment, demonstrated improved learning proficiency and problem solving, and were more active seekers as well as better users of information. On the other hand, externals' tendency to conform to the expectations of their superiors means that they should be easier to supervise (Spector, 1982), when assessed against their internal counterparts who tend to "... look to themselves for direction" (p. 486). Attributing consequences to themselves rather than to chance or powerful others, internals tend to believe that they have personal control over performance and rewards (Spector, 1982). Internals prefer participatory direction from their supervisors and thus appreciate autonomy and empowerment, whereas externals favor a directive leadership approach and conditions offering little ambiguity about task expectations and execution. Supervisory style patterns have also been recognized for internals and externals, with the former more likely to engage in persuasive appeals, and the latter, coercive tactics (Goodstadt & Hjelle, 1973; Spector, 1982). The literature also reports that internally- (versus externally-) oriented leaders are more confident in their capacity to inspire and sway others, and—being more creative and adaptive—believe that they can influence their environments and control their own destinies (Howell & Avolio, 1993). Cognizant of the direct relationship between their actions and outcomes, high internal LOC individuals are predisposed toward ethical conduct and disinclined to engage in immoral activities (Rotter, 1966). The literature provides ample support for this conjecture, with respect to an increased propensity for whistleblowing and prosocial actions, and antipathies toward cheating and kickbacks (Jones & Kavanagh, 1996). Consequently, internals (vs. externals) should be ill-disposed toward ecologically-harmful behavior.

Environmental Locus of Control

In psychology and other domains, equivocal findings cast doubt on the notion that LOC lies along a single continuum. Levenson's (1974) work on the dimensionality of LOC retained the internality aspect, but differentiated two classes of externality. Levenson conjectured cognitive and behavioral differences between those individuals believing their lives were controlled by powerful others versus those who felt that outcomes were ultimately determined by chance factors or destiny. The tripartite IPC (*I*nternal, *P*owerful others, *C*hance) LOC model has since been widely embraced (Bradley & Sparks, 2002), and its limited application to ecological contexts confirmed the IPC's improved predictive ability over Rotter's one-dimensional scale (Huebner & Lipsey, 1981). The corollary is that opinions of power over and responsibility toward environmental outcomes are also multifaceted. There are compelling reasons why these sentiments fluctuate across behavioral contexts, due to varying perceptions of choice options (selection, economic, and opportunity costs), effort required, personal efficacy, private versus public contexts, descriptive versus injunctive norms, and so forth.

Environmental locus of control pertains to perceptions regarding ascriptions of personal and outward obligations for environmental stewardship, which in turn derives from the person's beliefs concerning each party's relative abilities (or futility) to effectuate change. Operationally, ELOC is positioned between "general, dispositional measures of locus of control (LOC) and transitory, situation-specific attitudes" (Cleveland et al., 2005, p. 198). Internal-ELOC (hereafter, INELOC) denotes individuals' "multifaceted attitudes pertaining to personal responsibility toward and ability to affect environmental outcomes" (Cleveland et al., 2012, p. 293). Individuals can delegate responsibility for environmental sustainability to powerful others: politicians and public-policy shapers, corporations and senior management; or to a higher power. External-ELOC (henceforth, EXELOC) "encapsulates attitudes toward environmental outcomes that [individuals] believe are the result of extraneous forces beyond their volition" (Kalamas et al., 2014), divided into human and nonhuman control loci. The ensuing sections elaborate the sub-dimensions of ELOC embedded within these broader facets (Figure 9.1).

Internal Environmental Locus of Control

Several environmental dispositions intimate consequences sensed to be under volition. These can be divided into two broad categories: general attitudes toward the natural environment and/or some aspects thereof (e.g., overpopulation), and more focused attitudes relating to ecological actions, such as political activism and recycling (Hines et al., 1987; Kaiser et al., 1999). Regarding INELOC, the former is embodied by the green consumer dimension, whereas the latter is organized under the specific facets of recycling attitudes, activism, and advocacy.

Early research findings depict the green consumer as someone who is internally-controlled (Balderjahn, 1988) and numerous studies corroborate this conjecture. Of the four causal constructs examined (the others being knowledge, attitudes, and personal responsibility), Hwang et al. (2000) determined that (internal) LOC had the largest effect on intentions to undertake PEBs, and

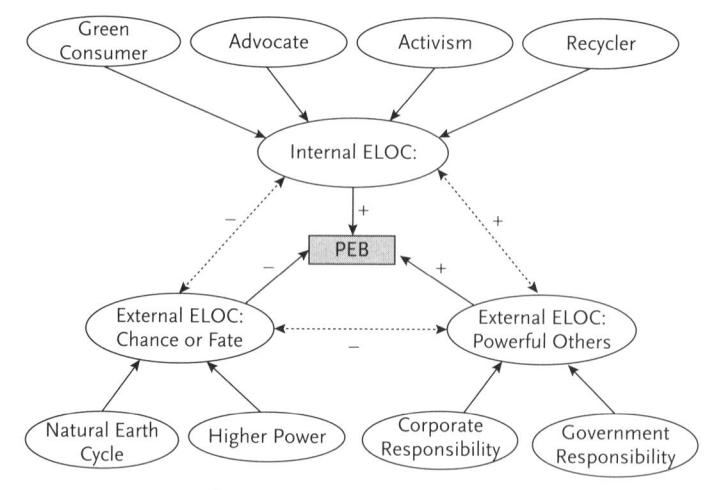

FIGURE 9.1 Environmental Locus of Control.[a]

[a]Modified from Cleveland et al. (2012) and Kalamas et al. (2014) (consult for corresponding measures).

the strongest direct effect on environmental attitudes. Fielding and Head (2012) found that pro-environmental perceived competencies, intentions, and behaviors were greater among those attributing ecological responsibility to themselves and to the local community; notably these same consequences were diluted among those shunting responsibility to the government.

For Moisander and Pesonen (2002), the archetype green consumer is an "exemplary citizen who tirelessly but with a relatively 'low profile' works toward sustainable development, doing small but momentous good deeds, guided and motivated by a rigid personal ethic and a firm confidence in his/her ability to 'make a difference'" (pp. 332–333). These individuals are intrinsically driven (notwithstanding extrinsic reinforcement) to reduce the ecological impact of their personal activities. This psychological motivation is particularly powerful when combined with the utilitarian benefit of saving money and/or the sociological benefit accruing from making a favorable impression (publically-visible behaviors, e.g., driving a hybrid: Chan et al., 2012). Indeed, individuals are more likely to undertake altruistic, pro-social behavior when they are informed it is common among their contemporaries (Cialdini et al., 1990; Goldstein et al., 2008), provided that this information is perceived as credible and not inflated or deceiving.

Recycling is analogous to a reverse-commons, given that the inconveniences are individual and immediate, whereas the benefits are communal and at some indeterminate period in the future. Cognitive dissonance theory (Festinger,

1957) provides justification for the important role played by recycling and other low-cost PEBs, as a gateway to more consequential and broad-based changes in ecological behaviors. Inconsistency in a person's beliefs, attitudes, or activities creates dissonance, which then provokes a drive to reduce the source of the dissonance by changing these beliefs, attitudes, or activities so that they are consistent. Small changes in environmental behaviors "can, by altering attitudes, produce larger changes" (Stern, 1992, p. 294). Recycling dispositions increase the probability of adopting ecologically-friendly products, and so forth. In this manner, the individual reveals an inherent shouldering of ecological responsibility by demonstrating the belief that his/her consumption activities impact the state of the environment (Straughan & Roberts, 1999).

The literature highlights the sway of reference groups on PEBs, in terms of imitation and social comparison (Welsch & Kühling, 2009). Environmental activists ". . . are committed to public actions intended to influence the behavior of the policy system and of the broader population" (Stern et al., 1999, p. 82). These include public forms of engagement with environmental movements and demonstrations (protesting, boycotting, etc.), as well as entreating others to act in kind. Environmental advocates are distinct from activists (Cleveland et al., 2012; Urien & Kilbourne, 2011), as the former are individuals who act on their environmental concern in a more passive, supporting fashion. These individuals undertake relatively inconspicuous and lower obligation activities, such as donating to conservational groups and supporting public policies that may entail incurring material sacrifices (e.g., higher taxes/prices), to lessen negative ecological effects. On the other hand, ". . . people often move back and forth, being activists for a time and then retreating to a less committed but still supportive role" (Stern et al., 1999, p. 82).

External Environmental Locus of Control: Powerful Others

People may assume the role of free riders in environmental harm-reduction endeavors (Cleveland et al., 2005). Even the most committed environmentalist is apt to experience feelings of impotency regarding how personal efforts could stand to make an impact in light of the collective activities and damage caused by billions of people and millions of firms. Corporations and governments collectively constitute the two most powerful societal actors (Kalamas et al., 2014). These entities can also be thought of as two forces lurking behind individual behavior. A good example is provided by Stern (1992) when describing the factors behind an automobile choice, which in addition to the preferences of the purchaser, ". . . depends on the price of gasoline, government emissions regulations, and the marketing strategies of manufacturers"

(p. 278). These extraneous contextual factors may loom larger than personal inclinations.

Large corporations have been denigrated for evading the full environmental costs of the actions they profit from (Ones & Dilchert, 2012), particularly given their economic and political clout (e.g., lobbying against environmental legislation). Many citizens believe that firms are not environmentally responsible. Numerous polls have reported consumers' cynicism of corporate environmental publicity as well as mistrust of eco-friendly product-labeling assertions (Shrum et al., 1995). The claims of many self-described green organizations/producers have been debunked, and even when they are genuine, consumers often greet such proclamations with skepticism (Cleveland et al., 2005; 2012), perceiving these as a marketing scheme or gimmick.

Hardin (1968) judges voluntary compliance and appeals to common good as ultimately futile, because the sacrifices are borne by the do-gooders who will not benefit in the face of the irresponsible activities of the free-loaders. Invoking mathematical and logical axioms that discount technical solutions, he resolutely concludes that the only solution to "treating the commons as a cesspool" is through mutual coercion, by way of forcible regulations and punitive taxing. Industries proclaim and follow voluntary agreements (e.g., LEED, ISO 14001 certification), yet only governmental entities are authorized to pass statutes (e.g., EPA) and compulsory standards (e.g., smokestack emissions), and enforce regulations intended to diminish environmentally-harmful conduct, as well as provide incentives for promoting benign or beneficial activities (e.g., subsidies and grants for implementing and researching waste treatment technology, respectively). The enactment of which, in democratic countries, will progress or be obstructed by public opinion (Leiserowitz, 2005), which in turn is a function of economic conditions, how salient and imminent the consequences are for dithering, as well as politicians' views regarding countries' ecological actions or lack thereof.

Thus, obligation for pro-environmental action is elusive when individual actions entail personal sacrifice but are deemed futile relative to the impact of more capable powerful others (Kollmuss & Agyeman, 2002). Evasion of personal responsibility is higher still for those crediting environmental circumstances to natural causes or fate.

External Environmental Locus of Control: Chance/Fate

Individuals holding an anthropocentric orientation see humans as the principal consideration: that the environment exists as a means toward human ends, and people are separate from other species. Individuals with an ecocentric orientation see humans as valuable, but as one of many species and ecological constituents, all having intrinsic worth (Stets & Biga, 2003). These ecological worldviews are not exclusive of religious beliefs (Greeley, 1993). In individualistic North American society, many Protestant denominations advocate to some degree literalist readings of the Bible, which in Genesis I implies that humankind has mastery over the earth (White, 1967). Such doctrinism has been negatively associated with environmental concern (Boyd, 1999). Relative to their Protestant counterparts, Catholics' interpretations are more subjective, espousing a more gracious (vs. Father figure) image of God. Kalamas et al. (2014) recently found that Protestants scored higher than Catholics, with both groups naturally scoring higher than secularists, on the higher power EXELOC sub-dimension. Compared to their more secular counterparts, highly religious people are prone toward fatalism, implying passive bearings toward the state of the environment; that is, God's will for humanity and the Earth (see Kalamas et al., 2014). Because apportionment of external responsibility is postulated to be higher, these individuals are presumably disinclined toward proactive PEBs. On the other hand, most major religions are diametrically opposed to materialism and self-centeredness (Cleveland & Chang, 2009). The corollary of spiritual peoples' reduced consumption is fewer negative ecological impacts.

The proportion of Americans denying or skeptical of anthropogenic climate change has been growing steadily. A recent report (Green Gauge Global, 2011) ranked the United States among the world's most environmentally-cynical nations. With a significant proportion of Americans denying or skeptical of anthropogenic climate change, politicians, corporations (e.g., BP, ExxonMobil), business leaders, and journalists are alleged to abet and exploit this diminished concern for the environment, which is exacerbated in the current era of austerity and economic difficulties. A Reuters study (2011) concluded that American and British newspapers devoted far more space to the opinions of climate skeptics versus those in Brazil, France, China, and India. This study also found more skeptical op-ed pieces in right-wing/conservative-oriented as opposed to left-wing/liberal-oriented newspapers. Leiserowitz's (2005) investigation of American environmental worldviews characterized the archetypal climate skeptic as an individualistic, Republican, and highly religious Caucasian male, who depicts climate change as a natural occurrence, propaganda, or at best, unfounded (the product of suspect science, e.g., in response to false climate change data conjured up by alarmists and scientific quacks). Cognizant of the skepticism spectrum, ELOC addresses individual environmental concerns, both inward- and outward-focused, and taps into the ensuing green behaviors (or lack thereof).

Environmental Locus of Control Interlinkages and Relationships to Pro-Environmental Behaviors

Kalamas et al. (2014) confirmed that INELOC was strongly positively associated with EXELOC-PO ($r = .59$) and negatively associated with EXELOC-CF ($r = -.25$). Sustaining the results from Guagnano's (1995) environmental application of Levenson's IPC scale, the two EXELOC dimensions associated negatively ($r = -.25$). The positive PO and INELOC link, in conjunction with the inverse PO-CF correlation, implies that individuals scoring high on the former are unlikely to ascribe outcomes to chance/fate factors; recognizing anthropogenic causes, they deem corporations and governments directly responsible not only for much environmental degradation, but also assign responsibility indirectly for the impediments obstructing consumers' abilities to behave in an environmentally-benign fashion. These findings demonstrate the compatibility of internal and external notions of control, insinuating that although many people are ready to do their part this motivation hinges on powerful societal actors assuming their fair share of the burden. Individuals are likely to believe that their personal ecoinitiatives are in vain if powerful others do not act in kind.

Strongly-held attitudes are more stable, easier to retrieve from memory, and thus more diagnostic of behavior (Fazio, 1995). Environmental dispositions are multifaceted: each may be held with varying degrees of conviction partly because of fluctuating perceptions of personal volition over and responsibility for environmental outcomes across circumstances. Consistent with the theory of planned behavior (Ajzen, 1985), which hypothesizes that the role of attitudes on behavior depends partly on contextual factors (e.g., social) and the underlying nature of the behavior (e.g., difficulty), studies demonstrate that the magnitude and directional influence of the various ELOC (sub-) dimensions vary across behavioral episodes. Whereas much earlier work on the environmental A-B relationship reports equivocal and/or nonsignificant findings (e.g., Balderjahn, 1988; Biswas et al., 2000; Hines et al., 1987; Kalafatis et al., 1999), Cleveland et al. (2012) found significantly positive relationships of INELOC to most behaviors examined (47 out of 50). However, and similar to their findings employing an earlier operationalization of ELOC (Cleveland et al., 2005), the magnitude of importance (explanatory power) of INELOC differed according to the context; that is, specific 3-R (reduce/reuse/recycle) activities, as well as behaviors corresponding to various forms of conservation, abstaining, activism, and environmental advocacy. The variable impact was more pronounced for EXELOC (Kalamas et al., 2014); further corroborating the inconsistency of consumers' pro-environmental actions. Significant for 18 out of the 50 behavioral contexts, the impact of EXELOC-PO was positive for all but one instance. The proclivity of activist behaviors like boycotting, eco-demonstrations, and donating to environmental charities; as well as the propensity of numerous conservation (e.g., waste reduction) behaviors rose along with higher PO scores. EXELOC-CF was negative for nine out of 11 significant relationships. For example, avoidance behaviors (abstaining from harmful products) were less frequent among those with higher CF scores. These findings highlight the unsuitability of categorizing individuals' notions of environmental responsibility along a single continuum ranging from internally to externally oriented, and moreover, disconfirm the simplistic presumption that individuals attributing control to powerful others will avoid PEBs due to perceptions of futility.

Applying Environmental Locus of Control to Organizational Contexts

Beyond marketing and public policy (see Cleveland et al., 2005, 2012), ELOC has numerous managerial applications and research implications, as detailed in the remainder of this chapter.

Practical Applications

The crucial difference between consumer and workplace PEBs is that although the former consists of "volitional behaviors rooted in individuals' own initiatives," the latter "... even when not prescribed by the organization or job duties, involve a certain degree of organizational oversight" (Ones & Dilchert, 2012, p. 452). Many employee behaviors are not entirely under their own volition. Borrowing from the ipsative theory of behavior (Frey, 1989), Tanner (1999) describes how a person's pro-environmental intentions can be thwarted by a real or imaginary lack of desirable alternatives, due to a personal view regarding the choice set (as opposed to the objective possibility set: Frey, 1989). Here, the individual's choice set is constructed on the basis of internal motivations that arise from personal relevancy and external conditions. Ipsative constraints (barring activation of a particular behavioral option) are distinct from subjective constraints (preventing preference for a specific alternative) and objective constraints (inhibiting performance of a particular option: Tanner, 1999). Whereas most psychological research has focused on the reasons for behavior, the ipsative perspective is concerned with explaining nonaction. The employee must first recognize the opportunity to act in a pro-environmental fashion, be motivated to act in kind, and not underestimate (overestimate) the probability that she or he can effectuate (be incapable of) change; based on a subjective impression of extenuating workplace factors. Managers must recognize how objective constraints (e.g., lack of knowledge/expertise, tools, procedures, alternatives) and subjective constraints (e.g., employees' beliefs about how their pro-environmental initiatives will be received by their supervisors) encumber ecoinitiatives. When employees are given discretion, considerations of convenience, cost and quality, as well as the need to justify decisions to superiors may trump ecological dispositions and even those corporate policies designed to encourage PEBs. The corollary is that organizational efforts devoted to increasing employees' awareness of ecological degradation and their agreement on the issue of joint responsibility will often be in vain, if lasting behavioral changes are improbable. This is aggravated by the short-term orientation of many executives whose focus on quarterly results is often at the detriment of pro-environmental action.

On the flip side, the multifariousness of environmental issues means that environmental management policies alone are insufficient, unless accompanied by voluntary ecoinitiatives proposed and assumed by firm employees independently of formal guidelines (Paillé et al., 2013). These discretionary activities can be regarded as a form of organizational citizenship behaviors (OCBs) applied to environmental contexts; distinguishable from those green tasks performed by employees as mandated by the organization (Ones & Dilchert, 2012). An employee's INELOC is bolstered by the proximity of like-minded personnel, supervisors, and organizational cultures; and the enactment of ecoinitiatives will be further enhanced when approbation from others is anticipated (Ramus & Steger, 2000). For these proactive behaviors to be sustained, employees must perceive the organization's stance as sincere and not a marketing ploy or merely prompted by pressure from external stakeholders (Paillé et al., 2013). Social exchange theory (Blau, 1964) is based on the reciprocity norm. When employees sense that the organization and particularly, their supervisors will value voluntary initiatives, they are motivated to engage in environmental OCBs, thereby increasing their emotional attachment and commitment to the firm (Paillé et al., 2013). Allegiance flows from employee satisfaction, which in turn is partly a product of social approval and intrinsic attraction (Blau, 1964). The approval of others helps the individual to rationalize his/her actions and decisions, and "the mutual attractiveness of persons (or entities) will be greater if they share the same opinions, values and/or norms" (Paillé et al., 2013, p. 6). Commitment rises when the firm's values and objectives overlap with those of the employee.

To reiterate, high INELOC individuals are intrinsically ecocentric and their motivation to assume environmental OCBs should be reinforced when supervisors and the greater organization are supportive; particularly when managers themselves convey similar ecological concern and model appropriate behaviors (Robertson & Barling, 2013). In this way, INELOC can be seen as an empowerment tool, which can be leveraged to encourage PEBs in the workplace.

Researchers have long recognized the vital role of executive and supervisory support in employee empowerment and creativity, and the literature suggests that this is especially true for fostering ecoinitiatives (Cronin et al., 2011; Ramus & Steger, 2000). Epitomizing internal LOC, transformational leaders focus on long-term goals, build a vision for the firm/unit, inspire and coach others to pursue and assume personal responsibility for achieving this vision, and if necessary, change workplace procedures/systems and encourage creative problem-solving so as to bring about this higher collective purpose (Howell & Avolio, 1993). The literature testifies that, compared to their externally-oriented counterparts, managers with high internal LOC have greater confidence, innovation, influence over others, and stress coping, as well as deliver higher levels of team and firm performance (see Howell & Avolio, 1993). Managers exhibiting environmental transformational leadership "might act as role models for employees by sharing their environmental values, discussing the importance of sustainability … taking actions that demonstrate commitment to addressing environmental problems … [and motivating] employees by providing an image of a future where work activities are more environmentally sustainable, talking about what the employees must do to create this future, and conveying confidence in employees' capabilities" (Graves et al., 2013, p. 82).

Thus, transformational leadership stimulates bottom-up ecoinitiatives. Transactional leadership (ensuing from legitimate power/authority) is effective for coercing employees to comply with top-down environmental directives, but these are unlikely to persist upon discontinuation of the intervention (Heiskanen et al., 2010). By encouraging innovative solutions from those harboring an elevated sense of control over environmental outcomes, the green firm may derive pecuniary, reputational, and other advantages over grayer competitors. It is true that eco-pioneering organizations assume the most risk but also stand to capitalize from first-mover advantages, particularly from a positioning perspective, in terms of attracting and retaining both customers (e.g., Toyota Prius owners) and employees (e.g., Whole Foods). Firms' green initiatives signal social responsibility, aiding the recruitment, commitment, and retention of talented, ecologically-oriented employees. Social identity theory (Tajfel & Turner, 1986) is concerned with how social perceptions and attitudes flow from self-perceived membership in a group. Social identity is defined as "that part of an individual's self-concept which derives from his knowledge of his membership of a group (or groups) together with the value and emotional significance attached to that membership" (Tajfel, 1978, p. 63). The theory "… suggests that a job seeker would expect to experience an enhanced self-concept from being employed by a reputable, environmentally-conscious organization" (Behrend et al., 2009, p. 348). Also, according to the person-organization fit perspective (see Behrend et al., 2009), individuals should be attracted to those firms whose organizational cultures are compatible with their personal values. Finally, signaling theory implies that would-be recruits make inferences about potential employers, drawing from incomplete sources of information they might come upon while on the job hunt (Behrend et al., 2009). Turban and Greening (1997, p. 659) state that a firm's "social policies and programs may attract potential applicants by serving as a signal of working conditions in the organization." Firms advocating a participatory decision-making work atmosphere should be attractive to prospective employees scoring high on INELOC. Firms looking to intensify their reputation for sustainability should seek out recruits who embody the organization's environmental stance.

Collating the early literature on the linkages between LOC and organizational behavior, Spector (1982) noted that so-called internals likely seek out conditions offering the potential for shaping outcomes. High INELOC individuals may be attracted to and remain at firms where they perceive that they are able to effectuate pro-environmental outcomes. Given their proclivity toward compliance (Spector, 1982), EXELOC individuals should be motivated to follow top-down organizational ecoinitiatives. For individuals espousing beliefs that dovetail with the powerful-others EXELOC aspect, the stimulation of personal motivation is perhaps conditional, subsequent to nontrivial green activities undertaken and encouraged by managers. Environmental management practices (in conjunction with extrinsic rewards) as well as public policy initiatives (educational forums, economic incentives, etc.) can further inspire these employees to assume personal control toward ecological outcomes. Self-perception theory (Bem, 1972) proposes that people form their beliefs and attitudes based on observations of their own behavior (vs. the standard hierarchy of internal cognitions and affective responses leading to behavior). Following this, inducing people to repeatedly perform responsible behavior eventually leads to the cultivation of intrinsic feelings of ecological stewardship.

From a managerial perspective, the notion of powerful others encompasses influential external stakeholders other than employees and executives, including upstream and downstream firms in the value chain, shareholders, competitors, customers, public opinion, as well as politicians and regulatory agencies. Even while trumpeting their green credentials for publicity, many executives hesitate to embark on costly reorganization and retooling if they fear that such procedures could put their firms at a competitive disadvantage, particularly against foreign firms not facing sustainability pressures (Kalamas et al., 2014). Well-publicized cases of greenwashing have exacerbated public opinion skepticism regarding the sincerity of organizations' green activities (Englis & Phillips, 2013). Talking green is insufficient; pro-environmentalism must pervade the entire organization

(Cleveland et al., 2005). Government intervention—additional regulations and punitive taxation for bad behavior versus rebates and incentives for good behavior—may compel companies into pro-environmentalism, yet too much interference may hurt productivity and, ultimately, competitiveness on the world stage. The carrot and stick approach therefore necessitates a balance between corporate and government responsibility, and hence, facets of EXELOC. As employees and other firm stakeholders high in EXELOC look to governments and firms for pro-environmental solutions and answers, green accountability will weigh heavily on society's most powerful.

Research Implications and Directions

Evaluating the effectiveness of individual- and firm-level ecoinitiatives is made difficult given that success ultimately rests upon a complex interaction of factors operating at these two levels, as well as the broader setting (Stern, 1992). Self-determination theory (Ryan & Deci, 2002), which conjectures two impetus categories, could further elucidate employees' determination to engage in PEBs. Thematically similar to INELOC but exclusive of notions of accountability and capability, autonomous motivation describes how employees intrinsically pursue environmental activities because of a personal commitment to sustainability or because these tasks are inherently gratifying (Graves et al., 2013). Evoking injunctive norms, external contingencies and instrumental conditioning, with controlled motivation, employees pursue PEBs to (avoid) achieve (un)desirable outcomes (e.g., sanctions or approval/rewards from peers and supervisors), or as a way to insulate themselves "from the negative self-assessments and feelings that might occur if they fail to perform PEBs" (Graves et al., 2013, p. 82). Related issues deserving of inquiry include examining the roles played by various values, specifically those inculcated from the institution juxtaposed with the broader social environment. Culture, whether at the organizational or societal level, shapes and directs human conduct, including economic behavior "by imposing obligations, enabling and disabling particular choices, and creating social or communal identities" (Berglund & Matti, 2006, p. 551). Examinations across firms and sectors, various nations/cultures, and combinations would test the generalizability of the theory and yield auxiliary insights into the nature and outcomes of ecological loci.

Too many green studies are cross-sectional and too few explicitly examine the effectiveness of various interventions (e.g., information/policies). The relative absence of field experiments is an especially glaring omission given the high cost, time/effort investment, and advertising clutter associated with real-life campaigns. From a communication and training perspective, environmental intervention studies are quite rare (Hanss & Böhm, 2013; Ones & Dilchert, 2012), although anecdotal evidence supports the effectiveness of community-based approaches to promoting green behavior (Heiskanen et al., 2010; Peattie, 2010). Social desirability biases are problematic when researching consumers' and employees' pro-environmental attitudes and behaviors (e.g., understating deviant activities, over-reporting benign behaviors). Social desirability is an issue associated with subjects in treatment versus control groups due to the interactive testing effects caused by priming. Future research should investigate, with longitudinal designs, the persistence of modified attitudes/behaviors. It would be particularly beneficial to see how the new attitudes/behaviors translate into more active forms of environmentalism within organizational settings, for example, persuading other employees at various levels of the corporate hierarchy. To the extent that ELOC affects behavior, the outcomes may then reinforce notions of internal and external control (Spector, 1982). Heiskanen et al. (2010) aver that "[f]eedback is an important aspect of empowerment because the problem itself is invisible, and people have no way of knowing whether they are making a difference" (p. 7588). The sense of competence derived by empowerment, when combined with knowledge about ecological collaborative efforts within the unit, firm, and/or industry, should counteract individuals' perceptions of helplessness.

Relationship configurations in networks result in different communication consequences; meriting research from the perspective of how environmental ascriptions are inculcated. Strong ties involving recurrent exchanges with similar individuals are suitable for conveying implicit information, whereas weak ties characterized by intermittent contact with a dissimilar group of persons are conducive for the transmission of explicit, novel information (Granovetter, 1973; Hargadon & Sutton, 1997). A person's location (e.g., executive, supervisor, front-line employee) within a network has an effect on his or her ability to influence others and on others' abilities to influence them. Position also affects the type of information sent to or sought from others. Network centrality is a relevant concept, comprising two dimensions: degree-centrality (quantity of relationship ties linked directly to the individual), and betweeness-centrality (boundary-spanning positions, e.g., between different units in an organization; or how the employee links otherwise unconnected members). The latter role is an important consideration for persuasion, opinion-leadership/seeking behaviors, and for other forms of information dissemination across the fabrics of networks. The number, station, and nature of association with colleagues provide insight into ecological consciousness, because they represent different socialization conditions in which the employee is situated (Balderjahn, 1988). The position(s) of individuals within/between networks evolves over time, necessitating longitudinal research.

The motivation to comply with social norms likely varies across organizational and social (e.g., ethnic) cultures. Some behavioral norms are formal and explicit (e.g., corporate policies, mission statement); most, however, are informal and implicit (e.g., organizational culture), and acquired over time through reference group socialization. Studies on green PEBs have focused mostly on the character of consumers and their activities as individuals; with much less attention paid to the sociological dimensions, in terms of how green behavior is shaped by "cultural conventions and shared meanings, routines, cultural representations, and the tacit rules that govern appropriate behavior in different social contexts" (Peattie, 2010, p. 211). Compliance likelihood also depends on the nature of the sender (direct vs. indirect supervisor, colleague, etc.) and her or his perceived ability to reward/apply sanctions for appropriate/undesirable employee responses. Several researchers submit that social factors are at least as powerful a motivator for PEBs as are personal environmental concern and economic reasons (Griskevicius et al., 2010). Other people's opinions rate among the strongest drivers of visible behaviors like recycling (Vining & Ebreo, 1990)—which earlier was described as a gateway to more effortful PEBs—and conspicuous green purchases (e.g., the Prius; Chan et al., 2012). In public settings, people tend to refrain from (prolong) behaviors that might convey a negative (positive) impression or provoke condemnation (commendation) from others (He et al., 2012).

Individuals' environmental outlooks ensue from a composite of psychological states. Some states are transitory as a result of the circumstances at hand; others tend to endure due to personal values and social norms (Urien & Kilbourne, 2011). Behavioral effects of each ELOC dimension are context-specific as opposed to absolute (Cleveland et al., 2005; 2012; Kalamas et al., 2014). Ones and Dilchert (2012, p. 456) demarcate five categories of workplace PEBs, for which internal versus external attributions of accountability and control could vary: avoiding harm (e.g., preventing pollution), conserving (reducing, reusing, etc.), working sustainably (modifying procedures, selecting eco-benign alternatives), influencing others (motivating and training colleagues), and taking initiative (instigating and prioritizing environmental programs). Whether a sustainable initiative is relatively invisible to supervisors and colleagues may attenuate the strength of A-B linkages. A novel research direction would be to examine ELOC from a group perspective: how teams and other workplace units evaluate their collective responsibility for and ability to effectuate pro-environmental outcomes. Finally, research is needed on applying ELOC to more challenging ecoinitiatives; beyond those that save the firm money or generate positive publicity. Internal feelings of obligation are more indispensable once "the low hanging fruit has been plucked from the tree of eco-efficiency" (Tilly, 2000, p. 39).

Conclusion

Sustaining substantive environmental change necessitates bringing contemporary niche behaviors into the mainstream. Pro-environmentalism requires top-down (top management and department/division heads) and bottom-up (grassroots) proselytization. Employees' ability to perform in a pro-environmental manner may be hampered by corporate culture (e.g., apathetic leadership) or policies (e.g., budgetary constraints, a lack of incentives, recognition, green workplace options); however, it can also be encouraged. Recycling stations, "green ideas" hotlines and contests, and green components embedded in employee evaluations and training seminars demonstrate top management commitment. Other concrete steps to help employees reduce their carbon footprint (and stress corporate pro-environmentalism) include electric charging stations for hybrid/electric automobiles, discounted transit passes, carpooling, and ecomonitoring dashboards for tracking energy usage. Incentives for ecoinitiatives that positively impact the ecology and the bottom line set the stage for a green organization.

Knowledge and skills are indispensable—without which individuals lack the facts and ability to make informed choices even if they do care—but ineffectual if obligation and enfranchisement are lacking. To model proper behavior, organizations should fast-track employees who have high INELOC. As supervisors, these individuals will reinforce the organization's pro-environmental commitment as they are looked to by others high in EXELOC-PO to take action. Firms should also hire candidates who identify with a particular green lifestyle, as self-identity strongly predicts identity-relevant behaviors, including PEBs. These beliefs stem from deep-rooted personal values, which can be gainfully leveraged if the corporation would only listen and react, to ensure that sustainable performance becomes an integral part of the firm's mission.

Suggested Additional Readings

1. Commoner, B. (1990). *Making peace with the planet*. New York: Pantheon.
2. Friedman, T. L. (2009). *Hot, flat, and crowded 2.0: Why we need a green revolution—and how it can renew America*. London: Picador.
3. Gould, K. A., Schnaiberg, A., & Weinberg, A. S. (1997). *Local environmental struggles: citizen activism in the treadmill of oroduction*. New York: Cambridge University Press.
4. Porter, M. E., & Kramer, M. R. (2006). Strategy and society: The link between competitive advantage and corporate social responsibility. *Harvard Business Review, 84*(12), 78–92.

References

Adler, B., & Adler, B. Jr. (1998). *The Reagan wit: The humor of the American president*. New York: William Morrow and Company, Inc.

Ajzen, I. (1985). From intentions to actions: A theory of planned behavior. In J. Kuhl, & J. Beckmann (Eds.), *Action control: From cognition to behavior* (pp. 11–39). Heidelberg, Germany: Springer-Verlag.

Balderjahn, I. (1988). Personality variables and environmental attitudes as predictors of ecologically responsible consumption patterns. *Journal of Business Research, 17*, 51–56.

Bamberg, S., & Moser, G. (2007). Twenty years after Hines, Hungerford, and Tomera: A new meta-analysis of psycho-social determinants of pro-environmental behavior. *Journal of Environmental Psychology, 27*, 14–25.

Bandura, A. (1997). *Self-efficacy: The exercise of control*. New York: Freedman.

Behrend, T. S., Baker, B. A., & Thompson, L. F. (2009). Effects of pro-environmental recruiting messages: The role of organizational reputation. *Journal of Business and Psychology, 24*, 341–350.

Bem, D. J. (1972). Self-perception theory. In L. Berkowitz (Ed.), *Advances in experimental social psychology* (Vol. 6, pp.1–62). New York: Academic Press.

Berglund, C., & Matti, S. (2006). Citizen and consumer: The dual role of individuals in environmental policy. *Environmental Politics, 15*, 550–571.

Bickman, L. (1972). Environmental attitudes and actions. *Journal of Social Psychology, 87*, 323–324.

Biswas, A., Licata, J. W., McKee, D., Pullig, C., & Daughtridge, C. (2000). The recycling cycle: An empirical examination of consumer waste recycling and recycling shopping behaviors. *Journal of Public Policy and Marketing, 19*, 93–105.

Blau, P. M. (1964). *Exchange and power in social life*. New York: John Wiley & Sons.

Boyd, H. H. (1999). Christianity and the environment in the American public. *Journal for the Scientific Study of Religion, 38*, 36–44.

Bradley, G. L., & Sparks, B. A. (2002). Service locus of control its conceptualization and measurement. *Journal of Service Research, 4*, 312–324.

Busseri, M. A., Lefcourt, H. M., & Kerton, R. R. (1998). Locus of control for consumer outcomes: predicting consumer behavior. *Journal of Applied Social Psychology, 28*, 1067–1087.

Chan, C., Berger, J., & Van Boven, L. (2012). Identifiable but not identical: Combining social identity and uniqueness motives in choice. *Journal of Consumer Research, 39*, 561–573.

Chung, Y. Y., & Ding, C. G. (2002). Development of the sales locus of control scale. *Journal of Occupational and Organizational Psychology, 75*, 233–245.

Cialdini, R. B., Reno, R. R., & Kallgren, C. A. (1990). A focus theory of normative conduct: recycling the concept of norms to reduce littering in public places. *Journal of Personality and Social Psychology, 58*, 1015–1026.

Cleveland, M., & Chang, W. (2009). Migration and materialism: The roles of ethnic identity, religiosity, and generation. *Journal of Business Research*, *62*, 963–971.

Cleveland, M., Kalamas, M., & Laroche, M. (2005). Shades of green: Linking environmental locus of control and pro-environmental behaviors. *Journal of Consumer Marketing*, *22*, 198–212.

Cleveland, M., Kalamas, M., & Laroche, M. (2012). 'It's not easy being green': Exploring green creeds, green deeds, and environmental locus of control. *Psychology & Marketing*, *29*, 293–305.

Collins, C. M., Steg, L., & Koning, M. A. S. (2007). Customers' values, beliefs on sustainable corporate performance, and buying behavior. *Psychology and Marketing*, *24*, 555–577.

Cronin, J. J., Smith, J. S., Gleim, M. R., Ramirez, E., & Martinez, J. D. (2011). Green marketing strategies: An examination of stakeholders and the opportunities they present. *Journal of the Academy of Marketing Science*, *39*, 158–174.

Englis, B. G., & Phillips, D. M. (2013). Does innovativeness drive environmentally conscious consumer behavior? *Psychology & Marketing*, *30*, 160–172.

Fazio, R. H. (1995). Attitudes as object-evaluation associations: Determinants, consequences, and correlates of attitude accessibility. In R. E. Petty, & J. A. Krosnick (Eds.), *Attitude strength: Antecedents and consequences* (pp. 247–282). Hillsdale, NJ: Erlbaum.

Festinger, L. (1957). *A theory of cognitive dissonance*. Evanston, IL: Row Peterson.

Fielding, K. S., & Head, B. W. (2012), Determinants of young Australians' environmental actions: The role of responsibility attributions, locus of control, knowledge, and attitudes. *Environmental Education Research*, *18*, 171–186.

Fishbein, M., & Ajzen, I. (1975). *Belief, attitude, intention, and behavior: An introduction to theory and research*. Reading, MA: Addison-Wesley.

Fishbein, M., & Ajzen, I. (2010). *Predicting and changing behavior: The reasoned action approach*. New York: Psychology Press.

Frey, B. S. (1989). Ipsative and objective limits to human behavior. *Journal of Behavioral Economics*, *17*, 229–248.

Furnham, A. (1986). Economic locus of control. *Human Relations*, *39*, 29–43.

Goldstein, N. J., Cialdini, R. B., & Griskevicius, V. (2008). A room with a viewpoint: Using social norms to motivate environmental conservation in hotels. *Journal of Consumer Research*, *35*, 472–482.

Goodstadt, B. E., & Hjelle, L. A. (1973). Power to the powerless. Locus of control and the use of power. *Journal of Personality and Social Psychology*, *27*, 190–196.

Granovetter, M. S. (1973). The strength of weak ties. *American Journal of Sociology*, *78*, 1360–1380.

Graves, L. M., Sarkis, J., & Zhu, Q. (2013). How transformational leadership and employee motivation combine to predict employee proenvironmental behaviors in China. *Journal of Environmental Psychology*, *35*, 81–91.

Greeley, A. (1993). Religion and attitudes towards the environment. *Journal for the Scientific Study of Religion, 32*, 19–28.

Green Gauge Global (2011). American consumers lead the world in environmental skepticism. Retrieved from http://www.prnewswire.com/news-releases/new-report-american-consumers-lead-the-world-in-environmental-skepticism-103520764.html on September 9, 2013.

Griskevicius, V., Tybur, J. M., & Van den Bergh, B. (2010). Going green to be seen: Status, reputation, and conspicuous consumption. *Journal of Personality and Social Psychology, 98*, 392–404.

Guagnano, G. A. (1995). Locus of control, altruism and agentic disposition. *Population and Environment: A Journal of Interdisciplinary Studies, 17*, 63–77.

Hanss, D., & Böhm, G. (2013). Promoting purchases of sustainable groceries: An intervention study. *Journal of Environmental Psychology, 33*, 53–67.

Hardin, G. (1968). The tragedy of the commons. *Science, 162*, 1243–1248.

Hargadon, A., & Sutton, R. I. (1997). Technology brokering and innovation in a product development firm. *Administrative Science Quarterly, 42*, 716–749.

He, Y., Chen, Q., & Alden, D. L. (2012). Social presence and service satisfaction: The moderating role of cultural value-orientation. *Journal of Consumer Behavior, 11*, 170–176.

Heiskanen, E., Johnson, M., Robinson, S., Vadonics, E., & Saastamoinen, M. (2010). Low-carbon communities as a context for individual behavioral change. *Energy Policy, 38*, 7586–7595.

Hines, J. M., Hungerford, H. R., & Tomera, A. N. (1987). Analysis and synthesis of research on responsible environmental behavior: A meta-analysis. *Journal of Environmental Education, 18*, 1–8.

Howell, J. W., & Avolio, B. J. (1993). Transformational leadership, transactional leadership, locus of control, and support for innovation: Key predictors of consolidated-business-unit performance. *Journal of Applied Psychology, 78*, 891–902.

Huebner, R. B., & Lipsey, M. W. (1981). The relationship of three measures of locus of control to environmental activism. *Basic and Applied Social Psychology, 2*, 45–58.

Hwang, Y-H., Kim, S-I., & Jeng, J-M. (2000). Examining the causal relationships among selected antecedents of responsible environmental behavior. *Journal of Environmental Education, 31*, 19–25.

Jones, G. E., & Kavanagh, M. J. (1996). An experimental examination of the effects of individual and situational factors on unethical behavioral intentions in the workplace. *Journal of Business Ethics, 15*, 511–523.

Judge, T. A., & Bono, J. E. (2001). Relationship of core self-evaluations traits—self-esteem, generalized self-efficacy, locus of control, and emotional stability—with job satisfaction and job performance: A meta-analysis. *Journal of Applied Psychology, 86*, 80–92.

Kaiser, F. G., Wölfing, S., & Fuhrer, U. (1999). Environmental attitude and ecological behaviour. *Journal of Economic Psychology, 19*, 1–19.

Kalafatis, S. P., Pollard, M., East, R., & Tsogas, M. H. (1999). Green marketing and Ajzen's theory of planned behavior: A cross-market examination. *Journal of Consumer Marketing, 16*, 441–446.

Kalamas, M., Cleveland, M., & Laroche, M. (2014). Pro-environmental behaviors for thee but not for me: Green giants, green gods, and external environmental locus of control. *Journal of Business Research, 67*, 12–22.

Kollmuss, A., & Agyeman, J. (2002). Minding the gap: Why do people act environmentally and what are the barriers to pro-environmental behavior? *Environmental Education Research, 8*, 239–260.

Leiserowitz, A. A. (2005). American risk perceptions: Is climate change dangerous? *Risk Analysis, 25*, 1433–1442.

Levenson, H. M. (1974). Activism and powerful others: Distinctions within the concept of internal-external control. *Journal of Personality Assessment, 38*, 377–383.

Maloney, M. P., & Ward, M. P. (1973). Ecology: Let's hear from the people. An objective scale for the measurement of ecological attitudes and knowledge. *American Psychologist, 28*, 583–586.

McCarty, J. A., & Shrum, L. J. (2001). The influence of individualism, collectivism, and locus of control on environmental beliefs and behavior. *Journal of Public Policy and Marketing, 20*, 93–104.

Moisander, J., & Pesonen, S. (2002). Narratives of sustainable ways of living: Constructing the self and the other as a green consumer. *Management Decision, 40*, 329–342.

Ng, T. W. H., Sorensen, K. L., & Eby, L. T. (2006). Locus of control: A meta-analysis. *Journal of Organizational Behavior, 27*, 1057–1087.

Ones, D. S., & Dilchert, S. (2012). Environmental sustainability at work: A call to action. *Industrial and Organizational Psychology, 5*, 444–466.

Paillé, P., Boiral, O., & Chen, Y. (2013). Linking environmental management practices and organizational citizenship behavior for the environment: A social exchange perspective. *The International Journal of Human Resource Management 24*, 3552–3575.

Peattie, K. (2010). Green consumption: Behavior and norms. *Annual Review of Environment and Resources, 35*, 195–228.

Phares, E. J. (1976). *Locus of control in personality*. Morristown, NJ: General Learning Press.

Ramus, C. A., & Steger, U. (2000). The roles of supervisory support behaviors and environmental policy in employee "ecoinitiatives" at leading-edge European companies. *Academy of Management Journal, 43*, 605–626.

Reuters (2011). *Poles apart: The international reporting of climate scepticism*. Retrieved from https://reutersinstitute.politics.ox.ac.uk/about/news/item/article/poles-apart-the-international-repo.html on September 9, 2013.

Roberts, J. A. (1996). Green consumers in the 1990s: Profile and implications for advertising. *Journal of Business Research, 36*, 217–231.

Robertson, J. L., & Barling, J. (2013). Greening organizations through leaders' influence on employees' pro-environmental behaviors. *Journal of Organizational Behavior, 34*, 176–194.

Rotter, J. B. (1966). Generalized expectancies for internal versus external control of reinforcement. *Psychological Monographs: General & Applied, 80*, 1–28.

Rotter, J. B. (1990). Internal versus external control of reinforcement: A case history of a variable. *American Psychologist, 45*, 489–493.

Ryan, R. M., & Deci, E. L. (2002). An overview of self-determination theory: An organismic-dialectical perspective. In E. L. Deci, & R. M. Ryan (Eds.), *Handbook of self-determination research* (pp. 3–33). Rochester, NY: University of Rochester.

Schwartz, S. H. (1977). Normative influences on altruism. In L. Berkowitz (Ed.), *Advances in experimental social psychology* (Vol. 1, pp. 221–279), New York: Academic Press.

Shrum, L. J., McCarty, J. A., & Lowrey, T. M. (1995). Buyer characteristics of the green consumer and their implications for advertising strategy. *Journal of Advertising, 24*, 71–76.

Skinner, E. A. (1996). A guide to constructs of control. *Journal of Personality and Social Psychology, 71*, 549–557.

Smith, A. (1977) [1776]. *An inquiry into the nature and causes of the wealth of nations*. Chicago: University of Chicago Press.

Smith-Sebasto, N. J. (1992). The revised perceived environmental control measure: A review and analysis. *Journal of Environmental Education, 32*, 24–33.

Spector, P. E. (1982). Behavior in organizations as a function of employee's locus of control. *Psychological Bulletin, 91*, 482–497.

Spector, P. E. (1988). Development of the work locus of control scale. *Journal of Occupational Psychology, 61*, 335–340.

Stern, P. C. (2000). Toward a coherent theory of environmentally significant behavior. *Journal of Social Issues, 56*, 407–424.

Stern, P. C. (1992). Psychological dimensions of global environmental change. *Annual Review of Psychology, 43*, 269–302.

Stern, P. C., Dietz, T., Abel, T., Guagnano, G. A., & Kalof, L. (1999). A value-belief-norm theory of support for social movements: The case of environmentalism. *Human Ecology Review, 6*, 81–97.

Stets, J. E., & Biga, C. F. (2003). Bringing identity theory into environmental sociology. *Sociological Theory, 21*, 398–423.

Straughan, R. D., & Roberts, J. A. (1999). Environmental segmentation alternatives: A look at green consumer behavior in the new millennium. *Journal of Consumer Marketing, 16*, 558–575.

Tajfel, H. (1978). Interindividual and intergroup behaviour. In H. Tajfel (Ed.), *Differentiation between groups: Studies in the social psychology of intergroup relations* (pp. 27–60). London: Academic Press.

Tajfel, H., & Turner, J.C. (1986). The social identity of inter-group behavior. In S. Worchel, & W. Austin (Eds.), *Psychology of intergroup relations* (pp. 7–24), Chicago: Nelson-Hall.

Tanner, C. (1999). Constraints on environmental behavior. *Journal of Environmental Psychology, 19*(2), 145–157.

Thøgersen, J. (2005). How may consumer policy empower consumers for sustainable lifestyles? *Journal of Consumer Policy, 28*, 143–178.

Tilly, F. (2000). Small firm environmental ethics: How deep do they go? *Business Ethics: A European Review, 9*, 31–41.

Turban, D. B., & Greening, D. W. (1997). Corporate social performance and organizational attractiveness to prospective employees. *Academy of Management Journal, 40*, 658–672.

Urien, B., & Kilbourne, W. (2011). Generativity and self-enhancement values in eco-friendly behavioral intentions and environmentally responsible consumption behavior. *Psychology and Marketing, 28*, 69–90.

Vining, J., & Ebreo, A. (1990). What makes a recycler? A comparison of recyclers and nonrecyclers. *Environment and Behavior, 22*, 55–73.

Wallston, B. S., Wallston, K. A., Kaplan, G. D., & Maides, S. A. (1976). Development and validation of the health locus of control (HLC) scale. *Journal of Consulting and Clinical Psychology, 44*, 580–585.

Welsch, H., & Kühling, J. (2009). Determinants of pro-environmental consumption: The role of reference groups and routine behavior. *Ecological Economics, 69*, 166–176.

White, L. Jr. (1967). The historic roots of our ecological crisis. *Science, 55*, 1203–1207.

III

THE ROLE OF ORGANIZATIONS IN PROMOTING WORKPLACE PRO-ENVIRONMENTAL BEHAVIORS

10 "GREEN ME UP, SCOTTY": PSYCHOLOGICAL INFLUENCE TECHNIQUES FOR INCREASING PRO-ENVIRONMENTAL EMPLOYEE BEHAVIOR

Kerrie L. Unsworth

It is now clearly recognized that the Earth is suffering and that we need to start becoming more environmentally friendly in our actions if we wish to survive. Many of the chapters in this book discuss this need and ways in which that can be achieved within organizations. In this chapter, I look specifically at the individual and psychological processes that we can alter to achieve increased pro-environmental employee behavior.

This chapter is based on the assumption that behavior is goal directed (Austin & Vancouver, 1996; Locke & Latham, 2013). I do not mean to suggest that at every waking moment you will be contemplating your goals and deciding how best to achieve them. Instead, it means that you are working toward achieving particular goals whether they be at a high level (i.e., abstract values) or low level (i.e., tasks or subtask actions), externally or internally derived, consciously or subconsciously. I will look at how pro-environmental behavior (PEB) interventions affect the goal-behavior process, and at how they relate to different types of goal activation—both conscious and nonconscious—and to different types of goals—both "environmental" and "nonenvironmental." In doing so, I hope to both provide an overarching theoretical framework to the PEB intervention literature and to stimulate thinking beyond traditional areas of intervention research.

An underlying premise of this chapter is that employees' behavior can change and that we can increase the amount of PEB in which they engage. A number of techniques have been developed over the years to create such change and a number of reviews already exist that systematically examine the efficacy of these techniques. Thus, I do not intend this chapter to simply review the techniques. Instead, I will look at the causal mechanisms that create the change and develop an understanding based on those core mechanisms. This is because these past reviews of PEB interventions have focused on the "what" of the intervention. I believe it is more important to understand the "how" and even more important to understand the "why" of the interventions. Why do particular interventions work? Why do particular combinations work even better? How are the interventions directed and what does this tell us about the mechanisms that are creating that change?

In this chapter I first give a brief overview of the types of PEB interventions that have been studied and the way they have been previously assessed and categorized. I will then demonstrate how the interventions overlap with the goal-behavior process and how this helps us to understand why the PEB interventions work. This overarching theoretical framework also then allows us to identify new types of interventions and effective combinations of interventions. I then look at how PEB interventions are constructed from a goals perspective and show that they can be placed into a matrix with two dimensions—the consciousness of the goal and the environmental content of the goal. Again, placing it into this framework allows us to identify new and potentially useful PEB interventions.

What Types of Interventions Have Been Studied?

As noted, there have been a variety of techniques used to influence PEB and a number of reviews of these have been conducted over the years (e.g., Abrahamse, Steg, Vlek, & Rothengatter, 2005; Davis & Challenger, 2012; De Young, 1993; Dwyer, Leeming, Cobern, & Jackson, 1993; Osbaldiston & Schott, 2012; Steg & Vlek, 2009). The most recent review of interventions to date identified 10 descriptive categories of interventions plus a miscellaneous category (Osbaldiston & Schott, 2012). These were:

- Making it easy—changing the situational conditions to make the behavior easier to do
- Prompts—reminders to complete a particular behavior
- Justifications—information about why you should perform the behavior
- Instructions—information about how you should perform the behavior
- Feedback—information about how well the participant performed the behavior
- Rewards—monetary gain that came directly from performing the behavior
- Social modeling or norms—information about what other people are doing with regard to the behavior

- Cognitive dissonance—highlighting to participants that their (anti-environmental) behavior does not match their pre-existing (pro-environmental) beliefs
- Commitment—making a verbal or written commitment to engage in the behavior
- Goals—asking participants to set a particular goal around the behavior
- Other miscellaneous—locus of control, personal satisfaction, message framing, decision making, religion and ethics contexts, and implementation intentions

As shown in Table 10.1, this broad descriptive categorization maps onto other narrower classifications, such as the antecedent/consequent categorizations, which differentiates interventions in terms of whether it alters an antecedent (e.g., commitment) or a consequent (e.g., reward) of the PEB (e.g., Katzev & Johnson, 1987; Lehman & Geller, 2004); as well as the informational/structural categorization that differentiates between changing the person's motivation and changing the situation (Steg & Vlek, 2009). The descriptive categorization by Osbaldiston and Schott (2012) also relates somewhat to De Young's (1993) framework that included the source of change (internal or external) as well as the category of intervention (information, positive motivation, coercion). Information techniques work by allowing people to understand why and how to change their behavior; positive motivational techniques provide extrinsic or intrinsic motivation for change; and finally, coercive techniques are those that constrain choice. Internal sources are those that come from within the individual, whereas external sources are those that come from outside (De Young, 1993).

These categorizations, however, do not tell us why a particular group of interventions work. In most cases, they are only describing what the intervention looks like. Moreover, each intervention has been based on its own psychological theorizing; for example, goal setting is based on goal-setting theory, rewards is based on operant conditioning principles, cognitive dissonance is based on cognitive dissonance theory, and so forth. This means that it is difficult to understand combinations of interventions and how they work together. The development and choice of a PEB intervention is also thus dependent upon the researcher's own expertise. Furthermore, without an underlying integrative framework it is difficult to identify new interventions that might complement or supersede what currently exists. This chapter aims to rectify these issues through identifying an overarching framework that both helps us understand why and how interventions work individually and in combination as well as being able to create new interventions.

Table 10.1 Integration of Some Descriptive Categorization Categories

Osbaldiston and Schott (2012)	Steg and Vlek (2009)	Lehman and Geller (2004)	De Young (1993)	Specific Examples
Easy	Structural	Antecedent		Moving recycling bins closer
Prompts	Structural	Antecedent	Information, External	Stickers saying "Turn it off"
Justifications	Informational	Antecedent	Information, External	Memo telling you why you should not cover the grate of the radiator
Instructions	Informational	Antecedent	Information, External	Notice telling you when and how you should drop and tilt the office blinds
Feedback	Informational	Consequence	Information, External	Graph on energy bill showing energy use
Rewards	Structural	Consequence	Positive motivational techniques, External	Lottery ticket
Social modeling	Informational	Antecedent	Positive motivational techniques, External	Information about how much energy people in your neighborhood are using
Cognitive dissonance	Informational			Making people feel hypocritical about their shower usage
Commitment	Informational		Positive motivational techniques, Internal	Pledge to use less energy
Goals			Information, Internal	Reduce energy use by 20%
				Direct experience, personal insight, self-monitored feedback
			Coercive techniques, External	Consumption-based taxes, social pressure, physical or legal barriers
			Coercive techniques, Internal	Sense of duty/remorse

Which Interventions Have Been Carried Out in Organizations?

To date, most PEB interventions have been conducted in a person's private life or private sphere. Indeed, even correlational type studies looking at psychosocial factors affecting engagement in PEBs are often conducted outside work with only a few exceptions (e.g., Bissing-Olsen, Iyer, Fielding, & Zacher, 2013; Carrico & Riemer, 2011; Greaves, Zibarras, & Stride, 2013; Robertson & Barling, 2013; Scherbaum, Popovich, & Finlinson, 2008). Of the studies that have been conducted within the workplace there are a few trends worth noting, however. First, the majority of PEB interventions have focused on reducing waste, and in particular paper recycling (e.g., Brothers, Krantz, & McClannahan, 1994; Ludwig, Gray, & Rowell, 1998); some have looked at reducing energy consumption (e.g., Siero, Bakker, Dekker, & van den Burg, 1996); whereas only a few have looked at transportation (e.g., Foxx & Schaeffer, 1981; Johns, Khovanova, & Welch, 2009). To our knowledge, no PEB intervention studies have examined purchasing or water consumption in the workplace. There is obviously a need for intervention studies to address a broader range of PEBs in the workplace.

Second, the types of PEB interventions most commonly examined are instructions and feedback. For example, Staats, van Leeuwen, and Wit (2000) gave office residents a brochure asking people to set the temperature of their radiator at a particular level (i.e., information) as well as providing both group and individual-level feedback on how often they had done so (i.e., feedback). Some studies combined instructions with prompts; for example, Luyben (1984) found that telling employees how and when to adjust their blinds (i.e., information) together with notices (i.e., prompts) changed employees' behavior. Other studies combined instructions with making it easier. Brothers et al. (1994) sent a memo to employees explaining what could be recycled (i.e., instructions) alongside a desktop recycling container (i.e., making it easier), and found significant effects for this intervention. Finally, a few studies, such as that by Foxx and Schaeffer (1981), combined instructions and feedback with a rewards scheme. Surprisingly few workplace intervention studies have looked at the effect of coercion, goal setting, social modeling and norms, cognitive dissonance, and commitment.

The third interesting trend in the workplace PEB intervention literature is the degree to which universities are the "workplace." Much like first-year university students were the basis for much of the early organizational psychology literature, a majority of the PEB intervention research has been conducted in university settings (e.g., Austin, Hatfield, Grindle, & Bailey, 1993; Kim, Oah, & Dickinson, 2005; Ludwig et al., 1998; Luyben, 1980, 1984; Staats et al., 2000). On the one hand, universities represent workplaces and as such employees of universities are valid populations to study. On the other hand, it would be good to have more PEB intervention studies in other workplace contexts to examine the generalizability of the results beyond university settings.

Why Do the Interventions Work?

As noted, this chapter uses a goal framework to understand psychological interventions designed to increase PEB. By looking through this lens, we are able to come to a deeper understanding of why the interventions are effective. As psychologists and organizational behaviorists we are generally not happy unless we know why something works—whether that be why some leaders are effective, why teams work, or why a particular intervention leads to increased employee PEB. Thus, a key aim of this chapter is to elucidate some of these underlying reasons why the PEB interventions might be working.

In undergoing any behavior, we generally: (a) choose a goal from among others that we hold based on the attractiveness of achieving the goal and our belief that we can achieve it; (b) commit to working toward it; (c) persist in working toward that goal depending upon the goal's specificity and difficulty; (d) regulate our behavior to stay focused depending on our personal abilities to self-regulate and emotions; and (e) attain or discard the goal and choose an alternative.[1] Given this overarching framework, how do PEB interventions fit in?

When we compare the intervention categories from Table 10.1 with this goal process, we can see five categories of extant interventions, those that affect: (a) goal attractiveness (justifications, rewards, modeling); (b) goal efficacy (easy, instructions); (c) goal choice directly (goal setting, coercion, prompts); (d) goal commitment more broadly (commitment, cognitive dissonance); and (e) self-regulation (feedback). I will now go through each of these intervention categories.

Interventions Affecting Goal Attractiveness

The first category of interventions contains those that affect the attractiveness of the PEB goal. In the goals process, I propose that these interventions affect the likelihood that the person will choose the PEB or a pro-environmental goal toward which to work. The interventions that I propose that work in this way include providing information about the benefits of engaging in the behavior (e.g., Kurz, Donaghue, & Walker, 2005), providing rewards

---

[1]. This is a vast simplification of a complex process. Interested readers should look to Locke and Latham (2013), Kanfer, Chen, and Pritchard (2008), and Austin and Vancouver (1996).

(e.g., Slavin, Wodanski, & Blackburn, 1981), as well as providing role models or credible message sources to highlight the importance of the behavior (e.g., K. R. Lord, 1994).

Changing attitudes and beliefs by providing justifications or rewards are likely to make the PEB goal more attractive—the person is more likely to want to engage in the PEB (Unsworth, Dmitrieva, & Adriasola, 2013). Social modeling and norm interventions let you know what is considered to be "good" behavior by your peers, colleagues, or neighbors (Cialdini, 2003; Schultz, Nolan, Cialdini, Goldstein, & Griskevicius, 2007). This makes the PEB more attractive by linking it to powerful subjective norms (Ajzen, 1985, 1991).

These attractiveness-type interventions have generally had mixed results at best (Osbaldiston & Schott, 2012; Stern, 2011). We believe that this is because the effect of the attractiveness intervention on change in PEB is moderated by self-concordance (i.e., the degree to which the PEB helps to achieve a person's longer-term goals and values). For example, if a person does not see how recycling paper will benefit him or her personally, then the person is less likely to take on board the justifications or social modeling information (Unsworth et al., 2013). In support of this, those attractiveness-type interventions that have been most successful have used personalized messages (Gonzales, Aronson, & Costanzo, 1988; Steg & Vlek, 2009), which most likely represents a direct attempt to increase self-concordance as well as increasing goal attractiveness.

Interventions Affecting Goal Efficacy

Just as expectancy theories of motivation focus on a combination of value and capability (Austin & Vancouver, 1996), PEB interventions have unwittingly looked not only at goal attractiveness (value) but also goal efficacy (capability). Some examples of interventions in this category include:

- Providing procedural instructions (e.g., Staats et al., 2000; Werner, Rhodes, & Partain, 1998)
- Specific tailored advice so that the person knows what he or she can do (e.g., McDougall, Claxton, & Ritchie, 1982–1983; Winett, Love, & Kidd, 1982–1983)
- Making the behavior easier (e.g., Brothers et al., 1994)
- Making competing behaviors more difficult (e.g., van Houten, Nau, & Marini, 1981)

Underlying all of these interventions is the premise that the person will perceive the goal to be within their reach. Knowing what to do and being able to do it easily enables a person to act on the goal attractiveness identified earlier when choosing a goal (Bandura, 1997). Thus, combinations of interventions that include both a goal attractiveness component and a goal efficacy component should be more effective than either on their own.

Interestingly, there is some research to show the way in which this combination may work. Pelletier and Sharp (2007) examined curbside recycling programs and compared the amount of recycling that occurred between neighborhoods that had an easy program (the recycling was picked up from outside the home) compared with those that had moderately difficult or difficult programs (in which people had to take their recycling elsewhere). They found that there was no difference in level of recycling in the easy program between people who believed in recycling and those who did not, but there was a difference between those groups for the more difficult programs; overall, there was less recycling in the difficult programs compared with the easy programs. In other words, when a person believed the goal was attractive, he or she engaged in recycling even with low goal efficacy, but the level of engagement was lower than when goal efficacy was high. Those for whom the goal was not attractive only engaged in the behavior when goal efficacy was high.

Overall, therefore, I suggest that one of the most effective combinations of interventions in organizations will be the blend of goal attractiveness and goal efficacy interventions; for example, telling employees about the health and environmental benefits of commuting via public transport (attractiveness) as well as providing bus and train timetables and flexibility in scheduling work (efficacy). Providing employees with a "why" as well as a "how" should increase employee PEB engagement.

Interventions Directly Affecting Goal Choice

In our daily lives we are constantly juggling our goals as we try to manage all the aspects of who we are—our performance goals, our collegiality goals, our family goals, our health goals, and so forth (e.g., Cropanzano, James, & Citera, 1993; Unsworth, Adriasola, Johnston-Billings, Dmitrieva, & Hodkiewicz, 2011). Given the mass of goals that each individual has, they must choose a particular goal to focus on at any point in time (Austin & Vancouver, 1996), whether that be a conscious or nonconscious choice (Bargh, Gollwitzer, Lee-Chai, Barndollar, & Trotschel, 2001). Although they do not explicitly consider this context of multiple goals, a number of PEB interventions operate to directly affect this goal choice. These interventions include goal setting, coercion, and prompts.

Goal-setting interventions are based, to a greater or lesser degree, around traditional goal-setting premises (Locke & Latham, 1990, 2002). At a bare minimum, participants are asked to set a goal for the particular PEB (e.g., McCalley

& Midden, 2002). Others have shown the increase in PEBs when goals are difficult (e.g., Becker, 1978) and when feedback on those goals is provided (e.g., Becker, 1978; Davis & Galvan, 2013). Given the origin of goal-setting theories in the workplace, surprisingly few studies examining the effect of goal setting on PEBs have been conducted in organizations. On the whole, however, goal-setting interventions obviously include a very deliberate attempt to make people choose the PEB goal as the focal goal toward which they are working.

Compliance and external control are also obvious ways that an organization can increase the number of PEBs engaged in by employees—in a more general context, legislation and regulation are often the first means taken by policymakers (Stern, 2011). And these compliance interventions do work to some extent, both in other organizational behaviors such as creativity (Unsworth, Wall, & Carter, 2005) and in household PEBs (Stern, 2011). I propose that such interventions directly affect the choice of the PEB goal such that the individual engages in the behavior to meet the behavioral goal.

These compliance interventions may also have a longer-term effect on goal persistence if they activate higher-order goals (Unsworth et al., 2013). Shah and Kruglanski (2003) found that engaging in related behaviors led to the activation of the associated higher-order goal—which then led to greater goal pursuit. Thus, if a person has an environmental goal within his or her goal hierarchy, then being required to engage in a PEB will result in greater motivation, because engaging in that behavior activates the higher-order environmental goal. Furthermore, engaging in a behavior that is strongly connected to an important goal generates positive affect (Fishbach, Shah, & Kruglanski, 2004), leading to further motivating potential (Louro, Pieters, & Zeelenberg, 2007). Nevertheless, from a wider organizational behavior perspective, we know that compliance can backfire (e.g., Amabile, 1996; Deci, Egharri, Patrick, & Leone, 1994; Hackman & Oldham, 1980). Thus, care must be taken when using compliance interventions to control a person's goal choice.

The third type of intervention that directly affects goal choice is prompts. Prompts can be seen in interventions such as the Turn It Off campaign, in which stickers are placed next to power points (e.g., Evans, Russell, Fielding, & Hill, 2012). Evaluations of such interventions have found generally positive effects. For example, Austin et al. (1993) examined how placing signs in academic office departments affected recycling behavior. In both departments they found that signs increased recycling, but that it was most effective when the sign was placed next to the bin (Austin et al., 1993).

When we consider the role of these goal-choice–type interventions in the goals process, these effects are not surprising. Self-set or other-set goals, external controls, and prompts act as markers that make a particular goal salient and make it the focal goal. Thus, initiatives that have been run by organizations such as the Earth Hour or Turn It Off campaigns may result in a cognitive switching to the environmental goal or the PEB as the focal goal. Although that goal is focal, all other goals, including the employees' performance goals, will be shielded and all resources will be allocated to the focal goal (McCullough, Aarts, Fujita, & Bargh, 2008; Shah, Friedman, & Kruglanski, 2002). Thus, if the environmental goal or PEB is the chosen goal at a particular point in time, then employees will be motivated to engage in PEBs to achieve that goal and any other goal will be forgotten.

On the other hand, these interventions in and of themselves will not always work. If another goal, such as a productivity or collegiality goal, is the chosen goal, then the environmental goal will be the one to be forgotten and/or shielded (Unsworth et al., 2013). This means that in situations in which conflicting goals are very strong for the employees, goal choice PEB interventions will not be particularly effective.

Interventions Affecting Goal Commitment

Goal commitment is the degree to which somebody is determined to reach a goal (Locke & Latham, 1990) and is central to whether or not a person strives for and/or attains that goal (Klein, Wesson, Hollenbeck, & Alge, 1999). Goal commitment often has been manipulated directly in PEB interventions. These interventions require the individual to make a public or private explicit commitment to engage in the behavior (e.g., Pallak & Cummings, 1976) and have been relatively effective particularly for fuel conservation and public recycling (Osbaldiston & Schott, 2012).

Another intervention that is likely to increase goal commitment is cognitive dissonance. Showing people how their behavior does not match their pre-existing beliefs appears to have strong effects on PEB (e.g., Dickerson, Thibodeau, Aronson, & Miller, 1992; Kantola, Syme, & Campbell, 1984). In other words, goal commitment is strengthened by creating a self-generated push to align one's behavior with one's goals.

Thus, the evidence suggests that increasing goal commitment, albeit directly or through cognitive dissonance, is likely to increase PEBs. However, when one considers its placement in the goals process, I suggest that it is likely to only have an effect once the goal has been chosen. A person cannot commit to a goal he or she does not hold. Therefore, an intervention that combines goal choice (e.g., prompts or goal setting) with goal commitment (e.g., pledge or cognitive dissonance) will be more effective than simply a commitment intervention on its own. For example, combining a Turn It Off sticker-prompting campaign with an individual employee pledge to turn off the computer and lights every day will be more effective than either intervention on its own.

Interventions Affecting Goal Self-Regulation

The way in which we regulate our behavior to achieve our goals is an incredibly complex practice, and there are a number of theories, not to mention empirical articles, about the processes and factors involved in it (Day & Unsworth, 2013). For example, self-monitoring, evaluation and self-reward or self-punishment were identified by Bandura (1991) as the key processes within self-regulation, whereas Austin and Vancouver (1996) identify planning, progress evaluation, error recovery, and goal revision. In general, this is a vast field of literature that identifies numerous factors and processes that affect goal attainment.

It is surprising, therefore, that so little of that work has come through in PEB interventions. To date, the only PEB intervention that falls into this category is that of providing feedback. These interventions have either provided feedback on how well the person is doing in relation to the goal or commitment (e.g., McCalley & Midden, 2002; Pallak & Cummings, 1976), or to other people and social norms (e.g., Midden, Meter, Weening, & Zieverink, 1983), or they have simply provided feedback on the behavior in question, such as energy usage monitors (e.g., Hayes & Cone, 1981).

The results regarding these interventions appear to be mixed (Osbaldiston & Schott, 2012). Once again, we can explain these results by looking at the placement of feedback within the goals process. Self-regulation, and in particular feedback, is only relevant if the person holds the goal in question and is committed to it. For example, De Leon and Fuqua (1995) compared a feedback-only condition with a feedback and commitment condition when examining recycling behavior; they found that only the feedback and commitment condition affected behavior. Thus, I propose that feedback interventions will only be effective when they are combined with goal choice, goal attractiveness, goal efficacy, and/or goal commitment interventions.

In addition to feedback, however, a number of other interventions can be identified under the banner of goal self-regulation. In the following, I have outlined Wood's (2005) summary of general self-regulation interventions and highlighted the implications for potential PEB interventions.

- Attention management—for example, you could provide visual and tactile cues that help employees to switch between their performance goals and their PEB goals

- Verbal self-talk—for example, asking employees to practise visualizing catching public transport to commute to work in the morning and modifying negative thoughts associated with it
- Accountability—for example, including PEBs in performance appraisals
- Organizational change—for example, redesigning tasks so that there are fewer anti-environmental behaviors (e.g., digital filing rather than paper-based filing)
- Personal challenges—for example, helping employees to deal with setbacks in moving toward incorporating more PEBs in their work environment
- Dysfunctional work cultures—for example, identifying any perceived inequities or threats that might emerge through increased PEBs
- Error tolerance—for example, getting employees to create a list of where they are still engaging in anti-environmental behavior and not punishing them for doing so
- Autonomy and flexibility—for example, allowing employees to decide when they are able to come in to work to best make use of public transport commutes
- Task support—for example, providing resources for changes in work redesign to incorporate new PEBs or change from anti-environmental behaviors
- Guided mastery approach for difficult tasks—for example, taking public transport first on days when the employee has no meetings and no deadlines, then gradually moving up toward taking public transport to commute to work on all days

These are simply a few ideas for how PEB interventions could use more of the extant self-regulation literature and there is likely to be a vast array of other potential interventions based on these ideas. Of course, like feedback, other self-regulatory PEB interventions would benefit from a combination with goal choice and goal commitment interventions to ensure that the employees hold the PEB goal.

Summary of Why Interventions Work and Their Implications

In summary, then, by looking at PEB interventions through a "goals" lens has allowed for a deeper understanding of why interventions work and when they are less likely to work. We can also see why certain combinations are particularly powerful, whereas others that might be addressing the same point in the goals process may be less powerful. Finally, through taking this approach, a number of additional interventions also can be identified that might prove to be as successful or more successful than those already being used.

How Do the Interventions Work?

So far in this chapter we have examined why particular interventions work by looking at how they affect goal-directed behavior. In addition to looking at why they work, however, we can also look at how they work. Again, this goes far beyond the usual categorization of intervention techniques based purely on what they are doing. Instead, in this section, we look at the means through which the intervention is conducted. By examining the "how" we can get another perspective into what is actually happening psychologically during the behavior change process. And, similar to the exploration around why interventions work, I will be able to highlight many areas that are still left to be examined.

I propose that PEB interventions can be placed into a 2×2 matrix (see Figure 10.1). The first dimension is whether or not the participant is expected to be aware of the intervention. If he or she is not expected to be consciously aware, then the process is happening at a subconscious level, whereas if he or she is aware of it, then it is happening consciously. The second dimension is whether the intervention is specifically aimed at a participant's environmental goals or not. Combining these two dimensions gives us four quadrants: (a) conscious environmental interventions; (b) conscious nonenvironmental interventions; (c) nonconscious environmental interventions; and (d) nonconscious nonenvironmental interventions. I will now go through each of these quadrants, identifying which of the current interventions fit each quadrant and identifying new interventions that might be considered.

	Conscious Goal	Non-Conscious Goal
Pro-Enviro. Goals	Prompts Goal-setting Justifications Cognitive dissonance Commitment Feedback Coercion based on Enviro. Regs Making an enviro goal easier Instructions linked to an enviro goal *Creating habits*	Making it easier linked to "obvious" PEB *Subliminal Images* *Emotions*
Non-Enviro. Goals	Rewards Social modeling Coercion *Self-Concordance* *Making it easy linked to non-enviro goals* *Instructions linked to non-enviro goals* *Commitment for non-enviro goals* *Feedback for non-enviro goals* *Creating habits*	Making it easier linked to "non-obvious" PEB *Nudging* *Maintaining habits*

FIGURE 10.1 Matrix of how PEB interventions work. (New interventions are in italics.)

Conscious, Pro-Environmental Goal Interventions

To date, the majority of interventions have looked at conscious green interventions. More generally, we see that existing conscious interventions aimed at pro-environmental goals cover the range of underlying goal-oriented processes. This includes interventions aimed at goal attractiveness through justifications, goal efficacy through making specific goals (e.g., recycling) easier, direct goal choice through prompts and coercion, goal commitment through commitment interventions, and self-regulation through feedback on specific goals.

These types of interventions have been the traditional approach and have generally worked moderately well. However, regardless of the number of benefits and advantages described, there are some drawbacks. As noted, even a slight perception of external control can have negative repercussions (Deci & Ryan, 1985). In the realm of PEB, when a participant is conscious that the intervention is working toward increasing PEB (i.e., conscious, pro-environmental goal), then he or she might engage in counterproductive behaviors. For example, if the person does not consider that the environmental implications will affect people similar to him or her, then a boomerang effect can occur in which the person moves away from a persuasive PEB message (Hart & Nisbet, 2012); or if the person does not have a higher-order pro-environmental goal, then a rebound effect can occur in which he or she engages in an additional anti-environmental behavior (Unsworth et al., 2013).

Given these potential backlashes, it would be beneficial to examine other ways that we can increase PEB. By using the 2×2 framework, we can look at non-environmental goals and the effects that interventions focused on those might have, whether through conscious or nonconscious means, or we could look at interventions that focus on the environmental goal but do it subconsciously.

Conscious Nonenvironmental Interventions

Both De Young (2000) and Unsworth and colleagues (2013) suggest that other motivations can lie behind PEB other than a pro-environmental goal, such as competence, participation, frugality, and luxury. At a more general level, goal hierarchy and goal systems approaches help us to understand how these other motivations can be used to design interventions around non-environmental goals (Cropanzano et al., 1993; Kruglanski et al., 2002; Unsworth et al., 2013). For example, Unsworth et al. (2011) describe a goal hierarchy approach to improving motivation for completing paperwork—although the context is different, the application to PEBs would be similar. That approach involved identifying the values, identities, and goals that were most important to the population group in question and then creating a link between the behavior and those specific goals. Thus, it could be that if social justice goals are most relevant to a particular population group, then you create messages around how engaging in PEBs can help to achieve this. There is some evidence that this approach might be successful. Bain, Hornsey, Bongiorno, and Jeffries (2012) found that linking climate change to societal development affected the intentions of climate change skeptics, although at a more personalized level, Unsworth and McNeill (2013) found that prompting people to think about how specific PEBs helped them to achieve their important goals led to increased intentions to engage in those PEBs.

Moreover, the goal systems characteristic of multifinality means that if a particular behavior is linked to more than one higher-order goal, then it is more likely to be performed (Kruglanski et al., 2002). In essence, the more goals a particular PEB can be linked to, the better. For instance, catching public transport can help not only to achieve an environmental goal, but also a healthy goal and a relax/meditation goal. An employee who is aware of this and whose pattern contains all these connections will be more likely to commute to work using public transport than one who views it only as a means to achieving an environmental goal. A key implication for increasing PEBs thus rests on the degree to which an organizational initiative can influence employees to perceive the PEB to be related to their other important, nonenvironmental goals.

In addition, I suggest that this goal hierarchy approach can explain other interventions that are focused on nonenvironmental goals, such as rewards and social norms. Although there is some debate about the effect of rewards (Eisenberger & Cameron, 1996; Frey & Oberholzer-Gee, 1997), it is apparent that large, salient rewards can cause the individual to focus on the reward rather than the task itself (e.g., Amabile, Hennessey, & Grossman, 1986; Eisenberger & Armeli, 1997). From a goals perspective, this means that gaining the reward may well become the goal rather than completing the PEB. As such, it is likely that interventions that use rewards are tapping into the reward-based, nonenvironmental goals. Financial rewards are tapping into financial goals, whereas public recognition rewards are tapping into recognition and respect goals. I suggest that the key to determining effective interventions is to diagnose the goals that are held by the employee and ensure that rewards are based around those goals.

Next, as noted earlier, the use of social norms is another widely used conscious intervention designed to increase PEB. I suggest that these are tapping into a normative goal held by the participants; but of course, this goal would only be held to the extent that the participants identify with that social group. When they do identify with the group and hold the group social identity within their hierarchy, there will be a strong motivation to take on the goals and behaviors that are representative of that group (Ashforth & Mael, 1989; Tajfel & Turner, 1986; Turner, Oakes, Haslam, & McGarty, 1994); indeed Fielding and colleagues (2008) and Dono and colleagues (2010) found that group membership was significantly associated with increased intentions to engage in environmental activism. Using organizational social identity literature as my base (e.g., Ashforth, Harrison, & Corley, 2008; Haslam & Ellemers, 2005; Haslam, Postmes, & Ellemers, 2003; Turner et al., 1994), I propose that when an employee identifies with the social group from which the norm data emerge, then social norms interventions will work because the individual holds a goal of wanting to align with the group. If, on the other hand, the employee does not identify with the group (i.e., that social identity does not sit within his or her salient goal hierarchy), then the person is unlikely to attend to the information and the goal will not be pursued.

Interestingly, the interventions that emerge in the conscious, nonenvironmental goal category are predominantly based around increasing goal attractiveness. Are there other mechanisms that could be used in this approach? I believe so. First, although many of the goal efficacy interventions are either explicitly related to environmental goals through a combination of interventions (e.g., making it easy combined with justifications) or are not consciously related to any goals (e.g., instructions for using office blinds), the efficacy interventions could relate the behavior more specifically to nonenvironmental goals. For example, workplace composting bins could be placed next to tea and coffee facilities (making it easier to compost) and then used in a workplace vegetable patch from which staff are able to eat the vegetables at work (connecting to eating or gardening goals).

Second, goal commitment interventions can easily be applied to non-environmental goals, but with the effect of increasing overall PEBs. For example, committing to saving money by reducing the electricity bill would result in an overall increase in PEBs even though the conscious goal is financial. Finally, self-regulation and feedback interventions again can be easily applied to nonenvironmental goals. For example, providing information on money spent and/or saved compared with previous time points would allow people to see the relationship between the PEB and the nonenvironmental goal.

The most important issue when considering conscious, nonenvironmental goal interventions is that the chosen goal must be relevant and important to the employee in question. If the nonenvironmental goal is not relevant to the employees, then they will not engage in the behavior (Molina, Unsworth, Hodkiewicz, & Adriasola, 2013). This may mean that multiple interventions are personalized for particular sets of employees (e.g., there may be differences between young and old employees, male and female employees, married and single employees, left-wing and right-wing employees, professional and technical employees, and so forth; depending upon commonalities and differences in individual goals), or that a more generic goal is sought that most of the population would hold (Unsworth et al., 2011).

Nonconscious Pro-Environmental Goal Interventions

So far we have covered conscious, supraliminal interventions in which employees or participants are aware of the intervention being conducted, whether or not it is aimed at an environmental goal. But what about nonconscious, subliminal mechanisms? Priming people with subliminal goals through words hidden in word search tasks (Bargh et al., 2001; Chartrand & Bargh, 1996), background pictures (Shantz & Latham, 2009), or even abstract signals of the goal (Aarts, Custers, & Marien, 2009) has been shown to lead to pursuit of that goal—without the person's awareness (Aarts, Custers, & Marien, 2008; Bargh et al., 2001).

When considering pro-environmental goals, to date, the only interventions that might fit into this category are those focused on making an obvious PEB (e.g., recycling) easier to do or very subtle environmental prompts (e.g., pictures of a drought). Indeed, it is even difficult to find these in the literature. However, for example, it could be that providing offices with recycling bins close to their desks may activate the pro-environmental goal without conscious awareness. Alternatively, subtle environmental cues such as background pictures of a forest or a coal-burning energy station could prime an environmental goal and prompt engagement in PEBs. If the subconscious environmental goal complements the conscious performance, relationship, or environmental goal, then there will be increased attention, commitment, and performance to the goal; unfortunately, however, if the subconscious environmental goal and the conscious goal are in conflict, then performance on both drops due to divided attention (Legal, Meyer, & Delouvee, 2007). This will obviously be an issue in organizations with strong task performance goals.

Assuming there is no goal conflict, the question then becomes, what type of subtle cue would prime an environmental goal? One key area that is important in nonconscious goals is emotion; thus, for subtle cues, the role of emotions becomes paramount. In general, research into PEB suggests that both positive (K. R. Lord, 1994) and negative emotions induce PEB change (Dickerson et al., 1992; Kantola et al., 1984; K. R. Lord, 1994). Russell and Griffiths (2008) suggest that further research is needed to determine the differential effects of positive and negative affect on PEB. From a goals perspective, though, when a goal is subconsciously primed together with the inducement of negative affect people stop working on the goal (Aarts, Custers, & Holland, 2007); and people in a positive mood are more likely to adopt a goal than somebody in a negative mood (Fishbach & Labroo, 2007). Thus, a subtle "positive" environmental picture such as BP's flower logo (before it was associated with oil spills) would nonconsciously activate a goal that would be more likely to be committed to and pursued than a subtle "negative" environmental picture.

Nonconscious Non–Pro-Environmental Interventions

The final quadrant in the proposed matrix is for interventions that are nonconscious and focused on non–pro-environmental goals. In the extant literature, there are few, if any, traditional interventions that fall into this category. There is one, however, that stands out—if only because of the degree to which the community and the public sector have embraced it—and that is nudging.

Nudging is a term made popular by Thaler and Sunstein (2008) and is based around the idea of modifying the "choice architecture" so that the desirable option is the easiest and most attractive one to choose. Importantly, the individual is not aware of the modification or the goal; because of this it has been called *liberal paternalism* (Thaler & Sunstein, 2008). The paradigm has become very popular with policymakers. For example, both Thaler and Sunstein have advised the UK and US governments, respectively, and the UK's Institute for Government vigorously promotes the approach (Dolan, Hallsworth, Halpern, King, & Vlaev, 2010).

This work builds on psychological foundations such as bounded rationality (Simon, 1957), prospect theory (Kahneman & Tversky, 1979), and cognitive dissonance (Festinger, 1957). Yet only a couple of studies have looked at nudging interventions in PEB. For example, Kallbekken and Saelen (2013) examined how nudging through providing smaller plates in buffet restaurants affected food waste. They found that reducing the plate size by only 1 cm reduced food waste by 2.5 kg (7.4% of the control group mean). This evidence seems compelling; however, given the scarcity of data, more studies are definitely needed.

How could nudging be implemented? Moseley and Stoker (2013) and Bowman (2011) identify some pro-environmental policy options that could be used based on nudging. Most notable is to frame initiatives and behaviors in a way that makes the PEB the best option, for example, making green energy sources competitive with more traditional energy sources. However, these nudging interventions are designed to be completely nonconscious. There are some who argue that this will not be enough and that more explicit and traditional forms of regulation are still required (French, 2011; Selinger & Whyte, 2012). As of yet, we have too little information to be certain.

Implications for Organizations and Organizational Research

By examining why PEB interventions work and how they work through a unifying framework, many implications for organizations and organizational research emerge. Many suggestions are highlighted throughout the chapter; however, in addition to those I believe there are additional important implications for the workforce.

First, it is worthwhile noting that little research in the workplace has used the leader in the PEB intervention. Yet within the workplace, one of the most prominent social influences is that of the leader. Theoretically, Lord and colleagues (R. G. Lord & Brown, 2001; R. G. Lord, Brown, & Freiberg, 1999) have suggested that leaders can influence followers by priming existing goal hierarchy patterns and/or by developing new goal hierarchy patterns. Goal contagion research suggests that people infer goals from seeing others engage in a behavior and are more likely to choose and pursue that goal themselves (Aarts, Gollwitzer, & Hassin, 2004; Dik & Aarts, 2006); moreover, supervisors are more likely to engage in PEB in front of their followers when they believe the organization values those behaviors (Andersson, Shivarajan, & Blau, 2005). Integrating these lines of research, we find a strong role for leaders in influencing PEBs—when an employee sees the leader engaging in PEBs and/or when the leader helps the employee to see the relationships between the PEB and his or her other goals, then he or she will be more likely to engage in PEB.

Second, in an organization environmental goals are likely to come second place to performance or relationship goals. On the one hand, we can consider interventions that link the PEB to these non–pro-environmental goals as noted. On the other hand, we could consider a full-blown integrative set of interventions. One such approach is to address employees' habits. To date, there has not been a great deal of PEB intervention research that has looked at habits. However, it is one framework that includes all aspects of the goals process as well as covering conscious and nonconscious interventions tackling both environmental and nonenvironmental goals. As such, it could be one way through which PEBs could be increased substantially, regardless of the employees' organizational goals.

If an employee has performed an anti-environmental behavior many times (e.g., they always drive the car to work) then it is considered to be a strong habit (Danner, Aarts, & De Vries, 2008; Ouellette & Wood, 1998; W. Wood & Neal, 2007) which will likely overcome intentions to engage in a PEB (Danner et al., 2008). Yet, all is not lost, even when an employee has a habit that is not environmentally-friendly. Again, the key motivational mechanism relies upon the degree to which the PEB can be related to a higher-order goal: If an individual can identify a goal related to the non-habitual PEB then this can help shield the behavior from being overcome by the habit (Danner, Aarts, Papies, & de Vries, 2011; Shah et al., 2002). Research into implementation intentions shows that specifying a plan for exactly how and when a person will engage in the non-habitual PEB (i.e., increasing the efficaciousness of the behavior) can also help to change behavior, particularly if the habits are weak (Gollwitzer, 1990; Gollwitzer & Brandstatter, 1997; Sheeran, Milne, Webb, & Gollwitzer, 2005). Furthermore, Danner, Aarts and de Vries (2008) showed that changing the context of the behavior allows the intended behavior to overcome the habitual behavior and Laran, Janiszewski and Cunha (2008) found that goal release is more likely to occur in unusual contexts.

Thus, I propose that initiatives designed to increase employees' PEBs should help employees to identify a specific PEB and create a goal around that behavior. For instance, the behavior might be using public transport to get to work rather than habitually driving to work; the employee can then create a goal (e.g., using public transport three times a week) and design plans for how he or she will get to the bus or train station, what time the person needs to leave, whether he or she should take a book to read or clothing to change into, and how he or she will deal with conflicting goals such as high workload. To overcome a strong habit, the employee will also need help in trying to change the context. For instance, organizations could encourage people to take public transport on "retreat" days or other non-normal days.

Specific Research Questions

Many research questions have been uncovered by examining the "why" and "how" of PEB workplace interventions. Some of these include:

- Are combinations of PEB interventions that follow the goals process more effective than other combinations and more than individual PEB interventions?
- What other self-regulatory based interventions are effective in increasing PEB?
- What are the positive and negative effects for conscious environmental PEB interventions?
- Are nonconscious PEB interventions as effective as conscious interventions?
- Which are more effective—environmentally focused or non–environmentally focused PEB interventions—or does it depend on other contextual factors?
- Is a comprehensive suite of goal-focused interventions, such as looking at habits, worth the time and effort involved in its implementation?

Conclusion

In summary, in this chapter I overlaid a goals framework onto the PEB intervention literature. By doing so, I was able to demonstrate why particular interventions work through their effects on goal attractiveness, goal efficacy, direct goal choice, goal commitment, and goal self-regulation. Moreover, I was able to show how particular interventions work through the use of conscious or nonconscious goal activation and through pro-environmental or non–pro-environmental goals. This overarching framework highlighted many areas in the PEB intervention literature that have yet to be fully understood as well as many potential PEB interventions that have not yet been developed. I hope that this overarching framework proves useful to researchers and practitioners wishing to improve PEBs in organizations (Figure 10.1).

Suggested Additional Readings

1. Young, W., Davis, M. C., McNeill, I., Malhotra, B., Russell, S. V., Unsworth, K. L., & Clegg, C. W. (in press). Changing behavior: Successful environmental programmes in the workplace. *Business Strategy and the Environment*.
2. Osbaldiston, R., & Schott, J. P. (2012). Environmental sustainability and behavioral science: Meta-analysis of proenvironmental behavior experiments. *Environment and Behavior*, *44*, 257–299.
3. Austin, J. T., & Vancouver, J. B. (1996). Goal constructs in psychology: Structure, process and content. *Psychological Bulletin*, *120*, 338–375.
4. Unsworth, K. L., Dmitrieva, A., & Adriasola, E. (2013). Changing behavior: Increasing the effectiveness of workplace interventions in creating pro-environmental behavior change. *Journal of Organizational Behavior*, *34*, 211–229.

References

Aarts, H., Custers, R., & Holland, R. W. (2007). The nonconscious cessation og goal pursuit: When goals and negative affect are coactivated. *Attitudes and Social Cognition*, *92*, 165–172.

Aarts, H., Custers, R., & Marien, H. (2008). Preparing and motivating behavior outside of awareness. *Science*, *319*, 1639.

Aarts, H., Custers, R., & Marien, H. (2009). Priming and authorship ascription: When nonconscious goals turn into conscious experiences of self-agency. *Journal of Personality and Social Psychology*, *96*, 967–979.

Aarts, H., Gollwitzer, P. M., & Hassin, R. R. (2004). Goal contagion: Perceiving is for pursuing. *Journal of Personality and Social Psychology*, *84*, 23–27.

Abrahamse, W., Steg, L., Vlek, C., & Rothengatter, T. (2005). A review of intervention studies aimed at household energy conservation. *Journal of Environmental Psychology, 25*, 273–291.

Ajzen, I. (1985). From intentions to actions: A theory of planned behavior. In J. Kuhl, & J. Beckmann (Eds.), *Action control: From cognition to behavior* (pp. 11–39). Berlin: Springer-Verlag.

Ajzen, I. (1991). The theory of planned behavior. *Organizational Behavior and Human Decision Processes, 50*, 179–211.

Amabile, T. M. (1996). *Creativity in context*. Boulder, CO: Westview Press.

Amabile, T. M., Hennessey, B. A., & Grossman, B. S. (1986). Social influences on creativity: The effects of contracted for reward. *Journal of Personality and Social Psychology, 50*, 14–23.

Andersson, L., Shivarajan, S., & Blau, G. (2005). Enacting ecological sustainability in the MNC: A test of an adapted value-belief-norm framework. *Journal of Business Ethics, 59*, 295–305.

Ashforth, B. E., Harrison, S. H., & Corley, K. G. (2008). Identification in organizations: An examination of four fundamental questions. *Journal of Management, 34*, 325–374.

Ashforth, B. E., & Mael, F. (1989). Social identity theory and the organization. *Academy of Management Review, 14*, 20–39.

Austin, J. T., Hatfield, D. B., Grindle, A. C., & Bailey, J. S. (1993). Increasing recycling in office environments: The effects of specific, informative cues. *Journal of Applied Behavior Analysis, 26*, 247–253.

Austin, J. T., & Vancouver, J. B. (1996). Goal constructs in psychology: Structure, process and content. *Psychological Bulletin, 120*, 338–375.

Bain, P. G., Hornsey, M. J., Bongiorno, R., & Jeffries, C. (2012). Promoting pro-environmental action in climate change deniers. *Nature: Climate Change, 2*, 600–603.

Bandura, A. (1991). Social cognitive theory of self-regulation. *Organizational Behavior and Human Decision Processes, 50*, 248–287.

Bandura, A. (1997). *Self-efficacy: The exercise of control*. New York: Freeman.

Bargh, J. A., Gollwitzer, P. M., Lee-Chai, A., Barndollar, K., & Trotschel, R. (2001). The automated will: Nonconscious activation and pursuit of behavioral goals. *Journal of Personality and Social Psychology, 81*, 1014–1027.

Becker, L. J. (1978). Joint effect of feedback and goal setting on performance: A field study of residential energy conservation. *Journal of Applied Psychology, 63*, 428–433.

Bissing-Olsen, M. J., Iyer, A., Fielding, K. S., & Zacher, H. (2013). Relationships between daily affect and pro-environmental behaviour at work: The moderating role of pro-environmental attitude. *Journal of Organizational Behavior, 34*, 156–175.

Bowman, M. (2011). Nudging effective climate policy design. *International Journal of Global Energy Issues, 35*, 242–254.

Brothers, K. J., Krantz, P. J., & McClannahan, L. E. (1994). Office paper recycling: A function of container proximity. *Journal of Applied Behavior Analysis, 27*, 153–160.

Carrico, A. R., & Riemer, M. (2011). Motivating energy conservation in the workplace: An evaluation of the use of group-level feedback and peer education. *Journal of Environmental Psychology, 31*, 1–13.

Chartrand, T. L., & Bargh, J. A. (1996). Automatic activation of impression formation and memorization goals: Nonconscious goal priming reproduces effects of explicit task instructions. *Journal of Personality and Social Psychology, 71*, 464–478.

Cialdini, R. B. (2003). Crafting normative messages to protect the environment. *Current Directions in Psychological Science, 12*, 105–109.

Cropanzano, R., James, K., & Citera, M. (1993). A goal hierarchy model of personality, motivation, and leadership. *Research in Organizational Behavior, 15*, 267–322.

Dahlstrand, U., & Biel, A. (2006). Pro-environmental habits: Propensity levels in behavioral change. *Journal of Applied Social Psychology, 27*, 588–601.

Danner, U. N., Aarts, H., & De Vries, N. K. (2008). Habit vs intention in the prediction of future behavior: The role of frequency, context stability and mental accessibility of past behavior. *British Journal of Social Psychology, 47*, 245–265.

Danner, U. N., Aarts, H., Papies, E. K., & de Vries, N. K. (2011). Paving the path for habit change: Cognitive shielding of intentions against habit intrusion. *British Journal of Health Psychology, 16*, 189–200.

Davis, M. C., & Challenger, R. (2012). *A socio-technical approach to sustainable intervention design*. Paper presented at the Academy of Management Annual Meeting, Boston.

Davis, M. C., & Galvan, J. J. (2013). *Driving green behaviour: Goal-setting and feedback a predictors of pro-environmental behaviour and performance in an organizational environmental initiative at an auto manufacturing plant*. Paper presented at the 10th Industrial and Organizational Psychology Conference, Perth, Australia.

Day, D. V., & Unsworth, K. L. (2013). Goals and self-regulation: Emerging perspectives across levels and time. In E. A. Locke, & G. P. Latham (Eds.), *New developments in goal-setting and task performance*. New York: Taylor & Francis.

De Leon, I. G., & Fuqua, R. W. (1995). The effects of public commitment and group feedback on curbside recycling. *Environment and Behavior, 27*, 233–250.

De Young, R. (1993). Changing behavior and making it stick: The conceptualization and management of conservation behavior. *Environment and Behavior, 25*, 485–505.

De Young, R. (2000). Expanding and evaluating motives for environmentally responsible behavior. *Journal of Social Issues, 56*, 509–526.

Deci, E. L., Egharri, H., Patrick, B. C., & Leone, D. R. (1994). Facilitating internalization: The self-determination theory perspective. *Journal of Personality, 62*, 119–142.

Deci, E. L., & Ryan, R. M. (1985). *Intrinsic motivation and self-determination in human behavior*. New York: Plenum.

Dickerson, C. A., Thibodeau, R., Aronson, E., & Miller, D. (1992). Using cognitive dissonance to encourage water conservation. *Journal of Applied Social Psychology, 22*, 841–854.

Dik, G., & Aarts, H. (2006). Behavioral cues to others' motivation and goal pursuits: The perception of effort facilitates goal inference and contagion. *Journal of Experimental Social Psychology, 43*, 727–737.

Dolan, P., Hallsworth, M., Halpern, D., King, D., & Vlaev, I. (2010). *Mindspace: Influencing behaviour through public policy*. London: Cabinet Office; Institute for Government.

Dono, J., Webb, J., & Richardson, B. (2010). The relationship between environmental activism, pro-environmental behavior and social identity. *Journal of Environmental Psychology, 30*, 178–186.

Dwyer, W. O., Leeming, F. C., Cobern, M. K., & Jackson, J. M. (1993). Critical review of behavioral interventions to preserve the environment: Research since 1980. *Environment and Behavior, 25*, 275–321

Eisenberger, R., & Armeli, S. (1997). Can salient reward increase creative performance without reducing intrinsic creative interest? *Journal of Personality and Social Psychology, 72*, 652–663.

Eisenberger, R., & Cameron, J. (1996). Detrimental effects of reward: Reality or myth? *American Psychologist, 51*, 1153–1166.

Evans, A., Russell, S. V., Fielding, K. S., & Hill, C. (2012). *Turn it off: Encouraging environmentally-friendly behaviours in the workplace*. Paper presented at the 26th Annual Australian and New Zealand Academy of Management Conference, Perth, Australia.

Festinger, L. (1957). *A theory of cognitive dissonance*. Stanford, CA: Stanford University Press.

Fielding, K. S., Terry, D. J., Masser, B., & Hogg, M. A. (2008). Integrating social identity theory and the theory of planned behaviour to explain decisions to engage in sustainable agricultural practices. *British Journal of Social Psychology, 47*, 23–48.

Fishbach, A., & Labroo, A. A. (2007). Be better or be merry: How mood affects self-contro. *Journal of Personality and Social Psychology, 93*, 158–173.

Fishbach, A., Shah, J. Y., & Kruglanski, A. W. (2004). Emotional transfer in goal systems. *Journal of Experimental Social Psychology, 40*, 723–738.

Foxx, R. M., & Schaeffer, M. H. (1981). A company based lottery to reduce the personal driving of employees. *Journal of Applied Behavior Analysis, 14*, 273–285.

French, J. (2011). Why nudging is not enough. *Journal of Social Marketing, 1*(2), 154–162.

Frey, B. S., & Oberholzer-Gee, F. (1997). The cost of price incentives: An empirical analysis of motivation crowding-out. *American Economic Review, 87*, 746–755.

Gollwitzer, P. M. (1990). Action phases and mind-sets. In E. T. Higgins, & R. M. Sorrentino (Eds.), *Handbook of motivation and cognition: Foundations od social behavior* (Vol. 2, pp. 53–92). New York: Guilford Press.

Gollwitzer, P. M., & Brandstatter, V. (1997). Implementation intentions and effective goal pursuit. *Journal of Personality and Social Psychology, 73*, 186–199.

Gonzales, M. H., Aronson, E., & Costanzo, M. A. (1988). Using social cognition and persuasion to promote energy conservation: A quasi-experiment. *Journal of Applied Social Psychology, 18*, 1049–1066.

Greaves, M., Zibarras, L. D., & Stride, C. (2013). Using the Theory of Planned Behavior to explore environmental behavioral intentions in the workplace. *Journal of Environmental Psychology, 34*, 109–120.

Hackman, J. R., & Oldham, G. R. (1980). *Work redesign*. Reading, MA: Addison-Wesley.

Hart, P. S., & Nisbet, E. C. (2012). Boomerang effects in science communication: How motivated reasoning and identity cues amplify opinion polarization about climate change policies. *Communication Research, 39*, 701–723.

Haslam, S. A., & Ellemers, N. (2005). Social identity in industrial and organizational psychology: Concepts, controversies and contributions. *International Review of Industrial and Organisational Psychology, 20*, 39–118.

Haslam, S. A., Postmes, T., & Ellemers, N. (2003). More than a metaphor: Organizational identity makes organizational life possible. *British Journal of Management, 14*, 357–369.

Hayes, S. C., & Cone, J. D. (1981). Reduction of residential consumption of electricity through simple monthly feedback. *Journal of Applied Behavior Analysis, 14*, 81–88.

Johns, K. D., Khovanova, K. M., & Welch, E. W. (2009). Fleet conversion in local government: Determinants of driver fuel choice for bi-fuel vehicles. *Environment and Behavior, 41*, 402–426.

Kahneman, D., & Tversky, A. (1979). Prospect theory: An analysis of decision under risk. *Econometrica, 47*, 263–291.

Kallbekken, S., & Saelen, H. (2013). 'Nudging' hotel guests to reduce food waste as a win-win environmental measure. *Economics Letters, 119*, 325–327.

Kanfer, R., Chen, G., & Pritchard, R. D. (2008). *Work motivation: Past, present and future*. New York: Routledge.

Kantola, S. J., Syme, G. J., & Campbell, N. A. (1984). Cognitive dissonance and energy conservation. *Journal of Applied Psychology, 69*, 416–421.

Katzev, R. D., & Johnson, T. R. (1987). *Promoting energy conservation: An analysis of behavioral research*. Boulder, CO: Westview.

Kim, S., Oah, S., & Dickinson, A. M. (2005). The impact of public feedback on three recycling-related behaviors in South Korea. *Environment and Behavior, 37*, 258–274.

Klein, H. J., Wesson, M. J., Hollenbeck, J. R., & Alge, B. J. (1999). Goal commitment and the goal-setting process: Conceptual clarification and empirical synthesis. *Journal of Applied Psychology, 84*, 885–896.

Kruglanski, A. W., Shah, J. Y., Fishbach, A., Friedman, R., Chun, W. Y., & Sleeth-Keppler, D. (2002). A theory of goal systems. *Advances in Experimental Social Psychology, 34*, 331–378.

Kurz, T., Donaghue, N., & Walker, I. (2005). Utilizing a social-ecological framework to promote water and energy conservation: A field experiment. *Journal of Applied Social Psychology, 35*, 1281–1300.

Laran, J., Janiszewski, C., & Cunha, M. J. (2008). Context-dependent effects of goal primes. *Journal of Consumer Research, 35*, 653–667.

Legal, J. B., Meyer, T., & Delouvee, S. (2007). Effect of compatibility between conscious goal and nonconscious priming on performance. *Current Research in Social Psychology, 12*, 81–90.

Lehman, P. K., & Geller, E. S. (2004). Behavior analysis and environmental protection: Accomplishments and potential for more. *Behavior and Social Issues, 13*, 13–32.

Locke, E. A., & Latham, G. P. (1990). *A theory of goal setting and task performance.* Englewood Cliffs, NJ: Prentice Hall.

Locke, E. A., & Latham, G. P. (2002). Building a practically useful theory of goal-setting and task motivation: A 35 year odyssey. *American Psychologist, 57*, 705–717.

Locke, E. A., & Latham, G. P. (2013). *New developments in goal-setting and task performance.* New York: Routledge.

Lord, K. R. (1994). Motivating recycling behavior: A quasiexperimental investigation of message and source strategies. *Psychology & Marketing, 11*, 341–358.

Lord, R. G., & Brown, D. J. (2001). Leadership, values, and subordinate self-concepts. *The Leadership Quarterly, 12*, 133–152.

Lord, R. G., Brown, D. J., & Freiberg, S. J. (1999). Understanding the dynamics of leadership: The role of follower self-concepts in the leader/follower relationship. *Organizational Behavior and Human Decision Processes, 78*, 167–203.

Louro, M. J., Pieters, R., & Zeelenberg, M. (2007). Dynamics of multiple-goal pursuit. *Journal of Personality and Social Psychology, 93*, 174–193.

Ludwig, T. D., Gray, T. W., & Rowell, A. (1998). Increasing recycling in academic buildings: A systematic replication. *Journal of Applied Behavior Analysis, 31*, 683–686.

Luyben, P. D. (1980). Effects of informational prompts on energy conservation in college classrooms. *Journal of Applied Behavior Analysis, 13*, 611–617.

Luyben, P. D. (1984). Drop and tilt: A comparison of two procedures to increase the use of venetian blinds to conserve energy. *Journal of Community Psychology, 12*, 149–154.

McCalley, L. T., & Midden, C. J. H. (2002). Energy conservation through product-integrated feedback: The roles of goal-setting and social orientation. *Journal of Economic Psychology, 23*, 589–603.

McCullough, K. C., Aarts, H., Fujita, K., & Bargh, J. A. (2008). Inhibition in goal systems: A retrieval-induced forgetting account. *Journal of Experimental Social Psychology, 44*, 857–865.

McDougall, G. H. G., Claxton, J. D., & Ritchie, J. R. B. (1982–1983). Residential home audits: An empirical analysis of the ENEVERSAVE program. *Journal of Environmental Systems, 12*, 265–278.

Midden, C. J. H., Meter, J. E., Weening, M. H., & Zieverink, H. J. A. (1983). Using feedback, reinforcement and information to reduce energy consumption in households: A field experiment. *Journal of Economic Psychology, 3*, 65–86.

Molina, R., Unsworth, K. L., Hodkiewicz, M. R., & Adriasola, E. (2013). Are managerial pressure, technological control and intrinsic motivation effective in improving data quality? *Reliability Engineering and System Safety, 119*, 26–34.

Moseley, A., & Stoker, G. (2013). Nudging citizens? Prospects and pitfalls confronting a new heuristic. *Resources, Conservation and Recycling, 79*, 4–10. doi: http://dx.doi.org/10.1016/j.resconrec.2013.04.008.

Osbaldiston, R., & Schott, J. P. (2012). Environmental sustainability and behavioral science: Meta-analysis of proenvironmental behavior experiments. *Environment and Behavior, 44*, 257–299.

Ouellette, J. A., & Wood, W. (1998). Habit and intention in everyday life: The multiple processes by which past behavior predicts future behavior. *Psychological Bulletin, 124*, 54–74.

Pallak, M. S., & Cummings, W. (1976). Commitment and voluntary energy conservation. *Personality and Social Psychology Bulletin, 2*, 27–30.

Pelletier, L. G., & Sharp, E. C. (2007). *From the promotion of pro-environmental behaviors to the development of an eco-citizen: The self-determination theory perspective.* Paper presented at the the Annual Conference of the Canadian Psychological Association, Ottawa, Ontario.

Robertson, J. L., & Barling, J. (2013). Greening organizations through leaders' influence on employees' pro-environmental behaviors. *Journal of Organizational Behavior, 34*, 176–194.

Russell, S., & Griffiths, A. (2008). The role of emotions in driving workplace pro-environmental behaviors. *Research in Emotion in Organizations, 4*, 83–107.

Scherbaum, C. A., Popovich, P. M., & Finlinson, S. (2008). Exploring individual-level factors related to employee energy-conservation behaviors at work. *Journal of Applied Social Psychology, 38*, 818–835.

Schultz, P. W., Nolan, J. M., Cialdini, R. B., Goldstein, N. J., & Griskevicius, V. (2007). The constructive, destructive and reconstructive power of social norms. *Psychological Science, 18*, 429–434.

Selinger, E., & Whyte, K. P. (2012). Nudging cannot solve complex policy problems. *European Journal of Risk Regulation*, *3*(1), 36–41.

Shah, J. Y., Friedman, R., & Kruglanski, A. W. (2002). Forgetting all else: On the antecedents and consequences of goal shielding. *Journal of Personality and Social Psychology*, *83*, 1261–1280.

Shah, J. Y., & Kruglanski, A. W. (2003). When opportunity knocks: Bottom-up priming of goals by means and its effects on self-regulation. *Journal of Personality and Social Psychology*, *84*, 1109–1122.

Shantz, A., & Latham, G. P. (2009). An exploratory field experiment of the effect of subconscious and conscious goals on employee performance. *Organizational Behavior and Human Decision Processes*, *109*, 9–17.

Sheeran, P., Milne, S., Webb, T. L., & Gollwitzer, P. M. (2005). Implementation intentions and health behaviour. In M. Conner, & P. Markman (Eds.), *Predicting health behaviour: Research and practice with social cognition models* (pp. 276–323). Maidenhead, UK: Open University Press.

Siero, F. W., Bakker, A. B., Dekker, G. B., & van den Burg, M. T. C. (1996). Changing organizational energy consumption behaviour through comparative feedback. *Journal of Environmental Psychology*, *16*, 235–246.

Simon, H. (1957). A behavioral model of rational choice *Models of man, social and rational: Mathematical essays on rational human behavior in a social setting*. New York: Wiley.

Slavin, R. E., Wodanski, J. S., & Blackburn, B. L. (1981). A group contingency for electricity conservation in master-metered apartments. *Journal of Applied Behavior Analysis*, *14*, 357–363.

Staats, H., van Leeuwen, E., & Wit, A. (2000). A longitudinal study of informational interventions to save energy in an office building. *Journal of Applied Behavior Analysis*, *33*, 101–104.

Steg, L., & Vlek, C. (2009). Encouraging pro-environmental behavior: An integrative review and research agenda. *Journal of Environmental Psychology*, *29*, 309–317.

Stern, P. C. (2011). Contributions of psychology to limiting climate change. *American Psychologist*, *66*, 303–314.

Tajfel, H., & Turner, J. C. (1986). The social identity theory of intergroup behaviour. In S. Worchel, & W. G. Austin (Eds.), *Psychology of intergroup relations* (pp. 7–24). Chicago: Nelson Hall.

Thaler, R., & Sunstein, C. (2008). *Nudge: Improving decisions about health, wealth and happiness*. New Haven, CT: Yale University Press.

Turner, J. C., Oakes, P. J., Haslam, S. A., & McGarty, C. (1994). Self and collective: Cognition and social context. *Personality and Social Psychology Bulletin*, *20*, 454–463.

Unsworth, K. L., Adriasola, E., Johnston-Billings, A., Dmitrieva, A., & Hodkiewicz, M. R. (2011). Goal hierarchy: Improving asset data quality by improving motivation. *Reliability Engineering and System Safety*, *96*, 1474–1481.

Unsworth, K. L., Dmitrieva, A., & Adriasola, E. (2013). Changing behavior: Increasing the effectiveness of workplace interventions in creating pro-environmental behavior change. *Journal of Organizational Behavior, 34*, 211–229.

Unsworth, K. L., Wall, T. D., & Carter, A. (2005). Creative requirement: A neglected construct in the study of employee creativity. *Group and Organization Management, 30*, 541–560.

van Houten, R., Nau, P., & Marini, Z. (1981). Reducing elevator energy use: A comparison of posted feedback and reduced elevator convenience. *Journal of Applied Behavior Analysis, 14*, 377–387.

Werner, C. M., Rhodes, M. U., & Partain, K. K. (1998). Designing effective instructional signs with schema theory: Case studies of polystyrene recycling. *Basic and Applied Social Psychology, 24*, 185–203.

Winett, R. A., Love, S. Q., & Kidd, C. (1982–1983). The effectiveness of an energy specialist and extensions agents in promoting summer energy conservation by home visits. *Journal of Environmental Systems, 12*, 61–70.

Wood, R. (2005). New frontiers for self-regulation research in IO psychology. *Applied Psychology: An International Review, 54*, 192–198.

Wood, W., & Neal, D. T. (2007). A new look at habits and the habit-goal interface. *Psychological Review, 114*, 843–863.

Young, W., Davis, M. C., McNeill, I., Malhotra, B., Russell, S. V., Unsworth, K. L., & Clegg, C. W. (2013). Changing behavior: Successful environmental programmes in the workplace. *Business Strategy and the Environment*. doi:10.1002/bse.1836

11 ORGANIZATIONAL CHANGE

Matthew Davis and Phillipa Coan

"Implementation and organizational change are the key issues the sustainability agenda is demanding action on" (Millar, Hind, & Magala, 2012, p. 491). This chapter sets out to provide insight into how organizational change principles may be employed as a means of enacting Work Pro-Environmental Behaviour (WPEB) more broadly across an organization and addresses the current lack of clarity on how specifically to implement corporate sustainability (Linnenluecke & Griffiths, 2010). We argue that organization-wide change promotes a proactive approach to engaging with and addressing the environmental sustainability agenda within organizations.

Efforts to promote WPEB can be considered as one part of a wider process of organizational change whereby organizations seek to implement new ways of working to deliver greater environmental sustainability (Davis & Challenger, 2009; Dunphy, Benn, & Griffiths, 2003; Post & Altman, 1994). The role of individuals is paramount to successful organizational change, whether it be through involvement in designing initiatives, leading change, accepting changes to working practices, or cultivating a shared culture; although all of these areas influence WPEB, they also ultimately contribute toward the organization's wider environmental sustainability (Andersson & Bateman, 2000; Bansal, 2003; By, 2005; Kotter, 1995; Weick & Quinn, 1999).

In this chapter we make the link between wider organizational change theory and environmental sustainability concepts and research. There is a need to integrate these literatures and to move beyond what have often been technological, infrastructural, or environmental management-led change programs toward more balanced organization-wide change initiatives that involve users and promote

WPEB (Bansal & Gao, 2006; Davis, Challenger, Jayewardene, & Clegg, 2014). This is crucial because organizations are unlikely to be able to achieve environmental sustainability through technology innovation alone (DuBois, Astakhova, & DuBois, 2013); human behavior is key to long-term change (Steg & Vlek, 2009; Young et al., 2013). There are clear parallels to the failures experienced with technology-led business change initiatives in general (e.g., Baxter & Sommerville, 2011; Clegg & Shepherd, 2007), in which technological innovations have often turned out to be much less effective in practice than when they were conceived (e.g., Broadhurst et al., 2010; Eason, 2007; Thompson, Pithouse, & Davey, 2010), and in the introduction of more energy efficient technologies, for example, the poor energy performance exhibited in some new commercial buildings with automated heating and ventilation systems (e.g., Wener & Carmalt, 2006).

We acknowledge from the outset that it would have been possible to write individual chapters, and in some cases whole books, on the themes that we identify within this chapter. However, our intention is to highlight what we believe are the most salient aspects of change management that are relevant to promoting WPEB and environmental sustainability within organizations, as well as to identify key themes and challenges that face those researching or practicing in this area. In so doing, we hope that this serves as a useful introduction and starting point for those considering applying a change process to support WPEB.

To frame the topic, the chapter begins with a definition of environmental sustainability and its link to organizational change. Next, four key areas of change management are focused upon, namely (a) organizational culture, (b) leadership and change agents, (c) employee engagement, and (d) differing forms that change may take. These factors were selected based on their relatively consistent inclusion within key organizational change models (e.g., Burnes, 1996, 2004; By, 2005; Clegg & Walsh, 2004) along with their initial success in driving WPEB (e.g., Fernandez, Junquera, & Ordiz, 2003; Harris & Crane, 2002; Robertson & Barling, 2013). The role of each concept in supporting organizational environmental change is discussed, together with relevant research evidence drawn from the corporate sustainability; WPEB; management and organizational change literatures. Then, socio-technical systems thinking (STST) (e.g., Cherns, 1976, 1987; Clegg, 2000) is offered as a framework with which to approach the design and implementation of holistic organizational change. Finally, we outline a number of key research developments that are required to aid progression within this domain and offer practical recommendations for enacting organizational change for environmental sustainability.

Defining Environmental Sustainability within the Workplace

Pro-environmental behavior has been defined as "behavior that consciously seeks to minimize the negative impact of one's actions on the natural and built world" (Kollmuss & Agyeman, 2002, p. 240). Within an organizational context, Ones and Dilchert (2012) define employee green behaviors as "scalable actions and behaviors that employees engage in that are linked with and contribute to or detract from environmental sustainability" (p. 87). They have categorized these behaviors as working sustainably (e.g., creating sustainable products and processes); influencing others (e.g., educating and training for sustainability); avoiding harm (e.g., preventing pollution); conserving (e.g., reusing); and taking initiative (e.g., lobbying and activism; Ones & Dilchert, 2010). Within this chapter, in addition to these WPEBs we also consider environmental sustainability in its wider sense and draw upon research that has sought to impact on organization's overall environmental performance. Environmental sustainability within organizations broadly refers to seeking a balance between industry growth and preserving the natural environment for future generations (e.g., Jennings & Zandbergen, 1995; Ramus, 2002). However, the concept of environmental sustainability within organizations is also often defined within a broader framework of sustainability, corporate sustainability, or sustainable development, which all tend to integrate environmental, social, and financial considerations, referred to as the "triple bottom line" (Vanclay, 2004). Although some researchers emphasize the environmental dimension as most important (e.g., Starik & Rands, 1995), others subsume the environment under the social component (e.g., Sekerka & Stimel, 2011). Due to a larger proportion of research carried out on sustainability, this chapter includes research that focuses on both environmental sustainability and sustainability more generally (within organizations).

Organizational Culture

When implementing any change initiative, a consideration of the organizational culture is necessary (Weick & Quinn, 1999). Although there are varying definitions across the literature, many scholars adopt Schein's (2010) three-level model of culture that outlines (a) a "surface level" representing the visible artifacts, including published reports and communications; (b) the "value level," which are the values, norms, and ideologies of organizational members; and (c) the "underlying level" described as the organization's core assumptions that determine both thinking processes and behaviors. Schein (2010) posits that it is this final underlying level that fully captures the "essence of a culture" (p. 32). Researchers have consequently argued that in order for an organization to become sustainable, its underlying values and assumptions must be in line with sustainability issues (e.g., Russell & McIntosh, 2011). This next section reflects on research that has explored (a) how an organization's culture influences the way in which it responds to environmental sustainability; (b) how organizations might successfully enact environmental culture change; and (c) the influence of subcultures within organizations.

Organizational Culture and Responses to Environmental Sustainability

Russell and McIntosh (2011) present a typology of organizations based on their paradigmatic views and subsequent responses to sustainability. Building on previous classifications (e.g., Carroll, 1979), they discuss the importance of culture as organizations progress from a "reactive" to a "proactive" state (see also Colby's, 1991, five category typology of environmental management). They outline five classifications: toward one end of the spectrum reactive organizations tend to emphasize purely economic priorities, while ignoring sustainability issues; defensive organizations do only what is required to meet legislation; and accommodative organizations accept their social and environmental responsibilities and begin to integrate environmental issues into corporate strategy, although often external pressures serve as the main driver (Lee, 2011). At the other end of the spectrum organizations are more proactive; however, while actively engaging in sustainable management, some argue organizations in this category do not act out of any moral obligation but are keen to be leaders in their industry (e.g., Carroll, 1979). Finally, Russell and McIntosh (2011) introduce sustainable organizations, which have a longer-term perspective fully embedding sustainability principles within their values.

There is some debate in the literature regarding whether organizations need to have an underlying moral commitment to sustainability for associated behavior to be carried out (Russell & McIntosh, 2011; Stoughton & Ludema, 2012). Lenninleucke and Griffiths (2010), for example, present a range of organizational culture types with varying values and assumptions who may all pursue corporate sustainability but for different reasons. There is also some empirical evidence supporting the view that organizations can successfully enact sustainable practices without changing their core values (e.g., Fineman, 1997; Fineman & Clarke, 1996). Crane (2000) refers to this as the "amoralization" of corporate greening. Others, however, have emphasized the need for organizations to embrace a more radical paradigm shift in corporate culture developing an entirely new value system aligned to green issues (e.g., Crew, 2010; Fernandez et al., 2003; Galbreath, 2009; Harris & Crane, 2002; Johnson & Macy, 2001; Stead & Stead, 1994; Welford, 1995). This is supported by mounting empirical evidence that corporate environmental values directly relate to workplace environmental behavior (e.g., Andersson, Shivarajan, & Blau, 2005; Nilsson, von Borgstede, & Biel, 2004; Ramus & Steger, 2000; Sharma, 1999). Furthermore, by fully embedding sustainability, organizations are less at risk of *green washing* or appearing to merely bolt on sustainability to existing initiatives that may impede employee buy-in and engagement (Lazlo & Zhexembayeva, 2011).

How to Enact Organizational Culture Change toward Environmental Sustainability

Although research on organizational culture change toward environmental sustainability has been criticized for failing to provide practical suggestions for *how* to enact such change (e.g., Harris & Crane, 2002; Newton & Harte, 1997), there are some notable exceptions emerging from the literature. For example, linking culture to human resource management (HRM) practices, including selection and recruitment, training, performance appraisal, and rewards (Fernandez et al., 2003; Renwick, Redman, & Maguire, 2013; see also section on Engagement and chapter 12); ensuring buy-in and leadership support from senior management (e.g., Andersson & Bateman, 2000; Linnenluecke & Griffiths, 2010; Ones & Dilchert, 2012; see also, the section on Leadership and Change Agents and chapter 8); having a clear environmental policy, mission and strategy statements, which are effectively communicated (Post & Altman, 1994; Ramus & Steger, 2000); appointing key change agents or champions across the organization (e.g., Andersson & Bateman, 2000; Heijden, Cramer, & Driessen, 2012; see also, section on Leadership and Change Agents); and fostering a learning culture that promotes innovation and creative thinking around how the organization can successfully move toward a more sustainable future (Crews & Woman, 2010; Ramus, 2001).

The Presence of Subcultures

Although most definitions of organizational culture refer to a homogenous, unified set of shared values and norms (e.g., Schein, 2010), more recently a number of researchers have pointed to the existence of more fragmented subcultures within organizations influencing the extent to which sustainability issues are diffused throughout an organization (e.g., Harris & Crane, 2002; Howard-Grenville, 2006; Linnenluecke & Griffiths, 2010; Stoughton & Ludema, 2012). These subcultures can form across departments (e.g., Sackman, 1992), hierarchical levels (e.g., Riley, 1983), or personal networks and/or demographic groups (Suls, Martin, & Wheeler, 2002). Importantly, these different subcultures have been found to influence the way in which sustainability is interpreted (e.g., Linnenluecke, Russell, & Griffiths, 2009) as well as how problems are addressed and what strategies for action are adopted (e.g., Howard-Grenville, 2006). These findings suggest that taking a unitary top down approach to environmental culture change is unlikely to be successful given the presence of these intraorganizational differences. Instead, initiatives may be more effective if tailored to the different groups throughout the organization as well as involving employees from each group with any change intervention (Harris & Ogbonna, 1998; Linnenluecke et al., 2009).

Leadership and Change Agents

The critical role of leaders in guiding, supporting, and structuring organizational change initiatives along with generating a shared vision, reinforcing company values and building consensus is well recognized within the literature (e.g., Ferdig, 2007; Schein, 2010; Schneider, Ehrhart, & Macey, 2013; Weick & Quinn, 1999). It is therefore perhaps not surprising that initiating any change toward environmental sustainability within organizations similarly relies on good leadership (Millar et al., 2012; Stead & Stead, 1994). However, there is still some confusion in the literature regarding who actually takes on the role of a leader within an organization (Schein, 2010). Although the role typically falls with the CEO, a head of department or manager, Schein (2010) highlights how "anyone who facilitates progress toward some desired outcome is displaying leadership" (p. x). In line with this, many researchers have argued that anyone in the organization can become a "sustainability leader" or key environmental change agent regardless of his or her role or position (Ferdig, 2007; Post & Altman, 1994). The next section explores some of the research that has looked at the role of leaders in promoting WPEB, and then the role of employees as essential change agents for environmental sustainability.

The Role of Leaders

The influence of top management in driving forward environmental sustainability stems from their ability to direct corporate strategy along with organizational policies, programs, budgets, and reward systems (Branzei, Vertinsky, & Zietsma, 2000). However, as well as having the capacity to steer the organization at the corporate level, they also have been found to personally carry out WPEBs to a greater extent compared with non-managers (Ones, Dilchert, Biga,

& Gibby, 2010); and their WPEBs have been found to influence other organizational members' WPEB (e.g., Ones & Dilchert, 2012; Ramus & Steger, 2000). In a recent special issue in the *Journal of Organizational Behavior* on the topic of environmental sustainability within organizations, Robertson and Barling (2013) looked at the role of environmentally specific transformational leadership (ETFL). Environmentally specific transformational leadership encompasses sharing environmental values with employees, convincing followers they can achieve WPEBs, helping employees consider environmental issues in new and innovative ways, and establishing relationships with employees through which they can exert influence. Not only did they find that leaders' WPEB directly influenced both employees' environmental passion and their WPEBs (consistent with social learning theory; Bandura, 1977), they also found that ETFL increased employees' environmental passion, which had subsequent effects upon their WPEB. Reflecting traditional organizational change successes (e.g., Weick & Quinn, 1999), leaders therefore serve to influence and support employees' WPEB as well as model the desired WPEB themselves.

Although a number of motivations may be driving leader's WPEBs and associated strategic decision making, including, for example, government regulations, consumer demands, external pressure groups, and market competition, there is increasing evidence that the organizations that most successfully implement environmental practices and innovations have leaders who show a persistent commitment to improved environmental performance stemming from personal eco-centric cognitions such as pro-environmental values and attitudes (e.g., Bansal & Roth, 2000; Branzei, Vertinsky, & Zietsma, 2000; Burger, 1999; May & Flannery, 1995; Shrivastava, 1995; Stead & Stead, 1994), as well as previous experience with environmental issues from past roles (Walls & Hoffman, 2013).

The Role of Employees

Although traditional leaders of organizations may play a prominent role in directing sustainability efforts within an organization, many recognize that any employee who is able to successfully engage with others regarding sustainability issues can become a sustainability leader, environmental champion, or change agent (e.g., Andersson & Bateman, 2000; Crane, 2000; Fineman & Clarke, 1996; Post & Altman, 1994). Ferdig (2007) refers to these employees as "everyday leaders . . . who take up power and engage with others to make a sustainable difference to organizations" (p. 33). Sustainability leadership is therefore often dispersed across the organization rather than being held by a single individual helping to diffuse sustainability issues more widely (Redekop & Olson, 2010).

In the organizational change literature, traditional change agents use advanced interpersonal, networking, and influencing skills to mobilize change and elicit cooperation and consensus from diverse departments whose ways of working and personal interests may be challenged by the change initiative (Hartley, Benington, & Binns, 1997; Weick & Quinn, 1999). Environmental change agents enact this same role, promoting WPEB like any other change initiative and playing an active role in both facilitating the flow of environmental information across all employees and "sense-making" any new initiative or sustainability framework to enable shared understanding (Heijden et al., 2012; Post & Altman, 1994).

As well as communicating environmental issues and initiatives to other employees, environmental change agents may also need to persuade top management of the value of a proposed initiative for both the organization and wider society (Fineman & Clarke, 1996; Post & Altman, 1994). For example, it was the employees at Interface, Inc. who presented Ray Anderson, the CEO, with relevant reading material around environmental issues and asked him to articulate his environmental vision (DuBois et al., 2013). Through this process, he transformed his approach to conducting business successfully, directing the carpet manufacturing company from a resource intensive firm toward sustainability (DuBois et al., 2013).

Andersson and Bateman (2000) used both interview and survey findings to develop a framework for successful championing behaviors, including how to identify, package, and sell environmental issues to management. Although acknowledging that behaviors would need to be adapted to suit different organizational contexts and cultures, their framework highlights the need to appropriately: (a) research the environmental issue, gathering background information and discussing this with others; (b) frame the environmental issue, for example, as an urgent problem with financial and reputational opportunities; (c) present the issue in a traditional business-like manner using formal language and protocol; and finally (d) sell the environmental issue, for example, by appealing to management's aspirations and goals and forming coalitions with other respected employees. In line with traditional organizational change processes, both change agents and top management commitment are therefore integral to the success of any environmental change initiative to ensure that the environmental message is clearly communicated and disseminated to all employees.

Worker Engagement and Involvement

Employee engagement is recognized within numerous theories of organizational change as essential to gaining acceptance of new ways of working or shifts in business practices (Armenakis & Bedeian, 1999; Burnes, 1996; Kanter, Stein, & Jick, 1992; Kotter, 1995; Luecke, 2003; Weick & Quinn, 1999). Indeed, a failure to engage or involve staff during change processes has often been associated with unsuccessful outcomes (Holman et al., 2000). The principles of engagement and involvement may hold open the prospect of more successful implementation and better design of organizational change programs directed at increasing environmental sustainability and WPEB change (Ramus, 2001; Young et al., 2013). This section examines how employee engagement may be a necessary aspect of environmental change, considers research that has employed techniques to engage staff, and discusses the distinction between engagement and involvement.

Engagement

Engaging employees in the change process is considered a key aspect of enacting change and subsequently sustaining it (Kanter, 1983; Pasmore, 1994). Engaged employees can be a valuable resource in helping to build readiness for change and through "doing more of what needs to be done, changing what needs to be changed" (Macey & Schneider, 2008, p. 18) within organizations attempting to increase their environmental sustainability.

Organizations use a range of techniques to engage staff and motivate employees in environmental sustainability initiatives and change programs (Cox, Higgins, Gloster, Foley, & Darnton, 2012; Osbaldiston & Schott, 2012; Young et al., 2013). Similar to individual behavior change initiatives in the workplace and at home, we can expect engagement to be gained through the use of a number of differing techniques to appeal to a range of individuals (Unsworth, Dmitrieva, & Adriasola, 2013)—see chapter 10.

The use of communications and provision of information is the most common engagement technique employed in this domain (Osbaldiston & Schott, 2012) and this is reflected in studies that have sought to build engagement into change programs (e.g., Handgraaf, Van Lidth de Jeude, & Appelt, 2013; White, 2009). The value of such an approach in supporting large scale organizational change in general was demonstrated by Schweiger and Denisi (1991) who showed that the use of communications channels (e.g., telephone hotlines, newsletters, staff meetings) directed at keeping employees informed of progress on a merger significantly reduced negative effects on employees (e.g., stress, turnover intent) compared with employees who were not party to ongoing communications. These general principles have likewise been supported in relation to environmental sustainability; for example, McMakin, Malone, Lundgren (2002) used a variety of communication channels (including focus groups, informational leaflets, videos, together with formal feedback and communications through the military chain of command) to successfully engage military personnel and families in energy reduction. Similarly, Procter & Gamble sought to keep staff engaged in their ongoing sustainability program through the use of newsletters, podcasts, and site-wide events (White, 2009).

Establishing open and continuing communications during periods of change enables organizations to communicate their vision and keep employees informed of planned change—with the aim of reducing resistance and worker uncertainty (Weick & Quinn, 1999). Such communication also establishes a channel to enable employees to share their thoughts and opinions on proposed changes, which has been recognized as a key requirement for successful change (Dowie, McCartney, & Tamm, 1998; Morrison & Milliken, 2000).

A variety of incentives have also been offered by organizations to engage staff in desired environmental change, for example, cash incentives or days off for performing actions such as changing travel mode (Cox et al., 2012). Monetary incentives have been found to help build engagement in environmental initiatives and drive impressive changes in working practices within the construction industry (Chen, Li, & Wong, 2002; Li, Chen, & Wong, 2003). Non-monetary rewards have also been successfully employed, for example, environmental gifts and public status have been used as rewards for engaging in an environmental sustainability program in the automotive industry (Davis et al., 2014). Interestingly, Handgraaf, van Lidth de Jeude, and Appelt (2013) found that public rewards were more effective than private rewards and non-monetary rewards were more effective than monetary rewards in reducing energy use in a Dutch organization. Despite these successes, however, how well rewards can sustain engagement and change over time is unclear. Potential alternatives in the form of feedback and goal-setting (Locke & Latham, 2004) have helped to deliver employee engagement and motivate them to take part in workplace environmental sustainability programs over the medium term (e.g., Lingard, Gilbert, & Graham, 2001; Siero, Bakker, Dekker, & Van Den Burg, 1996).

If employees are not adequately engaged in the change process they may potentially resist and undermine changes that are asked of them (e.g., By, 2005; Davis, Leach, & Clegg, 2011; Weick & Quinn, 1999). Indeed, institutionalizing environmental sustainability, and changing associated culture and practices will require individuals not only to understand the proposed changes, but also to want to adapt and actively engage in WPEB to help to create a green organization.

Involvement

As discussed, many organizational efforts to "green" have been technologically or process led (Bansal & Gao, 2006; Davis & Challenger, 2014). Even among people led change programs there is a danger that it can become a process that is decided from on high and simply imposed on or implemented toward those employees below (Clegg & Shepherd, 2007; Guy, 2006). Although employee engagement goes some way to counter potential employee resistance, it does not necessarily mean that a change program is employee led.

Involvement of employees from an early stage and enabling meaningful participation in decision making can support a more "bottom-up" and emergent form of change (Armenakis & Bedeian, 1999; Burnes, 1996; Kanter et al., 1992; Weick & Quinn, 1999; Woodman, 1989). This is congruent with what has been described as "pull-based user-owned change" (Clegg & Walsh, 2004, p. 235), whereby end users pull the change project through to successful completion by taking ownership of, and having input into, the process, ensuring that it meets their needs. This form of change caters to the general desire for control (e.g., Bandura, 1997; Karasek & Theorell, 1990) and the observation that employees require influence in addition to simply information about the changes that are affecting them to maintain interest and support (Heller, Pusic, Strauss, & Wilpert, 1998).

An employee-led change process with high involvement also acknowledges that employees themselves hold information valuable to the design and implementation of environmental sustainability within organizations (Davis & Challenger, 2009; Rothenberg, 2003; Young et al., 2013). Employees often possess tacit knowledge about how organizations work in reality and how changes to practices may best be implemented (Bansal, 2003; May & Flannery, 1995). However, although "pull-based," user-driven change, may be highly desirable (Heller et al., 1998), there can be difficulties in practically facilitating employee involvement in change processes. A key constraint can be the time requirements on project staff to meaningfully involve large numbers of employees in the process or in managing expectations and varying skills levels (Adams & McNicholas, 2007; Kujala, 2003). Such difficulties are not insurmountable, however, and careful planning and a considered mix of face-to-face and electronic facilitation techniques may be highly effective in supporting meaningful employee involvement.

The Form of Change

The previous sections have demonstrated the many interlinking factors and considerations that are involved in supporting successful organizational change.

We have considered the organizational culture, the role of both leaders and change agents, together with the need to engage employees in successful environmental sustainability programs. These levers of change relate to differing views regarding how to approach organizational change, with two major perspectives dominating the literature (Armenakis & Bedeian, 1999; By, 2005; Weick & Quinn, 1999), namely, the planned approach and the emergent approach. In this section we discuss each of these perspectives in turn and briefly reflect upon the potential middle ground of a contingency approach.

Planned Change

The planned approach to change grew out of the early work of Lewin on organizational change and Lewin's (1946, cited in Burnes, 2004) three-step model of change. The three-step model describes organizational change as discrete steps whereby (a) the current static state of the organization is unfrozen and old behaviors and processes are discarded, (b) action is then taken to move the organization to the next level or state, and then (c) the organization is refrozen at the new level with the change accepted (Burnes, 1996; By, 2005). There have been many extensions and developments of this basic model (e.g., Bullock & Batten, 1985); however, the underlying premise that organizational change is a planned process led by management is consistent (Weick & Quinn, 1999).

This approach to change can be viewed as highly dependent upon the skills and knowledge of top managers, relying on them to initiate change and actively drive the process within the organization from the top-down (Burnes, 1996). This approach may not lend itself to the bottom-up, employee-led aspect of change discussed earlier; however, employee engagement and consultation in the process is encouraged (Kanter et al., 1992). A planned approach to change may be particularly helpful in situations in which an organization is responding to very specific environmental challenges and the objectives are clear to the management team involved. However, the reliance upon leaders for initiating and setting the parameters of the process means that the change initiatives may not be as responsive to the external environment, as flexible or open to innovation as under an emergent approach, and unable to produce the sorts of transformational change that may be necessary to adapt to climate change (e.g., Burnes, 2004; By, 2005; Dunphy & Stace, 1993).

Emergent Change

In contrast, models of emergent change (e.g., Kanter et al., 1992; Kotter, 1996; Luecke, 2003) stress that organizational change should not be wholly preplanned and conducted over a fixed time period (Burnes, 2004)—rather change should be an ongoing process in response to the evolving environment and business landscape (By, 2005). This perspective envisages a more active role for employees, with a largely nondirective, bottom-up initiation of change responses. Employees have a role in interpreting the situation and responding to change, driving emergent changes in the organization (Weick & Quinn, 1999). Managers' roles in this form of change can be seen more as facilitators, leading change but not necessarily defining it, helping to foster a learning culture that promotes innovation (Burnes, 1996; Crew, 2010).

The iterative and adaptive process supported by an emergent approach may provide a means for responding to the complex and evolving nature of environmental sustainability in particular (DuBois et al., 2013; Dunphy & Stace, 1993), for example, changes in legislation, pressure groups, and shifting agendas. Such responses, are, however, predicated on employees possessing or obtaining the necessary skills or knowledge to respond to the environmental challenges that they encounter. Furthermore, the flexibility that an emergent approach offers, through being bottom-up, may also result in employees' attention being focused on particular challenges that they have identified and not the environmental issues that management foresee as obstacles to future growth (c.f., Burnes, 1996).

Contingency or a Middle Ground

It has been suggested that there is not one best way or approach to managing and supporting organizational change (Burnes, 1996), nor are there sets of universal rules to guide the way (Pettigrew & Whipp, 1993). A contingency approach offers a middle ground, suggesting that the form of change most appropriate to an organization will be contingent upon the situational variables that an organization faces (By, 2005). The general principle suggests that the form of change an organization adopts may vary over time as the organization or its situation varies (Dunphy & Stace, 1993).

Despite criticisms regarding potential difficulties in moving between differing forms of change (Burnes, 1996), it is suggested that it is likely that the form most appropriate to an organization will depend upon the environmental sustainability change they are seeking to promote, for example, to adapt production processes to meet specific upcoming environmental regulation, encourage individuals to change their travel habits, innovate new products, or revolutionize their whole way of business. A combination of top-down and bottom-up is probably the most common solution to help meet differing needs and outcomes—see Table 11.1 for a comparison among these different forms of organizational change.

Table 11.1 Key characteristics of major approaches to managing change.

Planned Change	Emergent Change	Contingency
• Change is a planned process, led and directed by management. • Encourages employee engagement and consultation during process. • Most suited to situations with clear goals and acknowledged responses. • Reliant on skills, knowledge and expertise of leaders.	• Change should be an ongoing response and not rigidly planned. • Employees take on an active role, driving a bottom-up process, with leaders largely facilitators of change. • Responsive to changing environment and agendas. • Reliant on employees' knowledge, expertise and willingness to respond to challenges.	• No set way to approach managing change, will be contingent upon situational variables. • Approach to change may vary over time as external and internal conditions vary. • May utlize aspects of both planned and emergent approaches to change.

A Socio-Technical Approach to Organizational Change

Although the previous sections have highlighted aspects of organizational change theory that are relevant to the promotion and management of wide scale environmental change within organizations, there is limited specific guidance regarding how to go about designing environmental change initiatives. Indeed, a consistent criticism of the organizational change literature in general is the lack of a valid framework for pursuing organizational change (By, 2005). Socio-technical systems thinking (e.g., Cherns, 1976, 1987; Clegg, 2000) offers well-established sets of principles and frameworks that can be applied to the design of organizational interventions and change programs directed at encouraging environmental sustainability within the workplace. This seems particularly relevant as environmental sustainability has been identified as highly systemic in nature (DuBois et al., 2013; Schrader & Thøgersen, 2011; Starik & Rands, 1995) and the complex issues involved makes it suited to a socio-technical approach.

This section briefly introduces the concept of socio-technical systems thinking and introduces a framework for approaching and analyzing change.

Introducing Socio-Technical Systems Thinking

Socio-Technical Systems Thinking (STST) suggests that an organization can be considered as a complex system, consisting of numerous inter-related parts (Trist & Bamforth, 1951; van Eijnatten, 1997). For example, we would usually expect an organization to include: people—who may have differing skills, attitudes, and perspectives; work processes; set goals and objectives; shared culture; and various technologies; all taking place within physical infrastructure and buildings (see Davis et al., 2014). No organization exists in isolation and we would anticipate the regulatory and economic environments, together with stakeholder interests, to influence various parts of the system, for example, environmental regulation may set minimum standards for the work buildings and production processes in use. Figure 11.1 provides a simple yet powerful conceptualization of a generic organizational system, with interdependencies represented by lines between the nodes.

Socio-technical systems thinking argues that attempting to alter any part of this system, whether the introduction of a new technology, a new rewards system, or a business change program, without considering the implications on the other parts of the system is likely to limit the effectiveness of the change (Hendrick,

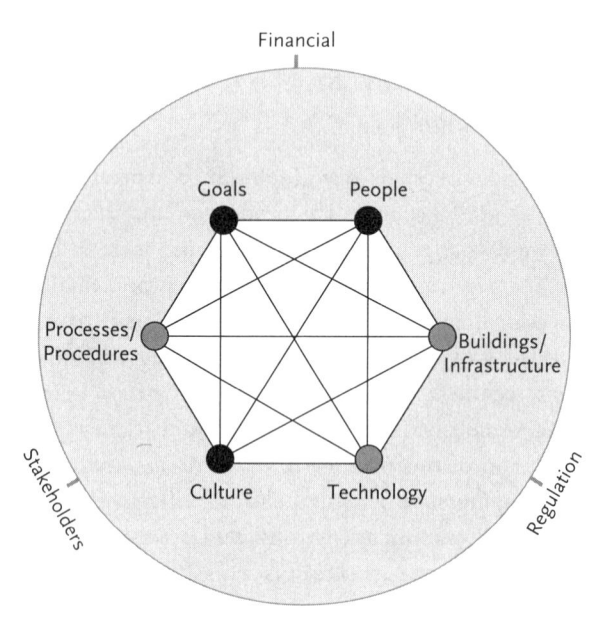

FIGURE 11.1 Socio-technical system, illustrating the interrelated nature of an organizational system embedded within an external environment.

Davis, M. C., Challenger, R., Jayewardene, D. N., & Clegg, C. W. (2014). Advancing socio-technical systems thinking: A call for bravery. *Applied Ergonomics, 45*(2), 171–180.

1997). At its heart STST concerns acknowledging the inter-relationships among different parts of the system, to pursue jointly optimized design, whereby both social and technical factors are simultaneously considered in the process (Cherns, 1976; Trist & Bamforth, 1951). This is of particular relevance to environmental sustainability given the dominance of organizational initiatives that are rooted in technological (e.g., more efficient information technology hardware), systems standards (e.g. ISO14001/EMAS), or buildings (e.g., Energy Performance of Building Directive)–based solutions and change. These initiatives and approaches rarely take account of employee behavior (e.g., Bansal & Gao, 2006; Davis et al., 2014) and their role in supporting wider organizational change is neglected. An STST approach to change management could help to not only improve the implementation of technical innovations (e.g., helping to predict how employees will react or behave within more sustainable buildings that may affect their subsequent environmental performance, Davis et al., 2011; Wener & Carmalt, 2006), but also to harness these technologies to help drive wider organizational change (e.g., to implement new smart meters to connect employees to their resource use or to act as the basis for competition).

If we seek to achieve meaningful and lasting change directed at greening whole organizations, then we need to examine how human behavior is embedded within the system and ensure that we both remove organizational or technological barriers wherever possible and identify strategies that make the system supportive of the intended behaviors and culture.

Applying a Socio-Technical Framework

The general principles of socio-technical systems thinking provide useful guidance regarding how to approach the process of organizational change and design (e.g., Cherns, 1976, 1987; Clegg, 2000; Mumford, 1983). Techniques such as scenario planning (e.g., Axtell, Pepper, Clegg, Wall, & Gardner, 2001), ETHICS (Mumford, 1995) and the socio-technical hexagon framework presented in Figure 11.1 offer specific structures for involving staff and other stakeholders in the process of organizational design and managing change. Common across these frameworks is the emphasis upon multi-disciplinary inputs to change, acknowledging that no one discipline holds all the answers to any particular problem (Clegg, 2000), and flexibility, to enable the process to reflect the organizational context and stakeholder interests. Each framework offers its own steps for tackling change.

The hexagon framework in particular has two potential uses here; it can be used to help analyze existing change programs and to involve staff in planning new initiatives (Davis et al., 2014). In both cases we can use it to consider inter-relationships between various factors involved in a change and the wider system, as well as identify potential conflicts and gaps in coverage. For example, through mapping elements of an existing change process onto the diagram, barriers to change may be identified, for example, rewards metrics that act as a disincentive to employees to pursue environmental goals. The framework promotes the identification (and removal) of conflicts to desired change and the inclusion of additional initiatives to address gaps in coverage across the organizational system, supporting the design of more holistic change programs (see, Challenger, Clegg, & Robinson, 2010; Davis et al., 2014, for guidance regarding applying the hexagon framework).

To illustrate this approach applied to analyzing an existing change program, we have used the hexagon to help map and understand a global manufacturer's environmental change program at one of their UK production plants (see Davis et al., 2014). Figure 11.2 captures and identifies the various approaches and techniques that the company has implemented to support environmental sustainability across the whole plant. The systems diagram illustrates the key steps that the organization has taken, which aspects of the system these steps have targeted, where the inter-relationships lie, and where least attention has been paid. It forms the basis for structured discussions with stakeholders and a framework for planning future program extensions.

The analysis demonstrates that culture and goals have received less attention than the more technological or process-driven aspects of the change program. The steps the organization has taken as a whole have primarily attempted to address core technology, infrastructure and training issues relating to WPEB, and environmental sustainability. The organization is now increasing the ambition of its employee engagement program to help widen and embed the organizational change, involving and capitalizing upon their human resources—building upon the technological investments already made. The analysis has helped to map the breadth of current initiatives and made explicit inter-relationships, as well as where efforts may be used to better reinforce one another (e.g., using the investment in buildings to emphasize environmental goals). Preliminary analysis has demonstrated the value of a holistic approach to change, with staff showing very high levels of engagement with the employee WPEB change program, positive pro-environmental attitudes site wide, ISO14001 certification, and the site has won sustainability awards for its efforts.

The STST framework offers guidance for approaching and designing change initiatives aimed at achieving greater environmental sustainability and WPEB. The way of thinking promotes a holistic approach to change and may lessen the chance that initiatives within an organization are either fragmented (being led by various departments or specialisms), fall into the trap of being technologically

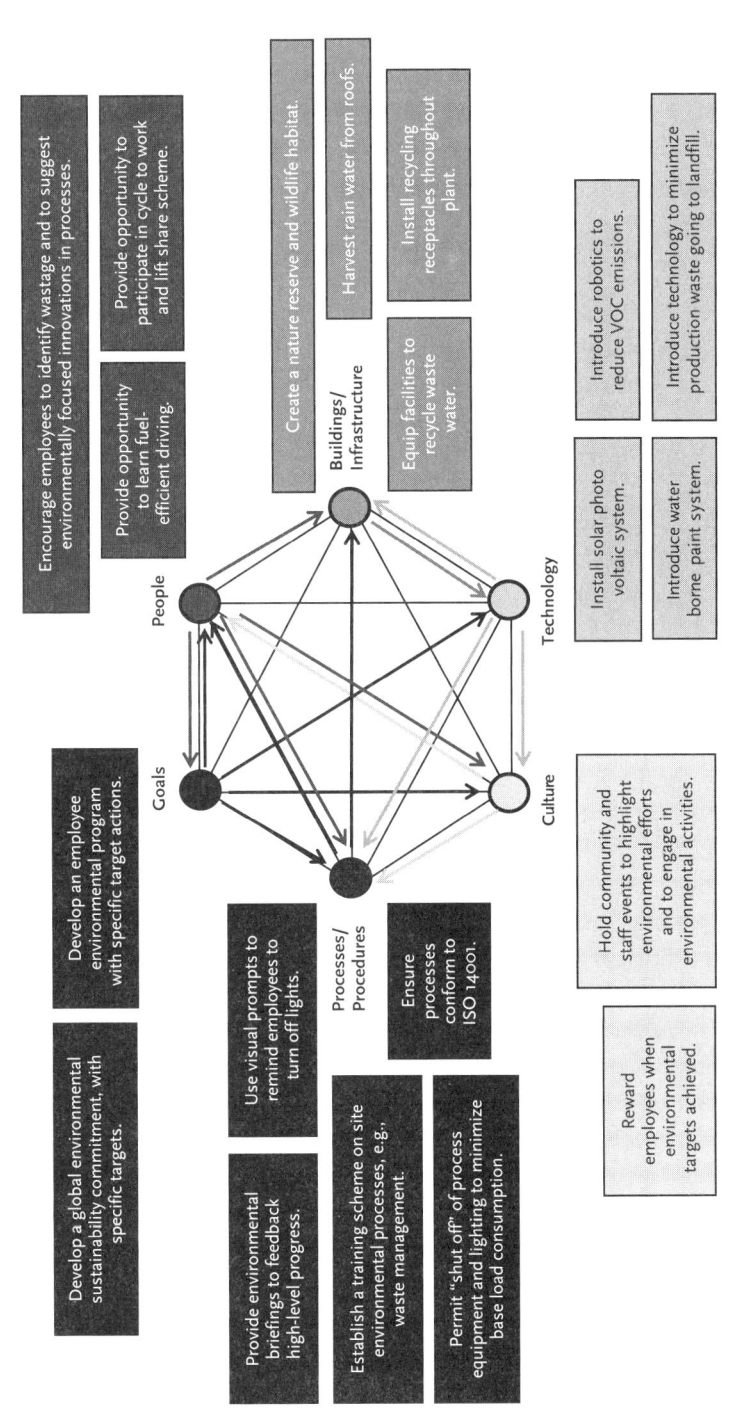

FIGURE 11.2 Approaches and initiatives implemented to support greater environmental sustainability at a major UK manufacturing plant. Davis, M. C., Challenger, R., Jayewardene, D. N., & Clegg, C. W. (2014). Advancing socio-technical systems thinking: A call for bravery. *Applied Ergonomics*, 45(2), 171–180.

led at the expense of social issues, or that behaviorally orientated change programs fail to recognize technological barriers or support (Davis et al., 2014; Young et al., 2013).

Future Research Directions and Practical Implications

This chapter has highlighted some central links across key success factors in traditional organizational change and environmental sustainability efforts within organizations. The literature on four key areas of change management have been reviewed, each of which it is argued requires simultaneous consideration if environmental change initiatives are to be successful: organizational culture; leadership and change agents; employee engagement; and choosing the right form of change that best suits the organization (Figure 11.3). Building upon this, STST has been offered as a framework that may aid the design and implementation of organizational change. Following on from this review, the current section proposes five key directions to help develop research in this area and then provides four main practical implications for organizations wishing to support environmental change.

Future Research Directions

First, more research is required that measures the extent to which environmental change initiatives have been successful. This would serve two purposes: (a) provide support for investment in further (successful) change initiatives by organizations, and (b) enable competing change management approaches to be tested and aid theorization. To assess the efficacy of change programs, success criteria need to be carefully chosen to reflect the aim of improving environmental sustainability. For example, a distinction needs to be made between simply the number of new initiatives being introduced and the subsequent impact on the environment (Ones & Dilchert, 2012). Furthermore, if the aim of a change program is to embed environmental sustainability across an organization, then it may be necessary to look below the organizational level and measure individual employees' WPEB (c.f., Weick & Quinn, 1999), as "the successful implementation of organizational environmental sustainability strategies ultimately depends upon the collective array of behavior changes from individual employees" (DuBois et al., 2013). Researchers also need to look beyond self-report measures to make better use of objective environmental data (e.g., energy performance data, product life cycle analyses, waste sent to landfill) or longitudinal behavioral data (e.g., diary studies, Robinson, 2010; see chapter 5) to support their validations.

Organizational Change • 263

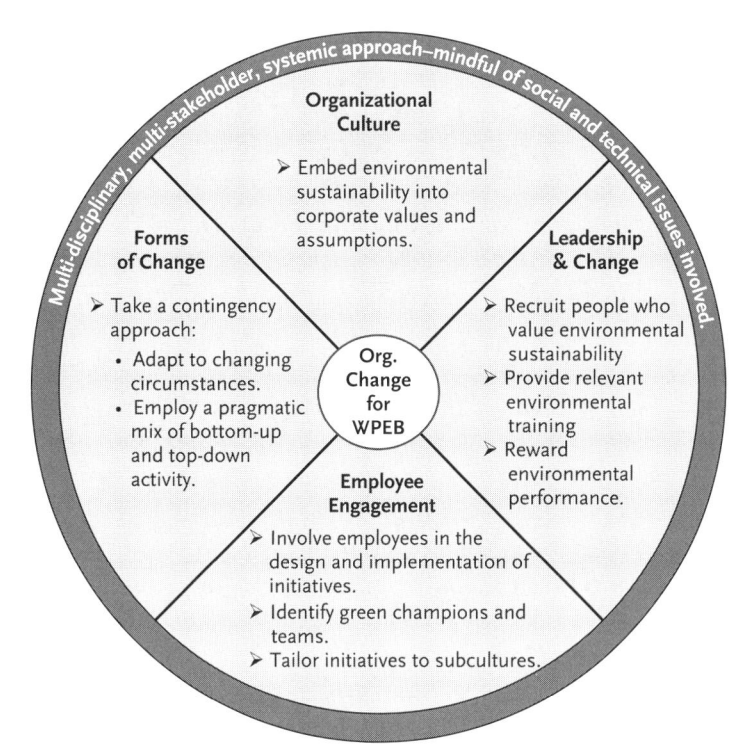

FIGURE 11.3 Summary of the approaches and practical steps for managing organizational change for WPEB.

Circle diagram centered on "Org. Change for WPEB" with outer ring labeled "Multi-disciplinary, multi-stakeholder, systemic approach–mindful of social and technical issues involved." Four quadrants:

- **Organizational Culture**
  - Embed environmental sustainability into corporate values and assumptions.
- **Leadership & Change**
  - Recruit people who value environmental sustainability
  - Provide relevant environmental training
  - Reward environmental performance.
- **Employee Engagement**
  - Involve employees in the design and implementation of initiatives.
  - Identify green champions and teams.
  - Tailor initiatives to subcultures.
- **Forms of Change**
  - Take a contingency approach:
    - Adapt to changing circumstances.
    - Employ a pragmatic mix of bottom-up and top-down activity.

Second, more research is needed to better understand what an environmentally sustainable organizational culture looks like and even whether a truly sustainable organization is possible to achieve. Russell and McIntosh (2011) highlight how there is little empirical evidence to demonstrate whether organizations *can* move to the level of the sustainable organization. Research is required to uncover how to move beyond compliance with environmental legislation and/or superficial efforts for sustainability (e.g., presence of relevant cultural artifacts, Schein, 2010), toward the adoption of voluntary proactive efforts with sustainability fully embedded into organizational values. One line of enquiry may be to explore cultural fragmentation across the organization. Although some researchers have begun to unpack the complexities of subcultures within organizations and how they influence the uptake of sustainability issues (e.g., Harris & Crane, 2002; Howard-Grenville, 2006), exploring how best to utilize subcultures, and in particular dominant subcultures, to better diffuse cultural change throughout the organization may be one useful avenue for future empirical research.

Third, it is unlikely that employees, including organizational leaders and environmental champions, consider environmental issues solely at work. An area of research that is currently underdeveloped is the potential spill over of environmental attitudes and behaviors across work and non-work domains (Muster & Schrader, 2011). Although there is some initial evidence for such spill over (Berger & Kanetkar, 1995; Tudor, Barr, & Gilg, 2007), more research is needed to uncover how organizations can facilitate a stronger link between environmental sustainability at work and during non-work time to positively impact corporate cultures, employee and leadership engagement, and subsequent environmental change initiatives. For example, asking employees to contribute toward green initiatives by considering their experiences from their non-work life may increase engagement. Similarly, by incorporating environmental behaviors that can be carried out during work *and non-work* time into workplace green initiatives, employees might start to consider environmental issues across multiple social contexts, thereby helping to develop more consistent environmental values and behavioral patterns. This stream of work may require new or amended self-report measures of WPEB, to enable researchers to measure general behaviors that employees could choose to engage in across a range of contexts.

Fourth, action research (e.g., Cassell & Johnson, 2006) should be applied to the study of environmental sustainability change. The approach offers researchers the opportunity to gain a greater understanding of the nature of change over time and to achieve direct impact on practice (Susman & Evered, 1978). For example, Adams and McNicholas (2007) adopted an action research methodology enabling them to observe and delve into a change process directed at improving sustainability reporting and provide feedback that inputted back into the change process. The realization of such mutually beneficial relationships is likely to be best supported by long-term cooperative relationships between organizations and researchers. These are challenging relationships to develop and maintain, however, the potential returns in theoretical insight and practical impact are significant.

Finally, we propose that research needs to more fully uncover the conceptual distinctions between traditional organizational change initiatives and environmental change initiatives specifically. This is similar to Lueneberger and Goleman's (2010) call for executives to understand how sustainability issues differ from other corporate initiatives. Although it is asserted that change management techniques should be broadly applicable to the management of environmental sustainability, the nature of the topic may require certain adaptations in how change is supported or engagement achieved. This would be comparable to the differences that are observed in the efficacy of behavior change techniques across differing WPEBs (Osbaldiston & Schott, 2012; Steg & Vlek, 2009).

Practical Implications

This review has highlighted a number of implications for practice. However, in this subsection we identify the recommendations that are thought to offer greatest impact on practice (see Figure 11.3), namely that organizations should: 1) cultivate the right corporate culture; 2) select in and train up leaders and employees who value environmental sustainability; 3) fully engage their employees; 4) take a contingency approach to organizational change towards environmental sustainability; and 5) take a multidisciplinary approach which utilizes socio-technical systems thinking. These will briefly be considered in turn.

First, although this chapter highlighted the debate in the literature as to whether organizations need to change corporate values to improve environmental performance, due to the steadily increasing number of papers showing direct links between an organization's environmental values and employee WPEB (e.g., Andersson et al., 2005; Nilsson et al., 2004; Ramus & Steger, 2000; Sharma, 1999), we argue that organizations should embed environmental sustainability into their underlying assumptions and values.

Second, HRM practices should be linked to an environmental sustainability-driven organizational culture by, for example (a) recruiting new employees and leaders into the organization who value environmental sustainability; (b) providing relevant training to employees and leaders to increase environmental awareness, knowledge, and skills. This could include training around environmentally related transformational leadership and management behaviors that facilitate environmental innovations along with how to successfully champion and communicate environmental ideas; and (c) rewarding environmental efforts via formal (e.g., performance management) and informal channels (e.g., praise and recognition, c.f., Renwick et al., 2013).

Third, there are a number of strategies that organizations can incorporate to ensure employees are aware of, and engaged with, green issues. Employee involvement has been labeled one of the most successful avenues for continued engagement (Renwick et al., 2013); encouraging employees to help in the design and implementation of any change initiative is likely to be critical to its success. Setting up organizational green teams and identifying green champions may also help facilitate the diffusion of environmental sustainability as well as targeting and tailoring initiatives to the different subcultures present within an organization.

Fourth, this chapter highlighted the differing approaches to managing change that organizations could follow when preparing to promote environmental sustainability and WPEB, ranging from planned to emergent and contingency forms of change (Burnes, 1996; By, 2005). A contingency approach offers companies the most flexible approach to the management of change, enabling leaders to adapt their plans in response to changing circumstances and should permit a practical mix of both top-down and bottom-up activities within a broad environmental sustainability change program.

Finally, we argue that any approach to environmental sustainability should adopt a systems view, taking into consideration the varied influences upon organizational environmental performance. Applying STST frameworks that promote bringing together multiple stakeholders, approaching change from a multi-disciplinary perspective in a flexible and ongoing manner maximizes the chance of social and technical issues receiving equal weighting and for the design of holistic initiatives.

Conclusion

This chapter has highlighted the potential for organizational change to be used as a means of supporting environmental sustainability and promoting WPEB. In particular, prominent aspects of organizational change, namely, organizational culture; employee engagement; leadership and change agents; and differing forms of change, have been identified as key components to focus on when managing change in this area. The danger of allowing change to become technology led has been discussed and STST offered as a means of approaching holistic change. This chapter has outlined some promising future directions for creating organization-wide change. We hope researchers and practitioners in the area act now to capitalize on the potential that these opportunities hold in helping to create a more sustainable future.

Suggested Additional Readings

1. Davis, M. C., Challenger, R., Jayewardene, D. N., & Clegg, C. W. (2014). Advancing socio-technical systems thinking: A call for bravery. *Applied Ergonomics*, *45*(2), 171–180.
2. Huffman, A. H., & Klein, S. R. (2013). Green organizations: Driving change with I-O psychology. Hove, UK: Routledge.
3. Russell, S. V., & McIntosh, M. (2011). Organizational change for sustainability. In N. M. Ashkanasy, C. P. M. Wilderom, & M. F. Peterson (Eds.), *Handbook of organizational culture & climate* (2nd ed.). Thousand Oaks, CA: Sage.
4. Weick, K. E., & Quinn, R. E. (1999). Organizational change and development. *Annual Review of Psychology*, *50*, 361–386.

References

Adams, C. A., & McNicholas, P. (2007). Making a difference: Sustainability reporting, accountability and organisational change. *Accounting, Auditing & Accountability Journal*, *20*, 382–402.

Andersson, L. M., & Bateman, T. S. (2000). Individual environmental initiative: championing natural environmental issues in U.S. business organizations. *Academy of Management Journal*, *43*, 548–570.

Andersson, L. M., Shivarajan, S., & Blau, G. (2005). Enacting ecological sustainability in the MNC: A test of an adapted value-belief-norm framework. *Journal of Business Ethics*, *59*, 295–305.

Armenakis, A. A., & Bedeian, A. G. (1999). Organizational change: A review of theory and research in the 1990s. *Journal of Management*, *25*, 293–315.

Axtell, C., Pepper, K., Clegg, C., Wall, T. D., & Gardner, P. (2001). Designing and evaluating new ways of working: The application of some sociotechnical tools. *Human Factors and Ergonomics in Manufacturing*, *11*, 1–18.

Bandura, A. (1997). *Self-efficacy: The exercise of control*. New York: W. H. Freeman.

Bansal, P. (2003). From issues to actions: The importance of individual concerns and organizational values in responding to natural environmental issues. *Organization Science*, *14*, 510–527.

Bansal, P., & Gao, J. (2006). Building the future by looking to the past: Examining research published on organizations and environment. *Organization Environment*, *19*, 458–478.

Bansal, P., & Roth, K. (2000). Why companies go green: A model of ecological responsiveness. *Academy of Management Journal*, *43*, 717–736.

Baxter, G., & Sommerville, I. (2011). Socio-technical systems: From design methods to systems engineering. *Interacting with Computers*, *2*, 4–17.

Berger, I. E., & Kanetkar, V. (1995). Increasing environmental sensitivity via workplace experiences. *Journal of Public Policy and Marketing*, *14*, 205–215.

Branzei, O., Vertinsky, I., & Zietsma, C. (2000). From green-blindness to the pursuit of eco-sustainability: An empirical investigation of leader cognitions and corporate environmental strategy choices. In S. Havlovic (Ed.), *Academy of Management best paper proceedings*. Toronto, ON: Academy of Management.

Broadhurst, K., Wastell, D., White, S., Hall, C., Peckover, S., Thompson, K., Davey, D. (2010). Performing 'initial assessment': Identifying the latent conditions for error at the front-door of local authority children's services. *British Journal of Social Work*, *40*, 352–370.

Bullock, R. J., & Batten, D. (1985). It's just a phase we're going through: A review and synthesis of OD phase analysis. *Group & Organization Management*, *10*, 383–412.

Burger, J. M. (1999). The foot-in-the-door compliance procedure: A multiple-process analysis and review. *Personality and Social Psychology Review*, *3*, 303–325.

Burnes, B. (1996). No such thing as . . . a "one best way" to manage organizational change. *Management Decision, 34,* 11–18.

Burnes, B. (2004). Kurt Lewin and the planned approach to change: A re-appraisal. *Journal of Management Studies, 41,* 977–1002.

By, R. (2005). Organisational change management: A critical review. *Journal of Change Management, 5,* 369–380.

Carroll, A. B. (1979). A three-dimensional conceptual model of corporate performance. *Academy of Management Review, 4,* 497–505.

Cassell, C., & Johnson, P. (2006). Action research: Explaining the diversity. *Human Relations, 59,* 783–814.

Challenger, R., Clegg, C. W., & Robinson, M. A. (2010). *Understanding crowd behaviours Volume 1: Practical guidance and lessons identified*. London: TSO.

Chen, Z., Li, H., & Wong, C. T. C. (2002). An application of bar-code system for reducing construction wastes. *Automation in Construction, 11,* 521–533.

Cherns, A. (1976). The principles of sociotechnical design. *Human Relations, 29,* 783–792.

Cherns, A. (1987). Principles of sociotechnical design revisited. *Human Relations, 40,* 153–161.

Clegg, C. W. (2000). Sociotechnical principles for system design. *Applied Ergonomics, 31,* 463–477.

Clegg, C. W., & Shepherd, C. (2007). The biggest computer programme in the world ever! Time for a change in mindset? *Journal of Information Technology, 22,* 212–221.

Clegg, C. W., & Walsh, S. (2004). Change management: Time for a change! *European Journal of Work and Organizational Psychology, 13,* 217–239.

Colby, M. E. (1991). Environmental management in development: The evolution of paradigms. *Ecological Economics, 3,* 193–213.

Cox, A., Higgins, T., Gloster, R., Foley, B., & Darnton, A. (2012). The impact of workplace initiatives on low carbon behaviours. Edinburgh, UK. Retrieved August 25, 2013, from http://www.scotland.gov.uk/Resource/0039/00390309.pdf.

Crane, A. (2000). Corporate greening as amoralization. *Organization Studies, 21,* 673–696.

Crew, D. E. (2010). Strategies for implementing sustainability: Five leadership challenges. *SAM Advanced Management Journal, 75,* 15–21.

Crews, D. E., & Woman, T. (2010). Strategies for implementing sustainability: Five leadership challenges. *SAM Advanced Management Journal, 75,* 15–22.

Davis, M. C., & Challenger, R. (2009). Climate change: Warming to the task. *The Psychologist, 22,* 112–114.

Davis, M. C., & Challenger, R. (2014). Environmentally sustainable work behaviors. In P. C. Flood, & Y. Freeney (Eds.), *Volume 7: Encyclopedia of organizational behavior,* in the *Wiley encyclopedia of management* (3rd ed.), Cary L. Cooper (Ed. in chief). Chichester, UK: Wiley.

Davis, M. C., Challenger, R., Jayewardene, D. N., & Clegg, C. W. (2014). Advancing socio-technical systems thinking: A call for bravery. *Applied Ergonomics*, *45*(2), 171–180.

Davis, M. C., Leach, D. J., & Clegg, C. W. (2011). The physical environment of the office: Contemporary and emerging issues. In G. P. Hodgkinson, & J. K. Ford (Eds.), *International review of industrial and organizational psychology* (Vol. 26, pp. 193–235). Chichester, UK: Wiley.

Dowie, W. A., McCartney, D. M. & Tamm, J. A. (1998). A case study of an institutional solid waste environmental management system. *Journal of Environmental Management*, *53*, 137–146.

DuBois, C. L. Z., Astakhova, M. N., & DuBois, D. A. (2013). Motivating behavior change to support organizational environmental sustainability goals. In A. H. Huffman, & S. R. Klein (Eds.), *Green organizations: Driving change with I-O psychology* (pp. 186–208). Hove, UK: Routledge.

Dunphy, D., Benn, S., & Griffiths, A. (2003). Organizational change for corporate sustainability. London: Routledge.

Dunphy, D., & Stace, D. (1993). The strategic management of corporate change. *Human Relations*, *46*, 905–920.

Eason, K. (2007). Local sociotechnical system development in the NHS National Programme for Information Technology. *Journal of Information Technology*, *22*, 257–264.

Ferdig, M. A. (2007). Sustainability leadership: Co-creating a sustainable future. *Journal of Change Management*, *7*, 25–35.

Fernandez, E., Junquera, B., & Ordiz, M. (2003). Organizational culture and human resources in the environmental issue: A review of the literature. *International Journal of Human Resource Management*, *14*, 634–657.

Fineman, S. (1997). Constructing the green manager. *British Journal of Management*, *8*, 31–38.

Fineman, S., & Clarke, K. (1996). Green stakeholders: Industry interpretations and response. *Journal of Management Studies*, *33*, 715–730.

Galbreath, J. (2009). Drivers of corporate social responsibility: The role of formal strategic planning and firm culture. *British Journal of Management*, *21*, 511–525.

Guy, S. (2006). Designing urban knowledge: Competing perspectives on energy and buildings. *Environment and Planning C: Government and Policy*, *24*(5), 645–659.

Handgraaf, M. J., Van Lidth de Jeude, M. A., & Appelt, K. C. (2013). Public praise vs. private pay: Effects of rewards on energy conservation in the workplace. *Ecological Economics*, *86*, 86–92.

Harris, L. C., & Crane, A. (2002). The greening of organizational culture: Management views on the depth, degree and diffusion of change. *Journal of Organizational Change Management*, *15*, 214–234.

Harris, L. C., & Ogbonna, E. (1998). Employee responses to cultural change. *Human Resource Management Journal*, *8*, 78–92.

Hartley, J., Benington, J., & Binns, P. (1997). Researching the roles of internal-change agents in the management of organizational change. *British Journal of Management, 8*, 61–73.

Heijden, A. V. D., Cramer, J. M., & Driessen, P. P. J. (2012). Change agent sensemaking for sustainability in a multinational subsidiary. *Journal of Organizational Change Management, 25*, 535–559.

Heller, F., Pusic, E., Strauss, G., & Wilpert, B. (1998). *Organisational participation: Myth and reality.* Oxford, UK: Oxford University Press.

Hendrick, H. (1997). Organizational design and macroergonomics. In G. Salvendy (Ed.), *Handbook of human factors and ergonomics* (pp. 594–637). New York: John Wiley & Sons.

Howard-Grenville, J. A. (2006). Inside the "black box": How organizational culture and subcultures inform interpretations and actions on environmental issues. *Organization & Environment, 19*, 46–73.

Jennings, P. D., & Zandbergen, P. A. (1995). Ecologically sustainable organizations: An institutional approach. *Academy of Management Review, 20*, 1015–1052.

Johnson, D. B., & Macy, G. (2001). Using environmental paradigms to understand and change an organization's response to stakeholders. *Journal of Organizational Change Management, 14*, 314–334.

Kanter, R. M. (1983). *The change masters: Corporate entrepreneurs at work.* London: International Thomson Business Press.

Kanter, R. M., Stein, B. A., & Jick, T. D. (1992). *The challenge of organizational change.* New York: The Free Press.

Karasek, R., & Theorell, T. (1990). *Healthy work: Stress, productivity, and the reconstruction of working life.* New York: Basic Books.

Kollmuss, A., & Agyeman, J. (2002). Mind the Gap: Why do people act environmentally and what are the barriers to pro-environmental behavior? *Environmental Education Research, 8*, 239–260.

Kotter, J. P. (1995). Leading change: Why transformation efforts fail. *Harvard Business Review, 73*, 59–67.

Kotter, J. P. (1996). *Leading change.* Boston: Harvard Business School Press.

Kujala, S. (2003). User involvement: A review of the benefits and challenges. *Behaviour & Information Technology, 22*, 1–16.

Lazlo, C., & Zhexembayeva, N. (2011). *Embedded sustainability: The next big competitive advantage.* Sheffield, UK: Greenleaf.

Lee, M. P. (2011). Configuration of external influences: The combined effects of institutions and stakeholders on corporate social responsibility strategies. *Journal of Business Ethics, 102*, 281–298.

Li, H., Chen, Z., & Wong, C. T. C. (2003). Barcode technology for an incentive reward program to reduce construction wastes. *Computer-Aided Civil and Infrastructure Engineering, 18*, 313–324.

Lingard, H., Gilbert, G., & Graham, P. (2001). Improving solid waste reduction and recycling performance using goal setting and feedback. *Construction Management and Economics*, *19*, 809–817.

Linnenluecke, M. K., & Griffiths, A. (2010). Corporate sustainability and organizational culture. *Journal of World Business*, *45*, 357–366.

Linnenluecke, M. K., Russell, S. V., & Griffi, A. (2009). Subcultures and sustainability practices: The impact on understanding corporate sustainability. *Business Strategy & the Environment*, *452*, 432–452.

Locke, E. A., & Latham, G. P. (2004). What should we do about motivation theory? Six recommendations for the twenty-first century. *Academy of Management Review*, *29*, 388–403.

Luecke, R. (2003). *Managing change and transition*. Boston: Harvard Business School Press.

Lueneburger, C., & Goleman, D. (2010). The change leadership sustainability demands. *Sloan Management Review*, *51*, 49–55.

Macey, W. H., & Schneider, B. (2008). The meaning of employee engagement. *Industrial and Organizational Psychology*, *1*, 3–30.

May, D. R., & Flannery, B. L. (1995). Cutting waste with employee involvement teams. *Business Horizons*, *38*, 28–38.

McMakin, A. H., Malone, E., & Lundgren, R. E. (2002). Motivating residents to conserve energy without financial incentives. *Environment and Behavior*, *34*, 848–863.

Millar, C., Hind, P., & Magala, S. (2012). Sustainability and the need for change: Organisational change and transformational vision. *Journal of Organizational Change Management*, *25*, 489–500.

Morrison, E. W., & Milliken, F. J. (2000). Organizational silence: A barrier to change and development in a pluralistic world. *Academy of Management Review*, *25*, 706–725.

Mumford, E. (1983). *Designing secretaries: The participative design of a word processing system*. Manchester, UK: Manchester Business School.

Mumford, E. (1995). *Effective systems design and requirements analysis: The ETHICS approach*. Basingstoke, UK: Macmillan.

Muster, V., & Schrader, U. (2011). Green work-life balance: A new perspective for green HRM. *German Journal of Research in Human Resource Management*, *25*, 140–156.

Newton, T. I. M., & Harte, G. (1997). Green business: Technicist kitsch? *Journal of Management Studies*, *34*, 75–98.

Nilsson, A., von Borgstede, C., & Biel, A. (2004). Willingness to accept climate change strategies: The effect of values and norms. *Journal of Environmental Psychology*, *24*, 267–277.

Ones, D. S., & Dilchert, S. (2010). *A taxonomy of green behaviours among employees. Shades of green: Individual differences in environmentally responsible employee behaviours*. Paper presented at the symposium conducted at the Annual Conference of the Society for Industrial and Organizational Psychology, Atlanta.

Ones, D. S., & Dilchert, S. (2012). Environmental sustainability at work: A call to action. *Industrial and Organizational Psychology: Perspectives on Science and Practice*, 5, 503–511.

Ones, D. S., Dilchert, S., Biga, A., & Gibby, R. E. (2010). *Managerial level differences in eco-friendly employee behaviors*. Paper presented at the Annual Conference of the Society for Industrial and Organizational Psychology, Atlanta.

Osbaldiston, R., & Schott, J. P. (2012). Environmental sustainability and behavioral science. *Environment and Behavior*, 44, 257–299.

Pasmore, W. A. (1994). *Creating strategic change: Designing the flexible, high performing organization*. New York: Wiley.

Pettigrew, A., & Whipp, R. (1993). *Managing change for competitive success*. Cambridge, UK: Wiley-Blackwell.

Post, J. E., & Altman, B. W. (1994). Managing the environmental change process: Barriers and opportunities. *Journal of Organizational Change Management*, 7, 64–81.

Ramus, C. A. (2001). Organizational support for employees: Encouraging creative ideas for environmental sustainability. *California Management Review*, 43, 85–105.

Ramus, C. A. (2002). Encouraging innovative environmental actions: What companies and managers must do. *Journal of World Business*, 37, 151–164.

Ramus, C. A., & Steger, U. (2000). The roles of supervisory support behaviors and environmental policy in employee "ecoinitiatives" at leading-edge European companies. *The Academy of Management Journal*, 43, 605–626.

Redekop, B. W., & Olson, S. (2010). *Leadership for environmental sustainability*. New York: Routledge.

Renwick, D. W. S., Redman, T., & Maguire, S. (2013). Green human resource management: A review and research agenda. *International Journal of Management Reviews*, 15, 1–14.

Riley, P. (1983). A structurationist account of political culture. *Administrative Science Quarterly*, 28, 414–437.

Robertson, J. L., & Barling, J. (2013). Greening organizations through leaders' influence on employees' pro-environmental behaviors. *Journal of Organizational Behavior*, 34, 176–194.

Robinson, M. A. (2010). An empirical analysis of engineers' information behaviors. *Journal of the American Society for Information Science and Technology*, 61, 640–658.

Rothenberg, S. (2003). Knowledge content and worker participation in environmental management at NUMMI. *Journal of Management Studies*, 40, 1783–1802.

Russell, S.V., & McIntosh, M. (2011). Organizational change for sustainability. In N. M. Ashkanasy, C. P. M. Wilderom, & M. F. Peterson (Eds.), *Handbook of organizational culture & climate* (2nd ed.). Thousand Oaks, CA: Sage.

Sackman, S. A. (1992). Culture: The missing concept in organization studies. *Administrative Science Quarterly, 41*, 229–240.

Schein, E. H. (2010). *Organizational culture and leadership*. San Francisco: Jossey-Bass.

Schneider, B., Ehrhart, M. G., & Macey, W. H. (2013). Organizational climate and culture. *Annual Review of Psychology, 64*, 361–388.

Schrader, U., & Thøgersen, J. (2011). Putting sustainable consumption into practice. *Journal of Consumer Policy, 34*, 3–8.

Schweiger, D. M., & Denisi, A. S. (1991). Communication with employees following a merger: A longitudinal field experiment. *Academy of Management Journal, 34*, 110–135.

Sekerka, L. E., & Stimel, D. (2011). How durable is sustainable enterprise? Ecological sustainability meets the reality of tough economic times. *Business Horizons, 54*, 115–124.

Sharma, S. (1999). Managerial interpretations and organizational context as predictors of corporate choice of environmental strategy. *Academy of Management Journal, 43*, 681–697.

Shrivastava, P. (1995). The role of corporations in achieving ecological sustainability. *The Academy of Management Review, 20*, 936–960.

Siero, F. W., Bakker, A. B., Dekker, G. B., & Van Den Burg, M. T. C. (1996). Changing organizational energy consumption behavior through comparative feedback. *Journal of Environmental Psychology, 16*, 235–246.

Starik, M., & Rands, G. P. (1995). Weaving an integrated web: Multilevel and multisystem perspectives of ecologically sustainable organizations. *The Academy of Management Review, 20*, 908–935.

Stead, E. W., & Stead, J. G. (1994). Can humankind change the economic myth? Paradigm shifts necessary for ecologically sustainable business. *Journal of Organizational Change Management, 7*, 15–31.

Steg, L., & Vlek, C. (2009). Encouraging pro-environmental behaviour: An integrative review and research agenda. *Journal of Environmental Psychology, 29*, 309–317.

Stoughton, A. M., & Ludema, J. (2012). The driving forces of sustainability. *Journal of Organizational Change Management, 25*, 501–517.

Suls, J., Martin, R., & Wheeler, L. (2002). Social comparison: Why, with whom and with what effect? *Current Directions in Psychological Science, 11*, 159–163.

Susman, G. I., & Evered, R. D. (1978). An assessment of the scientific merits of action research. *Administrative Science Quarterly, 23*, 582–603.

Trist, E. L., & Bamforth, K. W. (1951). Some social and psychological consequences of the longwall method of coal-getting: An examination of the psychological situation and defences of a work group in relation to the social structure and technological content of the work system. *Human Relations, 4*(1), 3–38.

Tudor, T., Barr, S., & Gilg, A. (2007). A tale of two locational settings: Is there a link between pro-environmental behaviour at work and at home? *Local Environment, 12*, 409–421.

Unsworth, K. L., Dmitrieva, A., & Adriasola, E. (2013). Changing behaviour: Increasing the effectiveness of workplace interventions in creating pro-environmental behaviour change. *Journal of Organizational Behavior, 34*, 211–229.

van Eijnatten, F. M. (1997). Development in socio-technical systems design (STSD). In P. J. D. Drenth, H. Thierry, & C. J. de Wolff (Eds.), *Handbook of work and organizational psychology. Volume 4: Organizational psychology* (pp. 61–88). Sussex, UK: Lawrence.

Vanclay, F. (2004). The triple bottom line and impact assessment: How do TBL, EIA, SEA and EMS relate to each other? *Journal of Environmental Assessment Policy and Management, 6*, 265–288.

Walls, J. L., & Hoffman, A. J. (2013). Exceptional boards: Environmental experience and positive deviance from institutional norms. *Journal of Organizational Behavior, 34*, 253–271.

Weick, K. E., & Quinn, R. E. (1999). Organizational change and development. *Annual Review of Psychology, 50*, 361–386.

Welford, R. (1995). *Environmental strategy and sustainable development: The corporate challenge for the twenty-first century*. London: Routledge.

Wener, R., & Carmalt, H. (2006). Environmental psychology and sustainability in high-rise structures. *Technology in Society, 28*, 157–167.

White, P. (2009). Building a sustainability strategy into the business. *Corporate Governance, 9*, 386–394.

Woodman, R. W. (1989). Organizational change and development: New arenas for inquiry and action. *Journal of Management, 15*, 205–228.

Young, W., Davis, M., McNeill, I. M., Malhotra, B., Russell, S., Unsworth, K., & Clegg, C. W. (2013). Changing behaviour: Successful environmental programmes in the workplace. *Business Strategy and the Environment*. doi:10.1002/bse.1836

12 HUMAN RESOURCE MANAGEMENT APPROACHES

Andrew Bratton and John Bratton

The world's leading climate scientists have recently reported that more than half of the global carbon dioxide allowance has been used up and, unless checked, the accumulation of carbon in the atmosphere will warm the planet by more than 2°C by 2045. This is significant because some have argued that this would result not so much in climate change, but ever more catastrophically, "climate chaos." The 2013 Intergovernmental Panel of Climate Change Working Group report states that:

> Warming of the climate system is unequivocal, and since the 1950s, many of the observed changes are unprecedented over decades to millennia. The atmosphere and ocean have warmed, the amounts of snow and ice have diminished, sea level has risen, and the concentrations of greenhouse gases have increased.

The scientific evidence from 209 leading climate scientists is clear: the planet is past halfway to triggering dangerous climate change, and they are "unequivocal" that global warming is a result of human actions (Harvey, 2013). That organizations are both part of the problem as well as part of the solution to carbon accumulation is not in doubt. The question examined in this chapter, however, is to what extent do people-oriented management practices contribute to changing behaviors that can create more environmentally sustainable workplaces?

This book examines a wide range of theories and research on the psychology of green organizations. Although other contributors have made direct or indirect reference to employment relations, there has been little discussion on employment relations (or human resource) practices developed by management. In recent years, the practices used to manage people in the workplace have assumed new prominence as concerns persist about global competition and environmental degradation. It is argued that market imperatives and environmental regulations require managers to change the way they manage the employment relationship to allow for the most effective use of people and the adoption of environmental sustainability initiatives in the organization.

Environmental sustainability has been defined as meeting "the needs of the present without compromising the ability of future generations to meet their own needs" (WCED, 1987, p. 43).[1] At the organizational level, corporate environmental performance refers to "organizational performance in managing natural resources and the natural environment in the process of conducting business" (Ones & Dilchert, 2012, p. 450). Corporate environmental performance includes both environmental outcomes and pro-environmental initiatives that organizations implement. The former represents the ecological impact or footprint of organizational activities; the latter focuses on what organizational *do* for environmental sustainability.

The 1990s were characterized by the increasing ascendancy and influence of the human resources function. During this period, a debate emerged on the concept of human resource management (HRM), which had its theoretical roots in US business schools (Blyton & Turnbull, 1992; Hendry & Pettigrew, 1990; Legge, 1995; Purcell, 1989; Storey, 1989). This debate, mostly among academics, produced normative models, evidence of a direct connection between "bundles" of best HRM practices and organizational performance, and exposed familiar conflicts in the social world of work. The term *human resource management* has been hotly contested; for some HRM is simply a grander term for personnel management, representing "old wine in new bottles." Others argue that HRM is quite distinct in theory and practice, and reflects a paradigm shift in the management of the employment relationship. The debate has been particularly fierce among British academics, and several conceptual models have been developed to explain the HRM phenomenon and the HRM-performance relation. Critical HRM scholars have linked the ascendancy of HRM, with its Protestant Anglo-Saxon individualist-oriented philosophy, to the rise of "Thatcherism": privatization, deregulation, and the decline of trade union bargaining power (Bratton & Gold, 2012; Delbridge & Turnbull, 1992; Godard, 1991; Townley, 1994). Most of the HRM literature examines a wide range of practices—recruitment and selection,

---

1. Environmentally focused reports, for example, the United Nations' Our Common Future (1987), commonly referred to as the Brundtland Report, have played a pivotal role in the development of sustainability concepts.

rewards, training, appraisal, employee relations—that seeks to make employees' behavior more predictable and manageable.

Scholarship investigating the nexus of HRM and environmental management has been called *green human resource management* (GHRM) (Renwick et al., 2013; Jackson & Seo, 2010). An early contribution was the Walter Wehrmeyer (1996) edited book, *Greening people: Human resources and environmental management*. In theory, HRM is associated with a distinctive organizational culture and set of best HR practices, which aim to recruit, develop, reward, and manage people in ways that create a sustainable commitment to what is sometimes called a *high-performance work system*. This suggests that there exists a bundle of HRM practices that generates superior organizational performance (Boxall & Macky, 2009).

The notion of the high-performance work system can be extended to what we call here a *low-carbon work system* (LCWS). We define LCWS as a planned approach to organization design, culture, and HR practices to deliver low-carbon outcomes in the workplace as well as to align the organization and its processes to achieve innovation and sustainable high-quality results for the organization, workforce, and customers. A LCWS requires new roles and behaviors for managers and nonmanagers. European research suggests that sustainable, low-carbon behaviors occur at three levels: individual, group, and material (Cox et al., 2012). Individual level influences act on individual motivations (e.g., personal rewards); group level influences act on employees when operating in teams or groups (e.g., social norms, shared understandings and communities of practice); and material level influences act on organizational structure and processes (e.g., products, technology, environment). The research by Cox et al. (2012) suggests that behavioral interventions tend to be most successful when they consider these three contexts—individual, group, and material—holistically, and not simply focus on trying to change individual attitudes or just installing new technology. In other words, when establishing an LCWS the goal should be to take an integrated approach that raises awareness and improves understanding with individuals and groups, builds social norms around low-carbon or "green" working practices, and supports employees with the technology they need, backed up with consistent policies.

Although the evidence base on low-carbon behavioral activities is not well developed, the extant studies suggest that green initiatives were more successful in organizations that were seeking to embed shared values about the importance of environmental sustainability into the organizational culture (Cox et al., 2012). Jackson and Seo (2010, p. 278) report that "the topic of environmental sustainability is not reflected in the research agendas of most areas of management scholarship. The field of [HRM] is one of the minimally engaged areas of specialization."

Just how important HRM practices are in helping us to understand how low-carbon behaviors can be nurtured and embedded in an organization is illustrated in the remainder of this chapter. We address a number of questions, some of which are essential to our understanding of how people behave in the contemporary workplace, and the role of HRM therein. What HRM practices have been used? How do HRM practices shape and change behavior? Is there a link between HRM practices and low-carbon behaviors? The debates bring out an important point: there are fundamental tensions and constraints that emphasize the complexity of a HRM approach to greening the workplace.

The Nature of Human Resource Management

To grasp the nature and significance of HRM it is necessary to remind ourselves why managing people is different from managing other resources. It is people in organizations who set overall strategies and goals, design work systems, produce goods and services, monitor quality, allocate financial resources, and market the products and services. People become human capital by virtue of the roles they assume in the organization. *Human capital* refers to the traits individuals bring to the workplace—intelligence, aptitudes, commitment, tacit knowledge and skills, and the ability to learn (Garrick, 1999). But as we have discussed earlier, the contribution this human resource makes to the organization is typically variable and unpredictable. It is this indeterminacy of an employee's job performance which, according to one management "guru," makes the human resource the "most vexatious of assets to manage" (Fitz-enz, 2000, p. xii).

The theory and practice of HRM draws heavily on psychology of work research, and is often viewed as a possible solution to such perennial problems as low worker commitment, low worker productivity, and worker resistance. One set of perspectives, drawing on psychology, suggests that human behavior in the workplace is a function of at least four variables: ability, motivation, role perception, and situational contingencies (Beer et al., 1984; Walton, 1985). Another set of perspectives, drawing on sociology, emphasizes the problematic nature of employment relations: contradictions and tension, and the perennial interrelated problems of control and commitment (Hyman, 1989). Human capital differs from other resources, partly because individuals are endowed with varying levels of ability (including aptitudes, skills and knowledge), with personality traits, gender, role perceptions and differences in experience, and partly as a result of differences in motivation and commitment. In other words, people differ from other resources because of their ability to evaluate and to question management's actions, and their commitment and cooperation always has to be earned. In addition, employees have the capacity to form groups and organize into trade unions to defend or further their economic interest.

The importance of the HRM function results from the dynamic nature of the relationship between the employee and the employer. First and foremost, the employment relationship embraces an *economic* relationship: the "exchange of pay for work" (Budd, 2004). The contract permits the employer to buy a potential level of physical or intellectual labor. The function of HRM is to narrow the gap between employees' potential and actual job performance: "[HRM] practices . . . offer a technology which aims to render individuals and their behavior predictable and calculable . . . to bridge the gap between promise and performance, between labour power and labour" (Townley, 1994, p. 14). The exchange, hierarchical and imbalanced power character of the employment relationship constitutes the distinctive attributes of an inclusive analysis of HRM: Managing people involves aligning internal human capabilities (Penrose, 1959) with strategic business plans, mobilizing greater discretionary effort from employees to close the gap between potential and actual performance and, at the same time, managing the unavoidable conflict between the parties.

Human resource management policies and practices shape the nature of work, the "psychological contract" (Rousseau, 1995) and regulate the behavior between the employer and employee, the employment relationship. Bratton and Gold (2012) identify eight key HRM activities or interventions that can change behaviors and build a green organization: strategic planning, staffing, training and developing employees, motivating employees, maintaining a safe and healthy workplace that complies with statutory standards and regulations, managing employee relations, managing change, and evaluating the value-added component of HRM practices and interventions. These HR activities are designed in response to organizational goals and contingencies, and are managed to achieve those goals. Each HR activity contains alternatives from which managers can choose.

These eight key HRM activities, however, give little indication of how power struggles inside the organization dictate the relative importance of HRM compared with other management functions. Within most organizations there are power struggles over which management functional area—finance, marketing, production, HRM—will dominate and fashion executive decisions. These disputes are partly the result of individual self-interest and power contests inside the management team, but they also represent differences on how best to compete in the marketplace, whether to emphasize market share and product price or high-quality branding and employee skill. As Jacoby (2005) contends, the role of HRM, how it is organized, and how much power it has relative to other management functions is affected both by internal factors unique to the organization (such as product or service range, and organizational culture) and by external contexts (such as labor shortages and national employment regimes). What makes HRM different from personnel management? Over the past 20 or so years, academics have given us something resembling Weberian ideal-type models that emphasize the alleged unique features of HRM, the integrated nature of HR activities, and HRM's strategic importance to the organization. It is to these theoretical models that we now turn.

Theoretical Models of Human Resource Management

So far we have focused on the meaning of HRM and the contribution it makes to the functioning of the work organization. We now turn to an important part of the HRM discourse, the search for its defining features, which potentially can demonstrate the connectedness between HRM and green behaviors and sustainable performance.

Academics in the United States and the United Kingdom have offered several different HRM models. The early Harvard model developed by Beer et al. (1984) has proven controversial among academics. For some, these models reflect a more individualistic-oriented culture, different management styles, and a general absence of trade union organization in the workplace (Bratton & Gold, 2012). The widely cited Storey (1992) model of HRM gives explicit attention to the role of transformative leadership and the wider culture and climate context in which HR practices are designed and executed. In the following section, we examine these two models and some of their strengths and weaknesses.

The Harvard Model of HRM

The analytical framework of the Harvard model offered by Beer and his colleagues consists of six complex components: (a) situational factors, (b) stakeholder interests, (c) HRM policy choices, (d) HR outcomes, (e) long-term consequences, and (f) a feedback loop through which the outputs flow directly into the organization and to the stakeholders.

The situational factors influence management's choice of HRM strategy. The model incorporates workforce characteristics, management philosophy, labor market regulations, societal values, and patterns of unionization and suggests a meshing of both product market and socio-cultural logics (Evans & Lorange, 1989). Analytically, both HRM scholars and practitioners are more comfortable with the contextual variables included in the model because it conforms to the reality of the employment relationship: an amalgamation of business and societal expectations (Boxall, 1992). The second component, stakeholder interests, recognizes the importance of trade-offs either explicitly or implicitly, between the interests of owners and those of employees and their organizations, the unions. Although the model is still vulnerable to the charge of unitarism, it is a much more pluralist frame of reference than is found in some other models.

The third component, HRM policy choices, emphasizes that management's decisions and actions in HR management can be appreciated fully only if it is recognized that they result from an interaction between constraints and choices. The model sees management as a real actor, capable of making at least some degree of unique contribution within environmental and organizational parameters, and of influencing those parameters themselves over time. The fourth component, the human resource outcomes, includes high employee commitment to organizational goals and high individual performance, leading to more cost-effective products or improved services. The underlying assumptions here are that employees have talents that are rarely fully utilized at work, yet they show a desire to experience growth through work. Thus, the Harvard HRM model takes the view that employment relations should be managed on the basis of the assumptions inherent in McGregor's (1960) classic approach to people-related issues, which he labelled *Theory Y*, or, to use contemporary parlance, in conditions of "human dignity at work" (Bratton & Gold, 2012, p. 20).

The fifth component, the long-term outcomes, distinguishes between three levels: individual, organizational, and societal. At the individual employee level, the long-term outputs comprise the psychological rewards workers receive in exchange for effort. At the organizational level, increased effectiveness ensures the survival of the organization. In turn, at the societal level, as a result of fully utilizing people at work, some of society's goals (for example, growth and environmental protection) are attained. The sixth component of the Harvard model is a feedback loop. The situational factors influence HRM policy and choices but conversely, long-term outcomes might influence the situational factors, stakeholder interests, and HR policies. The feedback loop therefore acknowledges this two-way relationship.

An advantage of the Harvard model is that it serves as a heuristic device for explaining the nature and significance of key HR practices. It also contains elements that are analytical (that is, situational factors, stakeholders, strategic choice levels) and prescriptive (i.e., notions of commitment, competence, and so on). Another advantage of the Harvard model is the classification of inputs and outcomes at individual, organizational, and societal levels, creating the basis for identifying and measuring what works for green behavioral interventions and what potential effects might be for the various stakeholders. A weakness is the absence of a coherent theoretical basis for measuring the relationship among HR inputs, outcomes, and performance (Bratton et al., 2010, p. 465).

The Storey Model of Human Resource Management

The Storey model shows the core features of HRM by creating an ideal type. The usage of an ideal type is a popular heuristic tool in the social sciences. It is a mental construct and, in its conceptual purity, cannot be found in any real workplace. Its purpose, as its originator, Max Weber explained is the comparison with empirical reality in order to establish its differences or similarities, and to understand and explain causal relationships (Bratton & Denham, 2014).

Storey's HRM model has four main components: (a) beliefs and assumptions, (b) strategic aspects, (c) role of line managers, and (d) key levers. The first component, the HRM recipe of ideas and assumptions, prescribes certain priorities. The most fundamental idea is that among all the factors of production, talented employees distinguishes successful firms from the mediocre. It follows logically from this premise that employees ought to be nurtured as a valued asset and not simply regarded as a cost. The second component, strategic aspects, emphasizes that HRM is a matter of critical importance to corporate planning. In Storey's words, "decisions about human resources policies should . . . take their cue from an explicit alignment of the competitive environment, business strategy and HRM strategy" (2007, p. 10). The third component, line management, argues that general managers, not HRM specialists, are vital to the effective delivery of HRM practices (Purcell et al., 2009). The fourth component, key levers, puts a spotlight on the methods used to implement HRM. What is persuasive about the HRM narrative according to Storey (2007), is evidence of a shift away from rules as a basis of good practice, to organizational culture and climate as proof of avant-garde workplace practices.

Building a Green Organization through Human Resource Management

Organizational cultures are stable and enduring. This has not prevented academics and practitioners from debating the role of HRM in changing an organization's culture. It has been argued, for example, "the HR professional must recognize, articulate, and shape a company's culture" (Brewster et al., 2008, p. 312). In mainstream definitions of the term, corporate sustainability is seen as a strategic goal that is underpinned by a strong culture expressing what the organization is and its relationship with customers and employees (Bratton & Gold, 2012, p. 163). A green organization can be senior management's "Big Idea" (Purcell et al., 2009). But, if sustainable low-carbon behaviors at individual, team, and material levels are to go beyond quaint rhetorical notions of going green, it is argued that managers collectively have to develop a "sustainability-oriented organizational culture" (e.g., Chen, 2011; Jabbour et al., 2010).

A green organization can be conceptualized as a *collective endeavor* and has the same attributes of strong corporate cultures wherein the culture acts as a metaphorical glue that binds employees and work processes together. As Purcell and his colleagues observe, although ad hoc HR practices can easily be replicated, "it is the mix of these practices with well-developed routines underpinned by values collectively applied and embedded which is so hard to imitate" (2009, p. 26). Scholarship on environmental sustainability affirms the importance of the efficient management of finite natural resources, the need to consult and "engage" the entire workforce, and the effective management of people (Arrowsmith & Parker, 2013; Macey & Schneider, 2008; Robertson & Barling, 2013). Moreover, it affirms the importance of convergence between low-carbon environmentally sustainable strategies; low-carbon behaviors, a culture based on ecological values and integrated HR practices (Fernandez et al., 2003). The established use of HR processes in health and safety, minimum waste production, and cultural management makes HRM well-positioned to coordinate the goal of a green sustainable organization (Jabbour et al., 2010; Oliveira & Pinheiro, 2009). In this context, HRM theorists have tried to identify effective ways to change manifestations of organizational culture: visible *artifacts*, including language and shared behavior; and work *values*, which are invisible, but can be espoused and various sets of HRM practices that change a culture. This section examines planned culture change toward a green organization through new HRM practices.

People are key carriers of values into the workplace. A cluster of HR practices is both a carrier through which dominant values are expressed and enacted and, by their outcomes, express deep-rooted shared values (Purcell et al., 2009). The extant literature on organizational culture and business strategy highlights how important it is that the prevailing business strategy and organizational culture are consistent with each other (internal fit) and with the wider operation of the organization (external fit) (e.g., Hau Siu Chow & Liu, 2009). Extending the best fit debate, a green HR strategy should coincide with the organization's business strategy and create an appropriate culture in which to enhance sustainable organizational performance. The emergent literature on green HRM emphasizes that a set of integrated HR practices covering recruitment, performance management and appraisal, learning and development, rewards, and employment relations can build a more environmentally sustainable workplace culture (Renwick et al., 2013). Broadly, the HRM approach to building a green organization is to develop and support the organization's low-carbon and environmental sustainability initiatives (Wehrmeyer, 1996; Ehnert, 2009).

So far, much of the GHRM research has focused on HR processes and practices: training and development (e.g., Sammalisto & Brorson, 2008); pay and rewards (e.g., Berrone & Gomez-Mejia 2009); and performance management and appraisal (e.g., Govindarajulu & Daily, 2004). More recently, Jackson and Seo's (2010) research examines the intersection of strategic HRM and environmental sustainability, and proposes research questions with the stated goal of encouraging more scholarship in the field. Existing GHRM studies highlight the opportunity for improved environmental performance when the goals, policies, and procedures of environmental management systems (EMS) are more closely aligned or "embedded" (Purcell & Kinnie, 2008, p. 546) with HR practices and wider organization activities (e.g., Brio et al., 2008; Chen, 2011; Jørgensen, 2000). However, this convergence, between HRM practices and organizational culture is considered secondary in classic studies of organizational sustainability (e.g., Shrivastava, 1995; Wehrmeyer, 1996). A central question that arises from the literature is whether effective environmental sustainability initiatives can develop from top-down management driven exercises, or are they more likely to be successful if part of a more grass-roots employee-led initiative for environmental sustainability in the workplace.

Recruitment and Selection

Environmental sustainability has become an important dimension shaping the recruitment and selection process. The environmental performance of an organization is increasingly used for attracting talented people and supporting a green organizational culture. Research suggests that attracting top candidates is easier for organizations known for superior environmental stewardship (Gully et al., 2013; Rupp, et al., 2013). One obvious way to build a low-carbon workplace is through self-selection of prospective employees. For example, German companies such as Bayer and Siemens use their environmental reputation to attract competent employees who are committed to the environment (Jabbour & Santos, 2008). The published research suggests that given a choice, people are attracted to green employers that are keenly attuned to climate change issues and have a strong ecological approach (Philips, 2007). Environmentally sensitive job previews combined with accurate portrayal of the organization's culture can attract talented people with values that match and sustain sustainability (Jabbour, 2011; Wehrmeyer, 1996).

Another way to embed a new Big Idea based on ecological values in the workplace is by selecting people with green-related skills and values. As Townley (1994) points out, selection practices are an important means of "knowing" and managing a culture change. The selection process may be designed to ensure that "employees committed to the environmental issue have a potential to be hired more than those who do not show an ability to lead the environmental management in a company" (Jabbour & Santos, 2008, p. 53). Studies also suggest that it may be expedient to start hiring managers who have a proven track record of environmental performance and value environmental protection (e.g., Ramus, 2002). Personality and competency-based tests provide one way of ascertaining the psychological factors that enable managers to find talented individuals who seem to fit the new culture. Employment selection tests based on attitudinal and behavioral profiling can be used to screen applicants for green values. However, the validity and predictive power of these assessment techniques have all been subject to challenge. Emergent studies in environmental management (Cox et al., 2012; Garavan & McGuire, 2010) suggest that in those organizations with proactive environmental sustainability programs, environmental criteria are systematically integrated further than just in the recruitment and selection process, reaching into employee performance appraisal, and the rewards and training dimension.

Performance Management and Appraisal

Performance appraisal programs are designed to improve the effectiveness of environmental management over time by guiding employees' actions toward the environmental performance outcomes desired by the organization. Milliman and Clair (1995) advocate for performance appraisal programs that encourage environmental activities at work. Jabbour et al. (2010) report that Brazilian manufacturing companies are establishing environmental objectives for their employees, whose performance is evaluated as one of the criteria of the performance appraisal. For example, the Xerox Company has a reward system that recognizes employees who meet certain levels of innovation in terms of how they deal with waste reduction, reuse, and recycling (Milliman & Clair, 1996).

Without performance appraisal and communication, employee environmental improvement efforts may come to a standstill. In order to achieve continued performance, most environmental programs need some form of review and feedback. Chinander (2001) highlights how many environmental management programs fail to emphasize the importance of feedback on environmental issues. Continual feedback ensures that employees are aware of their responsibilities and communicates the link between their environmental performance outcomes and rewards (Govindarajulu & Daily, 2004; Jabour & Santos, 2008).

Reward Management

Conventional wisdom suggests that a well-designed reward system can help motivate employees to achieve satisfactory performance levels, including environmental performance. The reward system provides a good indication of the seriousness of an organization's commitment to environmental sustainability management. It has been argued that the existence of rewards systems that take environmental performance into account is an indirect reflection of the level of management commitment to environmental management (Govindarajulu & Daily, 2004). Rewards can help to motivate and increase commitment from employees to be environmentally responsible (Jabbour & Santos, 2008; Patton & Daley, 1998). The rewards could be monetary or non-monetary, and could be tied to individual, group or organizational actions (Milliman & Clair, 1996; Ramus & Steger, 2000).

The use of contingent remuneration has been linked to superior environmental performance; and monetary rewards maybe one of the strongest motivators for encouraging employees to participate in environmental improvement activity (Govindarajulu & Daily, 2004; Ramus & Steger, 2000). For example, aligning compensation practices with environmental strategy has been implemented in North American companies such as Huntsman Chemical, Browning-Ferris Industries, and Coors Brewing Company (Milliman & Clair, 1996), where financial rewards are tied to employees' environmental performance. In this regard, management needs to determine if environmental responsibilities and initiatives should be incorporated into employees' performance appraisal, as it could be a significant motivating factor for some employees. However, Denton's (1999) survey suggests that even in some of the best-known companies for encouraging environmental initiatives, financial rewards, such as bonuses, incentives, or salaries were rarely tied to environmental performance.

To date, many workplaces are encouraging environmental activities with non-monetary rewards such as employee recognition schemes, time off from work, gift certificates, and paid vacations (Govindarajulu & Daily, 2004). For example, Dow Chemical, a leading American multinational corporation, motivates its employees by awarding plaques to employees who develop innovative waste reduction ideas (Denton, 1999). Some employees may be more motivated by formal or informal recognition rather than financial incentives. For example, empirical findings from six environmentally proactive European firms have shown that one of the most important factors for engaging employees and encouraging creative ideas is management support and company environmental awards (Ramus, 2001, 2002; Ramus & Steger, 2000). This suggests that front-line managers should seek environmental ideas from all employees, and seek opportunities to provide feedback to encourage employee engagement in environmental sustainability. Whether rewards are monetary or nonmonetary in nature, the reward system has to be supported by an effective communication plan (Parker & Wright, 2001), rewards must be tied to the achievement of environmental objectives (Starik & Rands,

1995), and must be consistent with other aspects of the rewards system (Dechant & Altman, 1994; May & Flannery, 1995).

Training and Workplace Learning

Training and workplace learning is a primary HR intervention for developing pro-environmental behaviors (Garavan & McGuire, 2010; Govindarajulu & Daily, 2004; Jabbour et al., 2010, 2011; Sarkis et al., 2010). Much of this training is related to improving employee health and safety, energy saving and waste management. For example, the US company 3M has encouraged employees to find creative ways to reduce pollution through their Pollution Prevention Pays (3P) program, which has saved the company close to $300 million (Renwick et al., 2008: 7). Training is a necessary component of advanced environmental management systems. The literature suggests that a major factor in a successful EMS is a comprehensive training program which provides all employees, at all levels of the organization, with the tools and understanding necessary to conduct themselves in an environmentally aware manner, foster innovation, make environmentally responsible decisions, and contribute to continued environmental improvements (Daily & Huang, 2001; Ulhoi and Madsen, 1996).

The level of employee environmental awareness is one of the most important predictors of the level of adoption and success of an organization's environmental initiatives. Perron et al. (2006, p. 553) report that the intent of clause 4.4.2 of ISO 14001 is to "ensure that employees at all levels of the organization understand the goals of the EMS and the ways their job activities impact the environment and the achievement of EMS goals." This understanding allows employees to participate in environmental management efforts, and could lead to improved environmental performance of an organization. Zilahy's (2003) study of the factors restricting the implementation of energy efficiency improvement indicates that perhaps the most salient restrictive factors were the level of employee environmental awareness. Research findings support the importance of employees being well versed in environmental issues, environmental processes, and the overall functioning of environmental management systems to ensure that an organization's environmental targets and objectives are achieved (Cohen-Rosenthal, 2000; Perron et al., 2006; Sammalisto & Brorson, 2008).

Employee Involvement and Participation

The GHRM literature suggests that environmental management requires employee involvement and participation (EIP) in the workplace (Brio et al.,

2007; Bunge, et al., 1996; Hanna et al., 2000; Lund, 2004). For example, Bernstein (1992) maintains that environmental change is impossible without employee engagement and participation, and participation is impossible without ecological understanding. This suggests that improved environmental performance heavily relies on employee engagement and learning (Zsoka, 2008). As Perron et al. (2006, p. 556) opine, "the many small actions and decisions that all members of an organization can make in their everyday work can cumulate to large improvements in the environmental impacts of the organization." The research suggests that when employees are "engaged" through EIP processes they will better understand how they can contribute toward environmental management. This highlights further that without the ingenuity and expertise of human capital environmental management initiatives may be limited and superficial.

Employee voice mechanisms such as suggestion schemes, "green teams" (Beard & Rees, 2000; Daily, Bishop, & Steiner, 2007), and "eco-champions" (Brosse, 2010) are major elements of the Green HRM strategy, largely because they provide workers with an opportunity to use their intimate knowledge *of* work and discretion *at* work to generate creative eco-friendly initiatives rather than rely solely on managers. The rationale for employee voice processes can be partly explained by the necessary human input into a successful sustainable strategy, a strategy based on low levels of carbon emissions, product differentiation, and high levels of value added and quality.

The Union Role in Workplace Sustainability

European trade unions have extended their traditional occupational health and safety focus by strongly supporting environmental improvements and green skills training. By responding to what has been described as one of the "big issues of the day" unions can influence sustainability in the workplace (Pearce, 2012). In the United Kingdom, the Trades Union Congress (TUC) has included climate change and environmental management issues in their union representative training, and called for investment in training as a cardinal principle in creating decent and green jobs. O'Grady (2010) describes the union position as follows: "Without green skills, there can be no decent green jobs; without decent green jobs, no flourishing green industries; and without these green industries, we will not—cannot—build a green economy."

In Canada and the European Union, trade unions have attempted to strengthen engagement in sustainable work at workplace level by calling for major investments in energy efficiency and renewable technologies, mandatory environmental audits, and bringing forward environmental sustainability issues into "mainstream" bargaining agendas (TUC, 2010). For trade unions, the low-carbon agenda is rooted in their long-standing aspirations for healthy working conditions, for social justice, for high-skill jobs, and for decent work (Mayer, 2009; Storey, 2004). The link between green working conditions and social justice is perhaps not self-evident, but exposure to toxic health hazards disproportionately affects blue-collar workers (Agyeman, Bullard & Evans, 2003; Agyeman & Evans, 2004; Dobson, 1998). As Mayer reminds us, workers are on the front line of the fight for removing toxic substances that threaten the health of workers *inside* the workplace and members of local communities *outside* the workplace (2009, p. 190).

Conclusion

In this chapter, we have defined core concepts and practices in HRM. The research reviewed emphasizes the importance of aligning HR practices with sustainability goals: "companies that are able to align practices and human resource dimensions with the objective of environment management can be successful in the organizational journey toward environmental sustainability," writes Jabbour (2011, p. 104). This chapter has offered a framework for examining HR interventions to create sustainable, green workplaces.

Several points relating to methodology and management philosophy and style can be summarized briefly. First, because environmental management is a process, we need to investigate the social interactions between knowledgeable line managers who execute HR green interventions and other employees at workplace level rather than rely solely on large-scale databases gathered from single responders such as senior managers. Second, research needs to be conducted within a theoretical paradigm that recognizes that the employment relationship is, by necessity, co-operative but it also entails conflict between the employer and employees. Third, research needs to be cognizant of organization or sector contingencies and to consider the forms HR interventions might take in contrasting workplaces. Moreover, research needs to be more sensitive to the broader sociocultural phenomenon that organizations are embedded in wider society (Watson, 2010). Although there is evidence that HR practices can contribute to the achievement of green organizations, there is also the problem of establishing the direction of the relationship or reverse causality. Green organizations operating as a monopoly or in favorable market conditions will both be able to meet the cost of sophisticated green HRM systems and invest in them (Purcell & Kinnie, 2008). Finally, with regard to management philosophy and style, green HR interventions tend to be more successful in organizations that seek to "embed shared values" (Cox et al., 2012). Evidence suggests that research should explore the contribution of employee voice, through EIP processes, to the achievement of green organizations.

Suggested Additional Readings

1. Boxall P., & Macky, K. (2009). Research and theory on high-performance work systems: progressing the high-involvement stream. *Human Resource Management Journal*, *19*(1), 3–23.
2. Bratton, J., & Gold, J. (2012). *Human resource management: Theory and practice* (5th ed.). Basingstoke, UK: Palgrave.
3. Bratton, J. (2015). *Work and organizational behaviour* (3rd ed.). Basingstoke, UK: Palgrave.
4. Legge, K. (2006) Human Resource Management. In S. Ackroyd, R. Batt, P. Thompson, & P. Tolbert (Eds.), *The Oxford handbook of work and organization* (pp. 220–241). New York: Oxford University Press.

References

Agyeman, J., Bullard, R., & Evans, B. (2003). *Just sustainabilities: Development in an unequal world*. New York: MIT Press.

Agyeman, J., & Evans, B. (2004). 'Just sustainability': The emerging discourse of environmental justice in Britian? *The Geographical Journal*, *170*, 155–164.

Arrowsmith, J., & Parker, J. (2013). Delivering employee engagement: A neo-pluralist departure for HRM?' *International Journal of Human Resource Management*, *24*(14), 2692–2712.

Blyton, P., & Turnbull, P. (Eds). (1992). *Reassessing human resource management*. London: Sage.

Beard, C., & Rees, S. (2000). Green teams and the management of environmental change in a UK county council. *Environmental Management and Health*, *11*(1), 27–38.

Beer, M., Spector, B., Lawrence, P. R., Quin Mills, D., & Walton, R. E. (1984). *Managing Human Assets*. New York: Free Press.

Berrone, P., & Gomez-Mejia, L. (2009). The pros and cons of rewarding social responsibility at the top. *Human Resource Management*, *48*, 957–969.

Boxall, P. F. (1992). Strategic human resource management: beginnings of a new theoretical sophistication? *Human Resource Management Journal*, *2*, 60–79.

Boxall, P. F., & Macky, K. (2009). Research and theory on high-performance work systems: Progressing the high-involvement stream. *Human Resource Management Journal*, *19*, 3–23.

Bratton, J., & Denham, D. (2014). *Capitalism and classical social theory*. Toronto: University of Toronto Press.

Bratton, J., & Gold, J. (2012). *Human resource management: Theory and practice* (5th ed.). Basingstoke: Palgrave.

Bratton, J., Sawchuk, P., Forshaw, C., Callinan, M., & Corbett, M. (2010). *Work and organizational behaviour* (2nd ed.). Basingstoke: Palgrave.

Brosse, M. (2010). Trends affecting the workforce. *Employment Relations Today, 36*, 79–84.

Brewster, C., Carey, L., Grobler, P., Holland, P., & Warnich, S. (2008). *Contemporary issues in human resource management*. Cape Town: Oxford University Press.

Brio, J. A., Fernandez, E., & Junquera, B. (2007). Management and employee involvement in achieving an environmental action-based competitive advantage: An empirical study. *The International Journal of Human Resource Management, 18*, 491–522.

Brio, J. A., Junquera, B., & Ordiz, M. (2008). Human resources in advanced environmental approaches: A case analysis. *International Journal of Production Research, 46*, 6029–6053.

Budd, J. W. (2004). *Employment with a human face: Balancing efficiency, equity, and voice*. London: Cornell University Press.

Bunge, J., Cohen-Rosenthal, E., & Ruiz-Quintanilla, A. (1996). Employee participation in pollution reduction: Preliminary analysis of the Toxics Release Inventory. *Journal of Cleaner Production, 4*, 9–16.

Chen, Y. (2011). Greening organizational identity: Sources and consequences. *Management Decision, 49*, 384–404.

Cohen-Rosenthal, E. (2000). A walk on the human side of industrial ecology. *American Behavioral Scientist, 44*, 245–264.

Cox, A., Higgins, T., Gloster, R., & Foley, B. (2012). *The impact of workplace initiatives on low carbon behaviours: Case study report*. Scottish Government. Retrieved from http://www.scotland.gov.uk/Publications/2012/03/2237 on September 29, 2013.

Daily, B. F., Bishop, J., & Steiner R. (2007). The mediating role of EMS teamwork as it pertains to HR factors and perceived environmental performance. *Journal of Applied Business Research, 23*, 95–109.

Daily, B. F., & Huang S. (2001). Achieving sustainability through attention to human resource factors in environmental management. *International Journal of Operations and Production Management, 21*, 1539–1552.

Dechant, K., & Altman, B. (1994). Environmental leadership: From compliance to competitive advantage. *Academy of Management Executive, 8*, 7–20.

Delbridge, R., & Turnbull, T. (1992). Human resource maximization: the management of labour under JIT system. In P. Blyton, & P. Turnbull (Eds.), *Reassessing human resource management* (pp. 56–73). London: Sage.

Denton, D. K. (1999). Employee involvement, pollution control, and pieces to the puzzle. *Environmental Management and Health, 10*, 105–111.

Dobson, A. (1998). *Justice and the environment: Conceptions of environmental sustainability and dimensions of social justice*. Oxford: Oxford University Press.

Ehnert, I. (2009). *Sustainable human resource management*. London: Springer.

Evans, A. L., & Lorange, P. (1989). The two logics behind human resource managemen. In P. Evans, Y. Doz, & A. Laurent (Eds.), *Human resource management in international firms: Change, globalization, innovation* (pp. 144–162). Basingstoke, UK: Palgrave Macmillan.

Fernandez, E., Junquera, B., & Ordiz, M. (2003). Organizational culture and human resource management in the environmental issue. *International Journal of Human Resource Management*, 14, 634–656.

Fitz-enz, J. (2000). *The ROI of human capital*. New York: AMACOM.

Garavan, T., & McGuire, D. (2010). Human resource development and society: human resource development's role in embedding corporate social responsibility, sustainability, and ethics in organizations. *Advances in Developing Human Resources*, 12, 487–507.

Garrick, J. (1999). The dominant discourses of learning at work. In D. Boud, & J. Garrick (Eds.), *Understanding learning at work* (pp. 216–229). London: Routledge.

Godard, J. (1991). The progressive HRM paradigm: A theoretical and empirical re-examination. *Relations Industrielles/Industrial Relations*, 46, 378–399.

Govindarajulu, N., & Daily, B. F. (2004). Motivating employees for environmental improvement. *Industrial Management and Data System*, 104, 364–372.

Gully, S. M., Phillips, J. M., Castellano, W. G., Han, K., & Kim, A. (2013). A mediated moderation model of recruiting socially and environmentally responsible job applicants. *Personnel Psychology*, 66, 935–973.

Hanna, M. D., Newman, W. R., & Johnson, P. (2000). Linking operational and environmental improvement through employee involvement. *International Journal of Operations & Production Management*, 20, 148–165.

Harvey, F. (2013). IPCC: 30 years to climate calamity if we carry on blowing the carbon budget. *The Guardian*, September 27, pp. 17.

Hau Siu Chow, I., & Liu, S.S. (2009). The effects of aligning organizational culture and business strategy with HR systems on firm performance in Chinese enterprises. *International Journal of Human Resource Management*, 20, 2292–2310.

Hendry, C., & Pettigrew, A. (1990). Human resource management: an agenda for the 1990s. *International Journal of Human Resource Management*, 1, 17–44.

Hyman, R. (1989). *The political economy of industrial relations*. Basingstoke, UK: Palgrave Macmillan.

Jabbour, C. J. C. (2011). How green are HRM practices, organizational culture, learning and teamwork? A Brazilian study. *Industrial and Commercial Training*, 43, 98 105.

Jabbour, C. J. C., & Santos, F. C. A. (2008). The central role of human resource management in the search for sustainable organizations. *International Journal of Human Resource Management*, 19, 2133–2154.

Jabbour, C. J. C., Santos, F. C. A., & Nagano, S. M. (2010). Contributions of HRM throughout the stages of environmental management: methodological triangulation applied to companies in Brazil. *International Journal of Human Resource Management, 21,* 1049–1089.

Jackson, S. E., & Seo, J. (2010). The greening of strategic HRM scholarship. *Organization Management Journal, 7,* 278–290.

Jacoby, S. M. (2005). *The embedded corporation: Corporate governance and employment relations in Japan and the United States.* Princeton, NJ: Princeton University Press.

Jørgensen, T. H. (2000). Environmental management systems and organizational change. *Eco-Management and Auditing, 7,* 60–66.

Legge, K. (1995). *Human resource management: Rhetoric and realities.* Basingstoke, UK: Palgrave MacMillan.

Lund, H, L. (2004). Strategies for sustainable business and the handling of workers' interests: Integrated management systems and worker participation. *Economic and Industrial Democracy, 25,* 41–74.

Macey, W. H., & Schneider, B. (2008). The meaning of employee engagement. *Industrial and Organizational Psychology, 1,* 3–30.

Marcus, A., & Fremeth, A. (2009). Green management matters. *Academy of Management Perspectives, 23,*17–26.

May, D. R., & Flannery, B. L. (1995). Cutting waste with employee involvement teams. *Business Horizons, 38,* 28–38.

Mayer, B. (2009). *Blue-green coalitions: Fighting for safe workplaces and healthy communities.* Ithaca, NY: Cornell University Press.

McGregor, D. (1960) *The human side of enterprise.* New York: McGrawHill.

Milliman, J., & Clair, J. (1996). Best environmental HRM practices in the U.S. In W. Wehrmeyer (Ed.), *Greening people: Human resource management.* Sheffield, UK: Greenleaf Publishing.

O'Grady, F. (2010). Keynote address to TUC Green Growth Conference, October 13. Retrieved from http://www.tuc.org.uk/soical/tuc-18662-f).cfm on October 15, 2010).

Oliveira, O. J., & Pinheiro, C. R. (2009). Best practices of the implantation of ISO 14001 norms: A study of change management in two industrial companies in the Midwest region of the state of Sao Paulo, Brazil. *Journal of Cleaner Production, 17,* 883–885.

Ones, D. S., & Dilchert, S. (2012). Environmental sustainability at work: A call to action. *Industrial and Organizational Psychology, 5,* 444–466.

Parker, O., & Wright, L. (2001). The missing link: pay and employee commitment. *Ivey Business Journal, 65,* 70–73.

Patton, K. R., & Daley, D. M. (1998). Gainsharing in Zebulon: What do workers want? *Public Personnel Management, 27,* 117–311.

Pearce, S., (2012). Tackling climate change: A new role for trade unions in the workplace? Advisory, Conciliation and Arbitration Service. Retrieved from http://www.acas.org.uk/CHttpHandler.ashx?id=3291&p=0 on September 29, 2013.

Penrose, E. T. (1959). *The theory of the growth of the firm*. Oxford: Blackwell.

Perron, G. M., Raymond, P. C., & Duffy, J. F. (2006). Improving environmental awareness training in business. *Journal of Cleaner Production, 14*, 551–562.

Philips, L. (2007). Go green now to combat climate change. *People Management*. Retrieved from http://www.cipd.co.uk/pm/peoplemanagement/b/weblog/archive/2013/01/29/gogreennowtocombatclimatechange-2006-11.aspx on February 22, 2014.

Purcell, J. (1989). The impact of corporate strategy on human resource management. In J. Storey (Ed.), *New perspectives on human resource management* (pp. 67–91). London: Routledge.

Purcell, J., Kinnie, N., Swart, J., Rayton, B., & Hutchinson, S. (2009). *People management and performance*. London: Routledge.

Purcell, J., & Kinnie, N. (2008). HRM and business performance. In P. Boxall, J. Purcell, & P. Wright (Eds.), *The Oxford handbook of human resource management* (pp. 533–551). Oxford: Oxford University Press.

Ramus, C. A. (2001). Organizational support for employees: Encouraging creative ideas for environmental sustainability. *California Management Review, 44*, 85–105.

Ramus, C. A. (2002). Encouraging innovative environmental actions: What companies and managers must do. *Journal of World Business, 37*, 151–164.

Ramus, C. A., & Steger, U. (2000). The role of supervisory support behaviours and environmental policy in employee 'eco-initiatives' at leading-edge European companies. *Academy of Management Journal, 43*, 605–626.

Renwick, D., Redman, T., & Maguire, S. (2008). Green HRM: A review, process model, and research agenda. Discussion Paper Series No. 2008.01 April. Sheffield, UK: University of Sheffield Management School.

Renwick, D., Redman, T., & Maguire, S. (2013). Green human resource management: A review and research agenda. *International Journal of Management Reviews, 15*, 1–14.

Robertson, J. L., & Barling, J. (2013). Greening organizations through leaders' influence on employees' pro-environmental behaviors. *Journal of Organizational Behavior, 32*, 176–194.

Rousseau, D. M. (1995). *Psychological contracts in organizations: Understanding written and unwritten agreements*. Thousand Oaks, CA: Sage.

Rup, D. E., Shao, R., Thornton, M. A., & Skarlicki, D. P. (2013). Applicants' and employees' reactions to corporate social responsibility: The moderating effects of first-party justice perceptions and moral identity. *Personnel Psychology, 66*, 895–933.

Sammalisto, K., & Brorson, T. (2008). Training and communication in the implementation of environmental management system (ISO 14001): A case study at the University of Gavle, Sweden. *Journal of Cleaner Production, 16*, 299–309.

Starik, M., & Rands, G. P. (1995). Weaving an integrated web: Multilevel and multisystem perspectives of ecologically sustainable organizations. *Academy of Management Review, 20*, 908–935.

Sarkis, J., Gonzalez-Torre, P., & Adenso-Diaz, B. (2010). Stakeholder pressure and the adoption of environmental practices: The mediating effect of training. *Journal of Operations Management, 28*, 163–176.

Shrivastava, P. (1995). The role of corporations in achieving ecological sustainability. *Academy of Management Journal, 20*, 936–960.

Storey, J. (1989). *New perspectives on human resource management*. London: International Thomson Business Press.

Storey, J. (1992). *Developments in the management of human resources: Analytical review*. Oxford: Blackwell.

Storey, J. (Ed.) (2007). *Human resource management: A critical text* (pp. 3–120). London: Thompson Learning.

Storey, R. (2004). From the environment to the workplace and back again? Occupational health and safety activism in Ontario, 1970s-2000. *Canadian Review of Sociology, 41*, 419–447.

Townley, B. (1994). *Reframing human resource management*. London. Sage.

Trades Union Congress (2010). TUC green growth conference. Retrieved from www.tuc.org.uk/social/tuc on September 29, 2013.

Ulhoi, J. P., & Madsen, H. (1996). The Greening of European Management Education. In W. Wehrmeyer (Ed.), pp. 289–300.

Watson, T. (2010). Critical social science, pragmatism and the realities of HRM. *The International Journal of Human Resource Management Studies, 21*, 915–931.

Walton, R. (1985). From control to commitment in the workplace. *Harvard Business Review*, March/April, 77–84.

Wehrmeyer, W. (Ed.) (1996). *Greening people: Human resources and environmental management*. Sheffield, UK: Greenleaf Publishing.

World Commission on Environment and Development (1987). *Our common future*. New York: Oxford University Press.

Working Group Contribution to the IPCC Fifth Assessment Report Climate Change 2013. The physical science basis summary for policymakers. Retrieved from http://www.climatechange2013.org/images/uploads/WGIAR5-SPM_Approved 27Sep2013.pdf on September 29, 2013.

Zilahy, G. (2003). Organizational factors determining the implementation of cleaner production in the corporate sector. *Journal of Cleaner Production, 12*, 311–319.

Zsoka, A. N. (2008). Consistency and "awareness gaps" in the environmental behaviour of Hungarian companies. *Journal of Cleaner Production, 16*, 322–329.

13 ERGONOMIC INITIATIVES

Andrew Thatcher

In the last few decades it has become increasingly apparent that resource limitations and the resultant disruptions to natural cycles (Bates et al., 2008; Vitsousek, 1994) have led to severe human tragedies such as negative impacts on human health and well-being (Pimentel et al., 2007), poverty and malnutrition (Hecht et al., 2012), and social system disruptions (Wilkinson & Pickett, 2009). In the words of Hecht et al. (2012, p. 64) the challenges for modern civilizations are multidisciplinary, immense, and complex:

> We must vastly improve infrastructure for water systems, sanitation, and urban development; lessen hunger, assuage poverty, and promote human dignity; curb greenhouse-gas emissions; avoid persistent, bioaccumulative, and toxic chemicals; and protect biodiversity.

Environmental sustainability is essentially concerned with resource scarcity or damage to ecosystems, either in the present or at some projected time in the future. Sustainability concerns usually manifest as (a) resource depletion or absence (e.g., lack of access to food, water, land), (b) resource degradation (e.g., biodiversity loss, soil erosion, marginal farming land), (c) the deliberate or accidental damage of resources for short-term gain (e.g., oil spills, strip mining, inadequate processing of waste), or (d) a misunderstanding of the complex interrelationships between different resources (e.g., global financial crises, fossil fuel use and the carbon cycle, agriculture fertilizers and the nitrogen cycle) (Daly, 1990). The term *sustainable development* is attributed to the World Commission on Economic Development (WCED, 1987), which defined sustainable development as "development that meets the needs of the present without compromising the ability of future generations to meet their own needs." Arguably, sustainable development is primarily a social justice project focusing on equitable development to meet human needs while still recognizing that the preservation of natural resources is necessary to fulfill these needs. Johnston et al. (2007) noted that the emphasis on sustainable development has meant that the focus has been away from the notion of resource limitation toward human development and a proliferation of definitions and modifications to the original WCED (1987) definition.

Thatcher (2012) noted that similar definitional problems have plagued the early work of "human factors and sustainable development." Recently, there has been increasing recognition by organizations that they have a significant role to play in ameliorating the negative impacts that human activities have on our planet and its ecosystems (Dyllick & Hockerts, 2002; Hawken et al., 1999; Senge et al., 2008). As a discipline related to organizational psychology, this chapter looks at the role that human factors and ergonomics (HFE)[1] in the workplace has begun to play in dealing with these global crises.

Over the last two decades several prominent ergonomists have emphasized the need for HFE to tackle the complex systemic social and environmental problems facing humanity such as global climate change, social inequalities, and poverty (Helander, 1997; Moray, 1993, 1995; Vicente, 2008; Wisner, 1997). Despite a number of initiatives, Martin et al. (2013) noted that the HFE response to these challenges has been limited. The earliest response came in the form of the term *eco-ergonomics*, first used as the theme to the Fourth Ergonomics Congress of Latin America. However, only a handful of papers at this Congress actually addressed issues related to global humanitarian and environmental crises. Eco-ergonomics has been used sporadically over the last 15 years, emphasizing the need for ergonomics to consider the well-being of the natural environment (Brown, 2007; Charytonowicz, 1998), although without suggesting any definitions or models of sustainability or sustainable development. The more recent approaches have been more firmly embedded in theoretical frameworks by introducing green ergonomics, ergoecology, and human factors and sustainable development.

---

1. The terms *ergonomics* and *human factors* are often used interchangeably in the literature, although sometimes with slightly different meanings. In this chapter the term *human factors and ergonomics* is preferred (abbreviated to HFE throughout the chapter) when referring to the disciplinary field in general. According to the International Ergonomics Association's website, the official definition of "ergonomics (or human factors) is the scientific discipline concerned with the understanding of the interactions among humans and other elements of a system, and the profession that applies theoretical principles, data and methods to design in order to optimize human well-being and overall system performance" (http://www.iea.cc).

This chapter first deals with the three theoretical approaches that address HFE and sustainability issues: human factors and sustainable development, green ergonomics, and ergoecology. Each of these approaches is briefly introduced and their primary underlying theoretical basis is presented. The chapter then provides an overview of the different HFE studies and interventions within the broad domain of sustainability. This section covers examples from the HFE literature on topics as diverse as organizational sustainability, sustainable work systems, social sustainability, task analysis and job design, design of the physical environment, and the design of products and interfaces to support sustainable behaviors and practices. The chapter concludes with commentary about the role of HFE in supporting green organizations.

Theoretical Approaches in HFE to Addressing Global Crises

Human Factors and Sustainable Development

The term *human factors and sustainable development* was first used by Steimle and Zink (2006), which preceded the establishment of an International Ergonomics Association (IEA) Technical Committee of the same name (Zink, 2008a). In a series of papers Zink and colleagues used a combination of the WCED (1987) definition, the triple bottom line (TBL) approach for sustainable organizations taken from Dyllick and Hockerts (2002), and Docherty et al.'s (2002) "sustainable work systems" as their formularization of human factors and sustainable development. Steimle and Zink (2006) argued that within wealthier nations environmental sustainability had been emphasized, with less attention being paid to the social aspects, and specifically to human factors. Steimle and Zink's (2006) original conceptualization encouraged ergonomists to make contributions by designing sustainable work systems, complementing the design process of sustainability-oriented products, ensuring the safe operation of complex systems to mitigate ecological and economic disasters, and using community ergonomics to help resolve social problems.

Zink et al. (2008a) extended Dyllick and Hockerts' (2002) TBL model to demonstrate how HFE interventions could address some of the TBL objectives (see Figure 13.1). Zink and Fischer (2013) outlined human factors and sustainable development principles that would (a) preserve and develop human and social capital; (b) acknowledge whole value chains across the development and use spectrum, not just end users; (c) take a life cycle approach that incorporates all aspects from manufacture, through use, to maintenance, and post use; and (d) helping systems cope with necessary change management to

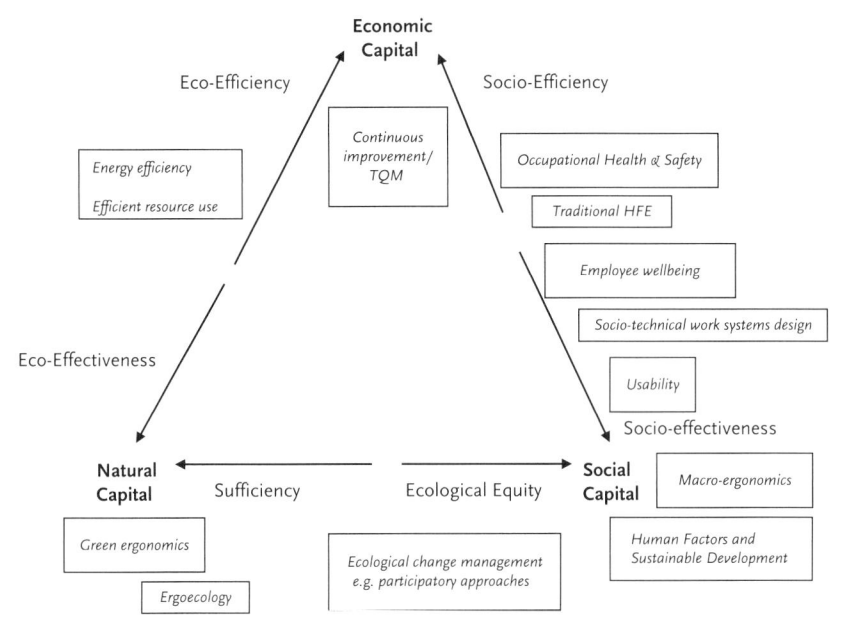

FIGURE 13.1 Organizational sustainability and HFE interventions.

achieve a sustainable society. Thus, Zink and Fischer's (2013) conceptualization is primarily based on achieving global social justice while acknowledging that the maintenance of natural resources is necessary. More recently, Zink (2013) acknowledged the limitation of the TBL approach: that it is based on the present. He proposed a TBL model that incorporates a time component, operationalized as the life cycle perspective that takes into account the whole work process over a period of time.

Green Ergonomics

Hedge (2008) and Hanson (2010) preferred the use of the term *green ergonomics*, which has been avoided by Zink and Fischer (2013) because of its implied reference to environmental issues, to the perceived exclusion of social and economic components. Hedge (2008) and Hanson (2010) both made practical suggestions for the application of green ergonomics, but neither of their articles referred specifically to any definition or model of sustainable development. The definition of green ergonomics comes from Thatcher (2013), who refers specifically to the same sets of definitions and models as Zink and his colleagues as background theory. Where Thatcher's (2013) definition differs is that green ergonomics is defined as a subcomponent of the broader term *human factors and sustainable development*, with the emphasis being on the maintenance and support of natural resources and systems. Green ergonomics comprises "ergonomics interventions that have a pro-nature focus" (Thatcher, 2013, p. 391), capitalizing on understanding the linkages and interplay between humans and their natural environment. This is captured in understanding how human systems preserve, conserve, and restore nature and enhancing the systems where humans benefit from the ecosystem services.

Ergoecology

Another approach to understanding the relationships between human factors and sustainable development that has recently emerged is the ergoecological approach (García-Acosta et al., 2012a). Originally proposed by García -Acosta (1996) in Spanish, this approach has taken some time to gain recognition in the mainstream human factors and ergonomics literature. García-Acosta et al. (2012a) draw on the WCED (1987) and the TBL approach but with additional cultural, technological, and political factors. Ergoecology is defined as "a scientific and technological multidiscipline systematically studying human beings and their relationships with the environment" based on an understanding of ergonomics (García-Acosta et al., 2014, p. 120). Ergoecology is the product of the interaction between an ergonomic system and this system's surroundings. The ergonomic system is defined as the human beings, objects/machines, and the physical space. The system's surroundings comprise political–legal, economic–financial, social–cultural, technological–scientific, and ecological–geographical, abbreviated as the PESTE factors. Ergoecology refers to the situation where there is a need for convergence on the ecological–geographical factor.

In parallel work, García-Acosta et al.'s (2012) ergoecological approach also draws on thermodynamic theories. To do this, they draw on classic thermodynamic theories that identify two types of energy, exergy and anergy. Exergy refers to the energy that is required by the system to maintain optimal performance. Anergy refers to any residual energy and includes waste products. Ergoecology calls for the maximum efficient use of exergy and the minimum resultant anergy.

Contributions from Human Factors and Ergonomics to Design and Work

Despite the relatively late development of theoretical approaches to sustainability issues in HFE, numerous HFE interventions have addressed sustainability concerns over recent decades. A systematic review of the HFE literature was conducted that included a review of articles published in the journals *Ergonomics, Applied Ergonomics, Human Factors, International Journal of Industrial Ergonomics, Behaviour & Information Technology, Ergonomics in Design, International Journal of Human Factors and Ergonomics, WORK,* and *Human Factors and Ergonomics in Manufacturing*. In addition, content that deals directly with sustainability was covered across a number of international and regional conferences (i.e., 2009 IEA Triennial Congress, 2012 IEA Triennial Congress, 2010 IEHF Conference), a book on sustainable development with a macroergonomics focus (Zink, 2008b), and two lead articles appeared in recent editions of the HFES Bulletin (Hedge, 2008; Sanquist, 2008). In recent years there has also seen an increased interest in how HFE has addressed global sustainability issues including a special edition of the journal *Ergonomics* (Haslam & Waterson, 2013).

Two limitations in the review that follows are acknowledged. (a) This review is not exhaustive but is intended to be illustrative; and (b) a great deal of design and evaluation research with an HFE focus also appears in print outside of the "traditional" HFE literature. There is a plethora of work in the psychology, design, sociology, and engineering literature across the last three decades that is not covered in this literature review (e.g., see Becker & Seligman, 1978; Brandon & Lewis, 1999; Benyus, 1997; Collier, Reeves, Stamp & Muckle, 2008; Maloney & Ward, 1973; McCalley & Midden, 2002; Tennessen & Cimprich, 1995; Ulrich, 1984). In this section, the examples cited predominantly review empirical (not theoretical) work published within the HFE literature.

Organizational Sustainability

One of the areas in which HFE has close links with organizational psychology is macroergonomics (Zink et al., 2008b). Macroergonomics emerged primarily from the realization that a number of small-scale HFE change interventions were not making a significant impact on bottom-line productivity for organizations (Hendrick, 1991; Kleiner, 2008). Although traditional HFE interventions made a significant impact on the work functioning and employee well-being of those directly affected by the interventions, they did not always effect significant productivity gains for the organization or work teams, and in some instances even increased job stress and job dissatisfaction (Meshkati, 1986). This realization led to the growth of a subdiscipline of HFE called Organisational Design and Management (ODAM; Hendrick, 1991), which was later changed to the term *macroergonomics* (Kleiner, 2008). Unlike traditional organizational development approaches, macroergonomics specifically emphasizes technology and the environment as focal elements in understanding the change processes for an entire organization.

There are different views about what constitutes organizational sustainability in HFE, including ensuring the long-term survival of an organization, supporting sustainable workplace practices and improvements, and enabling an organization to meet a TBL perspective. Each of these views is considered in Zink's (2008b) book on corporate sustainability. The stance taken by Zink is that HFE can contribute to creating sustainable organizations (although the emphasis was often only on the economic and social sustainability of the organization). The HFE approach most often referred to in his book is a branch of macroergonomics with links between total quality management and environmental management processes established in the early 1990s (Elkington, 1998). The basic premise is that business efficiencies achieved through total quality management processes and procedures can be applied to further improve the likelihood of the survival of the organization (Dahlgaard-Park & Dahlgaard, 2008; Dervitsiotis, 2008; Kanji, 2008). This is a rather narrow view of a sustainable organization. Other chapters in Zink's book take a broader view. More nuanced views recognize that taking a TBL perspective might enhance the organization's success and thereby its long-term survival (Cesarotti & Spada, 2008; Hermel, 2008; Zink, 2008c). These views recognize that organizations as complex systems have a duty to sustain their raw resource base, including the human resources that form part of the organizational system. The chapters by Kogi (2008), Tort-Martorell et al. (2008), and Vink (2008) look at different ways that HFE can assist in supporting sustainable improvements in organizations. Their concern is more with continuous development than with the TBL approach or green organizations. Again, these remain rather narrow conceptualizations that emphasize organizational longevity, biased toward an economic capital perspective.

In his chapter Karwowski (2008) challenged the ergonomics profession to think beyond a focus on human sustainability and rather to focus on sustainable lifestyles that integrate human well-being with environmental concern. Karwowski (2008) called for a new human factors approach, termed a "sustainable human-centered philosophy and design" (p. 125), which is built on the work of Fiksel (2003) who characterized long-lived organizations in terms of organic characteristics (i.e., diversity of organizational forms, sensitivity and adaptability to their environment, strong organizational cohesion, and efficient use of internal and external resources). Drury (2008) also encouraged the HFE community to become involved in producing a sustainable future in his chapter. He recognized the overlap of HFE and sustainability through their mutual emphasis on systems theory. Drury proposed that HFE should place an emphasis on sustainability at (a) the level of sustainable work (a concept not dissimilar to Docherty et al., 2002 and to Scott (2008) in the same book); (b) the design of products and the use of those products by consumers; and (c) the level of our own activities (which should apply to all humans), particularly through work on standards generation. From a systemic perspective, Drury (2008) noted that humans were particularly poor at understanding exponential relationships (i.e., population growth and the use of natural resources). He contended that HFE had a role to play in designing the way we present such resource use data to consumers and policy makers.

Zink's (2008b) book includes other studies investigating the role of HFE in supporting sustainable development. Continuing the work on using HFE to sustain an organization, various studies have looked at the application of HFE to sustaining organizations in the service industry (Karwowski & Ahram, 2012), in the minerals industry (Horberry et al., 2013), and in the tourism industry (Talsma & Molenbroek, 2012). Karwowski and Ahram (2012) use a user-centered design process to visualize the design of business management systems to deal with change. Each of these practical applications emphasized sustainable work and organizational success/longevity rather than a broader sustainability perspective.

Sustainable Work

Arguably a large proportion of the contributions from HFE have been about designing work that doesn't physically or psychologically damage the worker over the long term. This type of work is included in Steimle and Zink's (2006) early conceptualization of human factors and sustainable development as aligned with Docherty et al.'s (2002) sustainable work systems. Some of the research on corporate sustainability covered in the previous section (Drury, 2008; Horberry et al., 2013; Scott, 2008) also takes this view. Of course, these approaches are fairly narrow conceptualizations of sustainability (i.e., a focus on social capital) and it is not the purpose of this chapter to comprehensively review the HFE research focusing on creating work systems that support the health, safety, and well-being of workers. These aspects are important components of a fair and just workplace, but they do not obviously connect to sustainability and the recognized definitions of sustainable development and specifically there are no evident connections to the natural environment.

There is some published research on HFE that comes closer to acknowledging the broader definitions of sustainable development. Pitkänen and Louhevaara (2009) commented on the need to conceptualize work systems that are not only sustainable for the current worker, but also for future generations of workers emphasizing the intergenerational aspect of the WCED

(1987) definition. Hanson (2013) expanded on her earlier work by urging the HFE community to consider the health, well-being, and safety implications in the emerging green economy. She notes that green jobs such as the installation and maintenance of offshore wind turbines and solar photovoltaic batteries, work in organic farming and the recycling industries, and the design of low-energy public transport systems produce unique HFE challenges that require attention. Certainly there is a great deal that HFE has already accomplished in supporting work that is fair and that reduces the psychological and physical damage. However, further research is required to understand how the human aspects of work can contribute to sustaining natural resources rather than continually draining these resources, and findings from this type of research would have long-term implications.

Design of Tasks and Jobs

Another role for HFE is involvement in the design of tasks, jobs, work systems, and (ultimately) whole organizations. Much research is conducted in the HFE area on evaluating human work (task analysis in particular) and how these evaluations can be used for remedial action (Wilson & Corlett, 1999). However, relatively few studies have focused on jobs with a sustainability focus. Hanson's (2013) proposals would also fall into this category (i.e., the design of sustainable tasks and jobs), although she does not refer specifically to any empirical HFE studies that have investigated jobs in the green economy. A few innovative studies have begun to explore the links between task design and HFE while taking environmental sustainability into account. Torres et al. (2009) considered the task design of mussel farmers to enable sustainable farming practices. They suggested that monitoring of water quality, the mussel life cycle, and investigations to assess possibilities for waste usage would assist environmental conservation for sustainable farming. These tasks facilitate stewardship over the natural environment and simultaneously ensure the conservation of natural resources on which their jobs and tasks depend. Similarly, Celestino et al. (2012) assessed the task design of raft fishermen. Their investigations revealed that the fishermen required training on sustainable fishing practices, the development of stronger social and emotional bonds between the work groups to reduce wastage and pollution of the fishing grounds, and a cooperative program between stakeholders so that fishermen had a place to dock their rafts and hotel owners could simultaneously occupy beach space for their guests.

Other task design interventions in HFE have focused on designing work so that it can be conducted more eco-efficiently. Adams and David (2007) looked at ways of reducing errors in the fuelling of passenger vehicles. Their task analysis revealed several opportunities for HFE interventions to reduce fuel wastage and by doing so, also improve the eco-efficiency in this job task.

Although not specifically related to organizational psychology, a small number of HFE studies have examined how humans interact with technology to make those interactions more eco-efficient. Oliveira et al. (2012) conducted an analysis of how students undertook a simple cooking task. On the basis of this task analysis, the authors were better able to understand students' cooking behavior, and made several suggestions including (a) the development of a set of cooking guidelines and (b) the design of electrical appliances so that users were encouraged to use them more eco-efficiently. Similarly, Alli et al. (2013) conducted a careful task analysis of how students used three different types of public bathroom taps to wash their hands. Alli et al. (2013) produced design suggestions for public bathroom taps that would encourage more eco-efficient use. These studies show that task analysis might be used to design more eco-efficient work practices.

Another area in which HFE has the potential to influence work behavior is through training on how to use products and systems more eco-efficiently, which remains an under-researched area at present. Two studies focused on fuel-efficient driving behavior by bus drivers: af Wahlberg (2006) looked at the short-term and long-term (af Wahlberg, 2007) effects of a training program to help city bus drivers adopt more fuel-efficient driving styles. Neither the short-term nor long-term training effects were particularly encouraging, although fuel efficiencies were noted when additional feedback equipment was installed. The importance of feedback is a well-known component of successful training programs in the HFE literature.

Perhaps the most important role for HFE would be in facilitating larger, systemic behavior change. Sanquist et al. (2010) provided a number of suggestions (e.g., helping understand behavior change, helping present energy use information that is meaningful to users) wherein HFE might contribute to reducing energy consumption, but to date the only issue that has been assessed systematically is the HFE design of energy monitoring and management systems (covered in the section on product and interface design later in this chapter). Separately, Stanton et al. (2013) conducted a paper-based cognitive work analysis to understand the cognitive and practical constraints faced by commuters in moving to a mass-transport system that would reduce transport-based energy consumption. Their analysis identified new relationships between the identified constraints and possible HFE interventions. However, this was largely a theoretical exercise without access to actual commuters or other important stakeholders in the system. In the only empirical study (to date) that would fit into this category, a year-long study investigated how users' driving behavior changed when purchasing electric vehicles with regenerative braking systems (Cocron et al. 2013). The results of this study suggested that most drivers could adapt their driving style (particularly their braking habits) to maximize the regenerative benefits, and the authors provided design suggestions for making it easier for drivers to adapt to the changed driving demands and the systems easier to understand.

Social Sustainability

Arguably all the work on HFE in industrially developing countries has been about the equitable distribution of resources and knowledge (Kogi, 2006; Scott, 2009; Shahnavaz, 2000). Again, it is not the purpose of this chapter to outline all the work that is happening around the globe to uplift workers and communities from the more impoverished parts of the world (e.g., Ecuador, Mozambique, Turkey, Vietnam). This is a narrow view of sustainability that only takes the social and economic dimensions into account without necessarily understanding the complex interrelationships with natural systems. There has been an interesting array of studies that have purported to look at the relationships between sustainability and various different communities. Guimaraes (2012) borrows extensively from the macroergonomics tradition in looking at a sociotechnical design approach to understanding the sustainability needs of a medium size town in southern Brazil. This approach was used to identify seven focal areas for reducing the town's ecological footprint (i.e., energy, food, clothing, waste, sanitation, composting, and transportation) and three focal areas for human capital needs (i.e., employment, education, and health). Through using this approach Guimaraes (2012) demonstrated how HFE might be used for wider, community initiatives. With an increasing need for organizations to engage in corporate social responsibility initiatives, Guimareas (2012) provides a model for how organizational thinking might be applied to social and ecological upliftment.

In another approach, Hasle and Per Langaa (2012) looked at how HFE might be applied to improving global supply chains to improve the sustainability of communities internationally. They emphasized the role of participatory ergonomics in understanding the complex issues associated with global supply chain management, but also noted that there are several challenges posed by global supply operations that make traditional macroergonomic approaches difficult to implement. Hasle and Per Langaa (2012) argued that these are complex moral challenges that HFE will have to address if they are to contribute to ensuring equity in providing healthy and effective workplaces.

Environmental Conditions

The importance of a healthy physical environment on employee productivity and psychological well-being is well established in a number of disciplines. In HFE there has been a great deal of work on environmental ergonomics of the workplace, particularly in the built environment (e.g., sick building syndrome). Hedge (2000), for example, provided a review of studies investigating interventions related to lighting (especially daylight) and indoor air quality (including the use of indoor plants to remove pollutants), concluding that there were well-established human well-being and effectiveness benefits for interventions that focused on appropriate (day) lighting and indoor air quality that includes fresh air.

It is important to note that not every improvement in indoor environmental design quality necessarily results in greater environmental sustainability. For example, improved air quality might be achieved through an expensive heating, ventilation, and air conditioning (HVAC) system. Many HVAC systems may be more energy intensive and require greater resources to construct, maintain, and recycle. As a result, a number of studies have begun to explore the contributions that HFE can make to understanding whether green buildings improve work functioning and well-being at work. The work of Thatcher and Milner (2011, 2012, in press) examined which features of green buildings were most likely to lead to improved worker well-being and higher work effectiveness. They found that building features such as improved ventilation rates, increased daylight, and personal control of indoor environmental quality were the most significant components of green buildings. In similar work, Hedge et al. (in press) compared green buildings with a conventional building in Canada. They found that a range of environmental conditions (e.g., thermal conditions, office lighting, noise, satisfaction with the workstation) were not always significantly improved in green buildings. Additionally, Hedge and Dorsey's (2013) work found that green building designs largely ignore HFE contributions and focused rather narrowly on indoor environmental components to the exclusion of other important aspects such as furniture and fittings that incorporate HFE design and the design and layout of workspaces. This work is important because it has driven a worldwide trend to include HFE aspects as credits in green building rating tools. There is certainly a great deal of scope for HFE to continue to contribute to our understanding of what makes green buildings work appropriately for building occupants. Further work would also be necessary to understand whether working in a green building has an impact on general attitudes toward the environment and whether it changes other environmentally sustainable behaviors, such as recycling or traveling by bicycle to work.

Design of Products and Interfaces

The most obvious role for HFE (and where much of the research has been focused) is in the design of products to reduce or eliminate their resource load. Steimle and Zink (2006) emphasized the design and optimization of sustainable products as important for human factors and sustainable development; Tosi (2012) extended this notion by calling for design for sustainability to be an important component of HFE. Sauer and colleagues (Sauer & Rüttinger, 2004; Sauer et al., 2002, 2003, 2004; Wiese et al., 2004) investigated how simple changes in the design of product interfaces (e.g., the placement of controls and design of instructions) of basic household products (e.g., a domestic kettle, a vacuum cleaner, a central heating system) could enhance their eco-efficiency. They found that the placement of power controls (Sauer et al., 2002), automation (Sauer et al., 2004), and the labeling and instruction design (Sauer et al., 2002, 2003; Wiese et al., 2004) of these products benefitted eco-efficiency in terms of reduced energy and water consumption. Sauer and Rüttinger (2004) also considered other design features (such as the size and shape of a kettle). They found that a larger kettle resulted in more unused water, but its shape did not affect eco-efficiency. The context for these studies was in the domestic sphere, but these appliances are also used in organizations. There is also further scope to understand how the design of other workplace appliances (e.g., photocopying machines, laptops, mobile phones) might be further improved for eco-efficiency.

A fair number of HFE studies have investigated the design and efficacy of energy saving and monitoring systems. Kobus et al. (2013) investigated what factors lead to users of an energy management system changing their energy consumption behavior. Their findings offered several suggestions for the design and implementation of energy management systems, including interfaces that can distinguish between novice and expert users, the provision of feedback and prediction information, providing user control, and emotional rewards to encourage better usage. Sauer et al. (2007) studied the design of an interface for a central heating system; the interface provided the user with weather information, daily (i.e., energy consumption, energy wastage, energy cost, level of comfort), and monthly usage data. The results of their research showed that providing feedback significantly reduced energy consumption (Sauer et al., 2007). Peffer et al.'s (2013) analysis of the usability of a programmable thermostat interface led to several interventions that significantly reduced energy consumption (i.e., feedback provision, consistency in responses to user actions, clarity of displayed information) and suggested further interventions to the interface design that could improve energy consumption further. In a review of studies on energy saving and monitoring systems, Stedmon et al. (2013) suggested that HFE contributions could include the design of user feedback, the design of user-friendly interfaces, and understanding how these systems influence broader attitudes toward the environment.

The results of other HFE investigations have been less encouraging. Katzeff et al. (2012) used a participatory ergonomics design to develop an energy monitoring device that also provided feedback on how to reduce energy consumption, called EnergyCoach. Although this approach resulted in positive attitudes toward the device, there was considerable variability in its actual use. Fréjusa and Guibourdenche (2012) evaluated a real-time energy consumption display to determine whether this information would change behavior (in a household situation). The display increased users' awareness of their energy consumption but did not necessarily change their behaviors. Fréjusa and Guibourdenche (2012) discussed the ways in which user behaviors interfered with the efficacy of the display device. Similarly, Flemming and Jamieson (2009) found that an ecological interface (including functional information) did not reduce energy or water wastage compared to conventional feedback interfaces. What is common across these studies is that although an HFE approach leads to greater attitudinal acceptance of these devices, their usage varied considerably. In addition, all these investigations were conducted in domestic rather than office settings, which may be different because most employees are not directly responsible for the costs of buying resources (e.g., electricity, water, paper, etc.). This could change the dynamics of using an energy management system, and is worthy of further investigation.

Support for eco-driving behavior has somewhat more relevance for working contexts. Harvey et al. (2013) investigated perceptions toward eco-driving in a group of fleet drivers, people in the insurance industry, and traffic managers, and found that drivers did not see a link between driving efficiency, fuel savings, and their driving behavior. Instead, driving was primarily seen as a means for saving time and convenience. Thus, Harvey et al. (2013) found that the provision of feedback on eco-driving behavior was ineffective. Separately, Hilliard and Jamieson (2008) investigated the design of cognitive support tools for a solar-powered vehicle. Unlike conventional fossil-fuel and bio-fuel vehicles, solar powered vehicles do not carry their energy source on board, but derive their "fuel" from their environment. Solar-powered vehicles, therefore, need different driving skills and information requirements than on-board, fuel-based vehicles; they require information about the vehicle's functioning (e.g., solar array efficiencies, tire pressure, speed), traffic (e.g., traffic regulations, speed limits, traffic reports), and environment conditions (e.g., cloud cover, weather conditions, topographical details). These studies have direct relevance for organizations that rely on road transportation as an integral part of their business.

In other HFE investigations of energy consumption reduction, Oi, Yanagi, Tabata, and Tochihara (2011) studied energy savings from heated seats and foot heaters in motor vehicles. They found energy savings of about 10% from these devices compared to conventional air-based heating systems. In an interesting study, Anjos et al. (2012) showed that the usability of software was directly related to energy consumption: Specifically, software that was less usable resulted in tasks taking longer to perform and hardware having to work harder to deal with user requests, resulting in more energy consumption during task performance. Together, these studies demonstrate the complex relationships between human workers and the work technology with which they must interact, with scope for further research in understanding how these relationships can be optimized to ensure eco-efficient and eco-productive work.

Nadadur and Parkinson (2013) offer a different perspective on how HFE can contribute to the design of sustainable products. Using anthropometric population change dynamics, designers could develop products that have greater longevity and hence reduce the amount of raw materials required in the production of consumer products (Nadadur & Parkinson, 2013). This possible benefit rests on the assumption that historical patterns of population trends will remain consistent into the future and that the product does not become obsolete or degraded over time.

Human factors and ergonomics could also be used in the design of broader systems that reduce or eliminate resource loads. As one example, Mandavilli et al. (2008) investigated how the design of traffic circles could reduce motor vehicle emissions fuel consumption. In this study stop-controlled intersections were replaced with single-lane traffic circles, and the smoother traffic flow reduced carbon dioxide, carbon monoxide, nitrogen oxide, and hydrocarbon emissions. In addition, vehicles spent less time at the intersection, and therefore, less fuel getting to their destination. Replacing existing control mechanisms is a familiar strategy in many areas of HFE. In this case, the introduction of a traffic circle changed the traffic system functioning and positively affected eco-efficiency and psychological well-being (i.e., drivers arrived at their destinations sooner and with less traffic congestion).

Critique and Way Forward

Despite the recent emergence of theoretical frameworks to delineate the role of HFE in the sustainability space (Garcia-Acosta et al., 2014; Thatcher, 2013; Zink & Fischer, 2013), there is considerable variety in how sustainability is conceptualized. Interventions tend to focus on financial sustainability (e.g., the longevity of the organization or a particular product), social sustainability (e.g., sustainable work systems or sustainable communities), or environmental sustainability (e.g., energy consumption reduction). True sustainability likely requires some understanding of the balance among them.

Second, even the use of the term *green* within in the area of HFE and sustainability is contentious. For example, Zink and Fischer (2013) eschew the term *green* suggesting that it is an "environmentally oriented interpretation" (p. 354) consistently associated with an "ecological approach" (p. 353). Instead, while calling on the TBL perspective, they suggest that HFE is an anthropocentric discipline, and that it should focus on the social aspects. An emphasis on the social dimension would explain why so many of the HFE interventions are limited to sustainable work systems (Drury, 2008; Horberry et al., 2013; Scott, 2008), corporate longevity (Dahlgaard-Park & Dahlgaard, 2008; Dervitsiotis, 2008; Kanji, 2008 Kogi, 2008; Tort-Martorell et al., 2008; Vink, 2008), and social sustainability (Hasle & Per Langaa, 2012; Scott, 2009; Shahnavaz, 2000; Kogi, 2006). The danger in emphasising social sustainability factors is that many people in the HFE field likely believe that they are already contributing to sustainability, and might make little effort to strengthen their understanding of the complex interrelationships involved. This clearly was not the intention of Zink and Fischer (2013), who noted that HFE needs to extend its understanding of the complex interrelationships between humans and their external environments.

Third, the contributions that HFE has made to sustainability are wide ranging, but not always directly relevant for organizational functioning or for green organizations. For example, unless the organization is in the business of producing specific products, much of the prior research on the design of products and interfaces will only be of passing concern to most organizations. Still, understanding the design of kettles (Sauer et al., 2002, 2003; Wiese et al., 2004) when purchasing a kettle for the office, the likely energy saving benefits from installing an office energy management system (Fréjusa & Guibourdenche; 2012; Kobus et al. 2013; Peffer et al.; 2013; Sauer et al., 2007; Stedmon et al., 2013), or the likely fuel savings from purchasing electric cars for the company (Cocron et al. 2013; Harvey et al., 2013; Hilliard & Jamieson, 2008) could enhance organizations' environmental sustainability.

Other research in the HFE field is more directly relevant to creating green organizations. As one example, Anjos et al.'s (2012) research on the relationships between usable software, work efficiency, and energy consumption reduction is important for all organizations that use computing technology. The work in macroergonomics and ODAM might assist organizations in making the necessary changes required to be more holistically sustainable. Although practical examples of how macroergonomics might contribute are still lacking, the potential synergies are significant. HFE research on task analysis and job design (Alli et al., 2013; Adams & David, 2007; Oliveira et al., 2012) could add considerably to the methods and interventions applied traditionally in organizational psychology. Improving job design so that tasks use natural and human resources more effectively and efficiently can benefit the economic sustainability of the organization, the social sustainability of the employees, and the ecological sustainability of the planet. Research on workplace environmental design, particularly in green buildings (Hedge & Dorsey, 2013; Thatcher & Milner, 2011, 2012, in press) can significantly affect employee well-being and effectiveness, and contribute to more efficient use of natural resources.

Finally, an HFE approach effectively incorporates two options. First, HFE attempts to understand the tasks and roles that need to be performed to provide solutions for the tasks and or the supporting systems (e.g., technology). Second, HFE attempts to influence task behavior and roles through providing system (e.g., technology) constraints. This second instance is well recognized in aviation wherein the design of autopilot systems is intended to constrain flying behavior to make it safer and more efficient. Applying these options to sustainability, HFE can either provide the correct systems and designs to facilitate and support efficient and effective work (e.g., Hilliard & Jamieson, 2008) or use the technology to constrain the types of behaviors that are possible (e.g., Midden et al., 2008 propose an area of design called *persuasive technology*). Both these options would need to be considered depending on the work circumstances and the possibilities of the available technology.

Future Research

A great deal more research remains to be done to design work systems that are eco-efficient and eco-productive, ranging from introducing technology that is more eco-efficient, to understanding the interactions between technology and workers to ensure that they are used more eco-efficiently, to the design of work environments that leverage eco-efficiency. In particular there is a need to understand interactions between human users and biomimetic designs (i.e., designs that are based on, or mimic, natural systems). Such designs promise to be eco-productive rather than merely being more efficient. Different attempts to improve eco-efficiency in organizations involve technological intervention (e.g., green buildings, electricity monitoring devices, eco-efficient appliances) and yet we do not yet know whether these technologies result in a significant eco-efficient behavior change or not. Researchers should continue to evaluate the efficacy of technological interventions.

Future studies should also investigate how work design can be used to promote pro-environmental behaviors, both in the workplace and beyond (e.g., while traveling to work, in the general community). One specific research question might be whether a green workplace can lead to green behaviors beyond the workplace.

Hanson (2013) has suggested that some green jobs (e.g., installation and maintenance of offshore wind turbines and solar photovoltaic batteries, organic farming and the recycling industries, design of low-energy public transport systems) produce unique HFE challenges that require attention. How HFE might reduce the exposure to hazards that these jobs create (e.g., exposure to dangerous heights when installing skylights, solar panels, or wind turbines) needs to be investigated. There are also opportunities for HFE to explore work designs that incorporate the recreational and regenerative powers of natural systems. Work-life balance is an increasingly important component of modern workplaces and further work needs to be undertaken to understand whether natural systems provide benefits for effective work and appropriate work–rest cycles.

Conclusion

The response from HFE to the challenge of global climate change has been relatively slow, despite pleas over the past two decades (e.g., Moray, 1993). There has been a much more vigorous response over the last five years, a trend that will likely continue with upcoming special editions of the journals *Work* (dedicated to green ergonomics), *Ergonomics in Design* (dedicated to climate change), and *Applied Ergonomics* (dedicated to applied examples of designing a sustainable future). To date the responses have been in a wide array of areas from macroergonomic responses at the community and organizational level to microergonomic responses at the level of individual tasks and products Just what constitutes sustainability, however, remains varied. The theoretical approaches are fairly consistent in their portrayal of sustainability as multidimensional and complex, but practical implementations are dogged by misconceptions and narrow and naïve interpretations. Despite these problems, there are encouraging examples of multidisciplinary HFE work that addresses sustainability issues in complex and innovative ways. There is a considerable scope for HFE methods and interventions to work closer together with more traditional areas of organizational psychology and organizational behavior. Surviving the significant and complex problems facing our ecosystem and work systems will benefit from this multidisciplinary perspective.

Suggested Additional Readings

1. Anderson, R. (2009). *Confessions of a radical industrialist*. London: Random House.

2. Benyus, J. M. (1997). *Biomimicry: Innovation inspired by nature*. New York: William Morrow.
3. Drew, J., & Joseph, J. (2012). *The story of the fly and how it could save the world*. Cape Town: Cheviot Publishing.
4. Kellert, S. R., Heerwagen, J. H., & Mador, M. L. (2008). *Biophilic design: The theory, science, and practice of building for life*. Hoboken, NJ: John Wiley & Sons.

References

Adams, P., & David, G. C. (2007). Light vehicle fuelling errors in the UK: The nature of the problem, its consequences and prevention. *Applied Ergonomics*, 38, 499–511.

Alli, A., Maluleke, M., Bhana, S., Solomon, T., Klipp, Y., & Thatcher, A. (2013). Sustainability and usability of public bathroom taps. In M. Anderson (Ed.), *Contemporary ergonomics and human factors* (pp. 329–336). London: Taylor & Francis.

Anjos, T. P., Matias, M., & Gontijo, L. A. (2012). The usability of a product can be an ally of Sustainability. *WORK: A Journal of Prevention, Assessment and Rehabilitation*, 41, 2117–2121.

Bates, B. C., Kundzewicz, Z. W., Wu, S., & Palutikof, J. P. (Eds.) (2008). Climate change and water. Technical Paper of the Intergovernmental Panel on Climate Change. Geneva: IPCC Secretariat.

Becker, L., & Seligman, C. (1978). Reducing air-conditioning waste by signaling it is cool outside. *Personality and Social Psychology Bulletin*, 4, 412–415.

Brandon, G., & Lewis, A. (1999). Reducing household energy consumption: a qualitative and quantitative field study. *Journal of Environmental Psychology*, 19, 75–85.

Benyus, J. M. (1997). *Biomimicry: Innovation inspired by nature*. New York: William Morrow.

Brown, C. (2007). Eco-ergonomics. Proceedings of the New Zealand Ergonomics Society Conference, Waiheke Island, November 7-9, 2007.

Celestino, J. E. M., Bispo, C. D. S., Saldanha, M. C. W., & Mattos, K. M. M. D. C. (2012). Ergonomics and environmental sustainability: A case study of raft fisherman at Ponta Negra Beach, Natal-RN. *WORK: A Journal of Prevention, Assessment and Rehabilitation*, 41, 648–655.

Cesarotti, V., & Spada, C. (2008). The impact of cultural issues and interpersonal behavior on sustainable excellence and competitiveness: an analysis of the Italian context. In K. J. Zink (Ed.), *Corporate sustainability as a challenge for comprehensive management* (pp. 95–113). Heidelberg: Physica Verlag.

Charytonowicz, J. (1998). Ergonomics in architecture. In P. Vink, E. A. P. Konigsveld, & S. Dhondt (Eds.), *Human factors in organizational design & management VI* (pp. 357–362). Oxford: Elsevier.

Cocron, P., Bühler, F., Franke, F., Neumann, I., Dielmann, B., & Krems, J. F. (2013). Energy recapture through deceleration—regenerative braking in electric vehicles from a user Perspective. *Ergonomics*, 56, 1203–1205.

Collier, A., Reeves, K, Stamp, P., & Muckle, R., (2008). *A framework for pro-environmental behaviours*. DEFRA Report, January 2008 [Online]. Retrieved from http://www.defra.gov.uk/ on September 20, 2013].

Dahlgaard-Park, S. M., & Dahlgaard, J. J. (2008). A strategy for building sustainable innovation excellence—a Danish study. In K. J. Zink (Ed.), *Corporate sustainability as a challenge for comprehensive management* (pp. 77–94). Heidelberg: Physica Verlag.

Daly, H. E. (1990). Towards some operational principles of sustainable development. *Ecological Economics*, 2, 1–6.

Dervitsiotis, K. N. (2008). Developing sustainable competitive advantage through operational excellence and adaptation excellence with value-innovations. In K. J. Zink (Ed.), *Corporate sustainability as a challenge for comprehensive management* (pp. 37–55). Heidelberg: Physica Verlag.

Docherty, P., Forslin, J., & Shani, A. B. (Eds.) (2002). *Creating sustainable work systems: emerging perspectives and practice*. London: Routledge.

Drury, C. G. (2008). The future of work in a sustainable society. In K. J. Zink (Ed.), *Corporate sustainability as a challenge for comprehensive management* (pp. 199–214). Heidelberg: Physica Verlag.

Dyllick, T., & Hockerts, K. (2002). Beyond the business case for corporate sustainability. *Business Strategy and the Environment*, 11, 130–141.

Elkington, J. (1998). *Cannibals with forks: The triple bottom line of 21st century business*. Oxford: Capstone.

Fiksel, J. (2003). Designing resilient, sustainable systems. *Environmental Science and Technology*, 37, 5330–5339.

Flemming S. A. C., & Jamieson, G. A. (2009). Display design and energy conservation performance: a microworld study. International Ergonomics Association 17th Triennial Congress, August 9-14, 2009, Beijing, China.

Fréjusa, M., & Guibourdenche, J. (2012). Analysing domestic activity to reduce household energy consumption. *WORK: A Journal of Prevention, Assessment and Rehabilitation*, 41, 539–548.

García-Acosta, G. (1996). *Modelos de explicación sistémica de la ergonomía [Models of systemic explanation of ergonomics]* Master's thesis. Universidad Nacional Autónoma de México: México.

García-Acosta, G., Saravia Pinilla, M. H., Romero Larrahondo, P. A., & Lange Morales, K. (2014). Ergoecology: Fundamentals of a new interdisciplinary field. *Theoretical Issues in Ergonomics Science*, 15, 111–133.

García-Acosta, G., Saravia Pinilla, M. H., & Riba i Romeva, C. (2012). Ergoecology: Evolution and challenges. *WORK: A Journal of Prevention, Assessment and Rehabilitation*, 41, 2133–2140.

Guimarães, L. B. M. (2012). Sustainability and cities: a proposal for implementation of a sustainable town. *WORK: A Journal of Prevention, Assessment and Rehabilitation, 41,* 2160–2168.

Hanson, M. A. (2010). Green ergonomics: Embracing the challenges of climate change. *The Ergonomist, 480,* 12–13.

Hanson, M. A. (2013). Green ergonomics: Challenges and opportunities. *Ergonomics, 56,* 399–408.

Harvey, J., Thorpe, N., & Fairchild, R. (2013). Attitudes towards and perceptions of eco-driving and the role of feedback systems. *Ergonomics, 56,* 507–521.

Haslam, R., & Waterson, P. (2013). Ergonomics and sustainability. *Ergonomics, 56,* 343–347.

Hasle, P., & Per Langaa, J. (2012). Ergonomics and sustainability—challenges from global supply chains. *WORK: A Journal of Prevention, Assessment and Rehabilitation, 41,* 3906–3913.

Hawken, P., Lovins, A., & Lovins, L. H. (1999). *Natural capitalism: Creating the next industrial revolution.* Boston: Little, Brown & Company.

Hedge, A. (2000). Where are we in understanding the effects of where we are? *Ergonomics, 43,* 1019–1029.

Hedge, A. (2008). The sprouting of "green" ergonomics. *HFES Bulletin, 51,* 1–3.

Hedge, A., & Dorsey, J. A. (2013). Green buildings need good ergonomics. *Ergonomics, 56,* 492–506.

Hedge, A., Miller, L., & Dorsey, J. A. (in press). Occupant comfort and health in green and conventional university buildings. *WORK: A Journal of Prevention, Assessment and Rehabilitation,* in press.

Helander, M. G. (1997). Forty years of IEA: Some reflections on the evolution of ergonomics. *Ergonomics, 40,* 952–961.

Hecht, A. D., Fiksel, J., Fulton, S. C., Yosie, T. F., Hawkins, N. C., Leuenberger, H., et al. (2012). Creating the future we want. *Sustainability: Science Practice & Policy, 8,* 62–75.

Hendrick, H. W. (1991). Ergonomics in organizational design and management. *Ergonomics, 34,* 743–756.

Hermel, P. (2008). Social responsibility, strategic management and comprehensive corporate development: old roots, new issues? In K. J. Zink (Ed.), *Corporate sustainability as a challenge for comprehensive management* (pp. 217–229). Heidelberg: Physica Verlag.

Hilliard, A., & Jamieson, G. A. (2008). Winning solar races with interface design. *Ergonomics in Design, 16,* 6–11.

Horberry, T., Burgess-Limerick, R., & Fuller, R. (2013). The contributions of human factors and ergonomics to a sustainable minerals industry. *Ergonomics, 56,* 556–564.

Johnston, P., Everard, M., Santillo, D., & Robèrt, K. (2007). Reclaiming the definition of sustainability. *Environmental Science Pollution Research, 14,* 60–66.

Kanji, G. K. (2008). Performance excellence: Path to integrated management and sustainable success. In K. J. Zink (Ed.), *Corporate sustainability as a challenge for comprehensive management* (pp. 21–36). Heidelberg: Physica Verlag.

Karwowski, W. (2008). Building sustainable human-centered systems: A grand challenge for the human factors and ergonomics discipline in the conceptual age. In K. J. Zink (Ed.), *Corporate sustainability as a challenge for comprehensive management* (pp. 117–128). Heidelberg: Physica Verlag.

Karwowski, W., & Ahram, T. Z. (2012). Innovation in user-centered skills and performance improvement for sustainable complex service systems. *WORK: A Journal of Prevention, Assessment and Rehabilitation, 41*, 3923–3929.

Katzeff, C, Nyblom, A., Tunheden, S., & Torstensson, C. (2012). User-centred design and evaluation of EnergyCoach—an interactive energy service for households. *Behaviour & Information Technology, 31*, 305–324.

Kleiner, B. M. (2008). Macroergonomics: Work system analysis and design. *Human factors, 50*, 461–467.

Kobus, C. B. A., Mugge, R., & Schoormans, J. P. L. (2013). Washing when the sun is shining! How users interact with a household energy management system. *Ergonomics, 56*, 451–462.

Kogi, K. (2006). Participatory methods effective for ergonomic workplace improvement. *Applied Ergonomics, 37*, 547–554.

Kogi, K. (2008). Participation as precondition for sustainable success: effective workplace improvement procedures in small-scale sectors in developing countries. In . J. Zink (Ed.), *Corporate sustainability as a challenge for comprehensive management* (pp. 183–198). Heidelberg: Physica Verlag.

Maloney, M. P., & Ward, M. D. (1973). Ecology: Let's hear it from the people. *American Psychologist, 28*, 583–586.

Mandavilli, S., Rys, M. J., & Russell, E. R. (2008). Environmental impact of modern roundabouts. *International Journal of Industrial Ergonomics, 38*, 135–142.

Martin, K., Legg, S., & Brown, C. (2013). Designing for sustainability: ergonomics—carpe diem. *Ergonomics, 56*, 365–388.

McCalley, L. T., & Midden, C. J. H. (2002). Energy conservation through product-integrated feedback: The roles of goal-setting and social orientation. *Journal of Economic Psychology, 23*, 589–603.

Meshkati, N. (1986). Human factors considerations in technology transfer to industrially developing countries: an analysis and proposed model. In O. Brown, & H. W. Hendrick (Eds.), *Human factors in organizational design and management II* (pp. 343–350). Amsterdam: North Holland.

Midden, C. J. H., McCalley, L. T., Ham, J., & Zaalberg, R. (2008). Using persuasive technology to encourage sustainable behavior. Proceedings of Pervasive 2008, Sydney. Retrieved from http://web.stanford.edu/class/me221/readings/Persuasive_Tech_Sustainable_Behavior.pdf on September 10, 2014.

Moray, N. (1993). Technosophy and humane factors. *Ergonomics in Design, 1*, 33–39.

Moray, N. (1995). Ergonomics and the global problems of the twenty-first century. *Ergonomics*, *38*, 1691–1707.

Nadadur, G., & Parkinson, M. B. (2013). The role of anthropometry in designing for sustainability. *Ergonomics*, *56*, 422–439.

Oi, H., Yanagi, K., Tabata, K., & Tochihara, Y. (2011). Effects of heated seat and foot heater on thermal comfort and heater energy consumption in vehicle. *Ergonomics*, *54*, 690–699.

Oliveira, L., Mitchell, V., & Badni, K. (2012). Cooking behaviours: A user observation study to understand energy use and motivate savings. *WORK: A Journal of Prevention, Assessment and Rehabilitation*, *41*, 2122–2128.

Peffer, T., Perry, D., Pritoni, M., Aragon, C., & Meier, A. (2013). Facilitating energy savings with programmable thermostats: Evaluation and guidelines for the thermostat user interface. *Ergonomics*, *56*, 463–479.

Pimentel, D., Cooperstein, S., Randell, H., Filiberto, D., Sorrentino, S., Kaye, B., et al. (2007). Ecology of increasing diseases: population growth and environmental degradation. *Human Ecology*, *35*, 653–668.

Pitkänen, M., & Louhevaara, V. (2009). Mediating links between sustainable development and occupational wellbeing in the Finnish context. International Ergonomics Association 17th Triennial Congress, August 9-14, 2009, Beijing, China.

Sanquist, T. F. (2008) Human factors and energy use. *HFES Bulletin*, *51*, 1–3.

Sanquist, T., Moezzi, M., Vine, E., Meier, A., Diamond, R., & Sheridan, T. (2010). Transforming the energy economy—the role of behavioral and social science (pp. 763–765). Proceedings of the Human Factors and Ergonomics Society 54th Annual Meeting, Santa Monica, CA.

Sauer, J., & Rüttinger, B. (2004). Environmental conservation in the domestic domain: The influence of technical design features and person-based factors. *Ergonomics*, *47*, 1053–1072.

Sauer, J. Schmeink, C., & Wastell, D. G. (2007). Feedback quality and environmentally friendly use of domestic central heating systems. *Ergonomics*, *50*, 795–813.

Sauer, J., Wiese, B. S., & Rüttinger, B. (2002). Improving ecological performance of electrical consumer products: The role of design-based measures and user variables. *Applied Ergonomics*, *33*, 297–307.

Sauer, J., Wiese, B. S., & Rüttinger, B. (2003). Designing low-complexity electrical consumer products for ecological use. *Applied Ergonomics*, *34*, 521–531.

Sauer, J., Wiese, B. S., & Rüttinger, B. (2004). Ecological performance of electrical consumer products: The influence of automation and information-based measures. *Applied Ergonomics*, *35*, 37–47.

Scott, P. A. (2008). The role of ergonomics in securing sustainability in developing countries. In K. J. Zink (Ed.), *Corporate sustainability as a challenge for comprehensive management* (pp. 171–181). Heidelberg: Physica Verlag.

Scott, P. A. (2009). *Ergonomics in developing countries: Needs and applications*. Boca Raton, FL: CRC Press.

Senge, P., Smith, B., Kruschwitz, N., Laur, J., & Schley, S. (2008). *The necessary revolution: How individuals and organisations are working together to create a sustainable world*. London: Nicholas Brealey Publishing.

Shahnavaz, H. (2000). The role of ergonomics in the transfer of technology to industrially developing countries. *Ergonomics*, *43*, 903–907.

Stanton, N. A., McIlroy, R. C., Harvey, C., Blainey, S., Hickford, A., Preston, J. M., et al. (2013). Following the cognitive work analysis train of thought: exploring the constraints of modal shift to rail transport. *Ergonomics*, *56*, 522–540.

Stedmon, A. W., Winslow, R., & Langley, A. (2013). Micro-generation schemes: user behaviours and attitudes towards energy consumption. *Ergonomics*, *56*, 440–450.

Steimle, U., & Zink, K. J. (2006). Sustainable development and human factors. In W. Karwowski (Ed.), *International encyclopedia of ergonomics and human factors* (2nd ed.). London: Taylor & Francis.

Talsma, L., & Molenbroek, J. F. M (2012). User-centered ecotourism development. *WORK: A Journal of Prevention, Assessment and Rehabilitation*, *41*, 2147–2154.

Tennessen, C. M., & Cimprich, B. (1995). Views to nature: affects on attention. *Journal of Environmental Psychology*, *15*, 77–85.

Thatcher, A. (2012). Early variability in the conceptualisation of 'sustainable development and human factors. *WORK: A Journal of Prevention, Assessment and Rehabilitation*, *41*, 3892–3899.

Thatcher, A. (2013). Green ergonomics: definition and scope. *Ergonomics*, *56*, 389–398.

Thatcher, A., & Milner, K. (2011). Physical work environment, well-being, and productivity in a South African financial institution: implications for work and workplace design. In M. Göbel, C. J. Christie, S. Zschernack, A. I. Todd, & M. Mattison (Eds.), *Human factors in organisational design and management X* (Vol. *1*, pp. 75–80). Santa Monica: IEA Press.

Thatcher, A., & Milner, K. (2012). The impact of a 'green' building on employees' physical and psychological wellbeing. *WORK: A Journal of Prevention, Assessment and Rehabilitation*, *41*, 3816–3823.

Thatcher, A., & Milner, K. (in press). Changes in productivity, psychological wellbeing, and physical wellbeing from working in a 'green' building. *WORK: A Journal of Prevention, Assessment and Rehabilitation*, in press.

Torres, M. K. L., Teixeira C. S., & Merino, E. A. D. (2009). Ergonomics and sustainable development in mussel cultivation. International Ergonomics Association 17th Triennial Congress, August 9-14, 2009, Beijing, China.

Tort-Martorell, X., Grima, P., & Marco, L. (2008). Sustainable improvement: Six sigma—lessons learned after five years of training and consulting. In K. J. Zink (Ed.), *Corporate sustainability as a challenge for comprehensive management* (pp. 57–76). Heidelberg: Physica Verlag.

Tosi, F. (2012). Ergonomics and sustainability in the design of everyday use products. *WORK: A Journal of Prevention, Assessment and Rehabilitation, 41,* 3878–3882.

Ulrich, R. S. (1984). View through a window may influence recovery from surgery. *Science, 224,* 420–421.

Vicente, K. (2008). Human factors engineering that makes a difference: Leveraging a science of societal change. *Theoretical issues in Ergonomics Science, 9,* 1–24.

Vink, P. (2008). The influence of project duration and focus on involvement in participatory processes. In K. J. Zink (Ed.), *Corporate sustainability as a challenge for comprehensive management* (pp. 153–169). Heidelberg: Physica Verlag.

Vitousek, P. M. (1994). Beyond global warming: ecology and global change. *Ecology, 75,* 1861–1876.

af Wahlberg, A. E. (2006). Short-term effects of training in economical driving: Passenger comfort and driver acceleration behavior. *International Journal of Industrial Ergonomics, 36,* 151–163.

af Wahlberg, A. E. (2007). Long-term effects of training in economical driving: Fuel consumption, accidents, driver acceleration behavior and technical feedback. *International Journal of Industrial Ergonomics, 37,* 333–343.

Wiese, B. S., Sauer, J., & Rüttinger, B. (2004). Consumers' use of written product information. *Ergonomics, 47,* 1180–1194.

Wilkinson, R., & Pickett, K. (2009). *The spirit level: Why greater equality makes societies stronger.* New York: Bloomsbury.

Wilson, J. R., & Corlett, E. N. (1999). *Evaluation of human work: A practical ergonomics methodology* (2nd Ed.). London: Taylor & Francis.

Wisner, A. (1997). *Anthropotechnologie: Vers un monde industriel pluricentrique* [*Towards a pluricentric industrial world*]. Toulouse: OctarèsÉditions.

World Commission on Environmental Development (1987). *Our common future.* Report of the World Commission on Environment and Development. Oxford: Oxford University Press.

Zink, K. J. (2008a). New IEA human factors and sustainable development technical committee. *HFES Bulletin, 51,* 3–4.

Zink, K. J. (Ed.) (2008b). *Corporate sustainability as a challenge for comprehensive management.* Heidelberg: Physica Verlag.

Zink, K. J. (2008c). Human factors and comprehensive management concepts: A need for integration based on corporate sustainability. In K. J. Zink (Ed.), *Corporate sustainability as a challenge for comprehensive management* (pp. 231–253). Heidelberg: Physica Verlag.

Zink, K. J. (2013). Designing sustainable work systems: The need for a systems approach. *Applied Ergonomics, 45,* 126–132.

Zink, K. J., & Fischer, K. (2013). Do we need sustainability as a new approach in human factors and ergonomics? *Ergonomics, 56,* 348–356.

Zink, K. J., Steimle, U., & Fischer, K. (2008a). Human factors, business excellence and corporate sustainability: differing perspectives, joint objectives. In K. J. Zink (Ed.), *Corporate sustainability as a challenge for comprehensive management* (pp. 3–18). Heidelberg: Physica Verlag.

Zink, K. J., Steimle, U., & Schrőder, D. (2008b). Comprehensive change management concepts: development of a participatory approach. *Applied Ergonomics*, *39*, 527–538.

14   PRO-ENVIRONMENTAL ORGANIZATIONAL CULTURE AND CLIMATE

Thomas A. Norton, Hannes Zacher, and Neal M. Ashkanasy

Environmental sustainability is fast becoming a vital issue for business performance, growth, and survival in the twenty-first century (Dixon-Fowler, Slater, Johnson, Ellestrand, & Romi, 2012; Jackson, Ones, & Dilchert, 2012). Organizations pursuing such sustainability seek to achieve core business goals while minimizing harm to, and maximizing positive outcomes for, the natural environment (Starik & Marcus, 2000). We argue in this chapter that creating an organizational context that emphasizes values toward the environment (i.e., culture) in such a way that employees have shared perceptions of those values (i.e., climate) is therefore an imperative. In this instance, there is a large body of research that demonstrates the important role of culture and climate in achieving organizational goals (for reviews, see Ashkanasy, Peterson, & Wilderom, 2011; Schneider, Ehrhart, & Macey, 2013). To date, however, there appears to have been no real effort to develop an integrated model of pro-environmental culture and climate. In this regard, development of such a model should serve to benefit academic research as well as a facilitate the practical pursuit of environmental sustainability.

The goals of this chapter therefore are to introduce the concepts of pro-environmental organizational culture and climate and to examine how they might be integrated to create positive outcomes for organizations and the natural environment. Specifically, our focus is on explaining how the organizational context for sustainability, and employees' shared perceptions of this context, will impact employee behaviors that contribute to environmental sustainability in the workplace.

This chapter is structured in five sections as follows: First, we begin by establishing a case for pro-environmental organizational culture and climate. Second, we define and explain these concepts as well as the central characteristics. Third, we propose an integrative conceptual framework of pro-environmental organizational culture and climate based on a review of the theoretical literature and empirical evidence. Fourth, we describe how pro-environmental culture and climate can emerge (i.e., their antecedents) and how they may consequently influence prescribed and voluntary employee behavior, as well as broader organizational outcomes. Finally, we conclude by proposing areas for future research on pro-environmental organizational culture and climate, as well as recommendations for organizational practice.

Environmental Sustainability and Pro-Environmental Employee Behavior

There is now growing sentiment that sustainability makes good business sense from the perspective of well-established resource-, industry-, and stakeholder-centric theories (Fairfield et al., 2011). Furthermore, there is empirical evidence (e.g., see Kane, 2011) that being "green" is associated with lower operating costs, increased profit margins, and enhanced competitive advantage; occasioned in part to the favorable reputation developed through sustainable operation. For instance, recent research by Griffin, Lont, and Sun (2011) and Lourenco, Branco, and Curto (2012) highlights the financial benefits of being environmentally sustainable as reflected in share price growth and corporate economic performance. Thus, for many businesses, creating organizational conditions that support environmental sustainability are now seen to be a necessary requirement for pursuing sustainable development and for achieving long-term success (Accenture, 2013; Linnenluecke & Griffiths, 2010). Furthermore, these organizational conditions for sustainability should also promote pro-environmental behaviors among employees (Norton, Zacher, & Ashkanasy, 2012; Ramus & Steger, 2000).

An acknowledgment that organizational environmental sustainability hinges upon individual behavior is emerging from the literature (Bartlett, 2011; Paillé & Boiral, 2013). At this point, it is important to differentiate the terms *pro-environmental* and *environmental sustainability*. *Pro-environmental* refers to an attitude or behavior that is positively oriented toward the natural environment. *Environmental sustainability* in the organizational context, on the other hand, incorporates environmental considerations with business needs (e.g., productivity, profitability) in such a way as to reduce harm and promote benefits for the environment. Thus, pro-environmental attitudes and behaviors are necessary but not sufficient for environmental sustainability. Mesmer-Magnus, Viswesvaran, and Wiernik (2012) capture the relationship between the two concepts succinctly by defining pro-environmental behavior as individual actions that contribute to environmental sustainability. Similarly, Ones and Dilchert (2012) imply that environmental sustainability is an organization-level pursuit, facilitated in part through individual-level pro-environmental behavior.

In response to institutional pressures, organizations are increasingly introducing structural mechanisms (such as policies) to encourage pro-environmental employee behavior. However, the efficacy of such policies to engage employees across all levels of an organization is not clear. Ones, Dilchert, Biga, and Gibby (2010) suggest that pro-environmental behavior is more prevalent among senior organizational members such as executives and managers. Notwithstanding, the capacity for organizational initiatives to engage employees at lower levels appears to be weak. Ones and Dilchert (2012) indicate that organizations are increasingly requiring certain pro-environmental behavior from employees. In such circumstances, in which behavior is prescribed, the influence of an individual's pro-environmental attitude is reduced. Thus, it becomes necessary to consider factors above the individual-level of analysis, such as organizational culture and climate. We propose that creating a pro-environmental organizational context (i.e., culture and climate) may increase the reach of initiatives aimed at encouraging pro-environmental behavior throughout the organization, as well as being a necessary condition for environmental sustainability.

Scholars have identified both culture and climate as important influences on organizational and group outcomes as well as individual behavior both generally (e.g., see Hartnell, Ou, & Kinicki, 2011; Schneider et al., 2013) and with regard to environmental sustainability (Norton, Zacher, & Ashkanasy, 2014; Russell & McIntosh, 2011). For example, Walls and Hoffman (2012) demonstrated how board members influence an organization's pro-environmental culture by framing, interpreting, attending to, and making sense of issues in light of environmental sustainability. Linnenluecke and colleagues (Linnenluecke, Russell, & Griffiths, 2009; Linnenluecke & Griffiths, 2010) report in particular that the underlying ideological underpinnings of organizational culture shape the meaning environmental sustainability has for companies. Finally, researchers working in educational (Schelly, Cross, Franzen, Hall, & Reeve, 2010) and health settings (Tudor, Barr, & Gilg, 2007) have demonstrated that the existence and perceptions of pro-environmental organizational cultures lead to various individual- and organization-level environmental outcomes.

Throughout the chapter we refer to the example of the Sierra Nevada Brewing Company (Sierra Nevada; Casler, Gundlach, Persons, & Zivnuska,

2010; Sierra Nevada Brewing Company, 2012); this is an organization that we see to hold values and assumptions consistent with those of environmental sustainability. Founded in California in 1980 with the intention of operating in an environmentally sustainable manner, Sierra Nevada is now the sixth largest brewery in the United States (Casler et al., 2010), and is expanding its operation with a new facility in North Carolina (Sierra Nevada Brewing Company, 2012). Sierra Nevada employs approximately 400 workers, and currently produces approximately 900,000 barrels of beer per year. As a brewery, it relies on natural capital in order to provide its core product. Sierra Nevada supports such resources by using on-site compost to fertilize its hop and barley fields, operating a wastewater treatment facility to minimize its demand on local water reserves and encouraging suppliers to farm sustainably. Sierra Nevada also encourages pro-environmental employee behavior, for instance, by subsidizing employees who bike or bus to work. Finally, Sierra Nevada invests in the development of new technologies such as solar arrays, hydrogen fuel cells, biogas, and is committed to updating existing equipment when more energy efficient alternatives are available (Sierra Nevada Brewing Company, 2012).

Organizational Culture

Schein (2010), whose work has been instrumental in defining the nature of organizational culture, identifies growing concern on behalf of organizations regarding environmental sustainability as a key driver of research into culture. As environmental issues become more salient to business, the need to integrate sustainability into an organization's core mission is emerging as a necessary consideration. For many companies, this will require a potentially significant change to the existing culture. Moreover, and as Linnenluecke and Griffiths (2010) point out, culture is also an important consideration for practitioners: Without a cultural framework to provide meaning, interventions may only be short lived. Therefore, the manner in which organizations express their values toward environmental sustainability in cultural terms becomes vital in facilitating a successful and lasting transition.

Definition and Description

Organizational culture rose to prominence in the 1980s, owing in part to an attempt to explain performance disparity between US and Japanese companies (Ostroff, Kinicki, & Muhammad, 2013; Schein, 1990). In the following years, the assumption that culture is an important determinant of organizational, group, and individual behavior (Hartnell et al., 2011) drove a surge in attention. The concept is rooted in social anthropology and over time has become a feature of several disciplines, including organizational psychology and organizational behavior (Ashkanasy, Wilderom, & Peterson, 2000). The consequence of having such multidisciplinary appeal is a plethora of alternative definitions. There are, however, several common features of culture that Schein (2010, p. 18) includes in his comprehensive definition that scholars generally accept: A pattern of shared basic assumptions learned by a group as it solved its problems of external adaptation and internal integration, which has worked well enough to be considered valid and, therefore, to be taught to new members as the correct way to perceive, think, and feel in relation to those problems.

Theories of Organizational Culture

Hatch (1993) offers an extension to Schein's (1990) popular conceptualization of culture to address limitations surrounding the processes that link the key elements of culture proposed by Schein. As illustrated in Figure 14.1, this model includes two paths through which culture is formed, one prospective-proactive (clockwise), the other retrospective-retroactive (counter-clockwise). Hatch (2011) emphasizes that these two paths should be considered holistically, rather than focusing on the bidirectional effects of the four processes. Next we provide a brief description of the key elements and dynamic paths in Hatch's model.

Elements

Both Hatch (1993) and Schein (1990) recognize espoused beliefs and values as the foundations of culture. Thus, in much the same way as organizational

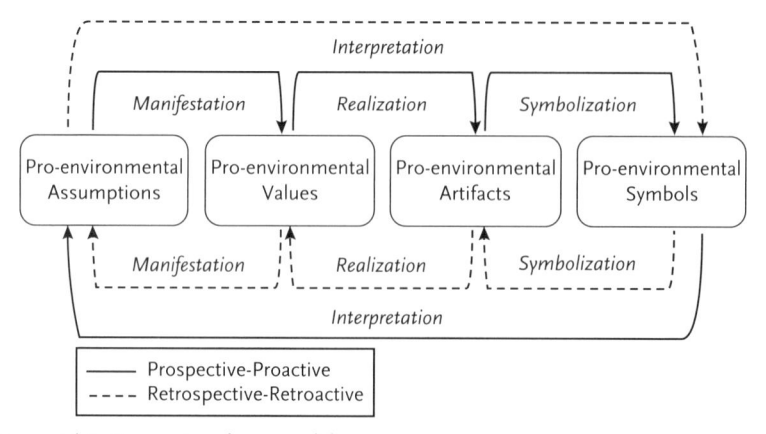

FIGURE 14.1 Dynamic culture model.

efforts for sustainability stem from individual actions (Ones & Dilchert, 2012), the dominant beliefs and values of an organization originate from individuals. Schein proposes further that crises offer opportunities for the beliefs and values of influential individuals (i.e., leaders) to be witnessed by a large audience; when crises arise, organizational members look to leaders to provide guidance. Members validate leaders' internalized values and beliefs empirically by evaluating their effect on performance, or socially through their shared experiences. This validation can transform beliefs and values over time into generalized assumptions (Schein, 2010).

Artifacts

Artifacts are the tangible manifestations of beliefs and values, such as objects, language, narratives, practices (Trice & Beyer, 1984), and organizational climate (Schein, 1990). Specifically, artifacts are representations of beliefs and values that possess literal meaning only (i.e., they are what they are), and may be considered static. Hatch (1993) distinguishes between artifacts and symbols on the basis of how organizational members use them, and the presence of literal and surplus meaning. Some artifacts become symbols when the members use them to convey additional or surplus meaning (Hatch, 2004), and thus may be considered dynamic (i.e., they are what they are *and more*). Objectively, artifacts and symbols appear the same (Hatch, 1993). Only members know the additional meaning inherent in symbols, which may be why Schein (2010) cautions against making inferences based on these surface-level manifestations of organizational culture. For non-members, it is difficult to ascribe meaning without the confounding influence of their own personal values and non-cultural elements.

Underlying Assumptions of an Organization

The deepest level of culture reveals the underlying assumptions of an organization. These may be considered the crystallized beliefs and values that, over time, have come to be taken for granted, and thus unconscious to the extent that any alternative is disregarded. Assumptions form the essence of culture and typically exist outside of consciousness (Schein, 2010). Members experience assumptions via the expectations to which they give rise (Hatch, 1993).

Dynamic Processes

Hatch (1993) also includes in her model the prospective-proactive (clockwise) and retrospective-retroactive (counter-clockwise) processes that describe the dynamics through which organizational members create and maintain a culture. These prospective-proactive processes then contribute to the formation of cultural material, such as values, artifacts, and symbols. Basic assumptions manifest in espoused values, which members realize into tangible artifacts. Some artifacts are used to supply additional meaning and become symbols, which members can then use to interpret assumptions. The retrospective-retroactive process evaluates the existing organizational culture. Members use their knowledge of assumptions to interpret the surplus meaning attributed to symbols, before evaluating these symbols relative to artifacts that possess only literal meaning. Members then appraise artifacts to verify the espoused values, which are evaluated to challenge or support fundamental assumptions.

Dimensionality of Culture

In addition to proposing a conceptualization of culture, including its elements and processes, it is also necessary to gain insights into how many cultures might exist within an organization. In this respect, Martin (2002) posits a collection of alternative perspectives. The first of these, an *integrationist* perspective, characterizes much of the early culture research, and assumes that within an organization there is but one *gestalt* culture, which all members of an organization share. Within this view, for something to be a feature of the culture, there must be consensus among members. Thus, anything about which opinions vary is not a feature of the culture. This perspective, though still dominant, has lost some credibility within the literature (Alvesson, 2011). In contrast, the *fragmented* perspective is based in the idea that it is unlikely that people across functional areas and organizational levels share similar experiences and meaning. As such, this perspective focuses on inconsistency, paradox, and contradiction.

As noted by Ostroff et al. (2013), scholars continue to debate whether disagreement within an organization indicates that a culture exists, that a fragmented culture exists, or that no culture exists. Sitting in between these two extremes is the *differentiation* perspective, which is based in the idea that numerous subcultures exist within organizations. In this case, differences at the group level result in different experiences, interpretations, and attributions of meaning (Linnenluecke & Griffiths, 2010; Martin, 2002). Zacher and Gielnik (2014) provide an example of how age subcultures emerge in an organizational context as a product of different assumptions and beliefs about younger and older workers. The most appropriate perspective to apply in the current context is the differentiation perspective, which allows for different subcultures, such as pro-environmental organizational cultures.

Culture and Environment

The concept of organizational culture also can be conceptualized with respect to an organization's internal and external environments. Dauber, Fink, and Yolles (2012) proposed a configuration model of culture that expands Hatch's (1993) conceptualization to include organizational strategy, structure, and operations as the internal environment (which could be argued are manifestations of the culture), task and legitimacy environments as components of the external environment, and dynamic relationships among the various elements. In proposing this model, the authors seek to emphasize the need to consider the organizational components that cultural assumptions and values shape, as well as the role external elements have toward influencing that culture. The concept of organizational culture can thus be conceptualized with respect to an organization's internal and external environments. For example, drawing from institutional theory (e.g., Scott, 2008), the pressures from regulatory, normative, and cultural-cognitive aspects of the broader environment shape an organization's response to strategic issues.

In summary, organizational culture may be considered a collection of elements and processes that create and reveal the unconscious or latent assumptions of an organization that guide its activities. Culture has a broad influence throughout organizations via the strategy, structure, and operations that enable a company to exist respective of the external environment. The differentiation perspective on the other hand is predicated on a notion that the way cultures manifest, even within a single company, is not necessarily uniform. In the next section we draw upon the competing values framework to investigate different forms pro-environmental organizational cultures might take in organizations.

Pro-Environmental Organizational Culture

Schein's (1990) definition of culture can easily be adapted to fit with environmental sustainability. The effect of human activity, and in particular economic activity (Wackernagel et al., 2002), on the natural environment clearly represents an external problem requiring organizational adaptation. The scope and chronic nature of this problem is such that it necessitates some form of response from most, if not all, organizations. The lessons learned from successful responses inform future actions and organizations then pass these lessons on to new members (Schein, 1990). Thus, we define a pro-environmental organizational culture as: *A pattern of shared basic assumptions learned by a group as it adapts to the challenges posed by human activity's impact on the natural environment in a way that permits day-to-day functioning, which has worked well enough to be considered valid and, therefore, to be taught to new members as the correct way to perceive, think, and feel in relation to environmental sustainability.*

Sierra Nevada is an excellent example of an organization with a strong pro-environmental culture (Casler et al., 2010). The brewery's continued growth and competitors' emulation of their sustainable practices validate the efficacy of their environmental beliefs and values. For example, like Sierra Nevada, MillerCoors, the second largest brewery in the United States, has formal structures in place that empower employees from across the business to shape the organization's approach to sustainability (MillerCoors, 2012). At the heart of Sierra Nevada's pro-environmental culture is the assumption that a clean environment produces the best beer (Casler et al., 2010). This assumption has manifested in the beliefs that to produce quality products the natural environment has to be maintained, and that the best way to maintain the environment is to operate in a sustainable way. These beliefs are deeply held to the extent that they are realized into cultural artifacts, such as policies and practices, across all aspects of the business: from recruitment to production, and from human resources to strategy (Casler et al., 2010). Sierra Nevada's values become shared employee values through recognition programs that reward and support individual pro-environmental behavior, and by investing in employee-focused initiatives such as garden plots (Casler et al., 2010).

In conclusion, shared experiences regarding the meaning of sustainability, which shape individual pro-environmental attitudes and behaviors through (shared) assumptions and expectations, create pro-environmental organizational cultures, such as the culture at Sierra Nevada. Consistent with Hatch's (1993) dynamic culture model, these subcultures may have different histories and be maintained in different ways. Thus, they may take different forms and have different underlying drivers, dependent upon the organizational context within which they emerge. Therefore, it is imperative to understand how organizations can vary in their orientation toward sustainability, and the influence this orientation has on the particular shades of green a pro-environmental culture may take. We address this in the next section.

The Right Culture for the Right Context: Different Shades of Green

To develop this idea, we refer to the competing values framework (CVF; Quinn & Rohrbaugh, 1983). This framework is appropriate because it provides a typology for culture that focuses on an organization's orientation on two key dimensions: internal versus external focus, and flexible versus

	Flexibility		
Human relations model		**Open-systems model**	
Theory	Participation fosters commitment.	Theory	Innovation fosters new resources
Goal	Cohesion and morale.	Goal	Growth and resource acquisition.
Sustainability focus	A way to benefit human capital.	Sustainability focus	A catalyst for innovation and competitive advantage.
Internal			External
Internal process model		**Rational goal model**	
Theory	Control fosters efficiency.	Theory	Competition fosters productivity.
Goal	Stability and control.	Goal	Efficiency and productivity.
Sustainability focus	A way to reduce costs and maximize profits.	Sustainability focus	A way to minimize the impact of poor environmental quality on organizational activities.
	Stability		

FIGURE 14.2 Competing values framework.

stable control (Figure 14.2). Companies vary on the first dimension depending on their focus on internal dynamics or the external environment. The second dimension describes the manner in which organizations exert control over their workforces. Stable organizations have a tendency to rely on formal mechanisms such as policies to create stability in the workplace. Conversely, flexible organizations use less rigid social mechanisms, such as norms to encourage desired outcomes.

Within this framework, we propose that there may be intra-organizational variation on these dimensions, based on functional, physical, and hierarchical separation of different groups. For example, the board of directors may have an external focus prioritizing stability in order to minimize shareholder risk, while the HR division is likely to have a more internal focus prioritizing flexibility to enhance employee well-being. Similar to the differentiation perspective of culture, which proposes that different cultures exist for different topic areas (e.g., pro-environmental, ethics, safety, age), this perspective suggests that different subcultures may manifest in different groups. This view is similar to Schein's (1996) proposition of the existence of executive, engineer, and operator cultures, which vary as a function of group focus.

Linnenluecke and Griffiths (2010) apply the CVF to discuss organizational culture in the context of environmental sustainability. In their analysis, the authors make several propositions regarding how each cultural orientation (according to the CVF) might influence an organization's approach to environmental sustainability. They suggest in particular that sustainability is not a one-size-fits-all concept, and thus pro-environmental organizational cultures may come in many different shades of green. Linnenluecke and Griffiths propose further that flexible organizations with an internal focus (i.e., a human relations model) should view sustainability in the context of human capital, and therefore should demonstrate a preference for interventions aimed at developing employee capacity and knowledge with outcomes for employee welfare.

Organizations with the same flexible approach, albeit with a more external focus (i.e., an open-systems model), should approach sustainability with a focus on generating competitive advantage (Linnenluecke & Griffiths, 2010). As with the human relations model, autonomy and discretionary behavior are important (Trist, 1981). On the other hand, in an open systems model, organizations are more sensitive to the external environment, and seek to capitalize on such flexibility by encouraging innovation and creating competitive advantage from a sustainability focus (Linnenluecke & Griffiths, 2010).

In contrast to flexible organizations, those that demonstrate a preference for stability and control rely on formalized structures that constrain the choices and actions through which employees can participate. In such organizations, Linnenluecke and Griffiths (2010) proffer that sustainability is seen in terms of efficiency. For such organizations that have an internal focus (i.e., an internal process model), the motivation to engage with sustainability is likely to peak when initiatives contribute directly to the financial bottom line. These organizations view sustainability as a way to maximize profits by increasing operational efficiency.

Finally, there exist companies that demonstrate a preference for stability, but with an external focus (i.e., a rational goal model). Linnenluecke and Griffiths (2010) suggest that organizations aligned with this model view sustainability as an imperative for ensuring long-term viability. These organizations recognize the importance of the broader environment within which they operate, and subsequently prepare for changes in environmental demands. Linnenluecke and Griffiths imply that the key distinction between these organizations and those aligned with the internal process model is an understanding of the environmental implications of creating efficiencies, and a more proactive approach, including the willingness to invest capital.

In summary, we have described in this section the elements and processes that constitute organizational culture. Furthermore, we used the example from Sierra Nevada to illustrate what a pro-environmental culture can look like in the real world. Finally, we used the CVF as a framework to describe how organizational preferences might influence the particular shade of green a pro-environmental culture takes. In the next section, we define and describe the related construct of organizational climate, and how this concept also relates to organizational environmental sustainability.

Organizational Climate

In contrast to culture, organizational climate represents a more objective and, arguably, a more practitioner-friendly approach to addressing the social context within the workplace (Ashkanasy et al., 2000). Climate focuses on the surface-level manifestations of the social climate, which makes it possible to quantify and compare these across organizations and, thus, more attractive to practitioners (Schein, 2010). From an organizational change perspective, climate is less stable than culture (Ashkanasy & Nicolson, 2003), and thus a more practical target for interventions. Despite existing in the shadow of its sister construct, organizational culture, for many years, there has been resurgent interest toward research on employee perceptions of the organization over the past two decades (Schneider, Ehrhart, & Macey, 2011). In the following section, we outline the climate construct in three stages. First, we define the concept and present an explanation for how individual and shared employee perceptions of their workplace influence individual behavior. Second, we review the impact of strategic climates on specific behaviors. Finally, we introduce the novel concept of pro-environmental organizational climate.

Definition of Organizational Climate

Whereas organizational culture reflects the intangible elements of the social context such as assumptions, beliefs, and values, organizational climate relates to employees' evaluations of tangible work environment attributes (James et al., 2008). Accordingly, Schein (1990) considers climate an artifact of culture. Theoretically, the concept is grounded in Lewin's (1951) field theory, which purports behavior as the product of an individual's experience of the work environment. A criticism of Lewin's theory is that it is only concerned with the influence of the environment on behavior, and not the potential contribution that an individual's behavior makes to the environment. This is in contrast to the theoretical underpinnings of culture, which emphasize the role individuals have in constructing their work environment.

There is considerably less conjecture regarding the definition of organizational climate compared with its multidisciplinary sister construct culture. Schneider and Reichers (1983) define climate as employees' perceptions of formal policies, the procedures that translate policies into tacit guidelines, and the practices that act upon them. Although Schein (1990) views these elements (i.e., policies, procedures, and practices) as artifacts, the literature also considers them to be the foundations for climate perceptions, thus providing the linking mechanism between the two constructs (Ostroff et al., 2013). We therefore conceptualize climate in terms of perceptions of cultural artifacts.

In order to resolve conjecture regarding the appropriate level of analysis to research climate, James (1982) proposes a compositional model of climate, which is widely accepted in the literature (e.g., see James et al., 2008; Ostroff et al., 2013; Schneider et al., 2011). In this sense, because individual perceptions provide the basis for climate, the construct's basal composition should be conceptualized to lie at the individual employee level. James and colleagues refer to perceptions at the individual level as "psychological climate." When a team or organization has shared perceptions (i.e., sufficient agreement exists among individuals), they can be aggregated to higher levels and then constitute a team or organizational climate. Thus, climate can be conceptualized at the level of the individual employee (psychological climate) and at broader organizational levels. James and colleagues consider the extent to which employees' psychological climate perceptions vary within teams or an organization a measure of a climate's strength, which Schneider et al. (2013) show to be an important moderator of climate outcomes. It is therefore critical that organizations striving to create a pro-environmental organizational climate communicate the company's attitude toward sustainability in such a way as to avoid ambiguity and encourage a common interpretation (James et al., 2008).

Litwin and Stringer's (1968) influential global climate model caused early research to operate for some years under the assumption that climate was a molar or unitary construct. Schneider (1975, 2000) criticizes this literature, however, for lacking strong theoretical foundations and for conceptualizing climate as a construct too generic to be useful. These criticisms may have been responsible for the decline in interest paid to climate (Kuenzi & Schminke, 2009). Nonetheless, the rise of multi-level organizational research over recent decades has seen a resurgence of studies on the influence of climate on employee behavior. A feature of this second wave of climate research is the abandonment of climate as a molar construct, and a focus instead on strategic climates. This shift in focus aims to enhance the validity of climate as a construct by conceptualizing it as a mediator in the relationships between organizational-level constructs (e.g., leadership) and specific organizational and employee outcomes (Ashkanasy et al., 2011; Kuenzi & Schminke, 2009).

Strategic Climates

Strategic climates focus on a specific facet of organizational life, and represent a molecular alternative to the molar conceptualization of climate that was prevalent in early research (Ashkanasy, 2007). Kuenzi and Schminke (2009) credit this strategic climate perspective for an increased understanding of individual and organizational outcomes of the broader social context. One of the earliest and, to date, most developed topics in this field is safety climate, which has been a feature of climate research for more than three decades (e.g., Zohar, 2000). Safety climate has implications at the individual and organizational levels, predicting accident and injury rates (Zohar, 2000), as well as safety motivation and participation (Neal & Griffin, 2006).

Pro-Environmental Organizational Climate

Recently, we suggested that a strategic climate aimed at environmental sustainability might be just as useful with regard to pro-environmental employee behaviors (Norton et al., 2012, 2014), and would add to the collection of organizational climates such as those for justice and customer service (Ashkanasy, 2007; Ashkanasy et al., 2011). We define pro-environmental organizational climate as employees' shared perceptions of pro-environmental policies, procedures, and practices that an organization rewards and supports (Norton et al., 2014). Given the repeated demonstration of efficacy that strategic climates present within the literature, it seems reasonable that such a pro-environmental organizational climate would offer a fruitful concept to investigate as an organizational-level predictor of employees' pro-environmental attitudes, engagement with the topic of environmental sustainability, and participation in associated workplace behaviors. Preliminary research demonstrates that pro-environmental climate at the individual (i.e., psychological) level acts as mediator between the perception of organizational policies for sustainability and pro-environmental behavior (Norton et al., 2014).

Organizational Climate and Pro-Environmental Employee Behavior

One of the strengths of research on strategic climates is the focus on positive behavioral outcomes such as citizenship behavior and employee performance (Kuenzi & Schminke, 2009). The perceptions implicated in climate reflect individual value-based schemas used to interpret workplace information (James et al., 2008). Thus, climate provides a perceptual lens through which employees decide what actions are appropriate in the work context. We have proposed that social norms may be the mechanism through which organizational policies for environmental sustainability influence pro-environmental employee behavior (Norton et al., 2014).

Specifically, we suggest that employee perceptions of the tangible aspects of their organization, including perceptions of organizational expectations but also of the typical behavior of their co-workers, reflect individual interpretations of social norms. Using the theory of normative conduct (Cialdini, Reno, & Kallgren 1990), we draw a parallel between the perceptions of organizational expectations and typical behaviors of co-workers, with the social psychological concepts of injunctive and descriptive norms (see also Norton et al., 2014). Injunctive norms refer to what is expected by and approved of by an organization, which we argue are reflected in the policies, procedures, and practices organizations adopt, reward, and support (Cialdini et al., 1990; Lo, Peters, & Kok, 2012). Descriptive norms in effect reflect what is typically done within that organization, and thus constitute the behavior of individuals within the organization (Cialdini et al., 1990; Goldstein, Cialdini, & Griskevicius, 2008).

These two distinct social norms motivate people by making salient the social outcomes of engaging (or not engaging) in distinct behaviors (Smith et al., 2012). First, using this approach, organizations that wish to encourage their employees to engage in pro-environmental behaviors in the workplace should foster injunctive and descriptive norms around environmental sustainability. Thus, in Norton et al. (2014), we found that the employees' perceptions of their organization's injunctive norms fully mediated the relationship between employees' perceptions of a policy for sustainability and prescribed task-related pro-environmental behavior. We found further no mediating effect of perceptions of injunctive norms regarding voluntary pro-environmental behavior. Second, employees' perceptions of the descriptive norms among co-workers in their organization fully mediated the relationship between perceptions of a policy for sustainability and voluntary pro-environmental behavior, but had no effect on required pro-environmental behavior.

Similarly, in a series of studies, Goldstein and colleagues (2008) demonstrate that using messages that contain social norms is more effective in terms of encouraging pro-environmental behavior than non-normative messages. In one study, these researchers expose hotel guests to either a standard message about a towel-reuse program focusing on the importance of protecting the environment, or a normative message demonstrating the extent to which other guests participated in the program. The effect of this manipulation was a 44% increase in participation among guests in the social norms condition compared with guests in the control condition. Thus, this empirical evidence appears to tell us that perceptions regarding environmental sustainability are important for engagement in pro-environmental behaviors, which is in line with research on organizational climate and associated behaviors in other areas, such as safety (e.g., Zohar, 2000).

An Integrated Model of Organizational Culture and Climate

As an outcome of the foregoing discussions, we propose an integrated conceptual model of organizational culture and climate (Figure 14.3). Our model marries Hatch's dynamic culture model (1993), itself an extension of Schein's (1990) influential model, with the conceptualization of climate grounded in Lewinian field theory (Schneider & Reichers, 1983). In doing so, we emphasize the dynamic processes that create and maintain a culture, and how culture leads to behavior. We next explain our model with regard to the integration of culture and climate in the central column.

In outlining our model, we refer readers to our earlier description of Hatch's (1993) dynamic culture model as an explanation of the processes that create and maintain a culture. The model differs from Hatch's in that we use climate to explain how the culture influences behavior, which we in turn have isolated from other artifacts. Schein (1991) asserted that local circumstances and immediate events influence behavior. We propose in particular that climate represents the nexus at which culture, local circumstances, and immediate events converge to influence behavior. Indeed, a large body of research on the strong relationship between climate and behavior (e.g., see Schneider et al., 2013) would seem to support this notion. Furthermore, we argue for a normative mechanism through which climate informs behavior. Culture influences behavior through employee perceptions of artifacts (i.e., climate), which translate organizational beliefs and values into behavioral norms.

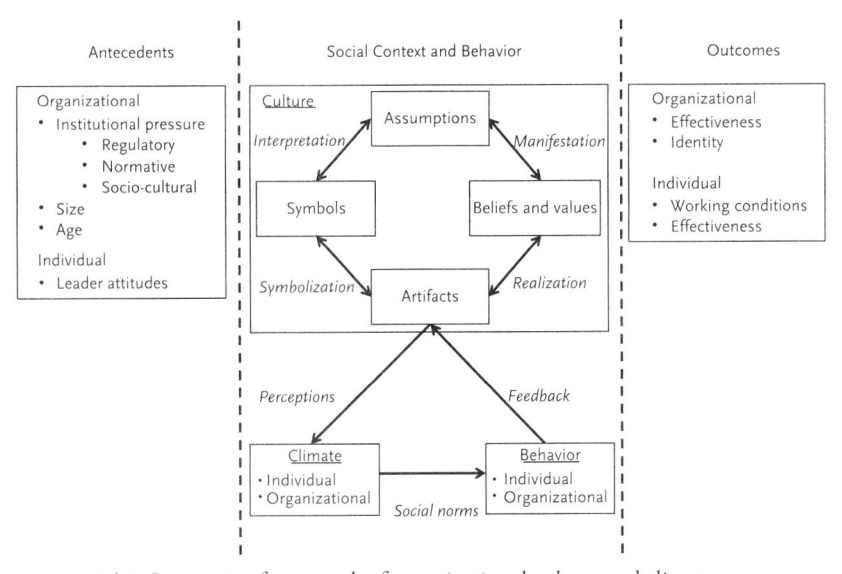

FIGURE 14.3 Integrative framework of organizational culture and climate.

Our model implies that an organization's social context is not an end-state, but a dynamic process through which an organization responds to external pressures. Thus, one outcome may be organizational effectiveness, although Hartnell and colleagues (2011) suggest that this relationship is complex. Moreover, the social context creates an identity for those that exist within it, which can be observed by external stakeholders (Schneider & Reichers, 1983). This identity may have subsequent implications for public image and investor interest. For individuals, the social context influences working conditions within the organization, which can influence individual effectiveness (Ostroff et al., 2013).

Pro-Environmental Culture and Climate

We now discuss our integrated model within the context of environmental sustainability. In the context of our model, we suggest that antecedents such as regulatory, normative, and sociocultural institutional pressure to engage with sustainability shape the pro-environmental values and attitudes held by those in positions of power within the organization (through a process of manifestation). To illustrate this (and returning to our example), we note that institutional pressures have resulted in other breweries beginning to emulate the sustainable production methods championed at Sierra Nevada. For example, strict environmental regulations for farming and brewing, consumer preferences (Tobler, Vischers, & Siegrist, 2012), and adoption of pro-environmental practices by major brewing conglomerates (e.g., MillerCoors, 2012), represent regulatory, cultural-cognitive, and normative pressures within the brewing industry.

Institutional pressures can influence the attitudes of those in charge of creating strategy within organizations, introducing policy, and influencing employee behavior (cf. Robertson & Barling, 2013). Thus the environmental attitudes of those in senior positions constitute an important antecedent for pro-environmental climate and culture (Linnenluecke et al., 2009; Norton et al., 2012). For example, Walls and Hoffman (2012) note that the influence of board members is a significant contributor to positive deviance from institutional norms regarding environmental sustainability, leading organizations to invest in sustainability above and beyond what is expected. In the case of Sierra Nevada, founder Ken Grossman has strong pre-existing environmental values, which he has imparted on the brewery for 30 years (Casler et al., 2010).

These beliefs guide activity within the company through a process of realization, whereby the firm produces artifacts such as formal pro-environmental policies and ways of work that foster employee engagement and commitment to organizational goals. Casler and colleagues describe the realization process at Sierra Nevada: "because sustainability is a natural element of its culture, a sustainable mindset directly feeds into its human resource policies and practices" (2010, p. 45). Examples of artifacts from Sierra Nevada include policies regarding waste management, using local ingredients, and energy efficiency (Sierra Nevada Brewing Company, 2012).

Employee perceptions of these and other cultural artifacts thus constitute pro-environmental climate. Climates can be encouraged through consistent communication of organizational values. Sierra Nevada encourages a pro-environmental climate through numerous initiatives that engage employees in environmental sustainability. Examples include environmental initiative recognition programs, subsidies for using public or alternative transport, and training programs that teach sustainable living (Casler et al., 2010). Such practices unambiguously demonstrate the company's environmental stance, which encourages shared employee perceptions.

By consistently communicating organizational values in such a way as to encourage a strong climate, organizations also create expectations regarding the types of behavior that it approves of, which constitute behavioral norms. Thus, pro-environmental climates may then translate into pro-environmental employee behavior (Norton et al., 2014). These activities at the individual and team level, in turn, feed back into the culture loop as behavioral artifacts. Employee-led innovations, participation in programs that benefit the natural environment, and the use of reusable shopping bags and coffee cups demonstrate how Sierra Nevada fosters a pro-environmental climate (Sierra Nevada Brewing Company, 2012).

In addition to this, certain pro-environmental artifacts will be granted additional meaning through a process of symbolization. For example, through symbolization, the literal meaning of using a reusable coffee cup as a convenient way to collect coffee may be complemented with the additional meaning that using the cup is a way to help the environment. Thus, the cup and its use become symbols for the organization's beliefs about environmental sustainability. The social context and behavior column in Figure 14.3 represents this process. Sierra Nevada-branded cycling apparel may be considered a symbol of the organization's pro-environmental culture as it represents minimal environmental impact and healthy living. Product labels may also constitute symbols, through their subtle use of environmental imagery, wherein only those with an appreciation of the brewery's environmental values perceive the surplus meaning.

Although researchers have only just begun to investigate within this field, the studies that have been done so appear to support the existence of specific favorable organizational outcomes of pro-environmental organizational culture and climate. For example, Kane (2011) shows that organizations that proactively engage with environmental sustainability experience more flexibility to operate, profit, grow, and enjoy an enhanced reputation as "smart" companies.

Using Sierra Nevada as a specific example of a company with a strong pro-environmental organizational culture and climate, we find that this firm's approach to sustainability has produced tangible benefits. For example, by embracing alternative fuel sources, redesigning product packaging, and becoming more water efficient, Sierra Nevada has found significant cost savings specific to the brewery's core business. Additionally, Sierra Nevada has also generated new revenue streams by selling packaging material to recycling companies, which generated $800,000 in 2008 (Casler et al., 2010). These and other initiatives have safeguarded Sierra Nevada against changes in the natural and economic environment, thus turning an external pressure into a strategic advantage, which has contributed to the brewery's exponential growth in a resource-dependent industry.

Recommendations for Research

Future research on pro-environmental organizational culture and climate should benefit from an integration of their respective theoretical literatures (cf. Ostroff et al., 2013; Schneider et al., 2013). We propose an integrative model applied to sustainability, and encourage organizational researchers interested in pro-environmental issues in the workplace to explore its validity. The next steps include testing the hypothesized links in the model, with a particular focus on determining the most important antecedents of pro-environmental culture and climate, the manifestation of culture and climate, and to identify important attitudinal and behavioral outcomes. In the following paragraphs, we identify three imperatives for research in this field.

Imperative 1: Identify Antecedents to Pro-Environmental Culture and Climate

The first imperative we identify is for researchers to establish a comprehensive list of antecedents to pro-environmental culture and climate (even beyond those we have nominated in this chapter). We further suggest that industries might be another important antecedent (Starik & Rands, 1995). Within this chapter we have offered examples from the brewing industry, which appears to be welcoming environmental sustainability. This may not be the case in other industries, however, in which environmental issues are not as salient.

Based on the literature we discussed earlier in this chapter, it is possible that a set of interrelated factors, namely industry, organizational size, and visibility, may interact to influence the extent to which an organization is susceptible to institutional pressures regarding environmental sustainability, and subsequently the form of its response. Finally, environmental attitudes at the employee level may moderate the extent to which employees interpret organizational policies as reflecting environmental values at the organizational level, and subsequently the emergence of pro-environmental climates.

Imperative 2: Investigate Organizational Responses to Institutional Pressures

The second imperative is consistent with the differentiated view of culture (Martin, 2002) and the interactive perspective of institutional theory (Gauthier, 2013). Specifically, we recommend that researchers begin to validate the theoretical position offered in this chapter by investigating if pro-environmental organizational cultures manifest differently according to an organization's response to institutional pressures, function, size, focus, and preference for flexibility or stability. We assert in this respect that practitioners with prolonged exposure to an organization have the best opportunity to examine culture, and should endeavor to uncover the hidden assumptions that are operating. For external practitioners hoping to investigate an organization's pro-environmental culture, we advocate the approach outlined by Schein (2003) whereby practitioners expose cross-functional groups to a variety of scenarios and ask them to generate responses to elicit the assumptions that underlie organizational activities.

Imperative 3: Investigate Pro-Environmental Culture/Climate Influences on Behavior

Our third imperative is for researchers to investigate the influence of pro-environmental culture and climate on a range of environmental behaviors, such as task-related, proactive, citizenship, and harmful behaviors (Bissing-Olson, Iyer, Fielding, & Zacher, 2013; Norton et al., 2014; Paillé & Boiral, 2013). It is apparent that, within this literature, there is a bias toward researching voluntary pro-environmental behavior. Indeed, much of the research typically considers pro-environmental behaviors as a special form of OCB. Estimates suggest however that organizations prescribe as much as one-third of all pro-environmental behaviors that occurs in the workplace (Ones & Dilchert, 2012). Thus, not all workplace pro-environmental behaviors are at the complete discretion of the employee, which opens up several possibilities for research.

Recommendations for Practice

Practically, organizations could generate pro-environmental organizational climates by complementing existing sustainability policies with concrete procedures and practices, and then communicating these in a way that facilitates a common perception among employees that the company authentically values environmental sustainability. Furthermore, we recommend that practitioners use the organizational culture frameworks reviewed in this chapter to identify the best way of understanding and framing the concept of environmental sustainability in organizations, and to enhance the likelihood of success for interventions.

With regard to culture, at a bare minimum, practitioners should be aware of the cultural components and the role employee perceptions (i.e., climate) play in translating organizational values into pro-environmental behavior. Beyond this, practitioners should also seek to facilitate the processes that link the various cultural elements to encourage the development of a pro-environmental culture. The next level of sophistication involves an appreciation of how an organization might view environmental sustainability in light of values regarding focus and control. This understanding should inform, at least to some extent, the types of initiatives to which an organization might respond.

For example, flexible organizations with cultures that align with the human relations model should view sustainability in reference to human capital, and demonstrate a preference for interventions that create direct benefits for staff by developing employee capacity and knowledge. Alternatively, organizations that align with the open-systems model may approach sustainability with a focus on generating competitive advantage. Such organizations may be particularly well suited to initiatives that facilitate new methods of work that maximize resource efficiency.

Stable organizations that align with the internal process model see sustainability in terms of efficiency (Linnenluecke & Griffiths, 2010). For such organizations, the motivation to engage with sustainability is likely to peak when initiatives contribute directly to the financial bottom line. Thus, the examples provided in the foregoing paragraphs would be less likely to succeed in an environment that emphasizes economic performance. Instead, these organizations may be more amenable to creating new revenue streams from by-products, where environmental and economic benefits exist alongside each other. Moreover, scholars recognize economics-driven approaches to sustainability as insufficient for organizations striving for overall sustainability (Linnenluecke & Griffiths, 2010). Stable organizations with an external focus, such as those that align with the rational goal model, view sustainability as an imperative for ensuring long-term viability (Linnenluecke & Griffiths, 2010). These organizations would demonstrate a preference for actions that minimize the impact of poor environmental quality on organizational activities.

For each of the preceding examples, organizations would have to interpret sustainability in such a way as to align it to existing values, whether the welfare of staff, creating competitive advantage, maximizing profits, or protecting natural resources. The ability to accurately determine an organization's priorities is critical for practitioners engaged in assisting organizations to strive toward sustainability. It is prudent to note that for each of the CVF typologies, a single company (i.e., Sierra Nevada) has provided the examples, demonstrating that organizations have the potential to integrate a range of initiatives. Indeed, the mark of a truly sustainable organization may be the presence of a sophisticated and multi-faceted complement of pro-environmental initiatives. Thus, we encourage practitioners to consider a variety of potential interventions, and interpret this section and the CVF as a framework to determine how a particular organization might approach sustainability, and to generate a range of initiatives from economic, environmental, social, and holistic perspectives (Linnenluecke et al., 2009).

In developing a pro-environmental organizational climate, practitioners should ensure that the organization's position toward the environment is visible. Importantly, this includes recognizing and rewarding desired behaviors to facilitate the creation and spread of social norms. For companies striving to create a pro-environmental culture, introducing behavioral requirements might be an important initiative. Thus, it is apparent that there is a need to use a broader conceptualization of behavior that includes such prescribed behaviors.

Conclusions

In this chapter, we provide an overview of the related concepts of organizational culture and climate, and how they relate to environmental sustainability at work. We propose in particular a model to facilitate understanding of how the two constructs of pro-environmental organizational culture and climate can be integrated. It is our intention that organizational researchers and practitioners interested in environmental sustainability use this model to study and facilitate pro-environmental social contexts in organizations. We hope that our model will shed light on how pro-environmental organizational cultures and climates emerge and influence various environmental activities at the organizational and employee levels. The model we propose allows in particular for pro-environmental cultures and climates to come in various shades of green, dependent upon a range of organizational considerations. These considerations can be used to guide research and inform practice on how organizations can engage with environmental sustainability, and hopefully, in the years to come, there will be many more environmentally sustainable organizations such as the Sierra Nevada Brewing Company.

Suggested Additional Readings

1. Benn, S., Dunphy, D. C., & Griffiths, A. (2007). *Organizational change for corporate sustainability: A guide for leaders and change agents of the future*. London: Routledge.
2. Jermier, J. M. (2013). *Corporate environmentalism and the greening of organizations* (Vols. 1–6). Thousand Oaks, CA: Sage.
3. Starik, M., Sharma, S., Egri, C., & Bunch, R. (2005). *New horizons in research on sustainable organizations: Emerging ideas, approaches and tools for practitioners and researchers*. Sheffield, UK: Greenleaf.
4. Worthington, I. (2012). *Greening business: Research, theory, and practice*. New York: Oxford University Press.

References

Alvesson, M. (2011). Organizational culture: Meaning, discourse, and identity. In N. M. Ashkanasy, C. P. M. Wilderom, & M. F. Peterson (Eds.), *Handbook of organizational culture & climate* (2nd ed., pp. 11–28). Thousand Oaks, CA: Sage.

Accenture. (2013). *UN global compact—Accenture CEO study on sustainability: Architects of a better world*. Retrieved from http://www.accenture.com/microsites/ungc-ceo-study/Pages/home.aspx.

Ashkanasy, N. M. (2007). Organizational climate. In S. R. Clegg, & J. R. Bailey (Eds.), *International encyclopedia of organization studies* (Vol. 3, pp. 1028–1030). Thousand Oaks, CA: Sage.

Ashkanasy, N. M., Wilderom, C. P. M., & Peterson, M. F. (2000). Introduction to the handbook of organizational culture and climate. In N. M. Ashkanasy, C. P. M. Wilderom, & M. F. Peterson (Eds.), *Handbook of organizational culture & climate* (pp. 1–18). Thousand Oaks, CA: Sage.

Ashkanasy, N. M., Wilderom, C. P. M., & Peterson, M. F. (2011). Introduction to the handbook of organizational culture and climate. In N. M. Ashkanasy, C. P. M. Wilderom, & M. F. Peterson (Eds.), *Handbook of organizational culture & climate* (2nd ed., pp. 3–10). Thousand Oaks, CA: Sage.

Bartlett, D. (2011). The psychology of sustainability in the workplace. In D. Bartlett (Ed.), *Going green: The psychology of sustainability in the workplace* (pp. 1–6). Leicester, UK: The British Psychological Society.

Bissing-Olson, M., Iyer, A., Fielding, S., & Zacher, H. (2013). Relationships between daily affect and pro-environmental behavior at work: The moderating role of pro-environmental attitude. *Journal of Organizational Behavior, 34*, 156–175.

Casler, A., Gundlach, M. J., Persons, B., & Zivnuska, S. (2010). Sierra Nevada Brewing Company's thirty-year journey toward sustainability. *People & Strategy, 33*, 44–51.

Cialdini, R. B., Reno, R. R., & Kallgren, C. A. (1990). A focus theory of normative conduct: Recycling the concept of norms to reduce littering in public places. *Journal of Personality and Social Psychology, 58*, 1015–1026.

Dauber, D., Fink, G., & Yolles, M. (2012). A configuration model of organizational culture. *SAGE Open*, *2*, 1–16.

Dixon-Fowler, H. R., Slater, D. J., Johnson, J. L., Ellstrand, A. E., & Romi, A. M. (2012). Beyond "does it pay to be green?": A meta-analysis of moderators of the CEP–CFP relationship. *Journal of Business Ethics*, *112*, 353–366.

Fairfield, K. D., Harmon, J., & Behson, S. J. (2011). Influences on the organizational implementation of sustainability: An integrative model. *Organization Management Journal*, *8*, 4–20.

Gauthier, J. (2013). Institutional theory and corporate sustainability: Determinant versus interactive approaches. *Organization Management Journal*, *10*, 86–96.

Goldstein, N. J., Cialdini, R. B., & Griskevicius, V. (2008). A room with a viewpoint: Using social norms to motivate environmental conservation in hotels. *Journal of Consumer Research*, *35*, 472–482.

Griffin, P. A., Lont, D. H., & Sun, Y. (2011). *The relevance to investors of greenhouse gas emission disclosures*. Retrieved from http://www.asb.unsw.edu.au/schools/accounting/Documents/D.%20Lont%20-%20The%20Relevance%20to%20Investors%20of%20Greenhouse%20Gas%20Emission%20Disclosures.pdf.

Hartnell, C. A., Ou, A. Y., & Kinicki, A. (2011). Organizational culture and organizational effectiveness: A meta-analytic investigation of the competing values framework's theoretical suppositions. *Journal of Applied Psychology*, *96*, 677–694.

Hatch, M. J. (1993). The dynamics of organizational culture. *The Academy of Management Review*, *18*, 657–693.

Hatch, M. J. (2004). Dynamics in organizational culture. In M. S. Poole, & A. H. Van de Ven (Eds.), *Handbook of organizational change and innovation* (pp. 190–211). New York: Oxford University Press.

Hatch, M. J. (2011). Material and meaning in the dynamics of organizational culture and identity with implications for the leadership of organizational change. In N. M. Ashkanasy, C. P. M. Wilderom, & M. F. Peterson (Eds.), *Handbook of organizational culture & climate* (2nd ed., pp. 341–358). Thousand Oaks, CA: Sage.

Jackson, S. E., Ones, D. S., & Dilchert, S. (Eds.). (2012). *Managing human resources for environmental sustainability*. San Francisco: Jossey-Bass.

James, L. R. (1982). Aggregation bias in estimates of perceptual agreement. *Journal of Applied Psychology*, *67*, 219–229.

James, L. R., Choi, C. C., Ko, E., McNeil, P. K., Minton, M. K., Wright, M. A., & Kim, K. (2008). Organizational and psychological climate: A review of theory and research. *European Journal of Work and Organizational Psychology*, *17*, 5–32.

Kane, A. (2011). Green recruitment, development and engagement. In D. Bartlett (Ed.), *Going green: The psychology of sustainability in the workplace* (pp. 6–17). Leicester, UK: British Psychological Society.

Kuenzi, M., & Schminke, M. (2009). Assembling fragments into a lens: A review, critique, and proposed research agenda for the organizational work climate literature. *Journal of Management*, *35*, 634–717.

Lewin, K. (1951). *Field theory in social science*. New York: Harper & Row.
Linnenluecke, M. K., & Griffiths, A. (2010). Corporate sustainability and organizational culture. *Journal of World Business*, 45, 357–366.
Linnenluecke, M. K., Russell, S. V, & Griffiths, A. (2009). Subcultures and sustainability practices: The impact on understanding corporate sustainability. *Business Strategy and the Environment*, 18, 432–452.
Litwin, G. H., & Stringer, R. A. (1968). *Motivation and organizational climate*. Boston: Harvard University Press.
Lo, S. H., Peters, G. Y., & Kok, G. (2012). Energy-related behaviors in office buildings: A qualitative study on individual and organisational determinants. *Applied Psychology: An International Review*, 61, 227–249.
Lourenco, I. C., Branco, M. C., & Curto, J. D. (2012). How does the market value corporate sustainability performance? *Journal of Business Ethics*, 108, 417–428.
Martin, J. (2002). *Organizational culture: Mapping the terrain*. Thousand Oaks, CA: Sage.
Mesmer-Magnus, J., Viswesvaran, C., & Wiernik, B. M. (2012). The role of commitment in bridging the gap between organizational sustainability and environmental sustainability. In S. E. Jackson, D. S. Ones, & S. Dilchert (Eds.), *Managing human resources for environmental sustainability* (pp. 155–186). San Francisco: Jossey-Bass.
MillersCoors. (2012). *Sustainability report*. Milwaukee: MillerCoors.
Neal, A., & Griffin, M. A. (2006). A study of the lagged relationships among safety climate, safety motivation, safety behavior, and accidents at the individual and group levels. *Journal of Applied Psychology*, 91, 946–953.
Norton, T. A., Zacher, H., & Ashkanasy, N. M. (2012). On the importance of pro-environmental organizational climate for employee green behavior. *Industrial and Organizational Psychology*, 5, 497–500.
Norton, T. A., Zacher, H., & Ashkanasy, N. M. (2014). Organisational sustainability policies and employee green behaviour: The mediating role of work climate perceptions. *Journal of Environmental Psychology*, 38, 49–54.
Ones, D., & Dilchert, S. (2012). Environmental sustainability at work: A call to action. *Industrial and Organizational Psychology*, 5, 444–466.
Ones, D. S., Dilchert, S., Biga, A., & Gibby, R. E. (2010, April). Managerial level differences in eco-friendly employee behaviors. In S. Dilchert (Chair), *Organisational and group differences in environmentally responsible employee behaviors*. Symposium conducted at the 25th Society for Industrial & Organizational Psychology Conference, Atlanta.
Ostroff, C., Kinicki, A. J., & Muhammad, R. S. (2013). Organizational culture and climate. In I. B. Weiner, N. W. Schmitt, & S. Highhouse (Eds.), *Handbook of psychology* (2nd ed., Vol. 12, pp. 643–676). New York: Wiley.
Paillé, P., & Boiral, O. (2013). Pro-environmental behavior at work: Construct validity and determinants. *Journal of Environmental Psychology*, 36, 118–128.

Quinn, R. E., & Rohrbaugh, J. (1983). A spatial model of effectiveness criteria: Towards a competing values approach to organizational analysis. *Management Science*, *29*, 363–373.

Ramus, C. A., & Steger, U. (2000). The roles of supervisory support behaviors and environmental policy in employee "ecoinitiatives" at leading-edge European companies. *The Academy of Management Journal*, *43*, 605–626.

Robertson, J. L., & Barling, J. (2013). Greening organizations through leaders' influence on employees' pro-environmental behaviors. *Journal of Organizational Behavior*, *34*, 176–194.

Russell, S. V., & McIntosh, M. (2011). Changing organizational culture for sustainability. In N. M. Ashkanasy, C. P. M. Wilderom, & M. F. Peterson (Eds.), *Handbook of organizational culture and climate* (2nd ed., pp. 393–411). Thousand Oaks, CA: Sage.

Schein, E. H. (1990). Organizational culture. *American Psychologist*, *45*, 109–119.

Schein, E. H. (1996). Culture: The missing concept in organization studies. *Administrative Science Quarterly*, *41*, 229–240.

Schein, E. H. (2003). Five traps for consulting psychologists: Or, how I learned to take culture seriously. *Consulting Psychology Journal*, *55*, 75–83.

Schein, E. H. (2010). *Organizational culture and leadership* (4th ed.). San Francisco: Jossey-Bass.

Schelly, C., Cross, J. E., Franzen, W. S., Hall, P., & Reeve, S. (2010). Reducing energy consumption and creating a conservation culture in organizations: A case study of one public school district. *Environment and Behavior*, *43*, 316–343.

Schneider, B. (1975). Organizational climate: An essay. *Personnel Psychology*, *28*, 447–479.

Schneider, B., Ehrhart, M. G., & Macey, W. H. (2011). Organizational climate research: Achievement and the road ahead. In N. M. Ashkanasy, C. P. M. Wilderom, & M. F. Peterson (Eds.), *Handbook of organizational culture & climate* (2nd ed., pp. 29–49). Thousand Oaks, CA: Sage.

Schneider, B., Ehrhart, M. G., & Macey, W. H. (2013). Organizational climate and culture. *Annual Review of Psychology*, *64*, 361–388.

Schneider, B., & Reichers, A. E. (1983). On the etiology of climates. *Personnel Psychology*, *36*, 19–34.

Scott, W. R. (2008). *Institutions and organizations: Ideas and interests*. Thousand Oaks, CA: Sage.

Sierra Nevada Brewing Company. (2012). *Biennial sustainability report*. Retrieved from http://www.sierranevada.com/brewery/about-us/sustainability.

Smith, J. R., Louis, W. R., Terry, D. J., Greenaway, K. H., Clarke, M. R., & Cheng, X. (2012). Congruent or conflicted? The impact of injunctive and descriptive norms on environmental intentions. *Journal of Environmental Psychology*, *32*, 353–361.

Starik, M., & Rands, G. P. (1995). Weaving an integrated web: Multilevel and multisystem perspectives of ecologically sustainable organizations. *The Academy of Management Review, 20*, 908–935.

Tobler, C., Visschers, V. H. M., & Siegrist, M. (2012). Addressing climate change: Determinants of consumers' willingness to act and to support policy measures. *Journal of Environmental Psychology, 32*, 197–207.

Trice, H. M., & Beyer, J. M. (1984). Studying organizational cultures through rites and ceremonials. *The Academy of Management Review, 9*, 653–669.

Trist, E. L. (1981). The evolution of sociotechnical systems as a conceptual framework and as an action research program. In A. H. Van de Ven, & W. F. Joyce (Eds.), *Perspectives on organization design and behavior* (pp. 19–75). New York: Wiley.

Tudor, T. L., Barr, S. W., & Gilg, A. W. (2007). A novel conceptual framework for examining environmental behavior in large organizations: A case study of the Cornwall National Health Service in the United Kingdom. *Environment and Behavior, 40*, 426–450.

Wackernagel, M., Schulz, N. B., Deumling, D., Linares, A. C., Jenkins, M., Kapos, V., . . . Monfreda, C. (2002). Tracking the ecological overshoot of the human economy. *Proceedings of the National Academy of Sciences, 99*, 9266–9271.

Walls, J. L., & Hoffman, A. J. (2012). Exceptional boards: Environmental experience and positive deviance from institutional norms. *Journal of Organizational Behavior, 34*, 253–271.

Zacher, H., & Gielnik, M. M. (2014). Organizational age cultures: The interplay of chief executive officers' age and attitudes toward younger and older employees. *International Small Business Journal, 32*, 327–349.

Zohar, D. (2000). A group-level model of safety climate: Testing the effect of group climate on micro-accidents in manufacturing jobs. *Journal of Applied Psychology, 85*, 587–596.

IV TYING IT ALL TOGETHER

15

SUSTAINABLE INNOVATION AT INTERFACE

WORKPLACE PRO-ENVIRONMENTAL BEHAVIOR AS A COLLECTIVE DRIVER FOR CONTINUOUS IMPROVEMENT

Steve Kennedy, Gail Whiteman, and Amanda Williams[1]

On the night of September 20, 1994, Ray Anderson, CEO and founder of a NASDAQ-listed company, had what he called an epiphany. Like a "spear through the chest," he realized that his way of doing business—of selling carpet to other businesses—was laying waste to the Earth in pursuit of profit. Heavily reliant on petrochemicals and a take-make-waste modus operandi, his company, Interface, had previously been content with a legal compliance strategy toward the environment. Yet from that day forth Ray vowed that his firm would do things differently.

Eighteen years later, Interface is a renowned leader in corporate sustainability (see DuBose, 2000; Elkington, 2012) and sustainable innovation (Carrillo-Hermosilla et al., 2010; Seebode et al., 2012). Corporate executives and staff have successfully made radical changes to their business model, simultaneously increasing profits and significantly reducing their negative impacts on the environment (Seebode et al., 2012). Interface started this journey like many companies, by

---

1. This study was made possible by a grant from the Dutch Ministry of Economic Affairs. We thank the Ministry for their interest and support for this work. We would like to give special thanks to the people from Interface for participating in this research and specifically to Geanne van Arkel (Sustainable Development), Mark Haverlach (Re-Entry Director), Peter Vogel (Director European Technology), and the Re-Entry 2.0 innovation team for their support. We would also like to acknowledge the generous introduction to the Interface Netherlands office organized by Ray Anderson in 2005, when the second author met him at the Academy of Management conference in Hawaii.

picking out the low-hanging fruit and seeking to gain efficiency savings where possible. By doing so, Interface has achieved over $450 million in efficiency savings alone, cut waste sent to landfill by 92% per unit of production, and reduced its carbon footprint by 41% per unit of production (Internal document 2013a, pp. 10–11). Interface has also attracted attention from other businesses curious to learn how they can take responsibility for the environment while positively impacting their economic bottom line. The company's approach has also fascinated management academics who have sought to learn the valuable business lessons from their novel strategy (Stubbs & Cocklin, 2008; Toffel et al., 2012).

Ray Anderson's epiphany in 1994 and subsequent personal action is a compelling example of workplace pro-environmental behavior (WPEB) at the executive level that had cascading effects over time. The main contribution of this chapter is to illustrate how both individual *and* organizational factors drive WPEBs. Even after Ray Anderson's death in 2011, his company has continued its pursuit of what Ray called Mission Zero—"our promise to eliminate any negative impact our company may have on the environment by the year 2020" (Interface, 2013). This mission is described as building processes that both support the environment and enable Interface to have restorative impact in both ecological and social respects on the places in which it does business (Interface, 2013).

Workplace pro-environmental behavior can be defined as "a broad set of proactive employee environmental activities that have the potential to transform work" (Graves et al., 2011, p. 2). Such behaviors are actions taken by employees with the intention of improving the overall environmental performance of the organization (Ramus & Steger, 2000). Examples of WPEBs at Interface include new product and process innovations to reduce greenhouse gas emissions and decrease the amount of virgin material used, as well as activities aimed specifically at closing the loop in the manufacturing and product use cycle and engaging other stakeholders in this mission.

What makes Interface such an interesting case for exploring WPEBs is that the organizational behavior of its employees encompasses much more than turning out the lights and printing less paper (although such activities are of course worthwhile). Interface is a compelling example of organization-wide set of WPEBs that have led to deep, transformational change within the company, and the rise of a new eco-centered business model. What makes Interface even more interesting is that Ray's WPEB is not an isolated case. Following Ray's epiphany in 1994, a raison d'être was born and cultivated. Among Interface employees, WPEB is widespread and purposefully promoted within the organizational culture. At all levels WPEBs have collectively resulted in continuous breakthroughs in sustainable innovation, and sometimes, unexpected new sustainable business opportunities.

In general, the literature on WPEB has focused on individual antecedents of WPEB at the micro-organizational behavioral level from a social psychology perspective. Although valuable, there have been few studies taking a more sociological and qualitative perspective on the organizational context under which WPEB thrives within an organization like Interface and across the value chain. In addition, Boiral and Paillé (2012) have called for more research on the role of corporate sustainability strategy and the diffusion of pro-environmental behavior within the workplace. These are gaps that our chapter seeks to address through a review of the literature and an empirical analysis of a recent process innovation—Re-Entry 2.0—at Interface.

Our chapter provides in-depth qualitative findings of the WPEB by innovation team members at Interface's European headquarters in the Netherlands, which resulted in what Interface calls Re-Entry 2.0. Re-Entry 2.0 is a new process innovation that enables scalable like-for-like recycling of carpet tiles. This is an innovation in closed-loop manufacturing that allows Interface to take back carpet tiles (its own and those of the competition) and re-use the material. Moreover, by gaining control of the used material flows, this innovation has opened the door for implementing new sustainable business models and for other Interface employees to enact further WPEB such as starting new bottom-of-the-pyramid initiatives.

This chapter describes how the pro-environmental behavior of the CEO, once translated into a corporate sustainability strategy, can inspire and diffuse WPEB through mechanisms such as organizational culture and collaborative work structures. The primary contribution of our chapter is to describe WPEB as a set of pro-environmental behaviors at the individual *and* organizational level, triggered by the pro-environmental behavior of one powerful figure head. Furthermore, our chapter illustrates how a multi-level WPEB climate can lead to radical sustainable innovation within, and beyond, the organization. In our discussion section, we also present a conceptual model of transformative WPEB at the organizational level to capture the upward spiral of individual WPEBs, which link together through a process of social diffusion between individuals, the organization structure and routines, and value chain actors (see Figure 15.1).

Workplace Pro-Environmental Behavior

Research on WPEB has originated from organizational behavior scholars adapting the concept of pro-environmental behavior in society at large to take into account the more specific context of organizational behavior within the workplace. This field is linked to the theoretical literature on value-creating pro-social behaviors and behavior intent models (Ramus & Killmer, 2007), with WPEB

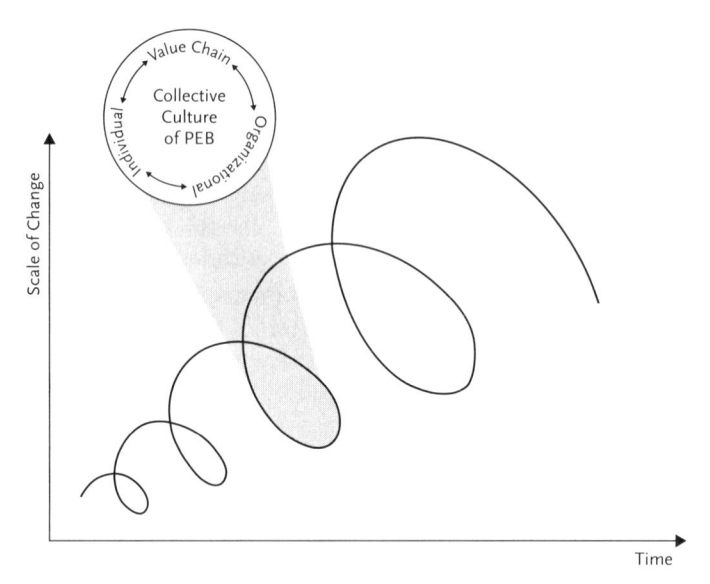

FIGURE 15.1 PEB as a systemic set of actions from a collective of organizational actions across a company.

often seen as a mixture of self-interest and pro-social behavior (Bamberg & Möser, 2007; Lo et al., 2012). Researchers have explored determinants of WPEB at the individual, group, and organizational level, but the interaction between individual and organizational levels as collective drivers of behavior remains underexplored.

Individual Level Determinants of Workplace Pro-Environmental Behavior

At the individual level factors such as attitudes, beliefs, personal norms, social norms, self-efficacy, and past behavior have all been found to be determinants of WPEB (Lo et al., 2012). Attitudes have been found to predict intention to act in a pro-environmental manner (Jones, 1990; Scherbaum et al., 2008) but correspond less well with actual behaviors (Andersson et al., 2005; Scherbaum et al., 2008). The literature linking beliefs (WPEB as the right thing to do) to actual behavior (WPEB) does not show consistent results (Lo et al., 2012). For instance Tudor et al.'s (2007) study shows that beliefs are moderately correlated to recycling behavior, whereas Marans and Lee's (1993) research shows only a weak correlation between beliefs and recycling behavior. Similarly personal norms, beliefs about what one should do or what one is responsible for, do predict WPEB (Scherbaum et al., 2008). In their review of WPEB determinants, Lo et al.

(2012) conclude that "The effect size of personal norms varied according to the degree of correspondence between personal norm and the dependent variable, and whether the dependent variable was intention or behavior," (p. 2946). Social norms have been found to predict individual actions such as levels of recycling behavior (Jones, 1990) and waste management behavior (Tudor et al., 2007), but evidence in the workplace remains limited (Lo et al., 2012). Self-efficacy, the belief that one has control over one's behavior, has also been linked to WPEB (Cordano & Frieze, 2000; Tudor et al., 2007). Studies show that individual success with WPEB increases people's their belief that they are capable of the same results in the future and they become more likely to engage in WPEB (Cordano & Frieze, 2000; Walls & Hoffman, 2013).

Finally, Russell and Griffiths (2008) highlight the fact that most research has focused on linking attitude theories with pro-environmental behavior, leaving the role of emotional and affective factors under studied. Yet their findings suggest that emotions are an important aspect of workplace behavior and deserve further attention in the WPEB literature.

The Role of Champions

Previous studies have shown that individual environmental "champions" can be critical to the environmental innovativeness of the firm (Andersson & Bateman, 2000) and to the formation and implementation of so-called green strategies (Branzei et al., 2004; Walley & Stubbs, 2000). Individual champions scan the organizational environment to identify the salient ecological issues, and then frame these issues in a manner that can gain the attention of top management (Andersson & Bateman, 2000). Successful champions have been found to exhibit behaviors such as issue scanning, issue framing, issue presenting, and influencing (Andersson & Bateman, 2000).

Organizational Level Determinants of Workplace Pro-Environmental Behavior

Contextual variables at the organizational level, such as environmental policies, involvement of superiors, physical facilitation (Lo et al., 2012), management commitment, employee empowerment, rewards, and feedback (Govindarajulu & Daily, 2004) have all been explored in the literature. Fineman (1996) found that managers culturally engineer WPEB and attach different emotional meanings to pressures to engage in green commitment. In this way, organizational commitment to sustainability has been shown to determine WPEB, depending on the way it is culturally engineered by leaders (Fineman, 1996). Similarly,

Aragón-Correa et al. (2004) found that the role of executives is crucial to improving corporate environmental commitment. Their findings show that executives influence environmental commitment through interpretations, preference, and decisions.

Others suggest that traditional cognitive models that assume environmental behavior is determined by linear and rational decision do not capture the complexity of the organizational context (Hargreaves, 2008). For example, Hargreaves (2008) found that WPEB is a collective and social process based on relationships between meaning and skill in a broad social space. Thus, WPEBs become salient normative issues through a process of re-socialization. In a related vein, Russell and Griffiths (2008) put forth the concept of pro-environmental climate, defined as "the organization's underlying characteristics that are supportive of issues of the natural environment" (p. 93). Their definition of pro-environmental climate aims to encompass all contextual variables and proposes that there is a direct impact on individual WPEB. Interestingly, recent empirical work also suggests that WPEB may act as a trigger and enabler of sustainable innovation (Kennedy et al., under review), but this area remains under researched.

Summary

Research on WPEB indicates that individual and organizational level determinants influence pro-environmental behavior in workplace settings. At the individual level, variables such as attitudes (Jones, 1990; Scherbaum et al., 2008), beliefs (Marans & Lee, 1993; Tudor et al., 2007), personal norms (Scherbaum et al., 2008), social norms (Jones, 1990), self-efficacy (Cordano & Frieze, 2000; Tudor et al., 2007), past behavior (Cordano & Frieze, 2000; Walls & Hoffman, 2013), and emotions (Russell & Griffiths, 2008) have all been found to determine WPEB. At the organizational level, scholars have shown that contextual variables (Lo et al., 2012) and organizational commitment (Aragón-Correa et al., 2004; Fineman, 1996) are linked with WPEB. The role and activities of individual champions for WPEB have also been explored, with studies beginning to give insight on how they may bridge between the individual level and the organizational context (Andersson & Bateman, 2000; Branzei et al., 2004).

In addition, studies on WPEB tend to adopt a micro-level organizational behavior focus instead of a multi-level perspective, which may allow for an embedded understanding (Andersson et al., 2013). Existing studies do not typically adopt a sociological perspective, although there is some research that suggests the importance of organizational climate and social interaction (Hargreaves, 2008; Russell & Griffiths, 2008). However, the literature has yet to describe WPEBs that are individually and collectively diffused throughout the organization and value chain. In addition, although researchers have determined some of the individual level determinants of WPEB, there is little understanding of how to link organizational factors including corporate sustainability strategy to WPEB and sustainable innovation, although it is clear that environmental champions and senior executives have an important role to play in diffusing WPEB throughout the organization.

Methods

Research Design

This chapter presents qualitative case study findings of a sustainable product and manufacturing innovation called Re-Entry 2.0 at Interface. These findings emerged out of a case study of Interface, investigating the organizational factors affecting sustainable innovation more generally. The focus of WPEB developed as our understanding of its significance to the innovation process unfolded and we came to appreciate the real detail of the *how* and *why* of events (Yin, 2003). Re-Entry 2.0 provides an excellent case from which to gain insight into the connection between WPEB and sustainable innovation, and the influence of corporate sustainability strategy. A case study design coupled with an inductive approach has allowed for an understanding to be developed that is grounded in the exploratory empirical research.

By studying the organizational process of Re-Entry 2.0, our research primarily operates at the project level unit of analysis, which allow us to gain a rich understanding of the complex organizational and individual level factors involved in WPEB.

Data Collection Methods

To investigate the Re-Entry 2.0 case we utilize the core strength of the case methodology and collate data from multiple sources: qualitative interviews, documentary evidence, and direct observations. These data collection methods are consistent with a qualitative approach, offer flexibility, and are sensitive to social context (Mason, 2002). The multiple sources approach offered opportunities for converging lines of inquiry and the processes of corroboration and triangulation (Yin, 2003).

Extensive access was granted to the first author of this chapter, with numerous visits made to Interface's European Headquarters in Scherpenzeel, Netherlands. Data were collected from July 2012 until June 2013. During this period, formal research methods were supplemented by informal discussions, casual observations of workplace operations, and four roundtable discussions on sustainable innovation (including specific to the case) conducted involving the authors of this chapter, representatives of Interface, and selected other multinationals. In total, seven field visits were made to Interface, a multitude of internal and external documents were analyzed, and a set of formal and informal interviews were conducted with Interface employees.

Semi-Structured Interviews

Semi-structured interviews were the primary method for this study, ranging from 30 to 120 minutes in length, with over 13 hours conducted. These interviews took place with multiple respondents from various hierarchical levels and functional areas, in particular including members of the innovation team. Interviewee positions include Senior Account Manager (Sales), Re-Entry Director, Senior Mechanical Engineer, Director European Manufacturing, Director European Technology, and Project Manager Sustainability–Process Material Research.

Interviewees were selected on a "snowballing" basis (Bryman & Bell, 2003), with interviewees asked to recommend further people to speak to. Interviews offered the potential for complex questions to be asked, non-verbal clues to be identified, and follow-up questions to be formulated based on responses. Interviews were all conducted on a one-to-one, face-to-face basis, except one was held on a one-to-two basis and audio recorded with the consent of the interviewee, allowing the first author, as the interviewer, to concentrate on the listening process. All interviews were conducted by the first author, except for one, which was conducted by a colleague within the same project team. Interviews were semi-structured in design, allowing flexibility for both the interviewer in the questioning and the interviewee in their responses (Bryman & Bell, 2003).

Observation

In total, seven field visits were made by the first author to Interface at Scherpenzeel, Netherlands, including an accompanied factory tour. Each of these visits represented an opportunity to make observations, which were recorded by photographed observations (with permission). Observations were principally useful in the initial exploratory phase of the study and were used to inform interview questions, generally help connect better with interviewees, and allow informed discussion.

Documentary Evidence

Our research made use of a range of publically (e.g., corporate websites, annual reports, and corporate brochures) and privately available information (e.g., internal presentations, and data sheets). Documentary evidence itself was cross-checked with evidence obtained in interviews to identify inconsistencies, which were subsequently investigated.

Data Analysis

Data were analyzed with the goal of producing a narrative of the case based on the analysis and connection of the primary themes (Dutton & Dukerich, 1991). Our analysis has generated an emergent understanding of the case starting from the empirical data, as an exercise of recognizing the patterns of relationships between categories of data and understanding their underlying logical reasoning (Eisenhardt & Graebner, 2007). We used an open and flexible approach to data analysis (Lofland et al., 2006). This helped to avoid problems associated with identifying themes at higher levels of abstraction (Easterby-Smith et al., 2002) and perceived forcing of data into categories (Glaser, 1992).

Data were analyzed using the computer qualitative analysis software (CAQDAS) NVIVO10 to identify and code data incidents, and subsequently compare and categorize patterns of similar incidents. By using tree nodes in NVIVO10, our analysis was structured by developing categories and subcategories and identifying linkages across data.

Case Study Findings

Interface, Inc. is the world's largest manufacturer of modular carpet for commercial and residential use, known as carpet squares or tiles (Interface, 2013). Interface, Inc. has its origins in the USA and is a global public limited company (listed on the NASDAQ Stock Market) with 3,146 employees and net sales of $932 million (Interface, 2012). The carpet industry traditionally has a slow pace of change with little disruptive innovation. Furthermore it was historically not an industry known for its sustainability activism, due to the reliance upon petrochemicals and business models built upon the need for consumption and replacement.

Led by its late Founder and Chairman, Ray Anderson, Interface has focused heavily on becoming a sustainable enterprise since 1994. This transition was triggered by an epiphany of the Chairman in 1994. Since that time, Interface has become well recognized for its proactive stance on sustainability, which has earned the company numerous accolades and awards (Interface, 2013). Interface also offers inspirational sessions to external audiences (including companies) called Cultural Immersions, and regularly accommodates visits from corporate executives from a range of industries and student groups eager to learn of the company's success.

The vision to be the first truly sustainable company is encapsulated in Interface's ambitious Mission Zero: The company's aim to completely eliminate the negative impact the company has on the environment by 2020. In 2012, Interface reported that its performance was already 80% toward this target (from a 1994 starting point). Corporate documents explain that these achievements are based upon "a culture of 'successful failure,' biomimicry and a strategy of 'open innovation'" (External document, 2011a). Fulfilling Mission Zero has also brought Interface many commercial benefits. The company has gained a great deal of brand reputation, has been able to take advantage of significant financial savings from eco-efficiencies, and is an appealing company to work for.

Like many of its counterparts, Interface began its journey with the 'low-hanging fruit' primarily through a waste elimination program named QUEST (quality utilizing employee suggestions and teamwork) (see DuBose, 2000 for the scope of this program and its impressive results). This program was the beginning of the environmental initiatives and formal structure at Interface. The QUEST program also created a common bond between employees and production locations (DuBose, 2000). Although eco-efficiency programs remain important to Interface, the company has now gone far beyond this program in its efforts toward Mission Zero, engaging with value chain partners on radical sustainable innovation and new sustainable business models.

Interface is now commonly perceived by its employees as an exemplar in transparency and openness, willing to share its sustainability lessons and creating voluntary environmental datasheets on products. The company uses Life Cycle Assessment studies and has openly identified raw materials (yarn) as the area of greatest environmental impact. As such, they aim to decrease corporate impacts through (a) reducing the amount used, (b) using greater recycled content, and (c) inventing new yarn. This chapter investigates how Re-Entry 2.0 emerged as a WPEB seeking to address this problem.

Re-Entry 2.0

Re-Entry 2.0 is a radical new process innovation developed by Interface, which enables scalable like-for-like recycling of carpet tiles. The technology is an industry first because it allows efficient separation of the nylon yarn and the bitumen backing from old carpet tiles while critically retaining the material value of each component. Only a small amount of material (<14%) currently cannot be recycled. Recycled nylon yarn is then sold back to a yarn supplier (dependent upon yarn type) and the backing material is fed into the on-site manufacturing process. Coupled with the technical development Interface upgraded its existent take-back scheme. This scheme received used carpet tiles from its customers for waste-to-energy schemes and now is organized for tiles to be recycled into raw materials. Used carpet tiles from other manufacturers are also accepted for recycling, but will go to waste-to-energy when not suitable for the process. This control of the material flows and capability for like-for-like recycling is most significant because Re-Entry 2.0 offers Interface the possibility of new sustainable business models to provide more conclusive solutions to achieving Mission Zero.

Radical Innovation

Re-Entry 2.0 represents a major breakthrough in closing the materials loop because it both diverts material from disposal and saves four times the energy of equivalent virgin materials in processing (External document, 2011a). Furthermore, it can fully recycle the nylon yarn—the most carbon intensive part of the carpet (External document, 2011a). It is the ability to separate the nylon yarn from its bitumen backing component that makes the recycling process significant, as this represents a first in the carpet industry. Competitors in the European marketplace have also begun to promote their own take-back systems, sending recycled yarn back to the same supplier. However, these recycling processes are unable to reclaim more than two-thirds of the yarn (Interviewee J) and do not produce backing of sufficient quality to be used back into the production stream. Instead, this material is downcycled for use in the road building and roofing industries.

Organizational Setting

Process innovations within Interface are conducted within the technical section of operations. The technical development of Re-Entry 2.0 was primarily carried out jointly between the Engineering and Process Material Research subdepartments. At a point at which an acceptable technical solution was found, the project broadened to encompass the manufacturing director, the sales director, and a sales account manager. In autumn 2012 a Re-Entry director was appointed who assumed responsibility for the innovation. In addition, a technical team in the USA has also been working on closing the loop and liaising with the European team during the developmental process.

Organizational Culture Promoting Workplace Pro-Environmental Behavior

It is difficult to have a conversation with someone at Interface about sustainability without them at least mentioning Ray Anderson. This indicates the influence and lasting impression of what most Interface employees considered to be a visionary leader of sustainable business. His picture alongside Paul Hawken's book, *The Ecology of Commerce* (which triggered Ray's epiphany), and numerous sustainability awards sits proudly in the office corridor of the European headquarters.

During interviews, both formal and informal, many employees directly quoted the late founder. For example: "You might have heard about a quote that Ray Anderson our founder once said. . . ." (Interviewee E). "But actually that's the vision of Ray Anderson. He said: 'I hope one day, that all our market, all our business is 100% sustainable, and then we can compete just on product and design'" (Interviewee J). "It is about, when Ray talks about cleaning oil, he talks about optimally become a restorative company, and putting more back than you take" (Interviewee K).

External documents (2010b) reinforce the power and impact of Ray's pro-environmental behavior and explicitly link this to employee behavior: "For many Interface employees, it's more personal than just achieving company sustainability goals—they don't want to disappoint Ray" (p. 6). This vision and Ray's numerous actions have inspired a culture that promotes employees to perform WPEB beyond what is expected of them. Interviewee K makes this clear: "the business could engage people in his vision. He did that in the 1990s, and then people took it on themselves to carry on with it. He didn't really have to keep saying 'don't forget to be sustainable,' it just happened."

The company strategy, Mission Zero, is central to understanding behavior and activities at Interface. Mission Zero is quantifiable and time-bound, making an internal and external reference point for Interface's commitment to sustainability. Mission Zero is well recognized by Interface employees and has been able to successfully inspire and drive the behavior of the European workforce. For example, Interviewee K notes its success in bringing focus to the company: "Because everybody is engaged in the mission, we have a very clear goal about zero emissions in 2020, so it is a real focus for the business." These sentiments are reinforced by formal Interface documents: "some people say it was naïve to think this is achievable. But it has inspired us to make fundamental changes in the way we work because whatever you do, you can always do better" (External document, 2011a, 3).

Interviewees spoke with enthusiasm of the next big step toward Mission Zero, were genuinely excited by the prospect of reaching the targets, and were actively looking for innovations. Based on our interview data and observations, employees at the European headquarters were actively engaged in WPEB because they wanted to help achieve Mission Zero and, critically, had the freedom within their respective roles to do so: "Because everybody knows where we are heading and everybody has the freedom within her or his role to contribute to that" (Interviewee A).

Past performance and ongoing achievements toward Mission Zero are discussed with much pride. Numerous instances of WPEB are retold alongside stories of Ray, which have turned into what can be described as workplace legends. A commonly recited story that came up during a number of informal interviews was also recorded in an external document giving status and honor to the employee involved.

> The head of engineering from a big multinational company visited our factory in LaGrange, Georgia, to hear about our approach to sustainability. She was highly skeptical during our presentation and couldn't understand why she'd been sent to a carpet mill in Georgia to learn about sustainability.
>
> During a break, she walked onto the factory floor and met forklift truck driver James Wiesner. When she asked him what he did at Interface, James replied, 'I come to work every day to help save the Earth' and then, after chatting with the visitor for a few minutes, added, 'I don't want to be rude, but if I don't get this roll of carpet to that machine in the next minute, our emissions are going to go out of control. I've got to go.'
>
> Our guest was stunned and returned to the seminar room with a whole new agenda. How could she get her own team that engaged in sustainability like this? How could she make sure they understand the vision and know what they as individuals need to do to achieve success for themselves, the company and the planet?
>
> *(External document 2010b, 2)*

Interface's organizational culture is perhaps partly due to recruitment of a particular type of employee with strong motivations for WPEB. The strong sustainability reputation of Interface has made it an attractive place to work, both for those within the carpet industry (Internal document, 2013b) and for talented individuals who otherwise would not work in the industry (Interviewee A). This does attract some workers inclined toward WPEB but Interface's recruitment policy is not dissimilar to a standard company, with only an expectation that applicants know the company's mission and have a view on it. Interviewee A explains: "Sometimes people ask us, you know, are we especially hiring people with a sustainability view. I didn't have a particular sustainability view when I started to work for Interface. I just looked at the company and thought oh ok, that's . . . it felt good."

More importantly, Interface formally offers an employee education scheme to help cultivate a culture of WPEB. This scheme is called Fast forward to 2020 and is positioned as a way to "get your colleague entrepreneurs out of the closet" (Internal document 2012d, 41). All employees are required to take the first level of this program to learn of the basics of sustainability, Mission Zero and the seven fronts of "Mount Sustainability" (the strategic ways of how to attain the mission). All managers are then obligated to take the second level, which links sustainability to their area of operations. Level three is a deep look at sustainability and requires a proposal of an idea to implement (Interviewee K). Such successfully realized ideas have included a carpet tile re-use project in Wales and a scheme to reduce emissions of company cars (Internal document 2012d, 42). Most significantly, on completion of level three, employees become sustainability ambassadors for Interface. This is promoted as a club with limited membership that is won on merit—by conducting a project in which employees combine their personal passion and interest into a contribution toward Mission Zero (External document, 2010b, 6; Interviewee A). Furthermore, ambassadors need to continually engage with sustainability issues to remain in the club.

Interface has a strong culture of promoting WPEB: "They (senior management) are encouraging us to do this. I mean we don't have to discuss this with them. It's so obvious for every one of us. It's in the genes of the whole company" (Interviewee D). Interviewee F comments on the strength of the culture by summing up the effect on new recruits: ". . . they want to work for Interface because they have sustainability values. Or if they don't have it, the culture internally is already that strong you get inspired . . . yeah you get inspired by it and you will change."

Innovation Driven by Workplace Pro-Environmental Behavior: Re Entry 2.0

"Closing the materials loop" is one of Interface's seven steps to achieving Mission Zero (Internal document 2013a). The principle idea of closing the loop is to break away from a linear model of consumption by collecting and recycling post-consumer waste to be once again used as raw materials for new products. Ray Anderson outlined many good business reasons for achieving this, including decreasing the quantity of virgin raw material that must be purchased and the company's dependence on increasingly scarce and polluting petro-based raw materials (External document 2009a, pp. 121–122).

Since 1994, Interface has made numerous ongoing attempts to close the loop both in Europe and North America. Within Europe, these efforts are primarily led by three individuals within the operations department; an employee of each of the Engineering and Process Material Research subdepartments, led by a technical director—hereafter referred to as the innovation team. This small team engaged with other members of the operations department when required and constantly engaged with their North American counterparts.[2] Though simple in concept, the realization of closing the loop has been exceedingly difficult. The technical ability to separate carpet tile into its component parts has proved to be a considerably difficult task: ". . . you know . . . because the thing with it right now, it was thought to be impossible 10 or 15 years ago. When I joined this company, we were already looking at separating the top cloth from the backing in a clean way" (Interviewee E). Interviewee H explains it as a type of self-punishment for the company, ". . . this sort of *self-punishment* . . . to continue to search, search, search . . . invest money in that . . . In our technical department, most of whom you've spoken to, we simply forced [them] to search and spend time and finally they come up with yet another potential process step." This process step was eventually called Re-Entry 2.0.

Idea Generation

The idea of Re-Entry 2.0 is rooted in a history of recycling efforts, but it is set apart from its predecessors most significantly by its successful, scalable, like-for-like recycling of carpet tiles. Past attempts were able to recycle carpet tiles to a certain extent, but were not deemed suitable solutions because they did not produce like-for-like products (e.g., significant material was lost or its value was downgraded). Interface employees said that although many companies deem such processes as closing the loop, this was not really the case and in fact created fuzziness over the meaning of the concept. For the innovation team of Re-Entry 2.0 (comprised of the same team working on previous recycling efforts) this was not acceptable, even if a successful business case could be made. Quite simply, if they did not achieve full separation of materials, maintaining the material value and without excess energy or labor (Interviewee B) they did not have a complete solution: "Yeah, it was common sense. Because we knew that the backing is relatively cheap and the yarn is a high quality part of the tile cost. Most . . . it was common sense to do this that we need to separate it. Otherwise, it was a crime. It would be downcycling. That's how it started" (Interviewee D).

Although a time-consuming and difficult task, the challenge to create a fully separable solution was not seen as a burden by the innovation team. Innovation

---

2. Although the principal aim remains the same, the North American team operates in quite a different context to the European and face different challenges. For instance, the technical composition of the carpets is different as is the operating environment, with the availability of a relatively inexpensive low-skilled labor force.

team members say that they have enjoyed the process and the opportunity to perform WPEB: "But we're not afraid of complexity. Like I said, that's fun. It's part of the fun. It's what we trained for, what we're educated for. I don't know about every technician, but I know that most of the technicians like to solve puzzles, explore things. At least, I like to do it. And these are puzzles too. And when you solve the puzzle it gives a big satisfaction" (Interviewee D). As such, Re-Entry 2.0 was also referred to as a *hobby garden* (Interviewee H) for the innovation team, whereby they have been given time and freedom to innovate and explore the ways in which they can achieve a radical solution. The company itself recognizes and promotes this as the best way to enable WPEB from these types of employees: "Engineers, for example, get excited by a technical challenge. Motivate them with an ambitious sustainability problem to solve and provide them with the time and resources to do it. They love toys (or machines) to play with. When people are given a great challenge, they can be inspired to come up with ground-breaking solutions" (External document, 2010b, 7).

Finding the Solution

To find the technical solution, the innovation team spent years engaging with a variety of machine suppliers. It was well known in the marketplace that Interface was seeking a full recycling solution, which meant that many suppliers would contact the innovation team to test (and normally rent) their equipment out on the problem. "The same company we visited about five times . . . and then the competitor we visited about three of four times. I mean, talking about all these years we've started from. We're talking about [19]98 until now. So there were many visits. Every time suppliers were thinking: 'Ok, we have a solution for your problem of how to grid the backing'" (Interviewee D).

This search led the innovation team down numerous unsuccessful paths as they tried to discover how the problem of separating the yarn and backing could be solved. It was at one of these machine tests when the innovation breakthrough was made, after a long day of trials. Interviewee D describes the moment and also illustrates the perseverance of the team to find a solution despite resistance: ". . . and then we saw this big [Machine part X]—'What if we try to put this in this [Machine part X]?' 'Ah, it's impossible . . . it can't work . . . No, no . . . we're not going to do it.' Because they (the equipment suppliers) were thinking, 'Ok, we have to clean the machine again.' But we paid money for this and said, 'Ok, we want to try . . . Just give it a try.' And by accident also on the out-feed shaft there were products coming out. They had these glass windows for testing, for the entire product. And we put a bunch of carpet tiles into the [Machine part X], and we saw this yarn coming by . . . 'Hey, what's going on here?' And that triggered it. And it works! We've separated the yarn from the backing."

Modestly, the innovation team attributes this discovery primarily to serendipity: "... and it was just coincidence and luck that we discovered it. Because if these windows weren't there we wouldn't have seen this—how this is going to separate it. If the machine ... if we would have listened to the suppliers and didn't put in the carpet tiles, then we wouldn't have discovered it. And we're still ... we're on our quest ... how to separate the yarn from the backing. So it was coincidence and sheer luck that we discovered it. It's not a development. I wish I could say that we were very bright, but it was just luck and discovery" (Interviewee D). Although good fortune may have played a role, it is evident that both the perseverance of the innovation team and their built-up tacit knowledge were critical to the breakthrough. Without this experience, an untrained eye would not have placed importance and connected what was being viewed. Interviewee D explains: "All these years, they were not a waste of time. This is building of experience, of know-how knowledge and without that we wouldn't have accomplished this. Even going the wrong path is a good way to do it."

At the point when a technical solution appeared, Interface set about organizing how to obtain a stream of used carpet tiles returned from the end-user to feed the recycling machine through a take-back system. The goal was to design a system whereby carpet tiles from all types of manufacturers could be returned and recycled, not just those originating from Interface. Interviewee F explains the goal: "Our aim is to get to prevent, let's say, carpet tiles being send to landfill because we don't want that. And that's not only for our material. That's for all carpet tiles." This aspiration meant tackling far more difficulties than the alternative of simply taking own made products for reasons such as needing to understand a wide variety of product compositions that affect the Re-Entry 2.0 machine calibration and how to handle the potential additional volume of used carpet tiles.

Market Launch of Re-Entry 2.0

Starting with near-zero information on issues such as the level and type of contamination expected in used carpet tiles, Re-Entry 2.0 was entered into the marketplace in a slow and cautious way to protect against reputational damage and potential large costs of waste disposal. Although successful in achieving these aims, this launch did not gain widespread support and momentum for Re-Entry because the innovation remained too technical: "The first offer we made with Re-Entry 2.0 was too much operation oriented and not sales oriented." (Interviewee J).

A year after the initial launch, a dedicated Re-Entry director was hired internally who possessed both an operations and sales background, with a zest for galvanizing stakeholders both internal and external to the company: "... and the system they wanted to start out was less service-based to the customer. But now with [the Re-Entry director] working re-introduction, I think he gets it. He knows what we have to do to make it a success" (Interviewee J). Critically the new Re-Entry director did not see his job as simply ensuring there was waste to feed the machine. Instead, the director took a systems perspective on end-of-life services such as product reuse and began to explore multiple options for how Interface, its value chain actors, and sustainability can gain shared value: "And what you say if you think of, let's say, closing the loop is bigger than Interface, is bigger than our Re-Entry 2.0. Then you get a whole different playing field. If you look at it from a, let's say, a recycling point of view, and if you see that are a lot of local initiatives. Why bring everything to Scherpenzeel? And what is the reason that we want to bring it to Scherpenzeel?" (Re-Entry director).

In addition, gaining control over the materials flow in Europe through Re-Entry 2.0 has finally allowed Interface to deliver on a vision that the company has been considering since the 1990s: "we now can reclaim the yarn . . . it's really. . . . and not only from our product but from other products as well. So that's a true game changer" (Interviewee A). These include extending the usage period of carpets by offering a tile maintenance service or changing the appearance of a space through a newly developed tile exchange service that offers good quality used products to, for example, less image-conscious customers; and leasing instead of selling carpets—a concept first introduced in 1996. The idea behind leasing—maintaining responsibility—has led to various product-service systems: "When we are responsible for the appearance of the carpet and there are damaged tiles, our partner replaces them and we take them back for recycling" (Re-Entry director, personal communication).

Inspiring Value-Chain Pro-Environmental Behavior

Interface employees also described how they felt a responsibility to seek buy-in and engage stakeholders on sustainability issues. This is also one of the company's seven fronts to "Mount Sustainability"–sensitizing stakeholders. Interviewee F explained that the sense of urgency to transform to a sustainable economy provides the responsibility: "you can't wait for legislation because if you wait for it is just too late and it will take ages. And if the industry is not ready for it, it will be delayed, and delayed, and delayed. So also as a company you have your responsibility to already start conditioning the market."

A critical example of how Interface employees actively encouraged pro-environmental behavior in the value chain can be found in the Re-Entry 2.0 project. At a very basic level, the process of Re-Entry 2.0 turns post-consumer waste back into virgin raw materials to be once again used for carpet tiles. The backing component is fed back into Interface's manufacturing processes, but for the yarn component a supplier is needed to convert it back into virgin material. Concurrent to the development of Re-Entry 2.0, a key supplier, Aquafil, took up the challenge to develop recycling machinery capable of this process. President and CEO of Aquafil Gruppo, Giulio Bonazzi explains how Interface inspired his company's own sustainability journey: "Interface(FLOR)'s bold mission for zero impact on the environment and questioning of the green credentials of its suppliers encouraged us to accelerate our own journey to sustainability" (External document 2012f, p. 11). This development by Aquafil was critical to the success of the innovation and is indicative to how a closing the loop initiative requires buy-in from the whole value chain.

With Re-Entry 2.0, its director states that he is explicitly seeking to provide inspirational leadership to all value chain actors on end-of-life solutions. This is not performed with a sole focus on making Re-Entry 2.0 a success, but also to inspire further sustainable value-creating initiatives: "So I have to inspire those guys (value chain actors) to get them on board on our Re-Entry proposition and make them feel connected. And if you then talk about leadership and if you talk about . . . it's more the transformational kind of leadership, where we empower the people" (Re-Entry director). Interviewee A also illustrates this approach by describing sustainability and Mission Zero as a 'relay' between actors striving in unison for a sustainable, circular economy: "So it's not a marathon anymore but it's a relay about exchanging information and helping each other to move further and then these breakthroughs. Yeah it's a relay" (Interviewee A).

Our case also indicates that Re-Entry 2.0 has inspired one new notable initiative for Interface and its value chain. Now that the European headquarters has the capability to accept and recycle yarn from carpet tiles, other products made from the same material—polyamide 6—can also potentially be taken back: "So we looked for other materials as well. This turned out to be fishing nets which were the same composition polyamide 6" (Interviewee A). Once employees at Interface realized this, one of the sustainability ambassadors came up with the idea to team up with the Zoological Society in London for a scheme called Net-Works, which collects discarded fishing nets in Danajon Bank, Philippines. This initiative helps to clean-up the environment of an endangered coral reef, offers local fishermen the ability to earn a little extra income from collecting the nets, and helps their long-term revenues by potentially improving their fishing catches. Net-Works provides an example of another pro-environmental behavior initiated by an employee but only made possible by WPEB among the technical team in the Netherlands, who were trying to solve another problem related to Mission Zero.

Discussion

Our qualitative case study of Re-Entry 2.0 illustrates a number of intriguing aspects of pro-environmental behavior, which have not been previously studied. Figure 15.1 captures our emergent research findings. At the core of these findings is a collective organizational climate of WPEBs, cultivated through myths, organizational routines, and material artifacts. Set within this culture is a systemic set of actions from individuals, within and across the organization and value chain members, which trigger a continuous stream of WPEBs. This diffusion of WPEB results in continued innovation and an upward spiral of organizational action, thereby increasing the scale of change. We discuss these findings in detail below.

First, pro-environmental behavior at Interface is not restricted to micro-level organizational behaviors in isolation. Whereas previous research focuses on outcomes such as recycling (Brothers et al., 1994) and waste reduction (Whitmarsh & O'Neill, 2010), our case captures how collective WPEB can lead to innovation and transformative change at the organizational level. Thus, our case contributes to an expanded definition of WPEB: that is, *transformative WPEBs can be conceptualized as a systemic set of actions from a collective network of organizational actors spread across a company, team, and/or value chain.*

Previous literature has focused on isolated examples of drivers of WPEB at the individual level, such as personal attitudes, beliefs, and norms (Bamberg & Möser, 2007). In line with previous studies, personal attitudes predicted WPEB at Interface. Employees were enthusiastic about their work and genuinely excited about Mission Zero. In addition, employees appeared to be driven by pro-social behavior and were not overly self-interested (Ramus & Killmer, 2007). Our findings also confirm that social norms such as not wanting to disappoint Ray, and to continue to strive for Mission Zero, triggered WPEBs among the innovation team, and other employees. Social norms also encouraged WPEBs. WPEB is expected from Interface employees, and they acted in a manner that others would approve. For example, employees wanted to avoid downcycling in the production process because this was considered a "crime." Although these factors can help to explain WPEB, the case at Interface also demonstrates that the organizational climate is an influential factor leading to transformative WPEB across actors. The WPEBs of the innovation team may have, in part, been inspired by personal and social norms (Bamberg & Möser, 2007) but also by organizational norms.

For example, Ray Anderson's own pro-environmental actions triggered change within his organization, but he also actively assumed the responsibility to create a pro-environmental climate within Interface (Russell & Griffiths, 2008) and was successful in doing so. His own identity (Mannetti et al., 2004) as an environmental champion created a lasting impression upon employees, both by instilling personal commitment to the organization (Fineman, 1996) and critically fostering a feeling of responsibility to the firm's sustainability goals, and to his legacy. The employees developed a personal belief that it was their responsibility to achieve Mission Zero and cited this as a driver for WPEB. The great affection in which employees speak of Ray Anderson creates a climate of personal obligation to WPEB, and an organizational identity that highlights the need to live up to his legend. Interface created an organizational climate that formally and informally diffused norms of engaging in pro-environmental behavior in order to help Interface collectively deliver on Mission Zero.

Second, WPEBs at the executive level may trigger an initial change in organizational action that result in pro-environmental behavior, but diffusion of WPEBs over time grows organically and purposefully and is related to organizational culture. Previous research on WPEBs points to organizational factors such as organizational commitment (Fineman, 1996), and a pro-environmental climate (Russell & Griffiths, 2008) as facilitators. Our findings confirm that a pro-environmental climate and organizational commitment to sustainability encourages individual level WPEBs, but that for continuous diffusion, other organizational routines and structures are required. Our findings also identify the organizational power of WPEB legends (Ray's epiphany; the forklift driver), and the use of material artifacts such as photos and the office display cabinet containing the book from Paul Hawken and other Ray Anderson memorabilia.

The pro-environmental climate (Russell & Griffiths, 2008) of Interface inspired employees to be conscious of their impact on the environment, to believe that they can make a difference and achieve the Mission Zero targets. Interface has not developed this culture by simply employing people with a certain set of pre-existing environmental values. Instead, an organizational culture of encouraging WPEB was actively formed through a program of employee education, setting, and acting in accordance to clear sustainability goals, fostering a passion of employees to contribute by engaging in WPEB, and by communicating various organizational narratives on WPEBs, which in some cases have achieved the status of legends or myths. Unlike the findings from Ramus and Steger (2000), which suggested that contextual variables at the organizational level such as environmental policies have little influence on WPEBs, the environmental strategy of Interface appeared to have a strong influence.

In this context WPEBs arise not at a 'cost to self,' but instead as a 'fun' challenge to solve. Although fun was not the initial motivator for WPEB within the innovation team, our findings identify it as a key facilitator, especially given the very long road to finding the solution. Although previous research suggests that intense emotions lead to WPEB (Russell & Griffiths, 2008), we believe that the role of fun is a novel finding within WPEB literature and one that deserves further research attention.

An organizational culture can also promote, reinforce, and perpetuate WPEB through the support and encouragement of organizational citizenship (Paillé & Boiral, 2013) and the engagement of environmental champions (Andersson & Bateman, 2000). The pro-environmental behavior of the innovation team was facilitated by the company's willingness to give them freedom to experiment— the team was confident that innovation would never be discontinued due to the integral importance of finding a solution to the problem of closing the loop within the manufacturing process. These results also reinforce the role of self-efficacy as a facilitator of WPEBs (Lo et al., 2012). Employees were driven by their past successes and ongoing achievements toward reaching Mission Zero. Individuals build self-efficacy from reflecting on past accomplishments and this was found in previous studies to predict WPEB (Walls & Hoffman, 2013). Such factors were part of the pro-environmental climate (Russell & Griffiths, 2008) fostered at Interface. This enabled the innovation team to not stop until they found the complete solution (i.e., no downcycling). Critically Interface employees believe that providing and acting upon this stimulus is their ongoing responsibility.

Finally, the WPEB diffusion at Interface is geared toward several long-term, visionary strategic outcomes including Mission Zero, with the ultimate goal of becoming a restorative company. Successful projects like Re-Entry 2.0 appear to energize the collective WPEB in a diffusion spiral that utilizes a range of affective and cognitive determinants and relies upon serendipity as well as corporate strategy. Corporate strategy enables WPEB over time and across the value chain. Our findings show that the Mission Zero strategy excited the European innovation team, made them feel good, and drove their behavior both cognitively (Bamberg & Möser, 2007) and affectively (Russell & Griffiths, 2008). The employees believed that every small behavior would influence the company's progress toward the corporate strategy of Mission Zero and therefore facilitated daily pro-environmental actions that over time resulted in radical organizational innovation in closing-the-loop in their manufacturing process. Although our data cannot shed psychological insight on if, and how, Interface's corporate strategy built behavioral intention to engage in WPEBs (Lo et al., 2012; Jones, 1990), it seems plausible that Mission Zero helped to socialize employees to embrace WPEB through increased behavioral intent.

Conclusion

Environmental psychology research has focused much attention on PEB in society, leaving WPEB under-researched (Andersson et al., 2005; McDonald, 2011).

By offering a case of WPEB, this chapter has provided insights to the individual *and* organizational determinants. Our case also illustrates how WPEB across a collection of actors can inspire and create continuous environmental improvement if supported by various organizational routines and culture.

Our definition and description of the process of transformative WPEB may have wider appeal than the case in question. In the latest UN Global Compact-Accenture survey of 1,000 CEOs, 93% believed sustainability was critical to the future success of their business. Moreover, 84% consider that business should lead the way on delivering global sustainability goals (UN Global Compact-Accenture, 2013). Drivers for establishing a sustainability strategy are varied but have generally centered on a business case, which sets sustainability as both a risk mitigation issue and a potential source of competitive advantage (Hall & Wagner, 2012; Hart, 1995). In addition, Starik and Kanashiro (2013) call for a multi-level, multi-system perspective of sustainability management. Theories of sustainability management are likely to draw conclusions at the individual, organizational, and societal levels of analysis, but more research is required to examine the interconnections between the micro and macro level of organization behavior. Andersson et al. (2013) follow this call and suggest that scholars should take a multi-level perspective of WPEB. They posit that a multi-level perspective allows the organizationally embedded nature of WPEB to be better described.

We contribute to this area by showing that individual level WPEB can lead to organization-wide impacts and create change across the value chain if an organizational culture of WPEB is developed and diffused. Our chapter suggests that the interaction between corporate strategy for sustainability, organizational climate, and WPEBs is an interesting area for future research. We believe that other organizations that wish to enhance WPEB could learn from the approach at Interface. Not all of the employees hired at Interface arrive with a drive to save the environment, but these employees also exhibit WPEB.

Based on our case findings, we recommend a few themes for future studies. First, we believe the influence of aspiration leadership to be a substantial determinant to WPEB and is deserving of more research attention. Second, the connection between an aspirational corporate sustainability strategy and WPEB needs further investigation. This relationship is currently poorly understood, and most studies draw upon established management theories such as goal setting. Third, although our case did not focus on power relations per se, we do note that the initial WPEB trigger from Ray Anderson was probably successful because of his personal and positional power within the organization. Yet the Re-Entry 2.0 case suggests that power relations governing WPEBs are not predominately positional in nature. Research on power and WPEBs and how this relates to the enablers and barriers to the diffusion of collective WPEBs would be welcome (Plank, 2011). Finally, the way in which WPEB can create value chain innovation and new sustainable business models offers a rich field of study. Understanding the mechanisms in which this takes place may be an essential part of creating sustainability transformations within industries.

Suggested Additional Readings:

1. Bartlett, D., & Kane, A. (2011). *Going green: The psychology of sustainability in the workplace*. (D. Bartlett, Ed.). Leicester, UK: The British Psychological Society.
2. Elkington, J. (2012). *The zeronauts: Breaking the sustainability barrier*. Abingdon, UK: Routledge.
3. Hawken, P. (1993). *The Ecology of commerce: A deceleration of sustainability*. London: Phoenix.

References

Andersson, L. M., & Bateman, T. S. (2000). Individual environmental initiative: Championing natural environmental issues in U.S. business organizations. *Academy of Management Journal*, 43, 548–570.

Andersson, L., Jackson, S. E., & Russell, S. V. (2013). Greening organizational behavior: An introduction to the special issue. *Journal of Organizational Behavior*, 34, 151–155.

Andersson, L. M., Shivarajan, S., & Blau, G. (2005). Enacting ecological sustainability in the MNC: A test of an adapted value-belief-norm framework. *Journal of Business Ethics*, 59, 295–305.

Aragón-Correa, J. A., Matías-Reche, F., & Senise-Barrio, M. E. (2004). Managerial discretion and corporate commitment to the natural environment. *Journal of Business Research*, 57, 964–975.

Bamberg, S., & Möser, G. (2007). Twenty years after Hines, Hungerford, and Tomera: A new meta-analysis of psycho-social determinants of pro-environmental behavior. *Journal of Environmental Psychology*, 27, 14–25.

Boiral, O., & Paillé, P. (2012). Organizational citizenship behavior for the environment: Measurement and validation. *Journal of Business Ethics*, 109, 431–445.

Branzei, O., Ursacki-Bryant, T. J., Vertinsky, I., & Zhang, W. (2004). The formation of green strategies in Chinese firms: Matching corporate environmental responses and individual principles. *Strategic Management Journal*, 25, 1075–1095.

Brothers, K., Krantz, P. J., & McClannahan, L. E. (1994). Office paper recycling: A function of container proximity. *Journal of Applied Behavior Analysis*, 27, 153–160.

Bryman, A., & Bell, E. (2003). *Business Research Methods*. New York: Oxford University Press.

Carrillo-Hermosilla, J., del Río, P., & Könnölä, T. (2010). Diversity of eco-innovations: Reflections from selected case studies. *Journal of Cleaner Production*, *18*, 1073–1083.

Cordano, M., & Frieze, I. (2000). Pollution reduction preferences of US environmental managers: Applying Ajzen's theory of planned behavior. *Academy of Management Journal*, *43*, 627–641.

DuBose, J. (2000). Sustainability and performance at Interface, Inc. *Interfaces*, *30*, 190–201.

Dutton, J. E., & Dukerich, J. M. (1991). Keeping an eye on the mirror: Image and identity in organizational adaptation. *Academy of Management Journal*, *34*, 517–554.

Easterby-Smith, M., Thorpe, R., & Lowe, A. (2002). *Management research*. London: Sage.

Eisenhardt, K., & Graebner, M. (2007). Theory building from cases: Opportunities and challenges. *Academy of Management Journal*, *50*, 25–32.

Elkington, J. (2012). *The zeronauts: Breaking the sustainability barrier*. Abingdon, UK: Routledge.

Fineman, S. (1996). Emotional subtexts in corporate greening. *Organization Studies*, *17*, 479–500.

Glaser B. (1992). *Basics of grounded theory analysis: Emergence vs forcing*. Mill Valley, CA: Sociology Press.

Govindarajulu, N., & Daily, B. F. (2004). Motivating employees for environmental improvement. *Industrial Management and Data Systems*, *104*, 364–372.

Graves, L. M., Sarkis, J., & Zhu, Q. (2011). Understanding employee proenvironmental behavior: A test of a theoretical model. *Academy of Management Annual Meeting Proceedings*, *8*, 1–6.

Hall, J., & Wagner, M. (2012). Integrating sustainability into firms' processes: Performance effects and the moderating role of business models and innovation. *Business Strategy and the Environment*, *21*, 183–196.

Hargreaves, T. (2008). Making pro-environmental behavior work: An ethnographic case study of practice: Process and power in the workplace. Unpublished doctoral dissertation, University of East Anglia, Norwich, UK.

Hart, S. (1995). A natural-resource based view of the firm. *Academy of Management Review*, *20*, 996–1014.

Interface. (2012). Annual Report 2012. Retrieved from http://www.interfaceglobal.com/Investor-Relations/Annual-Reports.aspx on 10/29/13.

Interface. (2013). Retrieved from http://www.interface.com/ on 10/29/13.

Jones, R. E. (1990). Understanding paper recycling in an institutionally supportive setting: An application of the theory of reasoned action. *Journal of Environmental Systems*, *19*, 307–321.

Kennedy, S., Whiteman, G., & van den Ende, J. (Under review). Enhancing radical innovation using sustainability as a strategic choice. *Long Range Planning.*

Lofland, J., Snow, D. A., Anderson, L., & Lofland, L. H. (2006). *Analyzing social settings.* Belmont, CA, Wadsworth.

Lo, S. H., Peters, G. J. Y., & Kok, G. (2012). A review of determinants of and interventions for proenvironmental behaviors in organizations. *Journal of Applied Social Psychology, 42,* 2933–2967.

Mannetti, L., Pierro, A., & Livi, S. (2004). Recycling: Planned and self-expressive behavior. *Journal of Environmental Psychology, 24,* 227–236.

Marans, R. W., & Lee, Y. J. (1993). Linking recycling behavior to waste management planning: A case study of office workers in Taiwan. *Landscape and Urban Planning, 26,* 203–214.

Mason, J. (2002). *Qualitative researching* (2nd ed). London: Sage.

McDonald, S. (2011). Green behavior: Differences in recycling behavior between the home and the workplace. In D. Barlett (Ed.), *Going green : The psychology of sustainability in the workplace* (pp. 59–64). Leicester, UK: The British Psychological Society.

Paillé, P., & Boiral, O. (2013). Pro-environmental behavior at work: Construct validity and determinants. *Journal of Environmental Psychology, 36,* 118–128.

Plank, R. (2011). Green behavior: Barriers, facilitators and the role of attributions. In D. Barlett (Ed.), *Going green: The psychology of sustainability in the workplace* (pp. 47–58). Leicester, UK: The British Psychology Society.

Ramus, C. A., & Killmer, A. B. C. (2007). Corporate greening through prosocial extrarole behaviors—a conceptual framework for employee motivation. *Business Strategy and the Environment, 16,* 554–570.

Ramus, C. A., & Steger, U. (2000). the roles of supervisory support behaviors and environmental policy in employee "ecoinitiatives" at leading-edge European companies. *Academy of Management Journal, 43,* 605–626.

Russell, S., & Griffiths, A. (2008). The role of emotions in driving workplace pro-environmental behaviors. In P. C. Stern (Ed.), *Research on emotion in organizations* (pp. 83–107). Washington DC: Emerald Group Publishing Limited.

Scherbaum, C. A., Popovich, P. M., & Finlinson, S. (2008). Exploring individual-level factors related to employee energy-conservation behaviors at work. *Journal of Applied Social Psychology, 38,* 818–835.

Seebode, D., Jeanrenaud, S., & Bessant, J. (2012). Managing innovation for sustainability. *R&D Management, 42,* 195–206.

Starik M., & Kanashiro, P. (2013). Toward a theory of sustainability management: Uncovering and integrating the nearly obvious. *Organization & Environment, 26,* 7–30.

Stubbs, W., & Cocklin, C. (2008). An ecological modernist interpretation of sustainability: The case of Interface Inc. *Business Strategy and the Environment, 17,* 512–523.

Toffel, M., Eccles, R., & Taylor, C. (2012). InterfaceRAISE: Sustainability consulting. *Harvard Business School Case* 611-069, May 2011.

Tudor, T. L., Barr, S. W., & Gilg, A. W. (2007). Linking intended behavior and actions: A case study of healthcare waste management in the Cornwall NHS. *Resources, Conservation and Recycling, 51,* 1–23.

UN Global Compact-Accenture. (2013). Architects of a better world. Retrieved from http://www.accenture.com/Microsites/ungc-ceo-study/Documents/pdf/13-1739_UNGC%20report_Final_FSC3.pdf on 12/12/13.

Walley, E., & Stubbs, M. (2000). Termites and champions. *Greener Management International, 29,* 41–54.

Walls, J. L., & Hoffman, A. J. (2013). Exceptional boards: Environmental experience and positive deviance from institutional norms. *Journal of Organizational Behavior, 34,* 253–271.

Whitmarsh, L., & O'Neill, S. (2010). Green identity, green living? The role of pro-environmental self-identity in determining consistency across diverse pro-environmental behaviors. *Journal of Environmental Psychology, 30,* 305–314.

Yin, R. K. (2003). *Case study research: Design and methods* (3rd ed). Thousand Oaks, CA: Sage.

INDEX

Page numbers followed by "f" and "t" indicate figures and tables.

ABI/INFORM database, 60
Ability, behavior in workplace and, 278
Accountability, 226
Action readiness, 142–143
Action research, 264
Activists, 195
Administrative leadership, 172
Advocates, 195
AET. *See* Affective events theory
Affect
   diary methods and, 106–107, 109
   emotions vs., 142
   interventions and, 231
Affect inclusion model, 143
Affective events theory (AET), 143
Affective motives, 43
Aggregation method, 71
Agreeableness, 131–132
Altruistic values, 35, 126, 190
Amoralization of corporate greening, 247
Analysis levels
   individual, 78–80
   institutional, 72–73
   organizational, 73, 78
Anderson, Ray, 251, 351–352, 359, 361–364, 370–371

Anergy, 300
Antecedent/consequent categorizations, 217, 218t
Antecedents, organizational culture and climate and, 337–338, 337f, 340–341
Antecedents of environmental leadership, 179
Anthropogenic change, 4, 197
Anthropogenic orientation, 196–197
Anthropometric population change dynamics, 310
Anticipated control, 191
Appraisal, human resource management and, 283–284, 285
Aquafil, 369
Archival data, 81
Artifacts
   human resource management and, 283
   organizational climate and, 333–334, 339
   organizational culture and, 327, 339
Ascription of responsibility
   environmental locus of control and, 193
   norm activation model and, 41, 41f, 125

Ascription of responsibility (*Contd.*)
  to self, 191
Ashkanasy's multi-level model of emotions
  group level emotions, 149–150
  interpersonal interactions and emotions, 147–149
  organization-wide emotions, 150–153
  overview of, 142–143
  within-person emotions, 143–144
  between-person emotions, 144–147
Aspiration leadership, 373
Assumptions, 282, 327
Attention management, 225
Attitude-behavior gap, 189–191
Attitudes
  behaviors and, 354
  leadership and, 168
  reasoned action and, 123
  theory of planned behavior and, 38
Attractiveness-type interventions, 221
Attribution, 190
Authentic leadership, 172
Automobile choices, 195–196
Autonomous motivation, 203
Autonomy
  competing values framework and, 332
  goal self-regulation and, 226
  job characteristics, workplace pro-environmental behaviors and, 109, 110–111
  perceived behavioral control and, 123
Autopilot, 312
Avoiding harm, 246
Awards, 177, 286
Awareness
  human resource management and, 287
  interventions and, 227, 227f
Awareness of consequences, norm activation model and, 41, 41f, 125

Behavioral frequency, habit vs., 128–129
Behaviors, pro-environmental (PEB)
  corporate greening through, 14–18
  definition and scope of, 18–27
  eco-innovations, knowledge management and, 17–18
  future research and, 28
  individuals and, 120–122
  internalization of environmental management practices and, 16–17
  mapping diversity of, 21–23, 22f, 24f
  as multifaceted umbrella concept, 19–21
  organizational citizenship behaviors, 23–27, 26t
  overview of, 12–14, 27–28, 33–34, 353–354, 354f
  for pollution prevention, 14–16
  theoretical frameworks for predicting, 34–45
Behaviors directed towards the environment, 19
Behaviors towards sustainability in the workplace, 19
Beliefs, 282, 354
Betweenness-centrality, 204
Between-person variables, 95–96
Bias, daily diaries and, 100
Biomimetic designs, 312
Biomimicry, 360
Biospheric values, 35
Bonzaai, Giulio, 369
Boomerang effects, 228
Bottom-up change, 254
Bottom-up ecoinitiatives, 201
Boundary-spanning positions, 204
Bounded rationality, 232
Breweries
  MillerCoors, 330, 338
  Sierra Nevada Brewing Company, 324–325, 330, 338–340

Steam Whistle Brewing Company, 165, 176–178
Broaden-and-build theory, 106–107
Bullfrog Power, 177

Capacity, perceived behavioral control and, 123
Carbon Disclosure Project, 64
Career choices, 145–146
Carpet industry. *See* Interface, Inc.; Re-Entry 2.0 case study
Case studies, 65–66
Catholics, 197
Cause-and-effect relationships, 64
CER programs. *See* Corporate environmental responsibility programs
Challenging of theoretical assumptions, 65
Championing activities
　change initiatives and, 251
　emotional climate and, 146
　importance of, 355
　types of individual environmental initiatives and, 23, 27
Chance, 193, 196–197
Change. *See* Organizational change
　anthropogenic, 4, 197
　anthropometric population change dynamics, 310
　bottom-up, 254
　climate, 3–6
　emergent, 255–256, 257t
　within-person, 96, 102–105
　planned, 255, 257t
　population change dynamics, 310
　pull-based user-owner, 254
　three-step model of, 255
　transformative, 370
Change management, 279
Choice, interventions directly affecting, 222–224
Choice architecture, modification of, 232

Choice sets, 199
Classification of environmentally responsible workplace behavior, 22–23
Climate, organizational. *See* Organizational climate
Climate change, 3–4
Climate change research
　organizational behavior and, 5–6
　psychology and, 4–5
　role of social science research in, 4
Climate chaos, 275
Closing the materials loop, 364–365
Coercive tactics
　interventions and, 219, 227f
　locus of control and, 192, 196
Cognition, emotions and, 143
Cognitive dimension, reasoned action and, 124
Cognitive dissonance
　goal commitment and, 224
　interventions and, 227f, 232
　locus of control and, 194–195
　overview of, 217, 218t
Collaborative leadership, 172
Collective endeavors, 283
Command control leadership, 172
Commitment, interventions and, 217, 218t, 224–225, 227f
Commons as cesspool, 196
Communication
　emotion and, 147–148
　employee engagement and, 252–253
　human resource management and, 285
　leadership and, 170
　organizational culture and climate and, 339
Company self-reporting. *See* Self-reporting data
Compensation, human resource management and, 286

Competence building, leadership and, 170
Competing values frameworks (CVF), 330–333, 331f, 343
Compliance interventions, 223
Compositional model of climate, 334
Compulsory standards, 196
Computer qualitative analysis software, 359
Conflicts, goals and, 224
Conscientiousness, 131–132
Consequences, 42, 280
Consumers, individual research and, 79–80
Consumer values and beliefs, 190
Contagion research, 233
Contextual factors, 45
Contingencies
 behavior in workplace and, 278
 change management and, 256, 257t
 human resource management and, 265–266
Contingent remuneration, 286
Convenience, emotionology and, 148
Conversation analysis, 85
Cooking behavior, 305
Corporate environmental responsibility (CER) programs, 46–47
Corporate greening, through employee pro-environmental behaviors, 14–18
Corporate social responsibility (CSR), 46–47, 145, 157
Corporate sustainability, 301
Correlational research, 63–64, 81
Costs, individuals and, 121
Creativity, 17–18, 178
Critical events, 132
Critical theory, 65
Cromwell, Greg, 176
Cross-norm inhibitory effect, 40, 48
CSR programs. *See* Corporate social responsibility programs

Culture. *See* Organizational culture
Customer service, 335
CVF. *See* Competing values framework
Cynicism, 197

Daily diaries, 99t, 100
Danish Ministry of Environment, 15
Data, types of, 68–72, 69–70t
Databases, 60, 62, 70
Data collection methods
 diary methods, 101–102
 organizational change assessment and, 262
 overview of, 67–68
 qualitative vs. quantitative, 84
 study of emotions and, 155–156
Data Envelopment Methodology, 85
Degree-centrality, 204
Denial, 148
Descriptive categorization categories, 218t
Descriptive norms
 leadership and, 169
 organizational climate and, 336
 overview of, 39
 reasoned action and, 123
Descriptive research, 64
Design. *See* Human factors and ergonomics
Diary methods
 daily diaries, 99t, 100
 event sampling, 99t, 100–101
 experience sampling, 98–100, 99t, 105
 future research and, 102–112, 103t
 job characteristics and, 109–112
 methodological issues and practical constraints of, 101–102
 overview of, 95–98, 97f
 psychological states and, 106–109

variation in types of workplace pro-environmental behaviors and, 104–106
Differentiation perspective of culture, 328
Difficulty, behavioral, 121
Diffusion of responsibility, 122
Dimensionality, of organizational culture, 328
Direct behavior, 22, 27
Discourse analysis, 68, 85
Discretionary behavior, 332
Dissonance, 195
Doctrinism, 197
Documentary evidence, 359
Dow Jones index, 70–71
Dynamic processes, 327–328
Dysfunctional work cultures, goal self-regulation and, 226

EBSCOhost database, 60
Eco-centric management, 166, 167–168
Ecocentric orientation, 196–197
Eco-champions, 288
Eco-civic engagement, as organizational citizenship behavior for the environment, 26t, 27
Eco-driving behavior, 309
Eco-effectiveness, 299f
Eco-efficiency, 299f
Eco-ergonomics, 297
Eco-friendly behaviors, 19
Eco-helping, as organizational citizenship behavior, 26t, 27
Eco-initiatives
   as organizational citizenship behavior, 26t, 27
   overview of, 20–21
   umbrella concept and, 19
Eco-innovations, 17–18, 19, 20–21
Ecological equity, 299f

Ecological footprints, 306
Ecological interfaces, 309
Ecology of Commerce, The (Hawken), 362, 371
Economics
   human resource management and, 279
   organizational sustainability and, 299f
   sustainability and, 342–343
Ecopreneurial behaviors, 105
Efficacy, of goals, 221–222
Efficiency, sustainability and, 342–343
Ego depletion, 49–50, 108
Egoistic values, 35
EIRIS. *See* Ethical Investment Research Service
ELM. *See* Environmental leadership model
Emergent change, 255–256, 257t
Emotional climate, 150–152
Emotional intelligence, 146–147
Emotional maturity, 146
Emotionology workers, 148
Emotions
   cross-level, 153–154
   defining, 142–143
   future research and, 154–157
   group level, 149–150
   individuals and, 129–130
   interpersonal interactions and, 147–149
   interventions and, 227f, 231–232
   organization-wide, 150–153
   overview of role of, 141–142, 158
   within-person, 143–144
   between persons, 144–147
Employee development, 279
"Employee Participation in the Introduction of Cleaner Technologies" program, 15

Employees. *See also* Individual determinants of behavior
　human resource management and, 287–288
　individual research and, 79–80
　Interface, Inc. and, 363–364
　organizational change and, 250–254, 263f, 264, 265
　organizational climate and, 335–336
　performance management and appraisal of, 285
　recruitment and selection of, 284–285
Employees' environmental commitment/involvement, 19
Employment relations. *See* Human resource management practices
EnergyCoach, 309
Energy management system design, 308
Engagement, organizational change and, 251–253, 263f, 265
Engineer cultures, 331
Environmental, social, governance (ESG) ratings, 62
Environmental leadership model (ELM), 168
Environmental locus of control (ELOC)
　attitude-behavior gap and, 189–191
　context of, 187–189
　external, 191–192, 194f, 195–197
　internal, 191–192, 193–195, 194f
　linkages and relationships to pro-environmental behaviors, 198–199
　locus of control and, 189–191
　overview of, 192–193, 194f, 206
　practical applications of, 199–203
　research implications and directions, 203–205
Environmentally-specific transformational leadership (ETFL), 173–176, 175t, 250
Environmentally sustainable behaviors, 19

Environmental performance, 21
Environmental/pro-environmental behaviors, 19
Environmental Protection Agency (EPA), 71. *See also* Toxics Release Inventory
Environmental self-identity, 42–43
Environmental sustainability, 19, 323–324. *See also* Sustainability
EPA. *See* Environmental Protection Agency
Epiphanies, 132
Ergoecology, 300
Ergonomic initiatives. *See* Human factors and ergonomics
Error tolerance, 226
ESG ratings. *See* Environmental, social, governance ratings
ETFL. *See* Environmentally-specific transformational leadership
Ethical Investment Research Service (EIRIS), 71
Ethical leadership, 172
EthVest Database, 70
Event sampling, 99t, 100–101
Event studies, 85, 111–112
Excellent in Corporate Responsibility award, 177
Executive cultures, 331
EXELOC. *See* External environmental locus of control
Exergy, 300
Experience sampling, 85, 98–100, 99t, 105
External control interventions, 223
External environmental locus of control (EXELOC), 193, 194f, 195–199
External influence, 166, 167
Externality, 191–192

Fast Forward to 2020, 364
Fatalism, 197

Fate, 196–197
Fear, motivation and, 148
Feedback
　employee engagement and, 253
　goal self-regulation and, 225
　interventions and, 216, 218t, 227f
　job characteristics and, 109, 111–112
　organizational interventions and, 219
　product design and, 308–309
Feedback loops, 280, 281
Field experiments, 203–204
Field theory, 333, 337
Financial sustainability, 310
Financial Times Global 500, 64
Fishing nets, 369
Fixed time-based sampling strategies, 98
Flexibility
　competing values framework and, 330–332, 331f
　goal self-regulation and, 226
　organizational culture and climate and, 342
Focus groups, 253
Fortune 500 index, 62
Fragmented perspective of culture, 328
Frameworks. *See* Theoretical frameworks
Framing. *See* Goal-framing theory
Frequency, behaviors and, 121

Gain goals, 36, 37–40
Gateway behaviors, 27
Genesis I, 197
German Journal of Research in Human Resource Management, 6
Gestalt culture, 328
GHRM. *See* Green human resources management
Global climate model, 334
Goal contagion, 233
Goal-framing theory, 35–37, 47
Goals. *See also* Model of goal-directed behavior
　interventions affecting attractiveness of, 220–221
　interventions affecting choice of, 222–224
　interventions affecting efficacy of, 221–222
　interventions affecting self-regulation of, 225–226
　socio-technical thinking and, 258f, 260, 261f
Goal-setting, interventions and, 227f
Gore, Al, 130–131
Gratitude, 145
Green, use of term, 311
Green behaviors, 19–20
Green buildings, 307
Green consumers, 193–194
Green ergonomics, 299–300
Green five taxonomy, 21–23, 22f
Green human resources management (GHRM), 277
Greening People: Human Resources and Environmental Management (Wehrmeyer), 277
"Green Management Matters" conference, 6
Green teams, 288
Green Toronto Award, 177
Greenwashing, 202–203, 248
Grossman, Ken, 338
Grounded theory approaches, 65, 84
Groups
　emotions and, 149–150
　environmental locus of control and, 205
　low-carbon work systems and, 277
Guided mastery approach, 226
Guilt, 107, 145, 146

Habits
  environmental behavior and, 44–45
  individuals and, 128–129
  interventions and, 227f, 233
Hardin, Garrett, 187–188
Harvard Model of human resources management, 280–281
Hatch's model of organizational culture, 326–329, 326f, 330, 337
Hawken, Paul, 362, 371
Heaps, Cam, 176–177
Hedonic factors, 43–44
Hedonic goals, defined, 36
Hedonistic values, 35
Helping behavior, 25, 26t
Heuristics, self-control and, 50
Hexagon framework, 258f, 259–260, 261f
HFE. *See* Human factors and ergonomics
Hierarchies
  interventions and, 228–229, 233
  organizational context and, 49
High-performance work systems, 277
Hobby garden, 366
Hope, 145
HRM practices. *See* Human resource management practices
Human capital, 278–279
Human dignity at work, 281
Human factors and ergonomics (HFE)
  contributions to design and work, 300–301
  critique and future of, 310–312
  environmental conditions and, 307
  ergoecology, 300
  future research on, 312–313
  green ergonomics, 299–300
  organizational sustainability, 301–303
  overview of, 296–298, 313
  produce and interface design and, 308–310
  social sustainability, 306
  sustainable development and, 298–299, 299f
  sustainable work, 303–304
  task and job design, 304–306
Human relations model, 332
Human resources management (HRM) practices
  building green organization through, 282–284
  employee involvement and participation, 287–288
  Harvard model of, 280–281
  nature of, 278–280
  overview of, 248, 275–278, 289–290
  performance management and appraisal, 285
  recruitment and selection, 284–285
  reward management, 285–287
  Storey model of, 282
  theoretical models of, 280
  training and workplace learning, 287
  unions and, 288–289

Idealized influence, 172, 174, 175t
Ideal types, 282
Identity
  environmental self-, 42–43
  individuals and, 132
  personal, 132
  task, 109, 110
IEA. *See* International Ergonomics Association
Implementation intentions, 234
Incentives, employee engagement and, 253
Income level, 131
In-depth analyses, 67
Individual determinants of behavior
  dynamics between, 133
  emotions and, 129–130

frameworks for, 122–128
future research on, 133–134
habit and unconscious influences of, 128–129
identity and, 132
interface with organizational determinants, 353
organizational climate and, 335–336
organizational culture and, 324
overview of, 119–120, 354–355
personal characteristics of, 130–132
workplace behaviors and, 120–122
Individual environmental initiatives, 19, 23
Individualized consideration, 172, 174, 175t
Individual level of analysis, 78–80
Individuals
influence of, 166
initiative of, 25
low-carbon work systems and, 277
organizational change and, 244, 249–254, 264, 265
socio-technical thinking and, 258f, 261f
Industrial organizational (I-O) psychology
climate change research and, 5–6
overview of, 86
pro-environmental employee behaviors and, 13
INELOC. See Internal environmental locus of control
Influence, 166, 246. See also Interventions
Informal/structural categorization, 217, 218t
Informational leaflets, 253
Information dissemination, 170, 252
Infrastructure, 258f, 261f
Initiative taking, 105
Injunctive norms, 39–40, 123, 336

Innovation
Interface, Inc. and, 360–361, 364–368
leadership and, 170
organizational culture and climate and, 339
pro-environmental employee behaviors and, 17–18
technological, 245
Inspirational motivation, 172, 174, 175t, 368–369
Institutional levels of analysis, 72–73
Institutional theory, 329
Instructions, interventions and, 216, 218t, 219, 227f
Instrumental leadership, 172
Integrationist perspective of culture, 328
Intellectual stimulation, 172, 174, 175t
Intensity, emotion, communication and, 147–148
Intent, reasoned action and, 123
Intentions, habits and, 44
Interactive leadership, 172
Interface, Inc. See also Re-Entry 2.0 case study
changing strategy of, 351–353
innovation and, 364–368
organizational culture and, 361–364
overview of, 359–360
overview of pro-environmental behavior and, 370–372
role of employees and, 251
Interface design, 308–310
Interfaith Center on Corporate Social Responsibility, 70
Internal environmental locus of control (INELOC), 193, 193–195, 194f
Internal influence, 166, 167
Internality, 191–192
International Ergonomics Association (IEA), 298

Interpersonal interactions, emotions and, 147–149
Interventions
  affecting goal attractiveness, 220–221
  affecting goal efficacy, 221–222
  affecting goal self-regulation, 225–226
  conscious, pro-environmental, 228
  conscious nonenvironmental, 228–231
  directly affecting goal choice, 222–224
  implications for organizations and organizational research, 233–234
  mechanisms of, 227, 227f
  nonconscious non-pro-environmental, 232
  nonconscious pro-environmental, 231–232
  overview of, 215–216
  reasons for success of, 220, 226
  that have been carried out in organizations, 219–220
  types of that have been studied, 216–217, 218t
Intervention studies, 203–204
Interviews, 358
Involvement, 254, 287–288
I-O psychology. *See* Industrial organizational psychology
IPC locus of control model, 193
Ipsative theory of behavior, 199–200
Irresponsible behaviors, 20
ISO 14001 standard, 16–17, 287

Job characteristics, 109–112
Job characteristics model, 110
Job design, 304–305, 311–312
Journal of Applied Psychology, 86
Journal of Occupational and Organizational Psychology, 86
Journal of Organizational Behavior, 6, 86

Justice, 335
Justifications
  goal attractiveness and, 221
  as intervention, 216, 218t, 227f

Kazdin, Alan, 5
Key levers, 282
Kinder, Lyndenberg, Domini (KLD) database, 62, 70, 71
Knowledge management, 17–18

LCWS. *See* Low-carbon work systems
Leadership
  case example of, 176–178
  characteristics of, 167–169
  environmental locus of control and, 201
  environmentally-specific transformational, 173–176, 175t
  frameworks for, 166–167
  future research on, 178–180
  individual research and, 79–80
  interventions and, 233
  organizational change and, 249–251, 263f, 265
  overview of, 164–165
  supervisory supportive behaviors and, 170–171
  transformational, 172–173
Leading Edge Consortium, 6
Legitimacy of organizational sustainability, 124
Lewinian field theory, 333, 337
Liberal paternalism, 232
Life cycle approach, 298
Life Cycle Assessment studies, 360
Limited-resource model of self-control, 108
Line managers, 282
LOC. *See* Locus of control
Local impact, 23

Locus of control (LOC), 189, 190, 191–192. *See also* Environmental locus of control
Longitudinal study designs, 66, 67
Low-carbon work systems (LCWS), 277–278

Macroergonomics, 301–302, 306, 311
Maladaptive behavior crisis, 189
Management of goals and responsibilities, 170
Material level influences, 277
Mediators, 73, 74–77t, 78, 80, 82–83t
MGB. *See* Model of goal-directed behavior
Middle ground, 256
MillerCoors, 330, 338
Minister's Award for Environmental Excellence, 177
Mission Zero, 360, 361, 362–363, 371
Model of goal-directed behavior (MGB), 129, 215
Moderators, 73, 74–77t, 78, 80, 82–83t
Molar construct, climate as, 334
Moods, emotions vs., 142
Moral evaluation, reasoned action and, 124
Morality, 127, 247
Moral norm activation theory, 190
Moral norms. *See* Personal norms
Moral obligation, 168
Moral responsibility, 107, 125
Motivation, 278, 279
Mount Sustainability, 364, 368
Multilevel research designs, 85
Mussel farmers, 304
Mutual coercion, 196

NAM. *See* Norm activation model
Natural capital, 299f
Nature protective behavior, 145

NEP. *See* New Ecological Paradigm
Nested research designs, 85
Network centrality, 204
Net-Works, 369
New Ecological Paradigm (NEP), 124–125
Newsletters, 253
Norm activation model (NAM), 41, 41f, 122, 125
Normative beliefs, 123
Normative conduct theory. *See* Theory of normative conduct
Normative goals
 defined, 36
 theories focusing on, 40–45, 41f
Nudging, 227f, 232
NVIVO10, 359

Objective constraints, 199
Objective data, 69t, 70
OB psychology. *See* Organizational behavior psychology
OCBE. *See* Organizational citizenship behaviors
Ontario, Canada. *See* Steam Whistle Brewing Company
Operator cultures, 331
Organisational Design and Management, 301
Organizational behavior (OB) psychology, 5–6
Organizational change
 culture and, 246–249
 forms of, 254–256, 257t
 future research directions for, 262–265, 263f
 goal self-regulation and, 226
 leadership and, 249–251
 overview of, 244–246
 practical implications of, 265–266
 socio-technical approach to, 245, 257–262, 258f, 261f

Organizational change (*Contd.*)
　worker engagement and involvement and, 251–254
Organizational citizenship behaviors (OCBE), 23–27, 26t, 170, 200
Organizational climate
　definition of, 333–334, 356
　integrated model of, 337–340, 337f
　overview of, 322–323, 333, 343
　pro-environmental, 335, 338–339
　pro-environmental employee behaviors and, 335–336
　recommendations for practice, 342–343
　recommendations for research on, 340–342
　strategic, 334–335
Organizational compliance, 25
Organizational culture
　change and, 246–249
　competing values framework and, 330–333, 331f
　definition and description of, 325–326
　environment and, 329
　goal self-regulation and, 226
　Hatch's model of, 326–329, 326f
　integrated model of, 337–340, 337f
　Interface, Inc. and, 361–364
　locus of control and, 203
　organizational change and, 246–249, 263f, 265
　overview of, 322–323, 325, 343
　pro-environmental, 329–330, 338–339
　recommendations for practice, 342–343
　recommendations for research on, 340–342
　socio-technical thinking and, 258f, 260, 261f
　three-level model of, 246

Organizational greening, 156
Organizational influence, 166–167
Organizational levels of analysis, 73, 78
Organizational loyalty, 25
Organizational sustainability, 301–303
Organizations
　as context with high level of formally shaped social interaction, 48–49
　defining organizational sustainability within, 246
　as depleting context, 49–50
　determinants of workplace pro-environmental behavior, 355–356
　implications for interventions and, 233–234
　interface with individual level, 353
　limiting autonomy over individual behavior, 47–48
　overview of importance of, 45–46
　as profit-generating context, 46–47
　types of interventions carried out in, 219–220
Outcome-efficacy, 41
Outcomes
　Harvard model of human resource management and, 280, 281
　overview of, 73–80, 74–77t, 82–83t

Packaging environmental issues, 23
Participation, human resource management and, 287–288
Participatory leadership, 172
PBC. *See* Perceived behavioral control
PEB. *See* Behaviors, pro-environmental
PEC. *See* Perceived environmental control
Perceived behavioral control (PBC), 38, 123, 191
Perceived environmental control (PEC), 191

Perceived (social) norms. *See also* Social modeling
  behaviors and, 355
  Interface, Inc. and, 370
  organizational climate and, 335–336
  overview of, 38
  reasoned action and, 123
Perceptions, leadership and, 168–169
Performance, diary methods and, 104–105
Performance management, 283–284, 285
Personal challenges, 226
Personal identity, 132
Personal norms
  behaviors and, 354–355
  habits and, 44
  norm activation model and, 125
  overview of, 127–128
Personal obligation, 107
Personnel Psychology, 6, 86
Person-organization fit perspective, 201–202
Persuasive appeals, 192
Persuasive technology, 312
PESTE factors, 300
Planned behavior. *See* Theory of planned behavior
Planned change, 255, 257t
Podcasts, 253
Policies
  Harvard model of human resource management and, 280, 281
  organizational culture and climate and, 324
Political orientation, 130–131
Pollution prevention, 14–16, 287
Pollution Prevention Pays (3P) program, 287
Polyamide 6, 369
Population change dynamics, 310
Powerful others, 193, 195–196, 202

Power relations, 373–374
Power struggles, 279–280
Pragmatism, reasoned action and, 124
Predictor-outcome relationship, 73
Predictors, 72–79, 74–77t, 82–83t
Pride, 146
Priming, 204
Privatization, 276
Proactive pro-environmental behaviors, 105
Proactive state, 247
Processes and procedures, socio-technical thinking and, 258f, 260, 261f
Product design, 308–310
Pro-environmental attitudes, 323–324
Pro-environmental behaviors (PEB). *See* Behaviors, pro-environmental
Profit, organizations and, 46–47
Prompts
  as organizational interventions, 219, 223–224, 227f, 231
  overview of, 216, 218t
ProQuest database, 60
Prospective-proactive path of culture formation, 326, 326f, 328
Prospect theory, 232
Protestants, 197
PsychInfo database, 60
Psychological contracts, 279
Psychological states, 106–109
Psychology, climate change research and, 4–5
Pull-based user-owner change, 254

Qualitative research
  intricate dynamics and, 132
  quantitative research vs., 63–67, 63t, 84
Quantitative research
  diary methods and, 98
  limitations of, 132

Quantitative research (*Contd.*)
    qualitative research vs., 63–67, 63t, 84
QUEST program, 360

Raft fishermen, 304
Rationalizations, 107
Reactive state, 247
Reasoned action. *See* Theory of reasoned action
Reciprocity norm, 200
Recruitment, 284–285
Recycling, 194–195. *See also* Interface, Inc.
Re-Entry 2.0 case study
    data analysis methods for, 359
    data collection methods for, 357–359
    findings of, 359–360
    finding solution and, 366–367
    idea generation and, 365–366
    innovation and, 364–367
    inspiring value-chain pro-environmental behavior and, 368–369
    market launch and, 367–368
    overview of, 353
    process studied in, 360–364
    research design of, 357
Reference groups, 195
Relationship configurations in networks, 204
Religion, 197
Research
    approaches and strategies, 63–67, 63t
    data collection methods in, 67–68, 67t
    data types in, 68–72, 69t
    levels of analysis in, 72–80, 74–77t
    observations and future directions for, 81–86, 82–83t
    overview of, 33–34
    overview of methods, 58–59, 60
    sample characteristics in, 61–63, 61t

scope of review of, 59–60, 60t
Resource degradation, 296
Resource depletion or absence, 296
Resource loads, 310
Retroactive beliefs, 191
Retrospection bias, 100
Retrospective-retroactive path of culture formation, 326, 326f, 328
Reverse causality, 64
Reverse commons, 188, 194
Rewards
    employee engagement and, 253
    goal attractiveness and, 221
    human resource management and, 283, 285–287
    interventions and, 227f, 229
    leadership and, 170
    overview of, 216, 218t
Risk Metrics Group, 71
Role perception, 278
Rotter, Julian, 191

Sacrifices, individuals and, 121
Safety, human resource management and, 279
Safety climate, 335
Safety-specific transformational leadership, 173
Sample characteristics
    diary methods and, 98
    in pro-environmental research, 61–63, 61t, 81
Sample recruitment, 102
Scalable actions, 246
Scanning behaviors, 23
Scenario planning, 259
Self-concordance, 221, 227f
Self-control, 49–50
Self-determination theory, 203
Self-development, 25
Self-efficacy
    attitude-behavior gap and, 190–191

as facilitator of workplace pro-environmental behaviors, 355, 372
norm activation model and, 41
perceived behavioral control and, 123
Self-interest, reasoned action and, 127
Self-perception theory, 202
Self-regulation, interventions affecting, 225–226
Self-reporting data
company, 68–70, 69t
stakeholder, 70t, 72
Self-transcendent values, 35
Selling environmental issues, 23
Semi-structured interviews, 358
Sense-making, 251
Shame, 146
Shared responsibility approach, 168
Sick building syndrome, 307
Sierra Nevada Brewing Company, 324–325, 330, 338–340
Signaling theory, 202
SIOP. *See* Society of Industrial and Organizational Psychology
Situational factors
goal-framing theory and, 37
Harvard model of human resource management and, 280
Skepticism, 197, 202–203
Skill variety, 109–110
Smith, Adam, 187
Snowballing interviews, 358
Social capital, 299f
Social desirability, 204
Social exchange theory, 200
Social identity theory, 201
Social influence, 166
Social modeling. *See also* Perceived norms
lack of workplace intervention studies on, 219
mechanism of, 227f
overview of, 216, 218t
reasons for success of inverventions and, 221, 229–230
Social norms. *See* Perceived norms
Social sustainability, 306, 310–311
Society of Industrial and Organizational Psychology (SIOP), 6
Socio-demographics, 131
Socio-effectiveness, 299f
Socio-efficiency, 299f
Socio-technical systems thinking (STST)
application of framework, 259–262, 261f
overview of, 245, 257–259, 258f
Sportsmanship, 25
Stability
competing values framework and, 330–332, 331f
organizational culture and climate and, 342
Staffing, 279
Stakeholder assessments, 70t, 72
Stakeholders, Harvard model and, 280–281
Standard and Poor's 500 index, 62
Statistics, sample size and, 62
Statutes, 196
Steam Whistle Brewing Company, 165, 176–178
Stimuli, emotions and, 142
Storey model of human resources management, 282
Strategic aspects, Storey model and, 282
Strategic climates, 334–335
Strategic leadership, 172
Strategic planning, 279
STST. *See* Socio-technical systems thinking
Subcultures, 248–249, 328
Subjective constraints, 199

Subjective norms. *See* Perceived norms
Subliminal images, 227f, 231–232
Sufficiency, 299f
Suggestion schemes, 288
Supervisory supportive behaviors, 170–171
Surface level of culture, 246
Surveys, 98
Sustainability. *See also* Organizational sustainability; Social sustainability
  defining within workplace, 246
  employee behavior and, 323–325
  overview of, 296–297
Sustainable development, 296–299, 299f, 303
Sustainable human-centered philosophy and design, 302
Sustainable work, 302, 303–304
Symbolic motivations, 43
Symbols, 327, 339

Target-specific transformational leadership, 173, 179
Task-related pro-environmental behaviors, 105
Tasks
  analysis of, 311–312
  design of, 304–305
  identity of, 109, 110
  significance of, 109
  support and, 226
Taxonomies, 21–23, 22f, 24f
Taylor, Greg, 176–178
Taylor, Sybil, 177–178
Technology
  organizational change and, 245
  persuasive, 312
  socio-technical thinking and, 258f, 260, 261f
Temporality, 191
Thatcherism, 276

Theoretical frameworks. *See also Specific frameworks*
  for behavior of individuals, 34, 50–51, 122–126
  competing values, 330–333, 331f, 343
  gain goals theories, 37–40
  goal-framing theory, 35–37
  hexagon, 258f, 259–260, 261f
  normative goals theories, 40–45, 41f
  reasoned action, 123–124
  value theories, 34–35
Theory elaboration, 65
Theory generation, 65
Theory of normative conduct, 336
Theory of planned behavior (TPB)
  environmental locus of control and, 191, 198
  individuals and, 122, 124
  leadership and, 168–169
  overview of, 37–39
Theory of reasoned action (TRA)
  environmental locus of control and, 191
  individuals and, 122, 123–124
  leadership and, 168–169
  value-belief-norm theory vs., 126–128
Theory testing, 65
Theory Y (McGregor), 281
Thermodynamic theories, 300
Third-party assessments, 69t, 70–71
Three-level model of culture, 246
Three-step model of change, 255
Time
  behaviors and, 121
  diary methods and, 98, 103
Toxics Release Inventory (EPA), 15, 62, 68–70, 85
TPB. *See* Theory of planned behavior
TRA. *See* Theory of reasoned action
Trades Union Congress (TUC), 288

Trade unions, 288–289
Tragedy of the commons, 121–122, 187–188
Tragedy of the Commons, The (Hardin), 187–188
Training
  eco-efficiency and, 305
  human resource management and, 279, 283, 287
Traits, emotions and, 144–145
Transactional leadership, 201
Transformational leadership, 172–176, 175t, 201
Transformational teaching, 173
Transformative change, 370
TRI. *See Toxics Release Inventory* (EPA)
Triangulation, 67, 84
Triple bottom line, 246, 298
TUC. *See* Trades Union Congress
Turn It Off campaign, 223–224
Type II errors, 62

Umbrella concept, 19–21
Underlying assumptions of organization, 327
Underlying level of culture, 246
Unifying leadership, 172
Unions, 276, 288–289
United Motor Manufacturing, 66
Universities, 219–220

Valence, 147–148
Value-added component, 279
Value-belief-norm (VBN) theory
  environmental locus of control and, 190–191
  overview of, 41–42, 122, 125–126
  reasoned action vs., 126–128
Value chains, 298, 368–369
Value level of culture, 246
Values. *See also* Competing values frameworks; Organizational climate and culture
  human resource management and, 283
  leadership and, 167–168
  organizational culture and, 247–248
  overview of theories on, 34–35
Variable time-based sampling strategies, 98
VBN. *See* Value-belief-norm theory
Verbal self-talk, 226
Videos, 253

Wealth of Nations, The (Smith), 187
WEB. *See* Workplace environmental behaviors
Website analysis, 85
Wehrmeyer, Walter, 277
Wiesner, James, 363
Within-person changes in behavior, 96, 102–105
Working sustainably, 246
Workplace environmental behaviors (WEB), 34
Workplace learning, human resource management and, 287